P9-CBQ-527

Roberta Russell
62 Settler's Way RR 4
Kemptville ON K0G 1J0

THE WAY IT WORKS

INSIDE OTTAWA

EDDIE GOLDENBERG

A DOUGLAS GIBSON BOOK

McCLELLAND & STEWART

Library and Archives Canada Cataloguing in Publication

Goldenberg, Eddie
    The way it works : inside Ottawa / Eddie Goldenberg.

"Douglas Gibson books".
ISBN 13: 978-0-7710-3352-0
ISBN 10: 0-7710-3352-4

1. Goldenberg, Eddie.   2. Canada – Politics and government – 1993-
3. Chrétien, Jean, 1934- – Friends and associates.   4. Liberal Party of
Canada – Biography.   5. Political consultants – Canada – Biography.
I. Title.

FC635.G64 2006   971.064'8'09   C2005-907316-0

We acknowledge the financial support of the Government of Canada through the Book Publishing Industry Development Program and that of the Government of Ontario through the Ontario Media Development Corporation's Ontario Book Initiative. We further acknowledge the support of the Canada Council for the Arts and the Ontario Arts Council for our publishing program.

Typeset in Janson by M&S, Toronto
Printed and bound in Canada

A Douglas Gibson Book

This book is printed on acid-free paper that is 100% recycled, ancient-forest friendly (100% post-consumer recycled).

McClelland & Stewart Ltd.
75 Sherbourne Street
Toronto, Ontario
M5A 2P9
www.mcclelland.com

1 2 3 4 5   10 09 08 07 06

To Caroline
and
to the memory of my father,
Carl Goldenberg

CONTENTS

Prologue

"**E**ddie, cancel this morning's meeting. Something else has come up that is much more urgent."

It was about 9:15 a.m. on March 17, 2003, and from the tone of Jean Chrétien's voice, I knew this was something serious. At 9:45, we had a meeting scheduled at 24 Sussex Drive, the prime minister's official residence, to discuss controversial proposed legislation to prohibit corporate bankrolling of Canadian political parties. I had been standing in my corner office on the second floor of the Langevin Building, which houses the Prime Minister's Office (PMO) and the Privy Council Office (PCO), gathering documents to take to the meeting when the phone rang. The prime minister, as always, got right to the point. He had just learned from his foreign policy adviser, Claude Laverdure, that the British government had contacted the Canadian Department of Foreign Affairs with four questions, which he proceeded to read to me.

"Will Canada provide political support for military action against Iraq?"

"What military capabilities will Canada contribute to such an action?"

"Is Canada prepared to make its position on this public?"

"What support will Canada provide to humanitarian assistance and reconstruction in Iraq?"

Worst of all, he added, "The British say that they and the Americans need an answer before noon – today. I want you to work right away with Claude to make recommendations on how we should respond."

I left my office at once, darted upstairs, and crossed into the connecting building that housed the foreign policy and defence secretariat of the Privy Council Office. Claude Laverdure, who headed the secretariat, was waiting for me in his office. On the walls were some souvenir photographs of Claude's long and distinguished career in the Canadian foreign service. On his desk were family photographs. In one corner – where we would spend most of the next three hours – was a standard-issue government conference table where we could sit, review documents, and write. From his window, I could see across Wellington Street to the Parliament Buildings and pick out the windows of the prime minister's own office, where the drama of the day would play out a few hours later.

Claude and I took as our starting point the fact that for months the prime minister had insisted publicly and privately that Canada would not participate in a war in Iraq without the approval of the United Nations (UN). So step one was to call Paul Heinbecker, the Canadian ambassador to the UN, to get an update from him as to what was happening there. We put him on the speaker phone and discussed for about twenty minutes the situation in New York. The ambassador told us that after weeks of debate and high-stakes drama on the international stage, it was now absolutely clear that there was no way that the UN Security Council would pass any resolution authorizing the use of force in Iraq.

For months, all of our discussions about Iraq had dealt with hypothetical situations. We now faced the ugly reality that Canada had moments earlier been confronted with an ultimatum by the United States and the United Kingdom, our two oldest allies. We were very surprised and puzzled that the Americans – who would lead the war effort – had not made a direct request to Canada for military assistance, but instead had used the British as an intermediary. But the surprising – and somewhat insulting – way they asked Canada didn't influence our decision. The bottom line was that the United States was going to war against Iraq, and wanted Canada to be part of it. The prime minister would have to make a final decision as to whether Canada would participate, and we were there to advise him. Now that the clock was ticking so fast, there was no time for more debate or broad consultation, no time for the prime minister to call a meeting of caucus or Cabinet. The British and the Americans had asked for an answer by noon, less than two hours away, and Parliament would be sitting for question period soon after that.

Heinbecker, Laverdure, and I had the same reaction to the demand for an answer by noon. Regardless of the deadline our friends and allies were trying to impose on us, we believed that Parliament should be informed ahead of foreign governments of a decision as to whether Canada would go to war. I pressed "o" on the telephone and asked the PMO switchboard operator to put us through to the prime minister. Within a minute, Chrétien was on the line, and I told him that I would put him on the speaker phone because I was with Claude. It was a brief conversation. Claude and I reminded him that there is no constitutional requirement to inform Parliament first, but our view was that as the House of Commons was sitting, it was the right place in which to provide the Canadian response to a request to go to war. We therefore recommended that he announce Canada's position at the beginning of the daily question period in the House of Commons, before our diplomats communicated it to Great Britain and the United States.

Chrétien agreed, saying, "We will be highly criticized in Parliament if the announcement of Canada's position leaks out of Washington or London before it is made public in Canada. I want to announce our decision in the House of Commons first." He instructed us to ask the Department of Foreign Affairs to inform the representatives of Great Britain and the United States in Ottawa that he would be responding first in the House of Commons at 2:15 p.m. Then he told Claude that the deputy minister of foreign affairs, Gaëten Lavertu, should arrange a meeting in the Lester B. Pearson Building, home of the Department of Foreign Affairs, with British and American representatives for a formal government-to-government response immediately after question period. Much later, some who disagreed with the decision not to participate in the war, including American ambassador Paul Cellucci, criticized Chrétien for the way in which he communicated with the United States at that moment. I have no doubt that they would not have been at all critical of first announcing the news to the House of Commons if the decision had been to go to war.

As the moments ticked away, Laverdure and I spoke again several times with Paul Heinbecker. We understood the gravity of a decision where Canada would be saying no to the United States on a matter of particularly high national security importance to the president, but Heinbecker was unequivocal that Canada should not participate. After reflecting on the principles that the prime minister and the government had articulated over the preceding weeks and months, the three of us agreed to recommend to the prime minister that our country not participate in the Iraq War.

Laverdure and I, and sometimes Michael Kergin, the Canadian ambassador to the United States, had been present at the weekly Tuesday-morning Cabinet meetings as the issue of Iraq was discussed in the months before any final decision had to be made. The first item on the agenda at each Chrétien Cabinet meeting was "general discussion." The prime minister often used this opportunity to express his initial thoughts and then get some reaction from other ministers on evolving policy issues that did not necessarily require immediate decisions. For months, the situation in Iraq was one of those issues discussed at length.

Claude and I were therefore well aware of the thinking of ministers and the prime minister.

Around noon we telephoned the prime minister again and gave him our recommendation not to participate in the war. He listened carefully and said that he, too, had come to the same conclusion. Then he said, "Eddie, prepare a statement for me for the House today. I will use it to reply to the first question from the Leader of the Opposition." I had been crafting statements for Jean Chrétien for thirty years, since the time I was a law student at McGill University and he was a young Cabinet minister in the Trudeau government. Some of the statements

I wrote over the years weren't always as important as I liked to think they were. This one was, and I knew this time that I had to get the words just right.

Ministers and prime ministers often compete to see who can obfuscate the best in responding to Opposition questions in the House of Commons. This time was different; the answer had to be short, clear, and to the point. We were constrained by the rules of the House of Commons. To maximize the number of questions that can be asked by the Opposition in the daily forty-five-minute question period, answers by ministers or the prime minister must be no longer than forty-five seconds, after which the microphone is automatically turned off. I sat at Claude's conference table and told him that I would take a little time to draft a few sentences that would articulate the Canadian position, which we could then refine.

The instruction from the prime minister was clear and unambiguous, so it was not hard for me to find the right words for him to use in the House of Commons. Within half an hour, Claude and I had fashioned a brief statement. We then ate a quick sandwich in his office while the PMO translator put our short draft into French so that we could give Chrétien a text in both official languages. Then around 1:00 p.m. we left for an historic meeting with the prime minister. We crossed Wellington Street as we had done so many times before on far less important matters, walked up Parliament Hill, and came into the building through the private entrance, used primarily by Cabinet ministers and members of Parliament (MPs), on the west side of the Centre Block. In our briefcases we had several copies of the seven sentences I had written.

As we got on the elevator to Chrétien's third-floor office, we met Francine Lalonde, an Opposition MP from the separatist Bloc Québécois. She told us how distressed she was, because she was certain that the government was about to support the American position in Iraq. We knew that she was not alone in her anxiety. There were many Canadians who did not expect the government to say no to Washington; some who hoped that Canada would not participate, and others who wanted Canada to participate in the war, all shared a perception that Canada was so closely intertwined with the United States that the American pressure would be too difficult to resist. We said nothing in response to Madame Lalonde, but smiled to ourselves and laughed nervously once we got out of the elevator, noting that on many issues that have nothing to do with the future of Quebec in Canada, the policy positions of the Liberal government and of the Bloc Québécois could often be the same.

Every day before question period, Chrétien met for about twenty minutes with his legislative assistant, his communications director, and his press secretary to be briefed on what the Opposition might ask. Often he would tease his assistants, proposing outrageous and sometimes very politically incorrect answers, which his staff always feared he might inadvertently let slip in the heat of parliamentary exchanges. The briefings were different when it was evident that major issues were likely to be raised in the House. Sometimes Cabinet ministers as well as other PMO senior staff, including me in my role as senior policy adviser, joined the briefing session. This was one of those times. Everyone recognized that the stakes were very high. As usual, the prime minister was sitting behind the large desk in his wood-panelled corner office. The office was decorated with family photos and an oil painting of his political hero, Sir Wilfrid Laurier. On one wall was a collection of paintings by the renowned Quebec artist Jean Paul Lemieux. The desk as usual was almost completely bereft of paper, as Chrétien did his paperwork early in the morning and later in the evening in his study at his official residence.

For this meeting, Chrétien had asked Minister of Foreign Affairs Bill Graham and Minister of Defence John McCallum to join the briefing, and they sat with Chrétien's legislative assistant, Ken Polk, his director of communications, Jim Munson, his press secretary, Steven Hogue, Claude Laverdure, and me in a small semicircle in front of his desk. Iraq was dominating national and international news, and we were therefore certain that the first question to the prime minister that afternoon from the Leader of the Opposition, Stephen Harper, would be about the prospect of war, even though the Opposition, like the Cabinet, was not aware of the requests that morning to the Canadian government from Great Britain on behalf of the United States. I handed the prime minister and the two ministers the draft statement. It was typed in a large font so that he could read it easily in the House without the reading glasses he never liked wearing. They read silently, and then Chrétien asked me to read the words aloud. Graham and McCallum listened intently and then each said that he was in full agreement.

The prime minister wanted to ensure that we all fully understood what was at stake. He reviewed our recommendations again. Typically, Chrétien's style was to keep all options open until the last possible moment and to play the devil's advocate before making final decisions. He threw questions at us. "Are you absolutely sure that I should speak today and not wait until tomorrow? Is it absolutely essential to make a decision today? Could the circumstances change overnight in the United Nations?" But he knew, as we did, that there could be no further delay; war was imminent. So to lighten the mood, I said, "Prime Minister, you should have made this decision yesterday. Can we compromise between yesterday and tomorrow by announcing it today?" He laughed, agreed, and started practising his delivery in both English and French. Ken Polk then left our meeting early to make sure that the Speaker's office was aware that the prime minister had an important answer on Iraq that might run longer than the forty-five-seconds rule. Polk came back to say that the Speaker would not cut him off before he finished his answer. At the end of the meeting, as we all stood up to leave, Chrétien – who normally preferred to undersell and hopefully outperform and leave history for the historians – told us very seriously: "This decision will be remembered as a significant event in Canadian foreign policy." We solemnly nodded in agreement and wished him well.

And then, accompanied by the minister of defence and the minister of foreign affairs, the prime minister walked down one flight of stairs past waiting reporters and television cameras and entered the House

of Commons. Laverdure and I followed into the government lobby –
just behind the House of Commons chamber – where we nervously
watched the proceedings on television. The first question from the
Leader of the Opposition at 2:15 p.m. sharp was, as expected, on the
subject of Iraq. Chrétien rose to his feet, paused for a moment, and
responded with the following words, which I knew very well:

> Mr. Speaker, I want to set out the position of the Government of
> Canada. We believe that Iraq must fully abide by the resolutions of
> the United Nations Security Council. We have always made clear
> that Canada would require the approval of the Security Council if
> we were to participate in a military campaign. Over the last few
> weeks the Security Council has been unable to agree on a new reso-
> lution authorizing military action. Canada worked very hard to find
> a compromise to bridge the gap in the Security Council. Unfortu-
> nately we were not successful. If military action proceeds without a
> new resolution of the Security Council, Canada will not participate.

All of the Liberal, New Democrat, and Bloc Québécois MPs rose with
a roar and gave Chrétien a standing ovation. The Opposition Canadian
Alliance members behind Stephen Harper sat in stunned silence,
their anger evident on their faces. The Progressive Conservatives were
divided and quiet. And Canada, for better or for worse, would not be
going to war in Iraq.

Getting Past the Snapshot

TELLING THE STORY this way of what happened on March 17, 2003,
provides little more than a snapshot, an image of an instant in time,
without the context of what happened before the photo was taken. In
fact, the announcement in the House of Commons that day was the
product of far more than a morning of meetings and a few phone calls.
This book tries to provide the context of what happens before and after
the photo is taken. Otherwise, such a snapshot can create an impression that decisions as important as the one not to participate in the war

in Iraq are made quickly one morning in a vacuum by very few people with no meaningful consultation and no real debate.

Major public policy decisions are the product of current events, personality, philosophy, and circumstance, influenced by experience, observation of government, and knowledge of history, politics, and international affairs. Debate and options start out broad and often involve wide consultations and analysis of public opinion. The Canadian decision on Iraq, for example, came after weeks and months of consultations with ministers, Canadian ambassadors, foreign policy advisers, foreign leaders, and members of Parliament. But to reach a final decision, debate has to narrow, much like a funnel. Sometimes decisions need to be made very quickly; in the end, only one person can make the decisions. That is what heads of government are elected to do. That is what leadership and governing are all about in a democracy.

From my perspective as an adviser and decision maker, it always seemed to me that the instant analysis of an important decision the next day by the pundits in the media, both written and electronic, can be incredibly superficial. In an era of twenty-four-hour news and immediate comment, public policy decisions are too often analyzed in the same way as sporting events from the night before. This approach may meet the needs of a media industry that requires identifiable winners and losers to sell newspapers or increase television ratings, because everyone understands a horse race or a hockey game. The real story behind a major decision, however, is often more complex and more interesting, but is always harder to write, and rarely fits into a television clip of a few seconds, which at best gives us a snapshot and, at worst, a misleading one.

The Decision-Making Funnel

DECISION MAKING IS an art not a science. The factors in the decision not to participate in the American-led war in Iraq illustrate the complexity and reality of decision making in Canada. Iraq is a perfect illustration of how highly intelligent, thoughtful people could take the same factors into account and, based on their own beliefs and knowledge, experience, and perspectives, come to very different conclusions. While hindsight more than three years later may make the Canadian decision look easy or obvious, it was definitely not so at the time. For example, our decision exposed tensions between the business community, fearful of offending their American customers and suppliers, and the federal government. It demonstrated the real differences between political parties in the House of Commons, where Stephen Harper was vocally in favour of Canadian troops being part of the American-led coalition. It also highlighted some differences within the Liberal Party itself.

The decision even reverberated in federal-provincial relations, where the premiers of Alberta and Ontario, Ralph Klein and Ernie Eves, angry at the prime minister for reasons that had nothing to do with Iraq, thought it appropriate to make very public declarations of disapproval of this foreign policy decision. And it played a role in Quebec's 2003 provincial election campaign. The government, of course, had more than domestic factors to consider. Among other things, it had to consider what the decision would mean for relations between Canada and the United States, whether there would be economic and political consequences, and, if so, how they could be managed. The decision had to be made in the context of September 11, 2001, an event that made it all the more difficult to deny our support to our friends, relatives, neighbours, and allies to the south.

The story of what happened on March 17, 2003, involves the prime minister and the PMO, the Privy Council Office, the House of Commons, the Cabinet, foreign and domestic policy, federal-provincial relations, Canada-U.S. relations, and national unity. In summary, the decision about the Iraq War – which is dealt with in greater detail in a later chapter – illustrates what this book is all about. This book tries to put the actions of a government into context, showing what goes on behind the scenes.

Chapter 1

THE SUMMER JOB THAT GREW

"A journey of a thousand miles must begin with a single step."
– LAO-TZU, 6TH CENTURY B.C.

First, a word about me. In early May 1972, at the end of my first year of law school at McGill University, I began what I thought was a four-month summer job in the office of Jean Chrétien, who was then the minister of Indian affairs and northern development. When I arrived in Ottawa that spring, Chrétien was a thirty-eight-year-old three-term member of Parliament. Despite already having been in the Cabinet for five years, he was still a relatively obscure junior minister and very much an outsider in the Liberal Party establishment. I knew of him through a friendship I had with John Rae, Chrétien's executive assistant from 1967 to 1971. John had told me over the years about the interesting job he had in Ottawa; so one day I asked him whether I could get a summer job in the office of the minister. "No one has ever asked for a summer job, but I'll see what I can do for you," he replied.

My summer job would last, in one way or another, for almost thirty-two years. I would never have dreamed that I would accompany Chrétien almost every step of the way on one of the most extraordinary journeys in Canadian public life, a journey that would take him through most of the senior departments of government all the way into the prime minister's office, where he would govern Canada with remarkable success for ten years, and place him at the Cabinet table for longer than anyone else in Canadian history. Nor would I have predicted that along that road, John Rae and I would help run two Liberal leadership campaigns for Chrétien, two Quebec referendum campaigns, and three winning national election campaigns.

Politics at Home

I DEVELOPED AN interest in government and public service at an early age. Like everyone, I was shaped by where I came from. I was born in Montreal in 1948 and grew up there. My grandparents were European immigrants who came to Canada, like so many others at the turn of the twentieth century, with nothing but the clothes on their backs and a burning ambition to make a good life for their children in a new land. My father, Carl Goldenberg, always reminded me that Canada welcomed his parents without caring about their skills, their incomes, their language or background. He loved the multi-ethnic character of this country and taught me that it is a source of great richness and great opportunity.

There was no prouder Canadian than my father, and he wanted his children to share his passion and love for Canada. When I was ten years old, my parents took my sister and me on the CPR's transcontinental train (appropriately named *The Canadian*) from Montreal to Vancouver. I spent days sitting in the dome car looking out the windows and absorbing the Canadian panorama. The next summer we drove from Montreal through Atlantic Canada. Those two trips – which I remember almost fifty years later as though they were yesterday – had a profound influence on me. As I grew up, I came to share my dad's passion and love for the country. Later in life, I fell in love with the magic of the North, and spent many summer holidays canoeing wild arctic rivers. This passion for Canada directed me to a career in public service.

My paternal grandfather early on became very interested in public affairs. He was a Laurier Liberal, like so many immigrants of his day, because it was under a Liberal Party government that they came to

Canada, and just as millions of immigrants have done in their own families for much the same reason throughout Canadian history, he passed on his support of the Liberal Party to my father.

Politics and public affairs were always a subject of conversation in our home. My father's sense of party loyalty seemed so strong to me that I remember as a young boy asking my mother very innocently whether it was possible to have friends who supported political parties other than the Liberals. She was horrified (perhaps because she usually voted for the CCF, and then the NDP, at least until 1993, when she knew that my job would be on the line if the Liberals lost) that we had been so partisan at home that I had not learned the basic principles of democracy. She quickly explained that our next-door neighbours, whom we liked very much, were Conservatives. That was a satisfactory lesson in democracy for me until she told the story over the back fence to Mrs. Hannon, who quickly set her and me straight. Our neighbours were lifelong Liberals!

Public service was always close to my father's heart. As a lawyer and academic, he spent a good deal of his life in public service advising federal, provincial, and municipal governments of different political stripes on matters as diverse as municipal taxation, labour law, federal-provincial relations, and the Constitution. He advised prime ministers from Mackenzie King through Pierre Trudeau to Jean Chrétien and served with distinction for eleven years in the Senate. My father was a genuine small-l liberal who believed in activist government as a force for good in society and treated public service as a means to make life better for those who are disadvantaged. And he tried to pass on those beliefs and values to me.

Universities were an important part of the life of our family as I grew up. Both my parents had lifelong associations with McGill University, my father as a lecturer after he graduated and later as a member of the board of governors, and my mother, Shirley Goldenberg, as a professor of industrial relations. Years later, as I describe in this book, developing a federal agenda for support of our universities became an important part of my work in the PMO.

The early 1960s was the time of the Quiet Revolution in Quebec, when Jean Lesage's provincial Liberals moved fast to bring modern government to the province. Our home in Montreal was always full of extraordinarily interesting friends of my father, including a University of Montreal law professor by the name of Pierre Elliott Trudeau. Politicians, academics, writers, public servants, labour leaders – French and English – often came together in my father's library. This exposure was part of my education and had a profound influence on my life and career, and may be one reason why Quebec's place in Canada played a big part in my career in government and is prominent in this book.

Early Encounters with Trudeau

I ENTERED THE faculty of arts at McGill University in 1965, set on studying economics and political science and then law. On September 10, the same week I began university, I was walking past the Mount Royal Hotel on Peel Street and ran into Jean Bazin, who a few years before had been my counsellor at summer camp, when I was fifteen years old. Bazin was a political junkie and an active Young Conservative, who more than twenty years later was appointed to the Senate by his friend Brian Mulroney. Jean grabbed my arm, saying, "Come with me. In twenty minutes there's going to be an interesting press conference in this hotel." We went in to see Trudeau, Jean Marchand, and Gérard Pelletier announce their intention to run as Liberals in the federal election that had just been called for November 1965. Prime Minister Pearson had wanted Marchand as a star candidate. Marchand only agreed to run on the condition that his two friends run as well, a precedent that I refer to in a different context in a later chapter in this book.

I had known Trudeau as a friend of my father, so I quickly volunteered to work in his campaign. As a freshman, I joined the McGill Liberal Club and soon was instrumental in inviting Trudeau to McGill to make his first political speech outside of his riding of Mount Royal. I will never forget sitting, with increasing alarm, on the platform as

Trudeau spoke about Plato, Aristotle, and Socrates, until the president of the student Liberals passed him a note suggesting he speak about the upcoming election. Trudeau smiled and said, "Your president wants me to speak about the election," talked for a few minutes about why he had come into politics, and then continued to discuss political philosophy. I was sure the president of the Liberal Club would never forgive me for my choice of speaker until, to my great relief, Trudeau received a prolonged standing ovation from an overflow crowd. It was an early introduction to a politician who didn't fit the usual mould. Later in that campaign, I attended an all-candidates meeting in Trudeau's constituency. When a woman asked him about the Divorce Act – a law he would radically reform two years later as minister of justice – Trudeau's reply was, "I'm sorry, madam, that you are having problems with your husband. I know how restrictive the law is, and that is why I haven't got married." I would not have predicted, at that moment, that Trudeaumania would sweep the nation less than three years later. In fact, when I heard his answer, I wondered whether he would even get elected at all in his riding.

Towards a Career in Government

AFTER OBTAINING my B.A. in 1969, I spent a year in France at the Institut D'Etudes Politiques in Paris, not long after the student turbulence of 1968 in Europe. I received my M.A. in economics and political science from McGill in 1971, and graduated from law school in 1974. During the years I was a university student, Canada had experienced both the excitement of Trudeaumania and the resulting disillusionment from the impossible expectations that were first created and then, inevitably, not met. I watched as Trudeau evolved, in the words of the satirist Larry Zolf, "from Philosopher King to Mackenzie King." During those years, Quebec experienced terrorist violence and the War Measures Act. It was a time of the civil rights revolution in the United States and the war in Vietnam, of revolutionary social change brought about by the women's movement, but also a time of disillusionment and cynicism about government in the United States and elsewhere as a result of the Vietnam War, and later of Watergate. I observed all of this as a student of government and as a self-confessed political junkie.

My career for the next three decades was intertwined with one of the most fascinating careers in Canadian politics, that of Jean Chrétien. I began my association with him as a student, and soon became an adviser, confidant, and lifelong friend. I started my career in government as a young man having the privilege to meet and learn from Canada's top mandarins and finished it at the very top myself. As a student during the Vietnam era, I wondered how middle-aged men in governments could bring themselves to send young soldiers into harm's way; as a middle-aged man in government – with the anti-war slogan, "Hey, hey, LBJ, how many kids have you killed today?" still ringing in my ears – I was involved in decisions to send young Canadians to the Balkans and Afghanistan and not to send troops to Iraq.

When Chrétien was minister of Indian affairs and northern development, he gave me the extraordinary opportunity as a student to see and learn about the Canadian North, to visit aboriginal communities and immerse myself in the issues facing our First Nations. I joined his ministerial staff full-time after I graduated from law school, and then worked directly for him on his staff in a variety of capacities over most of a twenty-year period, starting in the Treasury Board, then in Industry and Commerce, Finance, Justice, and Energy, Mines and Resources, and eventually as principal secretary in the Office of the Leader of the Opposition. Those years working in that extremely wide range of ministries gave me extraordinary opportunities to see first-hand the way it works in Ottawa, regardless of which party happens to be in power. By the time I became the senior policy adviser in 1993, I had many years of experience as a student of and a participant in government. I also had six years' experience practising law from 1984 to 1990, which gave me a perspective of the private sector from outside of government that was invaluable later in the PMO. I tried to apply the lessons I learned over those twenty years to my responsibilities advising a prime minister.

I had the opportunity to be involved in developing an agenda for government while in Opposition, and then moving from Opposition to government, and immediately advising on the formation of a Cabinet. I was part of the PMO for ten years. I observed Cabinets and caucuses, and I worked directly on maintaining a tenuous but essential relationship between a prime minister and his minister of finance. I was part of establishing and implementing government priorities, and I negotiated with provincial premiers, met with international leaders, and dealt with Quebec referendums and federal elections. Issues like the Clarity Act, the reform of political party financing, Canada-U.S. relations, the making of federal budgets, support for post-secondary education, crisis management, and the war in Iraq took a lot of my time. Most of all, I observed at close hand how a prime minister runs a government.

This Book's Aim

I AM VERY grateful that I had the opportunity to spend many years of my career in public service, where I saw first-hand that the cynicism about the motives of those in politics and public life is misplaced. This book is an attempt to explain the way it all works – the complexities of decision making, the crucial importance of personalities and relationships, the need for institutional memory, the influence of people and events in the rest of the world, how agendas are transformed by unforeseen events. I hope that this book will enable others to draw some lessons for the future.

My perspective over many years is largely the result of the long-standing, unique relationship I had with Jean Chrétien. But these pages are not a history of the Chrétien government. It has not yet been out of office long enough for its achievements and shortcomings to be placed in the perspective of the broad sweep of Canadian history. In this book I focus on matters in which I was particularly involved during the Chrétien government of 1993 to 2003 in order to set down my views about Canadian democracy, about how government works in practice, and about Canada at home and abroad. I was not, of course, involved in everything that the Chrétien government did. There was much of great importance where others played a major role and where they spent much of their time. But by drawing on my experience and my unique vantage point, I have tried to capture the essence of some of the important issues that have preoccupied Canadian politics for many years.

Any book like this one inevitably deals with the author's own participation, observations, and perspectives. Others had different vantage points, and as a result may have different viewpoints than mine. That is the nature of observations on public policy. However, my hope is that for those involved in politics, this book will draw lessons necessary for the challenges of governing in the years ahead. Even more important, I hope that it will provide a useful insight for Canadians outside government into what really goes on behind the scenes in Ottawa.

Chapter 2

EARLY BEGINNINGS IN OPPOSITION

"An opposition, on coming into power, is often like a speculative merchant whose bills become due. Ministers have to make good their promises, and they find a difficulty in so doing."

– WALTER BAGEHOT, 1867

New governments don't come into office free of constraints, and they never start – much as they might wish to – with a clean slate. A new prime minister finds a desk that is piled high with history, precedents, and successes and failures from the past. All new governments have to deal with the consequences, for better or for worse, of the decisions of their predecessors. They also have to deal with the consequences of their own words and actions when they were in Opposition before winning an election.

The success or failure of a new government coming out of Opposition is therefore often determined by how well it has prepared to take office while in Opposition. This was certainly the case for the Chrétien government; much of its agenda and many of its early decisions, good and bad, can be traced back to the three and a half years when Jean Chrétien was Leader of the Official Opposition. In June 1990, when he defeated Paul Martin at the convention to choose a successor to John Turner as leader of the Liberal Party and, as such, became Leader of the Opposition, Chrétien had spent almost all of his career in government and, despite his reputation as a street fighter, he had little experience in Opposition. I, too, had spent a decade in government and no time in Opposition when I became principal secretary to the Opposition leader and was asked to focus on policy and political strategy.

Party Unity: Martin and Chrétien

CHRÉTIEN KNEW THE fundamental rule in Canadian politics, both at the federal and provincial levels, that new leaders who do not reach out in a genuine way to their adversaries usually experience a rough ride. Those who immediately unify their parties, despite the inherent bitterness of leadership campaigns, make a difficult job far easier. Brian Mulroney's success in two elections was attributable in no small measure to the way in which he brought the almost perpetually warring factions of the Progressive Conservative Party together. Chrétien and I both knew that how he handled his relationship with Paul Martin would be crucial to the unity of the Liberal Party and to the eventual success of his government, if he ever formed one. The tone of the relationship that dominated the internal politics of the Liberal Party and the government of Canada for at least the next decade was set during the years in Opposition, from the time of the leadership campaign in 1990 until the formation of the government in 1993. I was in the middle of it for all of that time.

The very nature of political life and especially of life in broad-based political parties requires compromise and accommodation, with everyone putting a little water in their wine and setting bygones aside for the greater good of the party after a hard-fought campaign. We succeeded in doing so, but not without difficulty because some wounds inflicted during a campaign are harder to bandage than others. Martin's attack on Chrétien's Quebec policy during the leadership campaign was one of them. At the time of the last debate among the candidates in Montreal in June 1990, shortly before the Liberal leadership convention, Martin's organization had bussed in a great number of youth supporters from Ontario to yell "traitor" and "sell out" in French at Chrétien for opposing parts of the Meech Lake Accord. Many did not even know the meaning of the words *"traitre"* and *"vendu"* that they had been instructed to shout. But they are harsh, bitter accusations in any language. In the context of the political circumstances of the time in Quebec, they were particularly destructive and shortsighted, and could only give a boost to the separatist cause should Chrétien win the leadership.

It was no better at the Calgary convention. When Chrétien's victory was announced after the first ballot, a number of Martin's supporters from Quebec immediately put on black armbands in a gesture that obviously had been planned well in advance and must have been known to Martin and approved by him. Some of them, including Jean Lapierre (who fourteen years later became transport minister and Quebec lieutenant in Martin's short-lived government), immediately left the Liberal Party to join Lucien Bouchard in creating the separatist Bloc Québécois. Chrétien, who was proud to have dedicated his life to the cause of keeping Quebec within Canada, often noted that he had a lot of scars to show for his battles in the cause of Canadian federalism. He would not countenance attacks from within his own party on his loyalty to Quebec. Those attacks were beyond the pale for him and for his supporters. Chrétien, white with anger, never forgot and never forgave Paul Martin for what he and his supporters did.

It did not help that a few months after Chrétien became leader, Martin was asked as a gesture of unity to introduce the new leader at the annual Liberal Party fundraising brunch in Montreal. It is unheard of for an MP to refuse to introduce his leader at a party event. However, that is exactly what happened. Martin refused to introduce Chrétien, saying he was not yet comfortable enough to do so. This, too, was not forgotten, certainly not by Chrétien, but also not by me and others close to the leader. The only plausible explanation is that we were already in the early days of what became a thirteen-year underground campaign to undermine Chrétien's leadership.

Martin on Meech Lake and Trudeau

I FOUND THE vehemence of Martin's leadership campaign position on Meech Lake and Quebec particularly hard to accept. It was clearly not based on any philosophy of Canadian federalism, but solely on a perception of what he thought was good politics for himself in Quebec. In early 1989, shortly after Brian Mulroney had retained power in the general election of November 1988, a group of Liberals met at a conference at the Chateau Montebello hotel in Quebec, about a fifty-minute drive northeast of Ottawa. Paul Martin had just been elected for the first time to the House of Commons, and was interested in succeeding John Turner as leader of the Liberal Party. I had been friendly with him for a long time and was glad to see him at the conference. Running into each other on the first evening, we stopped to talk while looking down on the hotel's massive stone fireplace and its spectacular British Columbia cedar lobby. We chatted amiably for quite a while about how he was enjoying being in active politics. Then we discussed the Meech Lake Accord and how it was dividing the Liberal Party. I made no secret of my opposition to the accord.

To my amazement, Martin told me in no uncertain terms that he fully agreed with me; he, too, was against the accord. He said, however, that he had become convinced that it was not going to pass anyway, because the newly elected provincial Liberal government in New Brunswick was going to withdraw its consent before the constitutional amendments were proclaimed. So, as it was not going to pass, he did not have to oppose it. Instead, he could publicly support Meech Lake – knowing that it would fail – because, in his view, it was good politics in Quebec for federal Liberals to be seen to support it.

I was similarly concerned about – and, frankly, puzzled by – Martin's views on Quebec more than a decade later. In 2001, after Pierre Elliott Trudeau's death, his family proposed that the federal government endow a foundation for postgraduate scholarships and research in the humanities, as a national memorial to the late prime minister. Chrétien readily and enthusiastically agreed. Playing what had by then become my usual role as go-between in the discussions leading up to a budget, I discussed the idea with the finance minister while we were preparing the December 2001 budget. Martin had no objection to setting aside $125 million to fund the Trudeau Foundation, but insisted in doing so without specifying in the budget documents where the money was going. He made it clear to me that he was not prepared to be part of any government announcement in commemoration of Pierre Elliott Trudeau.

Later, in a meeting with Martin's chief of staff, Tim Murphy, I asked, half-jokingly, "Tim, why doesn't Paul agree to make the announcement himself? He could have his picture taken in the company of Mr. Trudeau's two sons, Sacha and Justin, for a future leadership campaign brochure that would trumpet his links to a Liberal icon and a Canadian hero." Tim sat on the couch in my office and replied very seriously, "Paul's Quebec people don't think it would be good for him to be associated publicly with anything in Trudeau's memory." I shook my head in disbelief: It was both disrespectful to the memory of a great Canadian and, in my view, terrible political judgment; most Liberals would have given their eye teeth to have an association – no matter how tenuous – with the Trudeau legend.

Building Bridges on Eggshells

DESPITE SERIOUS reservations about Martin's approach to Quebec issues, and the sour aftertaste of the leadership campaign, Chrétien and I knew that he and Martin would have to work together if the Liberal Party was to be united and have a chance to win the next election. My role from the day after the leadership convention was to act as a bridge between the two men. (Three years later, when the Chrétien government was about to take office, I sought advice about my general responsibilities as senior policy adviser from Tom Kent, who had played the same role under Lester Pearson as I did with Jean Chrétien. He told me that he had been required to spend a great deal of time managing the relationship between Paul Martin, Sr., and Pearson, and he expected that I would have a similar difficult diplomatic role in the new administration. I told him that I had already been doing that for three years in Opposition.)

Martin was extremely disappointed in the result of the 1990 leadership convention. He was still very ambitious, however, and did not want to remain as a Liberal MP in the Opposition for many years to come. He wanted to be a major player in the next government, even if he was not leading it, and so would do his part to help win the next election. But both he and Chrétien were extremely proud individuals and, as such, recognized and found slights even when they were not intended. That made the relationship particularly complicated to manage, but the management of difficult and large egos is part of what politics is about. People who are shy and retiring and hold a modest opinion of their own abilities do not tend to enter politics.

It helped that I had known and liked Paul Martin for a long time. Despite the closeness of my relationship to Jean Chrétien and my part in the Chrétien leadership campaign, there was a Goldenberg family friendship with the Martin family that went back many decades, and, indeed, our fathers had been friends since the 1930s. A few weeks after the leadership convention in 1990, I accepted Paul's invitation to spend a weekend with him on his farm near Knowlton in the Eastern Townships of Quebec. We had wide-ranging discussions throughout the weekend as we strolled through fields where his prize cattle were grazing or simply sat relaxing in his book-strewn living room looking out on the countryside.

Traditionally, seating arrangements in the Canadian Parliament – other than for Cabinet ministers – have a lot to do with seniority, and since Martin had been elected less than two years earlier, he did not then have a front bench seat. In the course of our talks, Paul told me frankly, "I would like a front bench seat in the House of Commons close to the leader." That weekend, Martin also told me he wanted to be the environment critic for the Opposition. I was surprised and asked, "Wouldn't you prefer to be the economic spokesperson for the Opposition? That's where your strengths are." His response said a lot about the man: "On the one hand, the environment is an important public policy issue and I can set out certain views. More important, if the Liberal Party forms a government after the next election, no one would expect me to be minister of the environment. On the other hand, if I am the finance critic in Opposition, everyone will expect me to become minister of finance after an election. If for any reason I am not appointed, it will appear that I have been downgraded, and I don't want to risk any potential future humiliation."

Then he spoke at some length about his father, reminding me that while his father did not achieve his ambition of becoming prime minister, he was responsible for a great deal of progressive social legislation during the 1950s when he was minister of health and welfare. "My dad proved that a senior minister can make a difference even without being prime minister." He talked about the partnership from 1948 to 1957 between Prime Minister St. Laurent and his minister of everything, C.D. Howe, who had played such an important role in transforming Canada into a modern postwar industrial economy. "I hope," he told me, "that Chrétien and I can develop the same type of partnership for the economy of the information age." (In fact, that is exactly what they did for nine years in government.) For that, Martin said that he wanted to be a major player in the policy development process leading up to the next election.

I reported all this back to Chrétien; he recognized what was necessary to unite the Liberal Party. He gave Martin a front bench seat, appointed him Liberal environment critic, and later named him co-chair of the Platform Committee to prepare for the next election.

Party Policy: Escaping a Time Warp

IN 1990, THE Liberals had already been in Opposition for six years, after suffering two crushing defeats by Brian Mulroney, first in 1984 and then in 1988. The party discipline in the parliamentary caucus was almost non-existent. Both Chrétien and I knew from our time in government that what was missing was the well-named "discipline of power" – where there are more immediate rewards for loyalty, and adverse consequences for disloyalty, than there are in Opposition. The normal problems all Opposition parties suffer were accentuated in the Liberal Party in the aftermath of the worst defeat in its history, under John Turner's leadership in the election of 1984. The divisive leadership rivalry between Turner and Chrétien that began when they ran

against each other in the leadership campaign of 1984 intensified after
the subsequent election, and was further exacerbated by the profound
split in the caucus in 1987 over Turner's support for the Meech Lake
Accord. The loss in 1988 threw party morale into a tailspin, and the
1990 leadership campaign created the Chrétien-Martin divide that I
have described.

Reaching out to Martin was an essential first step. But an Opposition party needs more than just caucus unity to present to the Canadian
public. Its policy positions are fundamental to establishing the credibility necessary to have a chance of winning an election. When I joined
the office of the Leader of the Opposition at the end of June 1990, I
was profoundly disturbed by what I found. The Liberal Party had
assumed a classic Opposition party mentality, whereby everything, at
least superficially, was black and white and consequently easy. The
government of the day was the adversary; it was always wrong, and a
change in government was all that was needed to reverse direction and
make the country better once again.

Although this had a certain appealing simplicity, it had its draw-
backs. The Liberal Opposition had demonized the Progressive Conservative government and its works out of all proportion to reality and
had equally unrealistically romanticized the Liberal Party's ideals. For
many Liberals, these took the form of an idealized Trudeau era – with
a strong national government never afraid to intervene in the economy,
never afraid of deficit spending, always willing to stand up to the United
States, as well as to provincial premiers, and never pandering to Quebec
nationalists. For some Liberals, the longer the Mulroney government
was in office, the more they longed for a Trudeau mode of government
that never really existed other than in their imagination, and that
Trudeau himself never would have recognized.

At the time, what troubled me most was that in general, the caucus
seemed to believe that nostalgia for the past combined with the seemingly immense unpopularity of the Mulroney government would be
good enough to win the next election. There wasn't much recognition
of the fact that the world had changed profoundly in many ways since

Trudeau had retired in 1984. The most vivid symbol of the change was the fall of the Berlin Wall in 1989 and the end of the Cold War. The neo-conservatism of Margaret Thatcher and Ronald Reagan had produced significant long-lasting effects on the role of government well beyond the borders of their countries. Like it or not, Mulroney was not alone in how he governed. Even more important, as technology and the information revolution were transforming the world, national economies were becoming much less constrained by borders than they had ever been, and were more affected than ever before by developments in other parts of the world. Globalization had become a fact of life. The impact of all of this on the role of national governments would be profound. To his credit, Mulroney had recognized this and had begun acting on it.

Chrétien understood that it was essential in 1990 for the Liberal Party to adapt to new realities if it was to have any chance of forming a government after the next election. But he had inherited a Liberal Party that was stuck in a time warp.

Shipwreck Survivors Will Cling to the Wreckage

I LATER DEVELOPED a theory that one of the problems facing all Opposition parties is that most of their MPs believe that they owe their election success in their own constituencies to stands they took on issues that actually were rejected in the election by the majority of the country as a whole. This causes a dilemma for them as the ship may have gone down, but the wreckage floated them safely ashore. These personal histories make adapting to changed circumstances difficult. The best example of my theory was the continuing opposition in the Liberal Party to free trade with the United States. In the election campaign of 1988, the Turner Liberals promised to "rip up" the Free Trade Agreement with the United States, which had been negotiated by the Mulroney government. The Liberals lost the election, but many of those who won their seats wanted to continue the fight, the election battle cries about the loss of Canadian independence still ringing in their ears. I had felt that it had been the wrong fight in 1988, but I was

certain in the new circumstances of a more globalized economy that it
was the wrong fight now.

Historically, the Liberal Party, ever since the time of Sir Wilfrid
Laurier, had always been the party of free trade. But as soon as the
Mulroney government accepted the recommendation of a royal commission appointed by the Trudeau government and chaired by Donald
Macdonald, a former Liberal finance minister, that Canada enter into
a free trade agreement with the United States, the Liberals under John
Turner put up ferocious opposition. It was a classic Opposition reaction to an initiative of a government: whatever the government is doing
must be wrong. Many Liberals simply dismissed their former colleague, Macdonald, as a turncoat, and Mulroney as a Ronald Reagan
acolyte, willing to put the economic destiny of Canada into the hands
of Washington. What they should have done was to examine the reasoning of the Macdonald Commission in the context of the new global
economic realities.

Promises in Opposition: A Cautionary Tale

BEING STUCK IN a time warp was one danger I identified in Opposition. A second danger is the matter of making promises to the electorate, either before or during an election, that will undoubtedly come
back to haunt a new government. Political parties, whether in Opposition or in government, have to be very careful about what they promise.
A government sometimes cannot fulfill promises made in Opposition
because of unforeseen changes in economic circumstances in the
country between the time the promise was made and the time it was to
be implemented. But if the government is unable to deliver because
the initial promise was irresponsible and never should have been
made in the first place, it seriously diminishes its own credibility and
increases public cynicism about the political process. Lyndon Johnson,
in his 1964 presidential campaign against Barry Goldwater, said he
would not send American boys to fight in Asian wars. Soon after his
election, he began large troop deployments to Vietnam, and his credibility was shattered. In 1974 in Canada, Trudeau campaigned against

the Opposition platform of wage and price controls as the only way to deal with serious inflation. His rhetoric was powerful. A vote for the Opposition Conservatives would mean "Zap, you're frozen." Soon after winning the election, he had to implement wage and price controls. As a result, zap, his credibility was badly damaged for a long time to come.

Chrétien and I knew those dangers. We understood that omelettes cannot be unscrambled, even when a new chef comes into the kitchen, and we both understood from our time in government that – like it or not – the economic, social, and administrative costs of changing some government policies and programs once they are in place are simply too great to be worthwhile. In 1989, the Mulroney government had introduced the new goods and services tax (GST). Canadians hated the GST and took out their anger on the Progressive Conservative government of the day. Liberals fought it with great ferocity before it passed the House of Commons. During the Liberal leadership campaign in 1990, both Paul Martin and Sheila Copps promised to scrap the tax if they were to form a government. Jean Chrétien, on the other hand, had been a member of the Trudeau Cabinet at the time of wage and price controls, and remembered very well how that government had suffered from accusations of flip-flopping. As a former finance minister in the Trudeau government, he also understood that it would simply not be possible to get rid of the GST once such a huge revenue source was in place. Therefore, unlike his two leadership opponents, he refused to promise to scrap it if he formed a government. In candidates' debates, Chrétien made a virtue out of being cautious and responsible, and he accused Martin and Copps of being irresponsible. He asked, "Where are you going to find alternative sources of revenue for the government?" They couldn't answer.

It was a few months later as leader of the party that he abandoned this responsible stand and made a big mistake that would affect his credibility as prime minister years later. As always, the context is important here. Chrétien's first months as Liberal leader were difficult. There were plenty of initial stumbles. He seemed unsure of himself and as a result, he received bad press, the polls were disappointing, and the caucus was restless. The leadership supporters of Paul Martin were – as became clear years later – hovering in the wings, waiting for an opportunity to pounce on the new leader. The caucus, with the exception of John Manley and Roy MacLaren, was insistent on promising to scrap the GST.

Brian Tobin was a great supporter of Chrétien's leadership bid, and like other caucus supporters, had agreed during the leadership campaign with his position on the GST. But unfortunately, Brian, who had considerable influence in caucus, always looked first and foremost to short-term, quick-result politics; he was the master of pithy media clips and, in fact, had persuaded John Turner to promise to "rip up" the free trade agreement. For those who believe a good Opposition politician is one who can go for the jugular of the government in office without thinking beyond the next election, then Tobin, who had been a charter member of Turner's Rat Pack, was a master. Not long after the leadership convention, he succeeded in convincing Chrétien that the only way to turn around his political fortunes in the Liberal Party and in the country was to reverse his position and promise to get rid of the GST once he became prime minister.

My advice over the years may not have always been right, but it was on the GST. I vividly remember the day Chrétien and I met after he had seen Tobin and been convinced by him to change his approach to the GST. We were in a large office he rarely used in the Opposition leader's staff quarters in the Wellington Building, diagonally across the street from Parliament Hill. He hunched behind a bare desk and I sat in front of him. It was one of the few memorably heated discussions we ever had – not that we always agreed with each other, far from it. But this time we both raised our voices. "You will regret this promise if you ever become prime minister," I told him very loudly. "You won't be able to keep it. You said as much during the leadership campaign. This will be for you what wage and price controls were for Trudeau." He became angry, less at me – although I bore the brunt – than at his political situation. Tobin had convinced him that there were short-term politics to consider. "Don't talk to me about when I am prime minister," Chrétien said. "I won't be prime minister if I lose the leadership of the party. Right now, my leadership is on the line. I can't afford to lose control of the caucus." I argued angrily that he could face down the caucus and win. I did not think his leadership was at risk. He disagreed. His political instinct after almost three decades in politics was clear: "I am not well enough established in the leadership to succeed." Then he said that once in government, he would find a way to change the tax. I told him, vehemently, that he was being unrealistic.

Our no-holds-barred conversation forced me to reflect on some of the very real constraints of Opposition leaders. Because their positions within their own parties are often precarious, inevitably the survival instinct comes to the fore. They face the dilemma of creating credibility problems for the future if they make what turn out to be unrealistic promises about reversing policies put in place by the existing government versus the credibility problems they create for themselves in the present if after fighting government measures tooth and nail before they pass, they then have to explain why the measures won't be changed if they succeed in forming the next government. Despite this, Chrétien made the wrong choice with respect to the GST. He had given in to immense pressure from his caucus, and try as he might to talk about the need to find ways to make up for lost revenues, he had created the public impression that a Liberal government would simply scrap the GST.

Well before the 1993 election, he recognized that he had to be clearer. I helped prepare a speech he delivered in Toronto early in 1993, where he moved from the caucus position of simply promising to scrap the GST – which he knew was totally irresponsible, because the tax raised many billions of dollars of revenue – to promising – and later repeating in the election platform – to replace it with a new and fairer tax that would generate equivalent revenues, and then he studiously avoided talking about the GST during the election campaign. But even this was not realistic.

It did not take long for the new Liberal government in office to discover, much to the prime minister's chagrin, that while the tax might have been structured differently before it had been put in place, it was too late to change the GST once it was in force. It took longer to figure out how to explain this conclusion to the public, particularly when Sheila Copps fulfilled her election promise to her constituents to resign if the GST was not scrapped. If Sheila Copps, the deputy prime minister at the time, thought the government was committed to scrapping the GST, it wasn't possible to explain to Canadians, even after Sheila had been re-elected in a quick by-election, that the fine print of the pledge was actually to find a replacement tax. When even that proved impossible for Paul Martin's finance team, there was no choice but to keep the hated GST. The saga of the GST undoubtedly affected the credibility of the government. It provides a lesson that Opposition parties should take to heart about knowingly making irresponsible promises.

Opposition: Making the Government Prove Its Case

IN AN ADVERSARIAL parliamentary system, one role of the Opposition is to attack the credibility of the government in place and create the conditions for its defeat in the next election. It is a truism that governments often defeat themselves, or at least create the conditions for their defeat. The Opposition is there to help them to do so. Chrétien fully understood what had to be done, and some of his MPs who had never been Cabinet ministers were very good at the attack role, something that is much harder for former Cabinet ministers, who usually find it difficult to adjust to Opposition. Chrétien certainly did, and was often uncomfortable as Opposition leader.

He knew that while opposing political parties have different philosophies and, as such, approach government in different ways, much of what any government does in its daily activities is what any Opposition party would also do if it were in power. In the privacy of his office, he would complain about the questions he was obliged to ask during question period in the House of Commons. He often said to me and other staff members, "I have been a minister. No minister comes into his office every day in the morning asking, 'How can I screw up today?'

They make mistakes in good faith. Why do I have to criticize them for doing what we would probably do in their place?"

I explained Chrétien's discomfort to his mentor in politics, Mitchell Sharp, whose wisdom from a half-century of public service and active politics was always invaluable. "Tell Jean," Mitchell said, "the role of an Opposition leader is like that of a defence lawyer. He isn't necessarily criticizing something he would do himself. His responsibility is to make the government prove its case."

Chapter 3

GETTING READY TO GOVERN

"He who is not ready today, will be less ready tomorrow."

– OVID

Keeping a government on its toes, and making it prove its case, is only half the job of an Opposition party; the other half is getting ready to govern. It was something Chrétien was determined to address from the start. The first step – which is easier said than done – was to build a strong team around him. It is something that takes patience, time and effort, and luck. Chrétien wanted to emulate his predecessor, Lester Pearson, whose team in Opposition from 1958 to 1963 later served him well in government. It included, for example, Tom Kent, Walter Gordon, Allan MacEachen, Maurice Lamontagne, Dick O'Hagan, Keith Davey, and Mitchell Sharp. Some served directly in his office; some worked out of Liberal Party headquarters; and others were part-time advisers who remained in the private sector but later ran as Liberal candidates and became ministers in Pearson's government. Chrétien knew, however, that since the Pearson days, recruiting good people – particularly into Opposition – had become even more difficult for a political party leader. In the intervening years, public cynicism about government and politics in general had increased; moreover, the difficulties that Pearson faced remained equally in force.

The pay in Opposition offices is poor compared to that of the private sector; there is no guarantee of winning the next election; and there is not the same job satisfaction that comes with success in a government.

Building a Team

WE BEGAN IN June 1990 with three huge holes in our organization. We needed a chief of staff to oversee overall planning and coordination, as well as a director of policy and a director of communications. There were no obvious candidates for any of the positions, and there definitely was no flood of unsolicited applications sitting on Chrétien's desk. In the end, we were highly successful, in considerable part through good luck, which, I learned, is as much a major ingredient in successful recruitment as is good management.

A Chief of Staff

THE CHIEF OF staff in any large political office is as important to political success as the conductor of an orchestra is to producing musical harmony. Chrétien needed someone he knew well, and in whom he had complete confidence, to manage the Opposition leader's office, to coordinate relations with the Liberal Party and the caucus, and to ensure that all pieces of the operation functioned smoothly and seamlessly. It was then politically important for Chrétien to choose a respected Quebecker, because he faced serious political problems at the time in Quebec as a result of his opposition to the failed Meech Lake Accord. But it was one thing to have a job description; finding qualified and willing candidates to fill it was something else. In this case, they were few and far between. Obviously, the job of chief of staff to the Opposition leader isn't one that can be advertised in the media; nor is it a position where the leader can delegate the choice, or even the search, to someone else. Chrétien thought long and hard, and spent months reflecting on who the right person might be, before he offered the job to his lifelong friend and classmate from high school, the former mayor of Quebec City, Jean Pelletier, a man who was highly

respected in Quebec and, who, as a former president of the Federation
of Canadian Mayors and Municipalities, had a tremendous network
right across the country. Pelletier was an extremely hard worker, had a
keen political sense and a reputation as a formidable administrator.
Chrétien could not have made a better choice, and was fortunate his
old friend agreed to take the plunge.

A Director of Policy

THE NEW OPPOSITION leader shared my discomfort with the negativ-
ity of the caucus and agreed with the need to bring the policy positions
of the Liberal Party into tune with the times. His approach was typical
of his style. Instead of micro-managing, he wanted a strong staff to
implement his overall directions. He knew from the beginning that he
was running a marathon and not a hundred-metre dash. He would
move the party gradually and methodically, while consolidating his
leadership over the caucus. Soon after he became leader, Chrétien
asked me to keep my eyes open for the person who could direct the
Liberal Caucus Research Bureau, reach out for ideas beyond the party,
and eventually help develop an election platform. It was a tall order,
and, at first, we didn't even know where to begin to look.

Then to our great good fortune, at least in terms of recruitment,
in September 1990, David Peterson's Liberal government in Ontario
was unexpectedly swept out of office in a provincial election. Most
observers immediately concluded that Peterson's defeat didn't augur
well for the federal Liberals. I saw his misfortune differently. His former
housing minister, Chaviva Hosek, was defeated in her riding. She was
exactly the person we needed in Ottawa. Chaviva had a lot going for
her. She had a doctorate from Harvard and a great reputation as an
academic at the University of Toronto. She had been president of the
National Action Committee on the Status of Women, a volunteer
position, while building her academic career. Then she had done a
stint with Gordon Capital, an investment house on Bay Street, before
going into active politics. She came to Canada as a child, the daughter of Holocaust survivors, grew up in Montreal, was extraordinarily

intelligent, thoughtful, intellectually curious, bilingual, committed to good public policy, was not too partisan, had an interesting and eclectic network across the country, and, last but by no means least, was exceptionally pleasant to get along with. In addition to all these impressive qualities, what was most important for us was that she woke up the morning after the Ontario election without a job.

I knew Chaviva well and phoned her that morning to commiserate on her defeat. I started with a joke. "I love the result of the election because now I can offer you a job."

"Go to hell, Eddie," she replied.

"I'm not kidding," I said. "Because, if you are interested, I might have a challenging job for you, but don't even think about it now. Get some rest and let's talk when you are ready."

Two days later, the phone rang at home. "Eddie, this is Chaviva. Were you kidding or were you really serious about a job for me? Tell me more."

I couldn't believe our luck. "Yes, of course I was serious." We talked it over for a while, and I suggested she come to see the Leader of the Opposition.

"Great. I'd love to talk to him." I immediately rushed to tell Chrétien what I had done. He was enthusiastic.

"I want to meet with her as fast as possible. We were colleagues in the late 1980s, when we were both advisers to Gordon Capital. She would be terrific, but is she really interested?" A few days later, Chaviva came to Ottawa and spent a couple of hours with Chrétien, who offered to make her director of the Liberal Research Bureau and senior policy adviser to the Leader of the Opposition. Over the next decade, Chaviva was crucial to almost everything we did well, first in Opposition and then in government.

A Director of Communications

ANOTHER MISSING piece of the puzzle was a director of communications who could write speeches and provide good strategic political communications advice. In the summer of 1990, Chrétien charged me with the difficult task of recommending a candidate to fill the job. Good communications advisers are crucial to any political operation, and are difficult to come by in the best of circumstances. There are a lot of people who think they are qualified for the job; in my experience, few are any good; fewer are very good; and someone outstanding is extremely rare. I consulted widely over a number of months with no success whatsoever in even identifying potential candidates. Then Lady Luck intervened once again. One day in March 1991, I was sitting on an airplane from Ottawa to Toronto. The flight was delayed on the tarmac, and I had time to read the *Globe and Mail* more closely than I usually do. I came across a small article by the journalist Michael Valpy, comparing two speeches that had recently been delivered. One was by Governor General Ray Hnyatshyn; the other was by Toronto Mayor Art Eggleton. Valpy wrote that Hnyatshyn's speech was mediocre, while Eggleton's was outstanding. He attributed Eggleton's success entirely to his assistant, Peter Donolo, whom he described as the best speechwriter/communications director he had ever seen. I didn't always agree with Valpy's columns, and didn't know Donolo, but decided that I had nothing to lose by calling him and asking for his advice as to whether he knew anyone in the communications field to whom I might consider talking. (It turned out to be one of the best decisions I ever made. Many years later, after we had been in office for a long time, the American ambassador to Canada, Jim Blanchard, told all and sundry that Donolo was a better director of communications than anyone he had ever seen performing a similar job in the White House.)

I called Donolo, introduced myself, told him that I would appreciate any advice he might have about our communications needs, and asked if we could meet. We set a time for the following week. I came to see him at his office at Toronto City Hall and discovered a thirty-year-old bilingual ex-Montrealer. This was a very promising start. Peter Donolo was a political junkie through and through, had been active in the Young Liberals, and was much more familiar than I expected with our needs. He began: "You guys are doing things eighty-five per cent right, but everyone is focusing on the remaining fifteen per cent. Here is what you should be doing to fix it, and here are a few names of people who might help you." His analysis was bang on. As he continued talking about his view of political communications in Canada, and then about his observations of what some American presidents had done well and why, and how Ronald Reagan's White House communications staff had been so successful, and which presidents were less successful communicators and why, I interrupted him, "Peter, forget the other names you're suggesting. I'm not interested in them. Could I put your name to Mr. Chrétien?" He told me months later that it was the one question he had hoped I would ask!

When Chrétien met Donolo, he was impressed by his intelligence and strategic thinking, his knowledge of Canadian and American politics, his ability to situate contemporary issues in a broader context, and his irreverent and irrepressible sense of humour, and immediately offered him the job. Like Chaviva, Peter was instrumental in all of our subsequent successes. Ironically, not long after Chrétien hired Donolo, Senator Keith Davey, who had been an integral part of Liberal election campaigns under Pearson and Trudeau, told me that we had made a big mistake bringing in someone as young as Donolo. What we really needed, said Davey, was someone like Dick O'Hagan, who had done a great job for Pearson and later for Trudeau, as their director of communications. "How old was Dick when he started with Pearson in Opposition? Wasn't he about Peter's age today?" I asked Keith. He smiled, took a deep breath, reflected on the importance that he had always accorded – at least in the abstract – to recruiting younger people, and admitted that I was right.

Recruiting both Chaviva Hosek and Peter Donolo may have been the most important long-term contribution I made to the ultimate success of the Chrétien government. They were critical players on the team, and also proved the axiom that good people recruit good people, as our team was immeasurably strengthened and deepened over the years by those Peter and Chaviva subsequently recruited to come in under them, including in particular Patrick Parisot as press secretary. After a year, the senior team – Donolo, Goldenberg, Hosek, Parisot, and Pelletier – was in place, and we could move forward on the three most important priorities for any Opposition party if it hopes to form a government: policy development, strategic communications, and election planning.

Policy Development

CHRÉTIEN'S GREATEST challenge after uniting the caucus and building his own team in his office was to refocus the Liberal Party to enable it to identify, understand, and adapt to the changes that had taken place in the world, both domestically and internationally, since its defeat in 1984. He was painfully aware that political parties that fail to adapt to changing times risk oblivion, or at least long periods in Opposition. New circumstances and the evolution of society at home and around the world are the driving factors in forcing change in the position of political parties. In Canada in 1945, Mackenzie King recognized the need for the Liberal Party to embrace the welfare state in preparation for demobilization at the end of the Second World War. He was re-elected, whereas the Conservative Party in Great Britain, which did not look to the future, was defeated despite the wartime leadership of Winston Churchill. Later, the great electoral successes of Tony Blair in Great Britain and Bill Clinton in the United States in the 1990s were in no small part due to how they brought their parties around to accepting that the world had fundamentally changed since their parties had last held office.

It was the same for Jean Chrétien in Canada. He knew that thirty years earlier, in 1960, his mentor, Mitchell Sharp, had organized the famous Kingston Conference, which had developed a platform for the then Liberal Opposition that served as the basis for much of what the Pearson government later accomplished. Almost thirty years before Kingston, the first Liberal Thinkers Conference had taken place in Port Hope in 1933, when Mackenzie King was also in Opposition. It prepared him for governing after he won the election of 1935. So now Chrétien asked Chaviva and me to organize a conference similar to Port Hope and Kingston to take place before the end of November 1991.

These conferences don't just happen. Organizing took months of concerted effort, and all the logistical, communications, and intellectual resources of the Office of the Leader of the Opposition and the Liberal Caucus Research Bureau. It took Chrétien's willingness as party leader to use his prestige and authority to get on the phone when necessary to invite speakers and cajole potential participants to attend.

Chrétien gave us a mandate to focus the conference on the future, reach out to bring renewal to the Liberal Party, and, to put it politely, to eliminate the tendency to look to an idealized past. The first decision Chaviva and I made was that the conference should bring together non-partisan experts from Canada and abroad to discuss the economic and geopolitical implications of globalization and to debate the scope of government in the 1990s, and particularly a government's role in a country's economy, and in social policy, environmental matters, health care, and science and technology. We succeeded in attracting speakers from Europe, Japan, and the United States, including Kenneth Courtis, a Canadian who was vice-president of Deutsche Bank (Asia) and a renowned expert on Asian economies; Guillermo de la Dehesa, who had been undersecretary of commerce and secretary of economy in Spain; as well such Canadians as Peter Nicholson, then senior vice-president of the Bank of Nova Scotia; Ken Battle, president of The Caledon Institute for Social Policy; and Geraldine Kenney-Wallace, then president of McMaster University.

Second, in order to be able to focus on the medium and long term, encourage renewal, and not be diverted by the partisan issues of the day and by the ideology of the previous election campaign, we decided to restrict the conference to 125 conference delegates, whom we invited primarily from outside the Liberal Party. Then, in a controversial move that did not increase my popularity in the caucus, we decided to keep caucus representation to a strict minimum, and invited only the chairs of caucus policy committees. Third, to provide symbols of continuity in the Liberal Party we invited Mitchell Sharp, who had organized the Kingston Conference, and (to my great personal satisfaction) both my father, Carl Goldenberg, and Paul Martin, Sr., who were the only two surviving delegates who had attended both Port Hope and Kingston. Fourth, we were able to organize extensive cable television coverage across Canada of the full conference, and finally, we decided to publish the proceedings of the conference in a book, *Finding Common Ground*, which Chrétien later sent, with a personal letter, to all the delegates to a National Liberal Party Policy Convention in February 1992.

"The Role of Government Is to Represent the Future to the Present"

THE AYLMER CONFERENCE (held in the Chateau Aylmer in Quebec across the river from Ottawa) took place from November 22–24, 1991. The keynote address was delivered by Lester Thurow, then dean of the Sloane School of Management at MIT. Thurow is a powerful, provocative, and entertaining speaker and soon had the audience eating out of his hand. His speech galvanized the conference. Business as usual, he said, is a path to declining living standards. Thurow painted a vivid picture of the competition North America faces as a result of globalization. He struck a chord with his comments that, "If you do not care about the future, you cannot deal with the present," and that, "The role of government is to represent the future to the present." Thurow and others concentrated their remarks on the emerging knowledge-based economy, and hammered home the need to focus government policy and investment on the promotion of innovation, knowledge, and research. The priority that the Chrétien government later attached to these areas was in no small part a direct result of the Aylmer Conference.

Chrétien concluded the conference on November 24 with a speech that firmly imprinted his own leadership and set a new direction for the Liberal Party. He made it abundantly clear that the Liberal Party under his leadership, as it prepared to govern in the 1990s, would move away from the protectionist and highly interventionist policies it had stood for in the 1988 election campaign. He said:

> One does not need a degree in political science or economics to see
> that the world of today is totally different from the world of yesterday.

> All of our points of reference have shifted; there is expectation in the air – but there is also uncertainty. At this conference we have learned that the old concepts of right and left do not apply in the world of today and tomorrow. . . . Protectionism is not left wing or right wing. It is simply passé. Globalization is not right wing or left wing. It is simply a fact of life.

The Aylmer Conference had just as much impact on the Liberal Party of the 1990s as the Kingston Conference did on the Liberal Party of the 1960s. It certainly helped to chart the ideological course for the Chrétien government. The conference, from my perspective, had the most significant impact of anything we did during the years we spent in Opposition, and is a model for what political parties can do to prepare to win back the confidence of the electorate.

Building an Election Organization

ONCE THE AYLMER Conference was over, Chrétien moved quickly to get ready for the next election. As his principal strategic adviser, I helped prepare three national general election campaigns, one from Opposition in 1993, and two from government in 1997 and 2000. I learned the surprising truth that election preparation is easier in most ways for an Opposition party than for an incumbent government. Its principal responsibility from the day after losing an election is to get ready for the next one. Fundamentally, it is all there is to do. It is the prime objective of parliamentary strategy. The Opposition leader can focus all his attentions on building his team, developing his policies, and putting a political organization in place. The best MPs have plenty of time on their hands to focus on getting the party ready for the next election, as they are not burdened with Cabinet responsibilities. The leader's staff can also focus all of its attention on planning for the election as it doesn't have any of the government responsibilities of the PMO. There are no diversions as a result of the exigencies of governing. So paradoxically, it should be better prepared for an election than the party in power, which has to work harder and faster to be ready.

Chrétien's four priorities were organization of the election campaign, recruitment of candidates, preparation of the policy platform, and preparation for a transition to government. The team he put in place to get ready for the eventual 1993 election campaign was very much a reflection of his management style. He prized competence, loyalty, experience, and inclusiveness. He appointed Chaviva Hosek and Paul Martin to be in charge of the platform committee. Chaviva had just organized the Aylmer Conference; Martin's policy sense was then widely admired and recognized; if his loyalty to Chrétien was uncertain, the appointment of a leadership adversary was a signal of inclusiveness in the party.

André Ouellet and Senator Joyce Fairbairn were put in charge of the election readiness committee. Both had considerable experience in Trudeau's campaigns; Ouellet was a former Trudeau minister who had been a great supporter of John Turner in the leadership campaign of 1984, and Fairbairn was a protegé of Trudeau. Most important, Chrétien named John Rae and Gordon Ashworth in charge of organization. Rae had been with Chrétien since he first joined Pearson's Cabinet in 1967, had organized both of his leadership campaigns in 1984 and 1990, and was a trusted and valued friend and confidant. Rae also was admired and well liked by all factions of the party and, as chairman of two leadership campaigns, had proven his organizational abilities. Gordon Ashworth was a former national director of the Liberal Party and had organized federal and provincial election campaigns for decades. He had more election experience than anyone else in the party and was the quintessential Liberal, loyal to whomever was the leader. Chrétien valued his loyalty, competence, and experience.

Finally, Chrétien asked David Zussman to prepare advice and materials to be ready to ensure a seamless transition to government after an election. Then dean of the School of Management at the University of Ottawa, he was an expert in government organization, had worked in the public service, from 1982 to 1984 had been a policy adviser in Chrétien's ministerial office, and then was a senior adviser in both Chrétien leadership campaigns.

Candidate Recruitment

IN PREPARING FOR an election, the party leader has the responsibility to field candidates who have the potential to be strong ministers. In the Canadian parliamentary system, the prime minister does not have the luxury that the president of the United States has (in a very different system of government) to choose the Cabinet from the population at large. With the exception normally of one or two senators, ministers in Canada come exclusively from among elected MPs, or must get themselves elected right after they are appointed to the Cabinet. That makes candidate recruitment particularly important. A party leader who intends to be prime minister and hopes to govern well cannot necessarily count on 308 individual constituency nomination meetings collectively producing all the Cabinet material he or she may need.

Furthermore, the electorate sees a political party as more than just the sum of its constituent parts, and judges a leader and potential prime minister in part on the quality of the team of candidates he or she presents to the country. The overall picture a leader wants to project of a team with, for example, gender and ethnic balance is not always completely compatible with depending entirely on 308 separate constituency nomination meetings.

Finally, a leader who tries to project a coherent approach to governing has to be able to stop special interest groups from abusing party democracy and taking over individual riding associations to impose candidates who don't reflect the policies of the party.

In most instances, people who want to run for office prepare themselves, join political parties, identify constituencies, and work hard to get nominations. They often make excellent MPs, sometimes become ministers, and eventually, like Jean Chrétien, who had been a long-time Cabinet minister, or like John Diefenbaker and Stephen Harper, who spent their parliamentary careers in Opposition, even one day become prime minister. But there are times when party leaders identify certain other individuals whom they particularly want to bring into public life. It is always hard to convince people to give up successful and lucrative careers outside of politics to run for office. Mackenzie

King did so with Louis St. Laurent; and St. Laurent did so in turn with Pearson. In both cases, they were given nominations in constituencies, immediately became Cabinet ministers, and later became Liberal Party leader.

Recruiting outstanding candidates is never easy at the best of times. It is even more difficult if the recruiting pitch is as follows:

> I would really like you to give up your current comfortable lifestyle for a job where you must be prepared to work seven days a week, twenty-four hours a day, see a lot less of your family, and face intense media scrutiny of everything you do. I can't guarantee when the election may be called, and of course, even if you win your seat, we could lose the election, and you will sit on the Opposition benches for four years. If that's no problem for you, then you can begin your adventure by trying to get a nomination.
>
> All you have to do is find yourself a constituency you want to run in, hope there aren't already several other potential candidates who have been signing up members for years, find organizers to sign up thousands of 'instant Liberals' for you from some ethnic group or another in the riding, make sure you have more 'instant Liberals' than the anti abortion candidate sponsored by Campaign Life (which has no Liberal Party affiliation), get them all to the nomination meeting, and good luck. By the way, you have a lot to contribute to Canada, and I really need you on my team.

Chrétien therefore convinced the Liberal Party at its biennial convention in 1992 to amend its constitution to give the leader the power to appoint candidates in ridings in exceptional cases, as opposed to the normal practice of candidates being elected at contested nominating meetings. It is a controversial power, sometimes criticized as being undemocratic, and should be exercised sparingly and judiciously. From my perspective, however, although appointing candidates may well appear undemocratic when looked at solely from the vantage point of an individual constituency organization, Canadian democracy is well served by its use at times in certain ridings. The use of the power – and the threat of its use – allowed Chrétien to keep special interest groups from hijacking riding associations, to bring in more women candidates than otherwise would have been the case, and to attract star candidates whom he appointed to the Cabinet. The final judge of the appropriateness of the use of the appointment power is always the electorate in the riding.

Preparing the Red Book

WHILE POLITICAL organization is easier in Opposition than in government, the preparation of a detailed policy platform is more difficult. The Liberal Party election campaign in 1988 suffered a body blow from which it never recovered when John Turner, at a disastrous press conference, was unable to explain the costs of a daycare promise that was the centrepiece of its social policy agenda. Chrétien wanted to erase that memory by presenting a detailed costed agenda for government to show Canadians that the Liberal Party knew exactly how it would govern, and to which he would be held accountable four years later. Paul Martin and Chaviva Hosek criss-crossed the country in 1992 seeking ideas and meeting Liberals, academics, non-governmental organizations, and a variety of interest groups. I worked closely with them throughout 1992 and the early part of 1993 to produce the now famous Liberal Red Book of 1993.

When we started, we knew some of the pitfalls of producing a detailed election platform. The first is that it is impossible to predict the future with any degree of accuracy. The inevitable result is that the more detailed an election platform is, the harder it will be to faithfully implement all of its commitments, because unforeseen circumstances will inevitably later require a government to shift some of its priorities. The second pitfall – which makes platform preparation so difficult – is that the public service resources available to the governing party to provide information about some of the real constraints that governments face are not available to Opposition parties. As a result, some promises that political parties make in good faith from Opposition are

invariably later found to be unworkable. Third, there are those promises that are later broken simply because they should never have been
made in the first place – such as our GST promise, which we knew we
would wear as an albatross around our necks. In 2006, Stephen Harper
made the same type of mistake when he promised that he would never
appoint senators, and then appointed a senator on his first day in office
and made him a Cabinet minister.

These are the generic problems of preparing election platforms for
any election. In addition, we had to tread carefully in 1993 because we
knew that while the Aylmer Conference had served the desire of the
leadership of the Liberal Party to move a long way from the policy
positions of 1988, there was still no unanimity in the party. In fact,
much of the caucus were still unsure that the new direction was necessary. It was not easy for them to come to the painful realization that
some of the accomplishments of their loathed and ostensibly wrong-
headed adversaries across the floor of the House could not be changed
or reversed. Many Liberal MPs continued to propagate the view that
the free trade agreement with the United States and the newly negotiated extended North American Free Trade Agreement between Canada,
the United States, and Mexico weakened east-west ties in Canada and
the Trudeau legacy of a strong national government.

Lessons from the Red Book

DESPITE THESE PROBLEMS – generic and specific – by the summer of
1993, the Liberal Party platform was ready. The Red Book, as it
became known from its cover, was made public during the second week
of the 1993 election campaign and was entitled, "Creating Opportunity: The Liberal Plan for Canada." It was released in the same way
as an important government document. There was a media "lockup,"
where reporters were given the document for three hours in advance
to allow them to study it carefully before it was officially made public
at a news conference for which Chrétien had been well briefed. The
document itself was designed to be, and to look, professional, almost
like a corporate annual report. Government departments immediately

snapped up copies so they could prepare to implement the Liberal platform if Chrétien won the election.

The breadth and scope of the Red Book took observers by surprise and undoubtedly contributed greatly to the election victory on October 25, 1993. It included a description of a general philosophical approach to government, specific targets and policy directions in a number of different areas, and a number of specific commitments with price tags attached to them. The reaction to the Red Book – both at the time of its publication and in the way it has been viewed and emulated by all parties since then – teaches a number of lessons.

First, an election should be about competing visions and different policy prescriptions. Therefore a political party has a responsibility to the electorate to produce a detailed, well thought out, and carefully costed policy platform.

Second, a thoughtful platform needs a number of simple, easy-to-understand commitments. For example, in 1993, the Red Book stated, "A Liberal Government will create a Canada Pre-Natal Nutrition Program. A Liberal Government will commit up to thirty million dollars a year for this program." This type of commitment is clear. Either it is kept or it is broken. Chrétien loved to hold up the Red Book as a prop at election rallies across the country and say, "This is what we stand for; the cost of our promises is on page 111; and you can hold me accountable in four years." Because the Progressive Conservative Party hadn't published a platform, he would then open and hold up an empty loose-leaf binder and say, "Here is the Tory platform in English," and would then stop while the audience laughed, turn the empty binder upside down for all to see, and add his punchline, "And here is the French version of the Tory platform."

Third, a thoughtful platform cannot be just a compendium of simple black-and-white pledges. The uncertainties of governing often require caveats. For example, the 1993 Red Book set out that:

A Liberal government, if it can obtain the agreement of the provinces, will be committed to expanding existing child care space in Canada

by 50,000 new quality child care spaces, in each year that follows a
year of three per cent economic growth up to a total of 150,000
new spaces, with 40 per cent federal funding, 40 per cent from the
provinces, and 20 per cent parental fees.

This was clearly not a commitment to new, unlimited, unconditional
federal funding of child care under any circumstances. It was carefully
and, we hoped, responsibly worded precisely because we could not
guarantee in advance that there would be provincial agreement forth-
coming, or that there would be sufficient economic growth to produce
the revenues needed to fund new child-care spaces. We wanted to show
that we understood that we weren't certain that it would be possible to
move forward. The Red Book commitment could easily and legitimately have been criticized by the Opposition for being vague and not
guaranteeing that there would be new child-care spaces created. When
the government failed to reach any agreements with the provinces it
would have been entirely legitimate to criticize that failure. Yet the
eventual criticism was different. The Opposition parties and the media
made the case that the government had cynically broken an unconditional promise to create new child-care spaces. In my view, that type of
criticism (and all parties are guilty of it), which deliberately distorts
something that has been carefully worded precisely to avoid contributing to cynicism about political promises, is not necessary, and only adds
to that cynicism. There is still room for plenty of legitimate criticism
to fuel vigorous political debate.

Fourth, the most important election commitments don't always
receive the most media coverage, and aren't always the principal focus
of speeches during a campaign. This is the fault of both the politicians
and the media. Some promises during an election campaign are simply
politically sexier than those that are far more fundamental to governing. The most important promise in the Red Book in 1993 was the
commitment to reduce the federal deficit to 3 per cent of gross domestic product within three years as a first step towards a balanced budget,
and implementing that commitment became the major focus of the

first years of the Chrétien government. But explaining that type of promise on the campaign trail in front of partisan audiences sounded too much like accounting and didn't create the type of excitement that the media look for when covering campaigns. So Chrétien focused his partisan speeches on a pledge to cancel the undertaking by the Mulroney government to buy almost $6 billion worth of new military helicopters, at a time the government was in deep financial difficulty. He argued in a way that resonated with voters, that just as a family often is forced to keep an old car and put off purchasing a new one until its financial situation improves, Canada's financial state was such that it could not afford new military helicopters. Therefore, the army would have to make do for years to come with its existing fleet. Chrétien's explanation was easy to understand, took only a few seconds to express in colourful language for a media clip, and served to symbolize his determination to reduce government spending. After the election, within hours of taking office, the first action of his Cabinet was to cancel the helicopter program to show that he would keep his promises. When the financial situation of the country later turned around, the government – like the family who eventually could afford a new car – finally ordered new helicopters almost ten years later.

Having been closely involved in both the preparation and implementation of three election platforms, in 1993, 1997, and 2000, I learned that political promises are meaningful, and it is far too facile to say that politicians rarely keep their word. Governments know they can be expected to be judged on their record, and usually do their best to keep as many of their commitments as they possibly can. But I suggest that the policy platforms of political parties should be looked upon in the same way as five-year corporate plans. They are not perfect. They don't and can't predict the future with complete accuracy. Shareholders and financial markets expect that corporate plans will be adjusted over time to take account of changing circumstances, and these adjustments to corporate plans aren't regarded as cynical breaches of trust. A successful corporate plan is not necessarily one that is followed to the letter. It is one that sets out a philosophy and some targets, and is judged a success if it is largely met. It should not be different for a four-year policy plan for a government, for whom circumstances are usually far more complex than for most corporations.

The First Test: Canada Stands Waist Deep in Boxes

REALITY HIT WITH a thud even before the government was formed. When we won the election on October 25, 1993, I had naively expected that we would at least have the time it took to pack our boxes for the move from the offices of the Opposition leader to those of the prime minister before we had to start to adapt to the hard realities of governing. I thought that the issues would probably come at us fast and furious after the new government was sworn in, but not before. I was wrong. The issue was North American free trade. There was no room for equivocation or delay, the timing was immediate, and the symbolism was enormous. It would be the first test of whether the new government had discarded an Opposition mentality.

Two days after the election, Chrétien appointed his senior staff, and announced that I would be senior policy adviser in the PMO. The next day, my telephone rang. It proved to be the American ambassador, Jim Blanchard. Jim and I were later to become close friends, but at the time we hadn't met. "The Clinton Administration is trying to get Congress to ratify NAFTA. It is very important to the president. We don't have enough votes yet to win. It's very tight in the House of Representatives. Canada can make it or break it, and we don't have a lot of time. Eddie, you will get a call later today from Mickey Kantor to see where Canada stands."

At the time, I knew exactly where I stood – waist deep in boxes preparing to move to my new office. Surrounded by packing crates, I had to pinch myself. Was this really happening? Did anyone really care what I thought? Who was I to tell the United States where Canada stands on NAFTA? As my new responsibilities sank in, I realized that it was a lot easier in the Opposition to give advice as to where Canada should stand on almost anything (a lot of people do that at their kitchen table, with about the same impact) than to speak on behalf of a government – even one that had not been formed – to one of the top officials of the U.S. administration.

Mickey Kantor, President Bill Clinton's one-time campaign manager, was now a Cabinet minister and the U.S. trade representative responsible for American trade policy around the globe. Clinton had not campaigned against NAFTA in the presidential election a year earlier, but rather on a pledge to make changes to the new free trade agreement with Canada and Mexico. He was a free trader in an increasingly protectionist Democratic Party, but had found enough face-savers after taking office to support ratification of the agreement. Chrétien was in the same boat. He, too, was a free trader in a party that, before he became leader, had fought tooth and nail against free trade with the United States. Both new leaders came to office determined to bring their parties into line with the changes that had taken place in the world during their time in the political wilderness. NAFTA – negotiated by their predecessors and opposed by the traditionalists in their own parties – was a tough test for both of them. Both leaders were walking political tightropes as they tried to move their parties to new positions. Chrétien, like Clinton, had been careful not to campaign against NAFTA, but rather to promise to make some changes. Liberals wanted to address the problem of weak dispute resolution guarantees in NAFTA. But the Liberal Red Book had moved a long way from 1988. This time it said: "Abrogating trade agreements should be only a last resort if satisfactory changes cannot be negotiated." However, members of both of their parties – Democrats south of the border and Liberals north of the border – who were strongly opposed to the agreement had trouble understanding the nuances. They both wanted to kill NAFTA.

What would Chrétien do? What would his decision mean for Canada-U.S. relations as he entered office? What type of Liberal was he?

These thoughts were all in my mind when Kantor called. I left a meeting in the boardroom of the Opposition leader, where we were planning for the change in government, and took the call in a small outer office that was so crammed with moving boxes that there was no chair to sit on. Kantor and I talked for a few minutes about common experiences in election campaigns, and then he came to the point. "We have to get NAFTA through Congress. It is crucial for the credibility of the president. What is the position of the new Canadian administration?" I explained the constraints we were under following the election campaign. "We also want to ratify NAFTA, but we are committed to making some changes and we have to find creative ways to meet our election commitments, otherwise it just won't be possible." He understood. "We had to do the same thing. We made the same type of commitments in our own campaign. We have found ways to meet the president's campaign commitments. I am sure we can work things out with Canada."

I explained the situation to Chrétien, who was to become prime minister officially a week later. I asked, "What do we do? You don't even have a trade minister yet."

"You handle it," he told me, "until we have a minister. Find ways for us to agree to ratify NAFTA."

I quickly arranged for briefings for myself from the senior Canadian trade officials, Al Kirkpatrick, the deputy minister of trade, and John Weekes, the assistant deputy minister responsible for the United States. Then I arranged for them to brief the incoming prime minister when they were ready with solutions, organized a meeting between Jim Blanchard and Jean Chrétien, kept in touch myself with Blanchard, and set up discussions between Canadian and American officials to identify ways of meeting our requirements. Over the next two days, there were more calls between Kantor and me, and more meetings with Chrétien to present to him different possible compromises and solutions, including side letters on certain issues between Canada and the United States, and the creation of Canada-U.S. working groups on disputed issues. After three days, our negotiations were successful enough in terms of our election commitments – particularly regarding our insistence on Canadian cultural protections – that even though we did not achieve all of our objectives, Chrétien agreed, even before the official change in government, that he would ratify NAFTA. He acted quickly and decisively because he was ready to govern.

Preparing the Transition

WHILE RAE, ASHWORTH, Ouellet, and Fairbairn were building a campaign team across the country, and Martin, Hosek, and I were preparing the election platform, David Zussman was quietly, behind the scenes, consulting and working on all the details of moving from Opposition into government. He used his expertise in government organization to prepare detailed recommendations for Chrétien on the structure of the PMO, the size and structure of the Cabinet and its committees, whether to maintain government departments as they were or engage in a reorganization, and how ministers' offices should be structured and staffed. Zussman met frequently with Chrétien before and during the election campaign to make his recommendations, and to obtain decisions that he transmitted to the Clerk of the Privy Council, who had to prepare for the eventuality of a change in government. For example, Zussman recommended that Chrétien have a much smaller Cabinet than Mulroney, that secretaries of state not be full ministers, and that reorganization of government departments be kept to a minimum. The transition documents prepared a strategy for the first Cabinet meeting and for the first meeting of deputy ministers with the new prime minister. Zussman and Chrétien agreed that new governments profit from continuity as well as change, and therefore there would be no firings of political appointees of the previous administration, and stability in the senior ranks of the public service would be the order of the day.

Zussman's work made it easier for us to focus on the NAFTA issue as well as everything else that had to be done in the ten days between the election and the formal transfer of power. The new prime minister was ready and able to demonstrate in the week before he was sworn into office that he and his government would not go back to what the

Liberals stood for in the losing campaign of 1988. Instead, he gave a strong signal that the new government would take into account the changes that had taken place not only in the country but in the world in the nine years since the Mulroney government had come into office in 1984.

Then he had to form his Cabinet.

Chapter 4

CABINET MAKING: CHOOSING THE TEAM

*"My Cabinet has 'shrunk' up North, and I must find a Southern man.
I suppose if the twelve Apostles were to be chosen nowadays, the shrieks
of locality would have to be heeded."*

– ABRAHAM LINCOLN, 1864

Sir John A. Macdonald once, somewhat facetiously, wrote *cabinet-maker* as his occupation when he signed a guest book. It was funny, but something more. For Cabinet making is one of the most difficult and loneliest parts of a prime minister's job, with the government's success or failure hanging on the success of the selection. The success or failure of a government, like that of any private enterprise, is dependent to a great extent on the quality and cohesiveness of the management team. The choice of senior executives by a chief executive officer in the private sector is usually made outside the public spotlight. Conversely, the choice of the Cabinet by a prime minister produces instant public winners and, worse, public losers. Ambitions are satisfied in some cases, but are disappointed in many more, because there is hardly a single backbencher, no matter how limited his or her talents may be, who does not believe that he or she deserves to be in the Cabinet.

In 1993, I advised a new prime minister as he selected his first Cabinet and then again whenever he shuffled his Cabinet over the following decade. When he formed his Cabinet, Jean Chrétien considered past practice, established his own criteria, consulted a few advisers, and

then made his own ultimate decisions. He had begun his career in politics as a young and ambitious backbencher hoping to get into Cabinet,
and then had sat as a minister in Lester Pearson's and Pierre Trudeau's
governments for seventeen years and had studied how those two prime
ministers and their successors – Turner briefly, Mulroney for nine
years, and Campbell briefly – chose and shuffled their Cabinets. He
had developed his own views of what they had done right and what he
would do differently. He had watched the workings of the government
caucus, the Cabinet, and the House of Commons over many years, and
had come to very definite conclusions about how best to choose ministers. As the election campaign of 1993 progressed, and as the prospect
of forming a government became more likely, Chrétien sat through
long campaign airplane flights jotting down names on small pieces of
paper that he would not show to anyone, and that he would carefully
fold and put in his wallet. He never wanted leaks about the people he
was considering for Cabinet.

First Things First: Party Solidarity

AS WE TRAVELLED in the campaign airplane, Chrétien explained to
me the three-dimensional jigsaw puzzle a prime minister has to put
together in forming his Cabinet. First, as a prerequisite for a successful government, a prime minister must ensure the unity of the political
party he leads. As a basic rule then, Chrétien understood that those
who had been his rivals for the leadership of the Liberal Party at the
convention in 1990 must be well treated in the formation of the government. He knew that party unity was one of the reasons that prime
ministers from King to St. Laurent to Diefenbaker to Pearson, Trudeau,
and Mulroney had all carefully placed their serious leadership rivals in
senior positions in their governments. In Chrétien's case, this meant
giving prominent positions to his two leading opponents, Sheila Copps
and Paul Martin.

    In the case of Copps, it was easy. While she had run a tough leader-
ship race, she always demonstrated loyalty to the leader, and would

not allow any future ambitions she might have to create division in the government. With Copps, what you saw was what you got. She was populist, feisty, partisan, combative, and always wore her heart on her sleeve. Chrétien was genuinely fond of her, but understood her strengths and weaknesses, and liked to joke that, as he was deaf in his right ear, he carefully placed Sheila, as his deputy leader, in the seat in the House of Commons at his left side while in Opposition, and then in the seat beside his right ear after he formed the government.

The case of Paul Martin was totally different. Martin could not hide his ambitions, and it was well known that he had a team in place, ready and anxious to profit from the slightest slip by the prime minister. While Chrétien always felt that he had to watch his back, his working relationship with Martin actually grew somewhat closer during their period in Opposition, particularly as a result of Martin's work on the platform. They could even make jokes at each other's expense. For instance, at one meeting of members of the Liberal Opposition caucus where he strongly disagreed with a position that Chrétien had taken, Martin began by saying, "With the greatest of respect, sir." Then he paused, laughed, and with a twinkle in his eye, added, "Now, Jean, you know that when I say 'with the greatest of respect,' I really mean you are full of . . . ," and everybody was able to laugh heartily. But the tension was always there.

Martin's political DNA was also a factor. I recounted to Chrétien just after he became prime minister what my father had told me: "Paul, Jr., will be as loyal to the Chrétien government as his father [who in 1958 had been defeated by Lester Pearson for the leadership of the Liberal Party, but whom Pearson had later made minister of external affairs] was to the Pearson government." That was the good news. Then my father added, somewhat ominously, "But if the prime minister were ever to be hit by a bus, Martin would be exactly like his father. He wouldn't call the ambulance!" Chrétien hardly needed to be told this, even though he was happy to name Martin as the minister of finance. He was well aware that prime ministers always face the danger of leadership challenges from within, particularly when governments go through tough times, as they all do.

Roman Guards, Old Hands, and New Blood

CHRÉTIEN'S SECOND criterion in forming a Cabinet was therefore clear: it is a law of politics that a prime minister needs at all times a core group of loyalists in Cabinet who will defend him from mutiny. Chrétien called these ministers his Roman Guard – ministers who would be prepared without hesitation to lay down their political life in order to protect the prime minister against a potential Brutus. The Roman Guard is always made up of unconditional, long-time, faithful political supporters. In Chrétien's first administration, these included, among others, David Dingwall, the minister of public works and government services; David Collenette, the minister of national defence; Ron Irwin, the minister of Indian affairs and northern development; and Sergio Marchi, the minister of citizenship and immigration; all had been tried-and-true political allies of the prime minister for many years.

The third political law is to choose some ministers who have served well as members of the caucus in the House of Commons in good times and bad, because the loyalty of caucus members to a government is dependent in part on the expectation that loyal service can have its rewards in Cabinet. For Chrétien, this meant appointing MPs who had served well in their days in Opposition, such as Brian Tobin, who became minister of fisheries and oceans, and Diane Marleau, who became minister of health.

Political life is difficult at the best of times, and bringing in new blood is nót easy for any political party. The fourth law of politics that Chrétien prized in selecting his Cabinet was, "Bring new blood into government." The appointment of Allan Rock as minister of justice and Marcel Massé as minister of intergovernmental affairs are two examples of star candidates immediately joining Cabinet. Rock was an extraordinarily successful Toronto lawyer when he decided to enter public life. Massé was a deputy minister at the top of the federal public service when he was convinced to gamble on the vicissitudes of public life.

Experience and Shooting Stars

ON THE OTHER HAND, Chrétien also prized experience as a fifth essential criterion for appointing ministers. He said that a successful Cabinet cannot be comprised only of rookies, and reminded his advisers that while some star candidates had been great successes in politics in the past, he had also seen many so-called star candidates in different governments, at both the federal and provincial levels, quickly become what he called "shooting stars," with the trajectory we associate with shooting stars in the night sky. Some who are very successful in business do not necessarily make great ministers, because the qualities that produce high achievement in business are not necessarily the same as those that lead to success in a political career. There is little substitute for experience in a profession as tough as politics. A successful minister has to be good in the House of Commons, so Chrétien also looked for those who had previously shown their mettle in the crucible of question period. This is why experienced performers in the House – in addition to whatever other qualities they possessed – like Lloyd Axworthy, Roy MacLaren, and André Ouellet, who had all served in Trudeau Cabinets, were obvious choices for Cabinet posts.

Ethnic, Gender, and Regional Balance – A Surprising Effect

MUCH HAS BEEN written about ethnic, gender, and regional balance, the sixth piece of Chrétien's jigsaw puzzle, as considerations for Cabinet. Critics of this approach to diversity argue that competence is sacrificed for purely cosmetic political reasons. Initially, I was sympathetic to the criticism. My views changed after watching the operation of Cabinet and Cabinet committees for a decade. I came to the conclusion that the criticism is too simplistic.

I attended one particular meeting of the Cabinet Committee on Social Policy where Claudette Bradshaw, a new and relatively junior minister from New Brunswick, was proposing a detailed initiative to combat homelessness. She faced stiff odds. Her proposals were strongly opposed by officials of the Department of Finance, who had briefed Paul Martin and convinced him to speak against them. On most public policy issues, gender is not a factor, but there are a few issues where for a variety of reasons, including life experience, it does matter. Women members of the Chrétien Cabinet attached a particular importance to combating homelessness. When Bradshaw made her proposal, and was supported one after another by each of the female members of Cabinet, who that particular day made up the majority of the attendees at the committee, the outgunned Martin threw away his briefing notes and gave her his support. A Cabinet with less gender balance almost certainly would have produced a different result.

In Canada, there is a long-standing and proper convention that every province has to have Cabinet representation. Cabinets that hear from ministers representing parts of the country outside the economic mainstream make very different decisions than would Cabinets composed primarily of members from Toronto or Calgary. This is as it should be, and this representative regional diversity is good for the most part, but it leads to difficult decisions in Cabinet making. Chrétien had to consider that his political base, after the election, was in Ontario, where he had won all but one of its ninety-nine seats in the House of Commons. Ontario had, as a result, to be well represented in Cabinet. But so did Quebec, for different reasons, since an upcoming referendum badly needed federal advocates in that province. Meanwhile, the Atlantic provinces had given him all but one of its seats, and the West had sent more Liberals to the House of Commons than it had for decades. Unfortunately, this need to balance regional representation sometimes results in excellent MPs not making it into Cabinet because of the abundance of potential ministers from their region.

As for ethnic balance, this has attracted some of the harshest criticism of all. Yet, in my experience, diversity brings a perspective to the table that would not be present in an ethnically homogenous Cabinet. I found that Cabinet discussions with the participation of ministers from different cultural backgrounds were therefore different and much richer than they otherwise might have been. A Cabinet whose composition reflects the diversity of the country also brings a perspective to decision making that unfortunately is still not present enough in the ranks of the senior public service.

Ethnic diversity in Cabinets serves an additional role in demonstrating for all to see the integration of new Canadians into the mainstream of Canadian society. Ethnic groups, of course, have often found that their active participation in the political system gives them recognition there far more quickly than they receive from other parts of society. This was the case of the Irish in the United States in the late nineteenth century and early twentieth century, and has been the case for different minorities in Canada at the end of the twentieth century. Ministers from different ethnic backgrounds often serve as role models for their communities, thus easing acceptance and integration in the country as a whole.

They serve another purpose that is little known but is becoming more and more important. In an era of globalization, the ethnic diversity of its government can provide Canada with an advantage in international relations. On travels abroad with the prime minister, I witnessed the respect and admiration leaders of other countries – such as China and India – had for Canada when they met Canadian Cabinet ministers like Raymond Chan and Herb Dhaliwal, who accompanied the prime minister to the land of their birth. These ministers – who were respectively the first Chinese and Indian immigrants to be appointed to the Cabinets of a western country – in addition to fulfilling their normal governmental responsibilities, were able to serve as valued ambassadors of Canada abroad.

Finishing Touches to the Jigsaw Puzzle: Assigning Positions

SUCCESSFUL POLITICAL parties in Canada have always been brokerage parties, and as a result, the Cabinet has to reflect the different ideological perspectives within the governing party. Chrétien led a Liberal Party that was socially progressive but had been brought around, reluctantly, to embrace fiscal prudence and free trade. He had more to consider, however, than just ideological balance. The most difficult part of completing the jigsaw puzzle is fitting prospective ministers into the right departments. It is not enough simply to select a few ministers from the right of the spectrum, some from the centre, and a few from the left. They have to be properly placed. The Cabinet has to be effective in dealing with the pressing issues of the day.

The Chrétien government came into office in November 1993 facing a difficult fiscal situation, with a federal deficit – more than 6 per cent of GDP – of $42 billion and rising. Thirty-seven cents of every tax dollar were going to pay interest on the debt. These were not abstract numbers. In the same way as a mortgage is less and less affordable when interest payments take up more and more of family income, governments are more severely constrained in meeting public needs when interest payments take up more and more of the collected tax dollars. To make matters worse, there was the imminent prospect of an election in Quebec with the strong likelihood of a Parti Québécois victory and another referendum on separation. The stakes were high, because the very future existence of the country was in question.

Chrétien took into account the fact that governments around the world were becoming less interventionist in the economy than they had been in the past. Therefore, he addressed ideological balance by appointing ministers on the right of the political spectrum to economic portfolios, with John Manley in Industry, Paul Martin in Finance, and Roy MacLaren in International Trade, while he appointed more left-of-centre ministers to social portfolios, with Allan Rock in Justice, Lloyd Axworthy in Human Resource Development, and Sheila Copps in Environment.

The key question, of course, in the formation of a Cabinet is who can best do a particular job. Chrétien's main criterion – like that of many of his predecessors – in assigning a minister was not necessarily his or her specialized knowledge or experience in the subject area of the department of government. The professional public service is there to provide the necessary knowledge and expertise in the ministry. The ability to be a problem solver or to bring a completely fresh approach to an intractable problem could be an even more important consideration. Chrétien vividly recalled the day in 1968 when Trudeau appointed him minister of Indian affairs and northern development. When he protested to Trudeau that he knew nothing about the subject, Trudeau's response was "I want a minister in that department with an open mind and no pre-conceived ideas." Twenty-five years later, Chrétien named Ron Irwin minister of Indian affairs and northern development in 1993 because of his confidence in Irwin's fearless ability to handle complex and often intractable issues.

Then again, in other circumstances, expertise in the subject area is a reason for a prime minister to choose a particular minister. So Justice was a natural fit for Allan Rock, as was Intergovernmental Affairs for Marcel Massé.

Chrétien did not see it as necessary or desirable for all Cabinet ministers to be media stars, and didn't look only for good communicators. His experience was that when all ministers are in a permanent competition for public attention, they don't focus on their work to the extent that they should, and good public policy suffers. He liked to remind his ministers that Trudeau once called him when he was minister of Indian affairs and said, "Jean, are you mad at me? You haven't called or asked to see me in a year." He replied, "No, I'm not mad at you. I'm just doing my job, and presume if you have problems with my work, you will call me." Trudeau responded, "I wish I had more ministers like you."

Chrétien selected his Cabinet with that conversation in mind. His approach was that while all governments certainly need a number of ministers who are well known, and that the prime minister should certainly not be the only member of the government with a high public profile, government isn't show business, and it badly needs ministers who can be counted on day in and day out to possess good judgment, run their departments well, solve problems, and not make mistakes. Politically, those low-key ministers are sometimes far more useful than the ones who seek a high public profile simply to get headlines to satisfy their own political ambitions (and in so doing, sometimes demonstrate a lack of judgment and wisdom). Ministers like Anne MacLellan

from Edmonton, first in Natural Resources, then in Justice, and finally
in Health, and Lucienne Robillard from Montreal, in Labour, then in
Citizenship and Immigration, and later in Treasury Board, never
sought a high public profile. But they could always be counted on to
perform well and make valuable contributions to the government. In
my view from the inside, they were two of the best ministers in the
Chrétien administration.

The Finalists

ONCE A PRIME minister has finished collecting the multiple factors
that go into Cabinet making, he has to rely on his sense of who will
make the best ministers. It is not an exact science and depends in the
final analysis on the instinct and judgment of the prime minister.
Chrétien once told me about a conversation he had with a Toronto MP
who had come to him after a Cabinet shuffle, complaining bitterly that
he should have been included because he knew he would have been a
great minister. The prime minister told him, "If I thought you would
be a great minister, I would have named you, but I don't think you
would be." It is not a way to win friends – the potential great minister
naturally soon became a great critic of Chrétien's, and eventually a not-
so-great minister in the Martin government – but it is the most succinct explanation of why some people are appointed to Cabinet and
others are not.

A prime minister rarely negotiates a Cabinet position with prospective ministers. Normally, a new prime minister calls in prospective ministers and informs them of their new job. "Congratulations, I am
naming you minister of transport." Unless they have a particularly good
reason to request another portfolio, such as a previous business interest
that could create a conflict, either they accept or they stay out of the
Cabinet. It is unusual, but not unheard of, that a potential minister
might be asked for a preference, or might express a wish for a particular portfolio. After the election, Chrétien readily agreed to Paul Martin's
request to be minister of industry. He then offered the job of finance
minister to a very surprised John Manley. A few days later, before the

Cabinet making was finished, Martin called back and said that he had thought it over and had changed his mind. He wanted to be finance minister. Chrétien accepted Martin's request, and breathed a sigh of relief that he had told each prospective minister that nothing was final until the government was sworn in, and that he reserved the right to change his mind. He then called Manley back, told him that there was a last-minute change, and he would be the new industry minister. The appointment of Martin as finance minister – despite the stormy personal relationship between him and the prime minister – turned out to be crucial to the long-term success of the Chrétien government.

The Last Hurdle: An Ethical Screen

THERE WAS ONE last hurdle for prospective ministers to overcome before being sworn into the Cabinet. Normally, an incoming prime minister – or a prime minister in office – provides a list of prospective ministers in advance to the Privy Council Office for security clearances. The names are then checked by the RCMP and the security services to make sure that no one is under criminal investigation or is considered a security risk. Chrétien went well beyond the normal relatively cursory checks, on the principle of better safe than sorry. He accepted a recommendation of David Zussman that each prospective minister be interviewed at length to ensure that there was nothing embarrassing in their past or in their personal lives that the prime minister should be aware of, and that there was nothing that could put them in any situation of conflict of interest as a result of previous business connections or family interests.

Chrétien asked his mentor of thirty years, Mitchell Sharp, and Allan Lutfy, who later became chief justice of the Federal Court of Canada, to conduct the personal interviews. It was an innovative process that worked well and prevented future embarrassment to the government. For example, one prospective minister was involved in a lawsuit against the government. He was told that regardless of the legitimacy of his claim, he could not be a minister of the Crown while he was suing the Crown. In this case, David Anderson agreed to drop his suit in order to serve in the Cabinet. There was another case where a prospective minister was in a business partnership that was also involved in litigation with the government. He was told that he would have to settle on the Crown's terms or stay out of Cabinet. He came to the conclusion that settling the matter on those terms would be unfair financially to his business partners, and so made the difficult decision not to enter Cabinet. In other matters, Sharp and Lutfy were able to give advice to prospective ministers on how to rearrange their personal affairs in such a way as to preclude any hint of perceived impropriety.

Planning Ahead

EVEN AT THE TIME he was forming his government, the new prime minister told me that he was looking ahead at his job as Cabinet maker during the course of his administration. In general, Chrétien believed that Cabinet shuffles during the course of an administration are required only to fine-tune the government, to deal with underperforming ministers, to promote some who outperform expectations, and to adapt to new political and policy circumstances. Since he valued a managerial style of government, he wanted his ministers to spend a considerable amount of time in their portfolios unless unforeseen problems arose that required a change. When ministers were doing well in their portfolios, he did not want to move them. He thought that both Trudeau and Mulroney had shuffled their Cabinets too often, and that ministers were moved before they really had the opportunity to get to know their portfolios. The more ministers moved, the less familiar they were with their departments, and consequently the less they decided themselves and the more the professional public service had to fill the vacuum.

However, as leader of his party and with years of experience in the House of Commons, Chrétien also knew that a government caucus gets restless and surly when there doesn't seem to be any hope of advancement for backbenchers. Less than a week after assuming office, the prime minister called me to his residence. As we walked in the garden before going in for lunch, he told me that he would follow the example of Lester Pearson, who appointed veteran members of Parliament to his first Cabinet, and then moved some out after a relatively short time in office in order to make room for promising new MPs. He said that he planned to ask André Ouellet and Roy MacLaren to retire after about two years. By then their experience would be less required, as the new government would already have found its feet, and their retirement would give him an opportunity to advance some backbenchers.

Chapter 5

THE PRIME MINISTER'S OFFICE

"I don't mind how much my ministers talk as long as they do what I say."
– MARGARET THATCHER

During the Chrétien years, the role of the Prime Minister's Office in the government of Canada became the subject of a great deal of myth. Books with the provocative titles *The Friendly Dictatorship* by Jeffrey Simpson, and *Governing from the Centre* by Donald Savoie helped to create an impression of an inordinate, inappropriate, and almost undemocratic concentration of power at "the centre" and, more particularly, in the PMO. Blaming the centre for wielding inordinate power is always convenient for critics of the actions or inactions of any government. However, my conclusion after ten years in the PMO is that the role of the office of the head of government is far too complex to be captured by pithy sound bites.

The prime minister is the head of government, is responsible for the management and decisions of the Cabinet, and is the principal spokesperson for the government in the House of Commons. He is responsible for federal-provincial relations and for Canada's relations internationally, and is also the leader of his political party. Everything he does and says sets the overall tone for the government. His desk, like Harry Truman's, could easily have a plaque on it saying, "The buck stops here." While there are obviously profound differences between the management of a government and the running of a business, the prime minister is still the chief executive officer of the largest and most complex corporation in the country. He has heavy responsibilities, and needs strong staff support to carry them out.

On October 26, 1993, the morning after the election victory, as the Liberal campaign plane took off from Trois-Rivières, just outside Shawinigan, for the flight back to Ottawa, Chrétien asked Jean Pelletier and me to join him at the front of the airplane, where he was sitting in the window seat in the first row on the right. As a result of the comprehensive transition materials David Zussman had prepared before the election, the new prime minister was ready to establish the PMO. "Jean, you will be my chief of staff and will manage the PMO. Eddie, you will be my senior policy adviser and will ensure the oversight and coordination of government policy. You will work a lot with ministers and deputy ministers and will attend all Cabinet committees as part of your duties." I could not have been more pleased – I would have a minimum of administrative responsibilities and plenty of time to focus on policy and strategy.

Ten days later, on the morning of November 5, 1993, the day after the government had taken office, in accordance with the transition plan that had been prepared for the first days in government, the prime minister met with all the deputy ministers in the government. Chrétien was well aware that the Diefenbaker government had failed in part, in the late 1950s and early 1960s, because of the animosity between the government and the public service, and that Mulroney got off to a bad start in 1984 when he promised in his election campaign to give public servants "pink slips and running shoes." Chrétien told the deputy ministers, as he had told the Cabinet at its first meeting the previous day, that he had learned from his experience in the Pearson and Trudeau Cabinets that governments only succeed when they trust the public service, and when the politicians and the public servants respect one another's roles, and then work seamlessly together. The prime minister said that he expected me as his senior policy adviser to work closely with deputy ministers and other senior public servants in the years to come to push forward the strategic policy agenda that was most important to him as prime minister. He saw his own policy role as focusing on a few priorities that he viewed as crucial to the government agenda. Helping him with those priorities would be my major responsibility for ten years.

Chrétien's Style: Teaching Tony Blair

CHRÉTIEN HAD STRONG views on what a prime minister should and shouldn't do. He didn't have the time or the inclination to be a details person, and was certain that wasn't the job of a prime minister. Rather he wanted to manage the big picture, and take time to himself for reflection and strategic thinking. I attended a meeting during the G-8 summit in Denver in June 1997 when Chrétien explained to Tony Blair how he believed prime ministers should function. It was their first meeting, just weeks after Blair became prime minister of Great Britain and a few days after Chrétien's re-election to a second term in office in Canada.

Shortly before the meeting, the Canadian High Commission in London informed Chrétien's foreign policy adviser, Jim Bartleman, that a junior minister in the new Blair Cabinet had made a statement earlier in the day to Parliament in Westminister that might lead to the restriction of exports of asbestos from Canada to Britain for environmental and health reasons. The Canadian industry had different views, and Bartleman brought the matter to Chrétien's attention. "Blair probably is unaware of this, but you could ask him to have his officials look into the issue." As we fully expected, the British prime minister didn't know about his minister's statement when Chrétien raised the subject. Blair was embarrassed, apologized, and said he would look into the matter immediately. Chrétien tried to put his counterpart at ease: "It happens to me all the time. My ministers decide and speak on many issues within the responsibility of their departments without my being aware. That is the very nature of government. Tony, you'll see that a prime minister cannot and should not know everything that goes on in the whole government."

Blair's response was interesting. "That's not my style," he said. "I want to know all about what all my ministers are doing." It was easy for him to say at the time, as he had only just been elected prime minister. I chuckled to myself and suspected his answer would be different years later.

The Role of the PMO

CHRÉTIEN EXPECTED the PMO to be a strategic player, but he didn't expect it to micro-manage the whole government. From his first day as prime minister, Chrétien insisted that the PMO is not there to second-guess ministers or to try to do their jobs for them. He did not want it to be intimately involved in all the priorities of every department of the government. In fact, when Chrétien was a Cabinet minister (and he served over time in nine different departments, and I was his executive assistant in most of them), he told me to stay away from the PMO except on the most important files, where it was obvious that it needed to be informed. "If you always ask them for advice on what to do about anything, they will give it, and we probably won't like it, but we will have to do as they say. But if you don't ask them, they will leave us alone to do our job." He didn't change those views about the role of ministers even as prime minister.

The evolution of the PMO's role has necessarily closely followed the expansion of the role of government and of the prime minister in Canada. Until the 1960s, the Prime Minister's Office, the Privy Council Office, the Department of Finance, the Department of External Affairs, and the Treasury Board were all small enough that they shared premises in one building – the East Block on Parliament Hill. Cabinet ministers themselves had very few staff. Ordinary MPs were two to an office, and they shared secretaries with each other at a time when the House of Commons only met a few months of the year. There was little need for earlier prime ministers to have much personal staff.

Mackenzie King even dictated many of his own letters in response to correspondence addressed to him. In the days of Prime Ministers King and St. Laurent, powerful regional ministers controlled what were veritable political fiefdoms in their own provinces without the prime minister of the day being very involved. Jimmy Gardiner, as minister of agriculture, was able, for example, to run the federal Liberal machine in Saskatchewan for twenty-two years between 1935 and 1957 without the involvement of the PMO.

By the 1960s, however, the role, size, and complexity of government had grown significantly in Canada. The more complex the issues were, the more they crossed departmental boundaries and, as a result, the more they required increased coordination from the centre. In addition, the rapidly growing importance of the media, and particularly television news, placed a new focus on the party leader during election campaigns and then on the prime minister as the central actor in the government. The attention given to a prime minister by the public and the media now precludes the emergence of old-style regional barons. For that reason, beginning with the administration of Lester Pearson, the Prime Minister's Office grew in size and responsibility. Today's prime ministers need staffs to do what King and St. Laurent in another era didn't have to do. For similar reasons, there was the same growth in the size and responsibility of the White House staff in Washington under President Kennedy in the early 1960s, and it was replicated later under Margaret Thatcher and particularly Tony Blair in the Prime Minister's Office in Great Britain.

The PMO has an oversight function that is essential in a modern government and that no one else in government is in a position to have, but it is not a parallel Cabinet or a parallel public service. Its role is to serve the prime minister; it doesn't operate on its own independently of the prime minister, and its style inevitably reflects the style of the prime minister himself. It is there to work with the Cabinet and the public service, and has a responsibility to ensure that the political collegiality of the Cabinet is maintained. As such, I often had to act as a mediator, helping to achieve a consensus among different ministers who held strongly conflicting views on how to address certain policy issues that affected the interests of their different departments in different ways. For example, the minister of health has a bias, by the nature of his responsibilities, to favour the generic drug industry, whereas the minister of industry is always more on the side of the research-based brand-drug manufacturers. When the two conflict, someone has to seek consensus or break a deadlock. Ultimately, that is the role of the prime minister or the PMO. Where issues are non-controversial and there is general agreement on how to address them, the PMO has less to do.

The Symphony Conductor

ONE OF THE sources of the mythology about excessive centralization or inordinate concentration of power is the way in which a modern PMO exercises its coordination function across the government. Yet coordination isn't something sinister; it is crucial to the success of any large enterprise. Just as musicians in an orchestra need a conductor to function in harmony, so a prime minister and a PMO need a chief of staff to work effectively. Jean Pelletier was that conductor for two and a half years in the Office of the Leader of the Opposition from 1991–3, and then for another seven and a half years in the PMO from 1993–2001, and his role was critical to the success of the Chrétien administration. He helped to pull the Liberal team together as soon as he joined the Opposition leader's office, and did the same again once we were in government. He came to the job as a serious, accomplished person with a long track record in public service. Pelletier radiated authority, integrity, and competence, and easily won the respect of the caucus, the Cabinet, and the public service. Chrétien counted heavily on the administrative abilities of his old friend, and also relied on his advice, particularly about all Quebec-related issues. When he left his post, he had established a reputation as having been one of the best chiefs of staff any Canadian prime minister ever had.

Pelletier had his own particular style, based on a very imposing personality and a no-nonsense approach to his job. Although he had been

mayor of Quebec City and had a high public profile himself in the
province of Quebec, he insisted that he, and indeed the whole PMO,
was not elected and so should stay out of the public limelight. He
wanted elected officials, not political staff, to be on television talking
on behalf of the government. Pelletier, like Chrétien, believed in the
importance of a strong team, and initially devoted a good deal of his
time to building a team that could make a transition to government in
a seamless fashion. He was an extraordinarily professional administrator, and made certain that whenever anyone left the PMO, their
replacement was chosen immediately.

He put the senior staff of the PMO in place as soon as the election
was over – Jean Carle as director of operations, Penny Collenette as
director of appointments, Peter Donolo as director of communications, Maurice Foster as caucus liaison, Bruce Hartley as legislative
assistant, Chaviva Hosek as director of policy, Michael McAdoo as
executive assistant to the prime minister, Patrick Parisot as press secretary, and me as senior policy adviser. Throughout the ten years of the
Chrétien government, the chief of staff chaired a meeting of the senior
staff every morning at 8:45, to ensure coordination within the office.
Most meetings were short and to the point, usually lasting less than
half an hour. Pelletier went around the boardroom table asking whether
anyone had anything to report. There would be a review of issues of
the day, discussion of the morning press, a review of the prime minister's schedule, and occasionally a discussion of longer-term strategic
political issues.

Pelletier understood the tendency in political offices for all of the
staff to want to participate in all of the files of the office. The senior
staff meeting was to inform and to coordinate, but he always warned
against "too many cooks in the kitchen," and he instilled a strict discipline ensuring that those responsible for particular areas ran them
without interference from others. The result was a PMO that worked
as a team, and was remarkably free of the internal politics that often
plague the offices of government leaders. His approach was to know
what was going on, coordinate the whole of the office, make sure it

operated professionally and efficiently, and ensure that all matters were dealt with properly and promptly, but he let his managers manage, never trying to do their jobs for them, and he didn't control direct access of any of the senior staff to the prime minister. Unlike some of his predecessors such as Tom Kent under Pearson, Marc Lalonde under Trudeau, and Derek Burney under Mulroney, Pelletier rarely got involved in policy issues; he left those to me and to Chaviva Hosek.

The chief of staff sees all the paper that crosses the prime minister's desk and much that doesn't get that far. Like a traffic cop, he makes sure that all the paper gets to the right place. He travels extensively with the prime minister overseas. His administrative and political responsibilities require at least fourteen-hour frenetic workdays packed with dozens of meetings and phone calls. Pelletier attended Cabinet meetings, met every morning for half an hour with the prime minister and the Clerk of the Privy Council, and then dealt with any political issues arising from that meeting, since one role of the chief of staff is to be a political problem solver for the prime minister. Many issues arise that MPs and Cabinet ministers believe are vital to their careers and often to their re-election prospects. Whether they are vital or not is irrelevant. What is relevant is that there are a lot of big egos in politics and they bruise easily. Chrétien counted on Pelletier to massage the bruised egos of Cabinet ministers and MPs. It is a time-consuming job, and he did it with aplomb, diplomacy, and firmness. He had the unpleasant task of saying no far more often than he could say yes to the many representations made to a PMO. Over time, Pelletier developed a reputation as "the velvet executioner." He was successful as chief of staff in great part because of his own abilities, but also because it was well known throughout the government that he had the complete confidence and support at all times of the prime minister.

Chrétien also believed in using whatever special strengths his advisers had, regardless of whether they had anything to do with their job description. Certainly relations with the president of France would not normally come within the ambit of the chief of staff of the prime minister of Canada. However, Jean Pelletier, during his tenure as mayor of

Quebec City, had established a very close personal friendship with Jacques Chirac, who was mayor of Paris at the same time. Their relationship proved very useful to the cause of Canadian unity.

The Parti Québécois had put enormous effort into cultivating relations with the French government in the twenty-five years that had followed General de Gaulle's famous "Vive le Québec Libre" speech in Montreal in 1967. When Chirac became president of France in 1995, he shared the long-standing Gaullist sympathy for the separatist movement in Québec, and during the 1995 Quebec referendum campaign let it be known that France would recognize a yes vote. France's possible support for an independent Quebec was a matter of grave concern to the Canadian government, and so, after the referendum, Chrétien gave Pelletier, instead of the Department of Foreign Affairs, the almost impossible task of converting his old friend into an ardent and public supporter of Canadian federalism, something he had never been before. Pelletier made several secret visits to Paris to meet with the French president, and also carefully managed all the relations and meetings over the years between Chrétien and Chirac. His diplomatic skills and his friendship with Chirac – much to the dismay and disbelief of Quebec separatists who saw a quarter-century of efforts go down the drain – were instrumental in achieving the desired result. By the end of Chrétien's term in office in December 2003, the two leaders had established such a close friendship and community of interests that Chirac gave a lavish and elegant state dinner (which I attended) in Paris, in the prime minister's honour, where Chirac asserted the essential role a united Canada plays as an example to the world. Pelletier deserved most of the credit.

Telling the Story

ALL GOVERNMENTS STRIVE, with more or less success, to tell a consistent story about what they are doing. Successful governments must combine long-term strategic communications thinking with short-term tactics. Whether it is a good or a bad story, there is no consistent story at all if you have more than two dozen Cabinet ministers all making announcements any time they see fit, about anything they want, without any planning or coordination. The PMO is uniquely placed to coordinate and manage the government's political and policy communications, which makes the role of the director of communications in the PMO pivotal to the overall success of the government.

Around the world, many communications advisers to heads of governments have short and unhappy careers, and leave their jobs blamed both by their bosses and the media for all the problems of the government. Stephen Harper's first communications director lasted all of one week in February 2006. George Stephanopoulos lasted only several months as director of communications in President Clinton's first administration. Peter Donolo, in the Chrétien PMO, was an exception. He was the right person in the right place at the right time. He is an example of how the job should be done. Part of Donolo's success, in addition to his professionalism, was simply the result of his own personality: a great sense of humour, a self-deprecating wit, a quick mind, an ability to get on with almost anyone, and an uncanny ability to win the respect and often the affection of the media.

His sense of humour was legendary. In April 1998, Chrétien made a state visit to Cuba. On the first day, as we drove to the Palace of the Revolution for the official welcoming ceremonies, we passed billboards in the streets of Havana proclaiming, "Socialism or Death!" Donolo and I then stood in a receiving line in front of the Palace of the Revolution, watching goose-stepping troops parade in front of us, while waiting for Fidel Castro to come by to shake our hands. Donolo had already recalled for me a recent visit to Ottawa by the Speaker of the Cuban Parliament. When he was criticized for receiving the Speaker of a one-party state, Gilbert Parent, then Speaker of the House of Commons, had somewhat improbably explained to the Canadian media that one-party states were no problem since, well, the New Brunswick legislature was made up of only Liberals, after Premier Frank McKenna swept every seat in the province in his first election in

1987. As Castro, wearing his trademark military fatigues, approached us in the receiving line, Donolo poked me in the ribs and whispered, "This is just like Fredericton, except with palm trees."

Donolo came to his job aware that it was well known in political and official Ottawa that Brian Mulroney's approach to communications was that a night when the prime minister was not on the national news was a wasted opportunity. Chrétien had different views – which Donolo shared – about the profile a prime minister should have. The prime minister didn't always agree with long-time Quebec Premier Robert Bourassa, but he certainly admired the way he had tried to manage his public image. Bourassa preferred to be known to be in charge, but he wanted to be underexposed himself. He put his ministers forward on most issues, on the grounds that overexposure of a leader considerably shortens his political shelf life. Donolo adopted the same approach in managing the Chrétien government's communications strategy. And Saskatchewan Premier Roy Romanow reinforced the same message when he recounted one day to Chrétien and to me that his father-in-law had once given him wise advice: "Roy, when you aren't on television, I presume you are working in your office and doing your job. When you are on television, I figure you are trying to explain your way out of problems!"

Donolo, as director of communications, had an overview of most issues facing the government. He was successful because he brought people together, consulted, and listened. He understood that a focus on the day to day, or the hour to hour, in response to the twenty-four-hour news cycle is only a small part of the job; a government soon comes adrift without the anchor of long-term policy and communications planning. Donolo held meetings every Monday at 9:30 a.m. in my boardroom with Chaviva Hosek, me, and those officials of the Privy Council Office responsible for keeping a rolling tab on all potential short- and medium-term government announcements. He chaired 10:00 a.m. Wednesday meetings with directors of communications of all regional ministers' offices, representatives of the Privy Council Office's communications secretariat, and communications directors from other ministers' offices as issues required, to discuss the week ahead, as well as specific communications challenges like budgets, foreign trips, or federal-provincial meetings, or more medium-term communications issues like an upcoming Throne Speech. He regularly held ad hoc meetings in his office with Cabinet ministers or ministerial staff and civil servants on specific problems or opportunities, and he was part of daily question period preparation of the prime minister.

Donolo was in a position to plan and coordinate overall government communications because (unlike less fortunate directors of communications in many governments) he was involved in discussions of policy before decisions were made and was able to provide us with communications input in advance. His knowledge of planned policy initiatives also helped him give strategic advice about which speaking invitations the prime minister should accept, what his message should be, where in Canada he should travel for maximum effect, and what other ministers should do to increase the impact.

A director of communications also has to be able to handle stressful and unpredictable situations that often crop up. In 1999, when Canada took in refugees from Kosovo, Donolo saw a great media opportunity for the prime minister and recommended that he meet some of the refugees at the Canadian Forces base in Trenton, Ontario, where they were temporarily housed. Chrétien arrived, got off the government plane, saw some of the Kosovar children playing basketball, and decided to join them. Unfortunately, the prime minister was wearing slippery dress shoes, and after immediately scoring one basket to the delight of press photographers, and especially of Donolo, he soon fell flat on his face, to the even greater delight of the media photographers. Donolo's happy visions of a compassionate Canadian prime minister dominating the news as he greeted and played with child refugees from a war-torn country were instantly transformed into a nightmare of pictures of a prostrate sixty-six-year-old prime minister splashed across the front pages of all the newspapers of the country the next morning. Donolo saved the situation by joking with the media, "Canadians love a down-to-earth prime minister." Sure enough, the next day many newspapers captioned the photo, "A Down to Earth Prime Minister."

In February 1996, the prime minister had grabbed a protester by the throat and pushed him aside. The protester immediately threatened to sue Chrétien for damage to a bridge in his mouth. Chrétien was shaken and nervous about the political implications of such a lawsuit. Donolo reassured him: "Don't worry, boss, the federal infrastructure program pays for bridge repairs." Chrétien repeated that line with great delight to a worried caucus and Cabinet. In both cases, Donolo's reaction not only relieved stress for the prime minister but, equally important, improved the mood of the caucus, Cabinet, and the PMO. That, too, is part of the job of managing communications.

It is very important for a director of communications to tell a prime minister when he is wrong as well as when he is right. Donolo was never intimidated and always gave honest, unvarnished advice. Of course, his advice, like that of any communications director, was not always taken, because good government is about much more than just communications and spin. Many policy decisions don't necessarily fit in to what a communications adviser would wish for, but Donolo understood that his job was to explain government policy, not to make it, although he never hesitated to make his own policy views known to anyone who would listen. He was always a good sport when his advice wasn't followed, and he never complained. On the other hand, after we fell into traps that he had warned about, he took great, perverse pleasure in being able to tell us that he had been right in the first place.

Giving Fashion Advice to Emperors on New Clothes

JUST AS DONOLO had no problem giving unvarnished advice to the prime minister, I certainly always told Chrétien what I thought, and so did Jean Pelletier. We were both brutally frank when necessary. Chrétien wanted and appreciated frank advice, and had little respect for those who didn't give it. There was one time in the early years of the government when I had tough advice (which I knew he wouldn't like) to give about a complicated personnel decision he had to make. I said, "If you just want me to tell you what I think you want to hear, invite me for relaxing fun social dinners at your house. But if you want me as an adviser, I'll always tell you what I think." He grumbled a little before agreeing with my recommendation, and then replied that just telling him what he wanted to hear would be the greatest disservice I could render to him.

Pelletier and I even made one exception to the rule that a prime minister, out of respect for the office, should always be called Mr. Prime Minister. We took advantage of the fact that we had both known Chrétien for decades, and we didn't hesitate to call him by his first name in private, although we never did so in front of ministers or public servants. It wasn't out of disrespect for the office, but because it is much easier to say face to face, "Jean, that is really a stupid idea and will get you into very deep trouble," than to say the same thing with as much force and emphasis and (ideally) effect, when the first words are necessarily "Mr. Prime Minister, sir."

One time early on in the government, Chrétien asked me for my views about an idea of his. I thought about it for a moment and told him right away that it didn't make much sense and couldn't work. He was genuinely surprised at my response, because he said he had already tested the idea with several people who really liked it.

"Who?" I asked, wondering to myself about whom he was consulting and the calibre of the advice he was receiving.

"Several members of Parliament," he responded.

"Of course," I said, "and how many of them hope to be ministers and want to please you by agreeing with you?"

His response was, "If they know me, they should know I would appoint the person who has told me what he really thinks." Chrétien might have really believed that; but in fact, too few people are prepared to give unvarnished advice, especially critical advice, to a head of government. Everything a prime minister says is unfortunately taken by some as coming from the fount of all wisdom. Often the prime minister is just throwing out an idea or suggestion for debate and discussion; yet, inevitably to his surprise, it is solemnly transcribed as if it were one of the Ten Commandments.

I never found a problem in "speaking truth to power." On the contrary, "power," in government, as in the corporate world, is normally receptive to hearing the truth. The problem lies with those who are afraid to tell it. I always made it clear to anyone going to see Chrétien that there was no point telling him what they thought he wanted to hear and then coming out of the meeting and complaining about the decision he had made. He actually wanted to know what they really thought. Unfortunately, that advice was not always taken, and I was the one who would often have to intervene in a meeting with the prime minister to give the less palatable advice while others, including ministers, who had told me ahead of time that they would give that same tough advice (and which he would have liked to receive from them), sat silent in his presence. After the meeting, Chrétien would then tell me that I was the only one disagreeing with him. I would explain what I had been told before the meeting, and would remind him that the excessive deference accorded to all heads of government leads to bad decisions.

Herding Cats

THERE ARE ALSO often important coordination functions that may appear, at first blush, to make the case about inappropriate centralization of power, but whose necessity on closer observation becomes obvious. For example, the PMO kept track of where every Cabinet minister was at all times. No minister was supposed to leave Ottawa without permission from the PMO, even though ministers never liked to be told to cancel travel plans, particularly when Parliament was not sitting, just because something unpredictable might happen.

Chrétien had a rule that there should be a minimum of six ministers in Ottawa at all times in case of unforeseen emergencies; and it was the responsibility of the PMO to enforce that rule. There was good reason for the policy. Important decisions benefit from discussion and debate where possible. In a system of Cabinet government such as ours, it is important for ministers to be able to express their views around the table and for the prime minister to have the benefit of their advice, so there always have to be some ministers in the capital. Even so, Cabinet ministers didn't always like their comings and goings from Ottawa dictated to them by the PMO; and in my experience, some complained bitterly about the seeming arbitrariness of our decisions. Yet, the events of September 11, 2001, reminded everyone of why it is important to coordinate ministerial travel.

September 11, 2001, was at the end of the summer; Parliament was not sitting; and it was a quiet time in terms of Cabinet business. Many ministers were in their constituencies. Some had departmental business to attend to outside of Ottawa, both in Canada and abroad, before Parliament resumed. Some were on vacation. So the PMO tried, for once, to be "nice guys," to accommodate the plans of ministers who wanted to leave Ottawa. It seemed to us that we didn't have any particular need to keep ministers in town other than in case of emergencies, and in early September 2001 there had not been an emergency for a long time. We learned that day that we had been too accommodating. The result of our nice-guy laxness was that there were only two ministers present in Ottawa on that fateful day. Worse still, all flights were grounded, making it difficult for ministers outside of central Canada to get back to Ottawa quickly. As a result, for several days the prime minister was unable to call a full Cabinet meeting to discuss the hugely important consequences of September 11.

The PMO doesn't have to keep ministers in Ottawa only for purposes of government business. It also has to judge the utility and sometimes the legitimacy of proposed ministerial travel to avoid potentially embarrassing political problems. Only the PMO can have an overview of the travel intentions of the whole Cabinet. With this overview, it can refuse travel requests so that the prime minister doesn't find himself in the position of having to explain publicly to some investigative journalist why half the Cabinet is pretending to have urgent government business in the Caribbean in January.

It is one thing if the minister of international trade has to attend a World Trade Organization meeting, with other trade ministers from around the world, that is held in Cancun in the winter; there would be no hesitation approving such a trip as legitimate public business. On the other hand, the PMO has the responsibility of ensuring that the ethical behaviour of ministers is unquestionable. Once, as winter was approaching, I refused the request of a junior minister to go to the Bahamas for five days, ostensibly to study the effect of the Haitian presence on local culture. He argued that his trip was required to understand the needs of the growing Haitian community in Quebec. Unfortunately for him, I didn't agree that such personal research was absolutely necessary and suggested, in quite colourful language, that the Canadian taxpayer would not take kindly to paying for his holiday. I gave him my opinion that the prime minister would not be amused by his request, and that I wasn't at all worried that he would complain to the prime minister about my decision – although I gave him full marks for imagination.

Handing Out Jobs

ANOTHER AREA THAT has been controversial in terms of the PMO is its role in appointments to government jobs. The prime minister has a legal responsibility to recommend to Cabinet a large number of Order-in-Council appointments: judges, senators, Lieutenant-Governors, deputy ministers, members of full-time and part-time boards and commissions. Chrétien focused his own attention primarily on the most significant ones: judges of the Supreme Court of Canada, the president of the CBC, the governor of the Bank of Canada, the members of the CRTC, and the lieutenant-governors of the provinces. He chose not to spend much time himself on other appointments, such as those to the many local Employment Insurance Boards of Referees, or Citizenship Court judges, or to a variety of other part-time jobs. In those cases, Chrétien generally relied on the recommendations of his ministers. But he insisted on linguistic, gender, regional, and ethnic balance in all government appointments. This required coordination.

One of the roles of the director of appointments in the PMO was to keep an overall scorecard of all appointments so as to ensure the balance that the prime minister wanted. The director of appointments (whether Penny Collenette, Percy Downe, or Manon Tardif) would often call a minister or a minister's staff to say, "What type of job search did you do? Where is your creativity? You may think you have a good candidate for a particular job, but the prime minister will not appoint another middle-aged, white male from Toronto. Surely you can find a young woman from British Columbia or from Newfoundland. And furthermore, your record when it comes to visible minorities is not very good. We want to see some improvement when you next have nominations to recommend, otherwise the boss won't approve them."

In filling government positions, like all prime ministers, presidents, premiers, and mayors, Chrétien was cognizant of partisan considerations – sometimes, in my view, too much so. The less important the job in question was, the more he took partisan considerations into account in filling it. There are a lot of part-time, low-paying government positions of little consequence. It is easy to appoint a political organizer in a constituency to a part-time job supervising a small ferry dock; the consequences to the country are not significant. Those appointments satisfy local MPs and Cabinet ministers who routinely pressure prime ministers to make them.

Such appointments, in my judgment, are counter-productive. The political organizer who is appointed to a government job is rarely grateful, and is usually convinced he or she received the appointment strictly on the grounds of merit; meanwhile, those organizers who are not appointed are upset with the lack of gratitude shown to them by the government. More important, the cumulation of such partisan appointments rightly creates public cynicism about cronyism in politics and inevitably loses a government far more votes in the next election than any political organizer, however grateful, who receives a government appointment, can win for it.

Political Appointments, Good and Bad

FOR THE MORE important positions, however, Chrétien, like many of his predecessors, looked primarily for competence. Most often appointments such as Louise Arbour to the Supreme Court of Canada,

Adrienne Clarkson as Governor General, and James Bartleman as Lieutenant-Governor of Ontario were non-partisan. But Chrétien also rightly argued that democracy is not well served if highly competent people interested in government and public service are discouraged from getting involved in the political process, because such involvement would constitute a bar to later government appointments for which they would otherwise be highly qualified. He therefore had no hesitation in appointing some very capable individuals with impressive professional credentials, who had once been involved in partisan politics, including Liberals such as Michel Robert as chief justice of Quebec, Carole Taylor as chair of the CBC, John Reid as information commissioner, and a Conservative like Roy McMurtry as chief justice of Ontario. Similarly, both Paul Martin and Stephen Harper made excellent appointments in Frank McKenna and Michael Wilson respectively as ambassadors to Washington.

The problems that arise aren't created by political appointments of highly qualified people. The bad ones stand out. Many heads of government understand in theory the political damage they cause to themselves by appointing political friends to positions for which they are not qualified, but they often ignore it in practice at their own peril. For example, George Bush's appointment of his political friend Michael Brown as head of the Federal Emergency Measures Agency turned out to be very damaging to the Bush Administration as Brown was blamed for the inadequate response to Hurricane Katrina. Chrétien also occasionally got himself in trouble for stubbornly insisting on rewarding certain political friends for past support, especially when they later performed badly in their government jobs.

Chrétien tried to rationalize, when he should have known better, either that his friend was actually qualified for the job or that the position he or she was appointed to did not require much competence. Ironically, the "friends" who later created the most trouble had never been particularly useful to him in their previous political service (although they may have convinced him that they had been), and even worse, none of them actually had ever been his close friends. I wondered why some of them even thought they "deserved" a reward, and how they managed to convince the prime minister to appoint them to anything. In some cases, such as the appointment of George Radwanski (who later had to resign because of a lavish expense account) as privacy commissioner, I concluded that they had been such nuisances that instead of sending them packing, as he should have, Chrétien (like many heads of government in similar situations elsewhere) felt sorry for them and made the mistake of giving them what they wanted, just to get them out of his hair.

In Canada, we have an ongoing debate as to whether some appointments to government positions are made in a too "political" and sometimes inappropriately partisan fashion, and whether a more "merit based" approach, with a smaller role for the prime minister and other politicians, is more desirable. In my view, there are fundamental flaws in the arguments of those who want to reduce the role of elected governments in making appointments. I remember a long discussion with Chrétien on this topic when he was minister of justice in 1981. There was a vacancy from Ontario on the Supreme Court of Canada, and he wanted to name the first woman judge to the court at the time the Charter of Rights was coming into effect. The best woman candidate was Justice Bertha Wilson of the Ontario Court of Appeal. The "establishment" in the Ontario legal community was shameless in making the case that she wasn't "ready," and that there were other (male) candidates who were better "qualified." Even Chief Justice Bora Laskin, who had his own preferred candidate at the time, made that argument very vociferously to Prime Minister Trudeau.

Chrétien and I shared the view that as long as Justice Wilson had the qualifications to sit on the Supreme Court of Canada, it was more important, in the context of the times, to appoint her than to appoint someone else who was male, even though he might arguably be "better" qualified with more experience as an appellate judge. Trudeau eventually agreed with the recommendation of his justice minister, and appointed Bertha Wilson, who in the course of her later career proved to be an outstanding Supreme Court judge. Hers was not a partisan appointment, but it was definitely a political decision, and one that may not have been made by a committee of non-political "experts" with no governmental responsibilities.

The case of Justice Wilson is a vivid illustration of a point that goes well beyond judicial appointments. It is not an accident that there are many more women on boards of directors of Crown corporations at the federal and provincial levels than on private sector boards. It is because elected governments decide to make appointments to government positions to reflect regional, linguistic, gender, and ethnic diversity. They should not be hamstrung by unaccountable committees examining each individual case with no thought of how it fits into the bigger picture. Furthermore, there is no guarantee that transferring appointments from the political realm to some supposedly non-partisan process will always produce better results. It isn't only politicians who make mistakes in choosing candidates for positions. In real life, not all individuals who are highly qualified on paper always perform as well as expected in the job. Human nature being what it is, there are as many examples of non-partisan appointments abusing expense accounts in as flagrant a way (but with less media coverage) as has occasionally been the case with partisan appointments. And human nature being what it is, it isn't only politicians who appoint their friends; non-political civil servants have been known to find ways to do so as well. At least politicians have to account for their decisions at election time, something committees don't have to do.

There are other good reasons that are not necessarily evident on the surface for so-called "political" appointments to be made. Prime ministers have a whole range of considerations in everything they do. In Canada, federal-provincial relations are always front and centre in the mind of a prime minister. I was involved in one case where a new provincial premier (of a different political stripe than the prime minister) wanted to make a personnel change in the senior ranks of the public service of that province. The premier rightly took advantage of his first meeting with Chrétien in the living room of 24 Sussex Drive.

He began by saying that he hoped they would establish a close working relationship between each other, and he was prepared to solve a lot of problems that had festered under his predecessor. Then he asked for a favour. "I need to change one of my senior officials, and it would make my life a lot easier if you could name that person to the bench." Chrétien was also anxious to have good relations with the new premier, so his instant response was, "I'll make the appointment as long as that person meets the qualifications to be a judge." I reported the gist of the conversation to the minister of justice. He checked the qualifications of the prospective appointee (who had not been on a list of possible judicial appointments), and when he was satisfied that they were in order, he took steps to speed up the normally slow approval process. Shortly thereafter, there was a happy new judge and, more important, a happy premier, and the prospect of solutions to long-standing differences between the two governments.

The Gatekeeper

COORDINATION ACROSS the government isn't the only function of the PMO. A prime minister needs staff and advisers to prepare for question period in the House of Commons; prime ministerial travel is complicated; responding to correspondence and e-mails from citizens is a labour-intensive job; relations with the parliamentary caucus are an essential part of leadership, as is the prime minister's role as leader of his political party. All of this requires staff support. It is why the PMO staff numbers around eighty – from the commissionaire at the front desk all the way up to the chief of staff. But one of the key roles in the PMO is that of gatekeeper.

The demands on the time of a prime minister are almost infinite: Cabinet, caucus, the House of Commons, meetings about government issues, delivery of speeches, foreign trips, receiving foreign visitors, meeting provincial premiers, spending evenings at partisan political events, as well as just staying home to read and think. This makes the time of a prime minister one of the most precious commodities of any government and it should be used as sparingly as possible. Managing a prime minister's time and the flow of thousands of documents a year to him is a twenty-four-hour-a-day job.

For eight years, the job of gatekeeper, or executive assistant, was carried out for Chrétien by Bruce Hartley, who performed a juggling act with great skill weekdays, evenings, nights, and weekends. Hartley had come to Parliament Hill out of university and started as a pageboy in the House of Commons. He soon found his way into the Office of the Leader of the Opposition helping on parliamentary strategy and, in 1993, became legislative assistant to Chrétien and, two years later, executive assistant to the prime minister. In that capacity, he saw the prime minister more than anyone else. He accompanied him on all his travel, both in Canada and abroad, and even walked him down the hall to his meetings in the Parliament Buildings. He controlled the prime minister's agenda. No one could see Chrétien without first asking Hartley. He had to know not only whom the prime minister needed to see or speak to, but also when, whom he should not see until certain issues had been dealt with, whom he should see at any time, and whom he should never see, which calls he should return, which calls should never be returned, which should not be returned until he had been briefed, and which documents he had to see right away and which could wait. He had to know what his family obligations were, and often dealt as well with Aline Chrétien on scheduling. Hartley had to say no far more often than he said yes, and he had to do it with the greatest of diplomacy. Sometimes he knew the answer himself; sometimes he consulted with Pelletier, me, or other senior staff members.

Hartley was the principal gatekeeper, but to a certain extent the role of gatekeeper is one that all of us played. I saw that part of my role was to resolve as many problems as possible without having to bring them to the prime minister for his decision. His job was to deal with problems others couldn't solve, so I considered a successful day to be one where I didn't have to talk to the prime minister. For example, I received countless calls from ministers and MPs that started out: "There is a big problem the PM needs to address immediately." Early on, I figured out that, ironically, the best way to keep problems away from the prime minister was to offer meetings with him. My response, after listening to the problem, was usually: "Why don't you call the prime minister on the telephone or go and see him if it is that important to you? He always makes himself available to a Cabinet colleague or an MP." Almost invariably (and not unexpectedly), the answer was, "Oh no, I wouldn't want to bother him about this. He's far too busy." I knew then that there was no issue of principle or real importance or even urgency involved. At that stage, I might suggest, "Maybe you and I can work it out together ourselves." They would usually agree. In the rare case when the answer was, "I would appreciate a call or an appointment," then I would try, through Hartley, to arrange it as quickly as possible, and he and I would ensure that the prime minister was well briefed on the subject before speaking to or meeting with the minister or MP.

The Mythology: Conversation Becomes a Command

DURING MY TEN years in the PMO, I was associated with a group of men and women who all worked ten hours or more a day, sometimes six and seven days a week, took their jobs very seriously, and were deeply committed to what they did but fortunately did not take themselves too seriously. As a result, we had trouble seeing ourselves as a powerful, fear-inspiring, mysterious organization. On my first day as senior policy adviser, however, I discovered that the myth about the PMO is real, and that regardless of what we thought, what senior members of the PMO say can be easily misinterpreted and given an unintended importance.

I was sitting in my new office arranging boxes and files in the first hours after the government had been sworn in. When the telephone rang for the first time, I wondered what important affairs of state were about to confront me. Instead, my caller introduced himself as a lawyer from Vancouver who had a client with an immigration problem; somehow the lawyer, whom I didn't know, had the phone number of the direct line to my desk. I told him that I knew from my years as a ministerial assistant that the PMO should stay away from individual cases, and that he should instead get in touch with the Immigration Department, but still, I dutifully took note of the lawyer's representation.

For much of the rest of the afternoon (unlike the fifty calls or more that I would get every day for the next ten years), the phone did not ring. Then my good friend Sergio Marchi, the new minister of immigration, called to ask how I felt about finally being in government after all of the leadership and election campaigns we had been through together. I told him that it was eerily quiet and laughed: "Serge, it's great that you called, because up to now the only call I have received is a strange request on an immigration matter. It's your problem, not mine, and here's the name and telephone number of my caller."

To my great surprise, the first call I had early the next morning was from the assistant deputy minister of immigration telling me how he was going to deal with the matter on which I had "given instructions." I told him the full story, and explained that I had not "given instructions." It was an instructive lesson for me in how ministers and officials view the PMO.

The next lesson came a few weeks later, shortly before Chrétien's initial federal-provincial meeting of first ministers. A senior official from the Intergovernmental Affairs Secretariat of the Privy Council Office asked to see me in my office late one afternoon to discuss the proposed agenda. She showed me a draft, which I read, and then commented that I had a few questions for her about the order of the agenda. She stopped me after my first question, asked if she could use my phone, and called her office. "Stop everything," she told her staff, "PMO doesn't agree with the agenda."

"Wait a minute," I protested, "I haven't even disagreed with you. We just started to talk and I'm only asking questions. When I hear what you have to say, I might very well agree with your approach." It hadn't crossed my mind that expressing an initial reaction to someone who asked me for my thoughts would be interpreted as an order.

Years later I was having lunch in the Parliamentary Restaurant with Senator Raymond Setlakwe. He was a fount of knowledge about the Liberal Party, having attended every party convention since 1948, and was an unconditional Chrétien loyalist, a member of what the prime minister liked to call his Roman Guard. We enjoyed each other's company and always had a lot of fun together. During the course of a wide-ranging, cheerful chat, he mentioned to me that the Senate might soon debate a motion condemning the Armenian genocide of 1915, and asked me what I thought. It wasn't something I was interested in, and as far as I was concerned, Senator Setlakwe was just making conversation. I told him candidly that I had never given any thought whatsoever to the matter.

I really wanted to change the subject, so in the same spirit of candour between old friends, I betrayed my own bias about the usefulness of the Canadian Senate. "I would have thought the Senate has more pressing matters to address than something that happened in another part of the world almost a century ago. I really don't care what the Senate does about it. As far as I'm concerned, if you want to waste your time on that type of resolution, go right ahead." Then we spoke about other things that I found more interesting and more useful. It didn't cross my mind that he was seeking my considered views as the senior policy adviser to the prime minister of Canada. I knew that he was a successful small businessman from the Eastern Townships of Quebec; I had no idea that he was of Armenian descent.

A few days later, I was the most surprised person in the world to learn that I had made an important decision. The word was out that I had reversed a long-standing position of the government (of which I was completely unaware), and that the PMO apparently no longer objected if the Senate was to proceed with the resolution on the Armenian genocide. I got frantic calls from Sharon Carstairs, the leader of the government in the Senate, and Lloyd Axworthy, the minister of foreign affairs, telling me that I might have caused a major problem in relations between Canada and Turkey by what I thought was an off-handed comment to my lunch companion, and certainly not a decision. I relearned an important lesson, which is that anything said by a member of the PMO is easily misinterpreted as instructions or orders when they are merely questions, thoughts, ideas, or personal views, or even just a matter of passing unsolicited representations on to someone else.

Focusing on Priorities

WHEN HE APPOINTED me as his senior policy adviser, Chrétien did not want me to work on every policy file of the government. He expected me to focus on his major policy priorities, and to work with Cabinet ministers and deputy ministers to implement them. In addition, because of our long experience together, he told me that my role would include providing advice on overall political strategy, federal-provincial relations, and much else as circumstances required. Chrétien also named Chaviva Hosek as his director of policy. The two of us, and later her successor, Paul Genest, were responsible for how the PMO managed and coordinated government policy priorities. We worked very closely together and, in fact, collaborated on all major issues. Chaviva focused more than I did on social policy, and I devoted more of my time than she did to economic issues and federal-provincial relations, but we worked together on both. She also had an overall policy coordinating role, and was responsible for the development of the election platforms of 1993, 1997, and 2000. Her staff took responsibility for making sure that all the Cabinet ministers followed through on election campaign commitments; they also carefully monitored the agendas of all Cabinet committees, identified problems between departments and ministers, offered advice, and worked to fix problems.

Chaviva and I had worked together almost like twins in Opposition and our relationship carried over into government. It could hardly have been better. Every Monday morning, she would come into my office, threaten to hit me between the eyes with a two-by-four, hoping that would get my attention, and then would give me a big hug to make me feel better. One of the two always worked.

Our job was particularly challenging because the coordination of government priorities requires management from the centre. We found that there is no other way.

Chapter 6

HOW CABINET WORKS

"Committees of twenty deliberate plenty,
Committees of ten act now and then,
But most jobs are done by committees of one."

– OLD RHYME

The overall priorities of a government are usually put forward first in election platforms. Then, after the election, they are set out under the direction of the prime minister in the Throne Speeches that open sessions of Parliament. Of course, election platforms and Throne Speeches usually leave room for later decisions on the determination and timing of initiatives, particularly for those that require government spending. It is also the case that new issues arise during the course of a government's term in office, and new priorities can arise as a result of changes in political, economic, and even international circumstances.

During the Chrétien years, there were a number of different – and unsuccessful – attempts made to involve the whole Cabinet in priority setting. In the end, it was the annual budget that became the primary instrument for allocating and implementing government priorities, with the final decisions on those priorities made solely by the prime minister and the minister of finance rather than by the whole Cabinet.

For example, the February 2000 budget provided significant new resources for the National Child Benefit and for a vastly expanded

system of parental leave, both under the responsibility of the Department of Human Resources Development. I met with Claire Morris,
the deputy minister of that department, shortly after the budget came
down. She was clearly delighted with its provisions but was puzzled by
how the decisions to allocate budget priorities had been made, because
her minister, Jane Stewart, had told her that they had not been made
by the Cabinet. Morris had recently joined the federal government
after lengthy experience as the senior public servant in New Brunswick.
"In New Brunswick," she told me, "we had lengthy Cabinet meetings
that could go on almost interminably until a consensus was reached on
the allocation of priorities. These would then be reflected in the next
provincial budget. It doesn't seem to happen that way here in Ottawa.
Am I missing something?"

"No, Claire," I said. "You aren't missing anything."

I explained, "In my experience in Ottawa, Cabinets don't seem to
work in a way that is conducive to achieving a consensus on what
overall government spending priorities should be. We have tried different approaches to involving the whole Cabinet in priority setting,
and have discovered that Cabinet is too large and diverse as a group to
be able to take into account the whole mix of considerations that go
into the allocation of spending priorities: past election platforms,
Throne Speeches, the next election, constraints of federal-provincial
relations, the volatility of financial markets, pressures from caucus and
non-governmental organizations, and sometimes even unanticipated
international events." I continued, "There is also a syndrome in the
Cabinet which I call PIMBY (Please In My Back Yard). The result of
PIMBY and all of the competing interests in any Cabinet is that only
the prime minister, usually in conjunction with the minister of finance,
can make the final decisions on the determination of spending priorities. That's what happened in this case."

The management and organization of Cabinet is one of the most
important prerogatives of a prime minister. Jean Chrétien had his own
style, and when he became prime minister, he decided to do things his
own way. He often told his staff and his ministers that he found

Pearson's Cabinet meetings too unfocused and Trudeau's Cabinet meetings too long; there were too many Cabinet committees; they took up much too much of the ministers' time and prevented them from having sufficient time to do their own departmental work. Chrétien was businesslike and preferred no more discussion than necessary to reach a decision. He was comfortable knowing that Cabinet decisions are the sole prerogative of the prime minister; there are no votes taken in Cabinet, and decisions aren't dependent on the number of ministers who have spoken on one side of an issue or another. As soon as discussion ended on an issue, he usually called his decision and moved onto the next item. Occasionally, where there was no apparent consensus and where he had no strong views, Chrétien would take an issue under advisement and would decide at a later date.

Chrétien was a firm believer that lengthy meetings are not synonymous with good decision making. His regular Cabinet meetings when Parliament was in session took place every Tuesday morning from ten o'clock until noon. He tried to keep interventions short and to the point, and always insisted on beginning and especially on finishing on time. If an item on the agenda was still proceeding at noon, unless it was extremely urgent, the prime minister would put it off until the next meeting, saying, "If we stay here late, the press outside the room will speculate that we are dealing with a crisis when we are not. And in any event, you have other meetings on your own agendas that are important for you to attend. I don't want ministers spending all day in Cabinet and Cabinet committee meetings."

Inside Weekly Cabinet Meetings – A Ten-Year Perspective

THOSE WHO DO not attend Cabinet meetings probably share an expectation, fed by the media and certainly fed to the media by political spin doctors, that the secret discussions in Cabinet are always weighty and serious, and produce profoundly important and rational decisions. There are, in fact, many times when Cabinet meetings produce important decisions impacting the whole country, such as the decision in 1999 to move forward with the Clarity Act. Sometimes I listened with considerable fascination to lengthy discussions about important matters of foreign policy such as whether to send troops to the Balkans, the situation in Iraq, Canada–U.S. relations, or major domestic political issues such as same-sex marriage, gun control, or an upcoming referendum in Quebec.

But the discussions weren't always like that. Despite the breathless anticipation of journalists and political assistants who wait outside the Cabinet room every week until the meeting is over so as to learn what important decisions were made, in my experience most Cabinet meetings dealt primarily with relatively routine administrative issues of importance to some ministers, but not necessarily to the whole country. These might include House of Commons business, reports from ministers who have attended international meetings or federal-provincial meetings, Order-in-Council appointments, ratification of decisions of Cabinet committees, or overviews of general issues involving a particular department of government.

The single most important rule I learned in understanding how Cabinets work is that they are made up of human beings. In every Cabinet, there are some ministers who are thoughtful, knowledgeable, and always listened to with interest and respect by their colleagues. But not all have something important, relevant, or interesting to say at all times. As in any large group of people, some ministers speak at greater length than others, and some try to speak on every subject under the sun. The most long-winded are usually the least relevant. Until they are cut short by the prime minister, they give their colleagues the opportunity to sign correspondence, get coffee, go to the washroom, or even go out to return telephone calls.

In my experience, the ministers who had the most impact in Cabinet discussions were the ones like John Manley and Herb Gray, who combined seriousness and intelligence with a good sense of humour, usually and importantly self-deprecating humour. They were listened to attentively. Other ministers unfortunately tried to carry the weight of the world on their shoulders and tended to make interventions that were far too often melodramatic, overly serious, and without any hint of humour or perspective. These ministers had limited success, as did those who were too politically partisan for their own good, when their partisanship blinded them to the realities of governing.

Some ministers who represented areas of the country outside of the economic mainstream were down to earth and capable of cutting through bureaucratic presentations with common sense. Chrétien identified with them. He was underestimated himself when he was in the Trudeau Cabinet, and he saw in some of his rural colleagues a reflection of his younger self. Coming from a small town, he took them very seriously. As a minister, he was a great fan of Trudeau's agriculture minister, Eugene Whelan, who came from Essex County in rural Ontario. In his own government, he was often impressed by the political acumen of Veterans Affairs Minister Lawrence McCauley, who came from Prince Edward Island, and by the populism of Sheila Copps. The influence of these ministers often escapes outside commentators who underestimate the sharp intelligence sometimes concealed under a "folksy" manner.

Scripting versus Spontaneity

IN MY OBSERVATION, when the regular Tuesday meetings of the Chrétien Cabinet addressed specific policy issues from individual departments, the debate often lacked the spontaneity that emerged in the general discussion of broader issues of foreign policy, national unity, and human rights. The Privy Council Office expected ministers to use speaking notes prepared in advance by their departments, and circulated to the PCO, which then provided those notes to the prime minister the evening before the meeting. The PIMBY syndrome was omnipresent, and it was easy to predict who would say what on any particular issue.

I could imagine a Cabinet discussion about Canadian interests on the moon. It would go this way:

> The prime minister: "The minister of agriculture has something to say. Go ahead, but please be brief."

The minister of agriculture: "Thank you, prime minister. As you are aware, this has been another bad year for lunar crops; indeed, it has undoubtedly been one of the worst years in history. There is little prospect for things to get better next year or even the year after. We have no choice but to immediately introduce temporary farm income stabilization programs on the moon. While they may be expensive in the short run, we will phase them out within three years, and in any event, even if it takes longer, surely we all agree that Canadians expect us to act now because they know that our farmers are the glue that holds society itself together on the moon."

The prime minister: "The minister of rural development wants to add something. Please be briefer than the previous speaker. We have many other items to finish before noon."

The minister of rural development: "Prime minister, it is not just farmers who are in need, far from it. They are almost irrelevant. I know that you understand from your own extensive travels that the rural parts of the moonscape have long been neglected by the central administration. I wring my hands in despair at the incomprehension of our colleagues despite, of course, your own best efforts, for which I am deeply appreciative. Nevertheless, I have to solemnly warn you that such continued neglect will lead to the government's inevitable defeat in the next election. We really have to put our priority and our money into small rural lunar communities"

The prime minister: "We are really running out of time. The minister of the environment has one minute to enlighten us about his views."

The minister of the environment: "Farming is not important today on the moon. Nor are a few small rural communities. I profoundly worry about the quality of the little remaining lunar air, and the rape of the lunar environment by multinational resource companies. We have no time to waste. Let me tell colleagues that the only way to solve these problems is by massive government investments today in environmental technologies that will save future generations untold tax burdens. May I elaborate?"

The prime minister: "No, you may not. I guess it is only fair to hear from the minister of natural resources for thirty seconds."

The minister of natural resources: "I have a different point of view on the urgency of developing lunar resources. There is absolutely no science to back up what my colleague, the minister of the environment, has said. My department tells me that he is relying too much on his departmental briefing notes. Prime minister, we all know that if Canadians don't develop lunar resources immediately, someone else will. I have a proposal for the minister of finance for small temporary tax incentives for resource development. They won't cost anything over the long run because they will eventually produce spectacular revenues for the government from the economic growth and employment they stimulate on the moon."

The prime minister: "I see the minister responsible for regional agencies has been trying to catch my attention. You have twenty seconds."

The minister responsible for regional agencies: "Prime minister, before you conclude, I have something urgent to say. As always, no one has spoken today about the growing alienation on the dark side of the moon. That is the real urgent problem to address. The rest, with due respect to our colleagues, can wait. My department has a plan, which I would like to go into in some detail now."

The prime minister: "Not now. We have heard enough for today. I want to reflect on this important matter before deciding. I see the minister of finance has something to say. Go ahead."

The minister of finance: "Prime minister, all of our colleagues have made excellent points. I fully agree with each and every one of them. Everything they have said is very very important and should indeed be our first priority. (As you know by now, I have many first priorities.) Unfortunately, my forecasters have just informed me of the possibility – indeed the probability – of meteorite showers striking the moon sometime over the next five million years in a manner which could negatively affect our fiscal position. Therefore we can't do anything for the time being."

The prime minister: "Colleagues, enough of this debate. I am going to have to decide myself because Cabinet can't seem to come to a consensus."

Seeking Priorities

CHRÉTIEN TRIED DIFFERENT approaches to involve the whole Cabinet in setting the overall spending priorities of the government. At the end of his second year in office, he asked Chaviva Hosek and me to interview each Cabinet minister for an hour or two at a time, to discuss what each person thought overall government priorities should be for the rest of the mandate. We found during the course of our interviews that most Cabinet ministers were so busy with their own departmental responsibilities that they had given little serious thought to what the overall priorities of the government should be. This did not come as a real surprise to me, because when I worked as a ministerial assistant to Chrétien when he was in the Trudeau Cabinet, he always focused on his own departmental responsibilities and rarely talked to me or others about the overall agenda of the Trudeau government.

Chaviva and I came out of our consultations with individual ministers with two kinds of priority lists. The first was always interesting, but was not really the object of our exercise. It was what each minister told us the government as a whole should be doing to implement the minister's own particular departmental priorities, and sometimes what to do to address the needs of the part of the country the minister represented in Parliament. The second list about what the government as a whole should do was much shorter than the first, and was usually very vague. As a result, the dialogue we had with all of the Cabinet ministers didn't allow us to narrow down priorities to make focused recommendations. Chaviva and I dutifully compiled what each minister had said and reported back in detail to the prime minister, and also informed the minister of finance, in more general terms, of what we had learned. The exercise was not rated a huge success.

Cabinet Retreats

CHRÉTIEN TRIED OTHER approaches to involve the Cabinet in discussing overall government priorities. Two or three times a year he convened Cabinet retreats lasting a full day, or a day and a half, to discuss the medium-term priorities of the government in a more relaxed and collegial atmosphere than the regular weekly meetings. The retreats were usually held in the Foreign Affairs Building, because it had a larger and more comfortable, albeit more formal, conference room than the Cabinet room on Parliament Hill. Chrétien stubbornly refused to hold the retreats in the comfortable rustic surroundings of the government centre at Meech Lake because he did not want his government to be associated in any way with the place where the Meech Lake Accord had been negotiated. Ministers dressed informally if they wished. Sports shirts and sweaters predominated over ties and jackets for men, and slacks over skirts or dresses for women. There was always a buffet lunch in pleasant surroundings on the top floor of the Pearson Building, where ministers could spend close to two hours in informal discussion sitting without assigned seats at tables for eight. The prime minister himself usually chose to sit with the most junior ministers. In the evening, there was a dinner for ministers and their spouses, along with senior advisers from the PMO and the PCO, at the residence of the Governor General, because the dining room at 24 Sussex Drive is not large enough to accommodate the Cabinet and their spouses.

Three of the retreats I attended over the course of ten years were particularly important. The first was held shortly before the budget of

1995, where the prime minister made crystal clear to those of his colleagues who were reluctant to agree to spending cuts that the minister of finance had his complete support in setting the country on course for balanced budgets. Chrétien told his ministers that the decisions had been made, and that if any of them continued to complain about cuts to their departments, he would cut that department by an additional 25 per cent. He would brook no criticism of, or deviation from, a policy of rigorous fiscal discipline.

The second retreat of real long-term significance was held in early February 1996, shortly after the Quebec referendum of 1995. It set the parameters for the government's Quebec strategy for years to come. The third one was in the early summer of 2003, where, following a controversial decision of the Ontario Court of Appeal, the government decided to press ahead with legislation legalizing same-sex marriage.

Chrétien managed retreats differently than regular Cabinet meetings. He wanted to hear from all ministers and even encouraged them to speak for longer than usual if they wished. The best discussions at retreats normally were about issues that did not involve the spending of public funds. National unity, foreign policy, or civil liberties and human rights are the type of subjects that most Cabinet ministers, like most Canadians, reflect on and have strong views that they are happy to express, even if such issues are not part of their day-to-day responsibilities. Cabinet retreats, nevertheless, proved to be just as unsuccessful in establishing spending priorities for the government as the process Chaviva Hosek and I went through in interviewing individual ministers, and for the same reasons.

The retreats invariably began with the prime minister asking the finance minister to give his colleagues an update on the fiscal situation of the government. As he was calling on Paul Martin to make his presentation, Chrétien always made clear that Martin's fiscal policies had his full support. He had already seen and approved the presentation that had been prepared by Martin and his senior officials, which they had worked on with me in my role as the senior policy adviser. Part of my job was to brief the prime minister ahead of time, seek his comments, and eventually obtain his final agreement on the presentation. Martin made his presentation in PowerPoint form, which meant that ministers could see it on the screen in both English and French while listening to what he had to say. There were charts and graphs about trends in government spending, projections about economic growth, interest rates, government revenues, and international economic trends. Martin, like any finance minister, would use these projections to try to dampen the spending expectations of his colleagues before the later discussion that would take place after the prime minister asked each of his colleagues to speak on what the priorities of the government should be.

The PIMBY Syndrome Continues to Thrive

INEVITABLY, TWO major problems – similar to what Chaviva Hosek and I had found when we interviewed ministers individually – became evident as soon as the Cabinet discussion turned to priorities involving the spending of public funds. First, despite the admonition of the prime minister to ministers to try to put aside their own departmental issues, take a step back, look at the broader picture, and speak about the government as a whole, most ministers – having long since succumbed to the PIMBY syndrome – talked primarily about their own narrow departmental and regional needs. Second, when ministers did speak about issues beyond their own departments, they began their remarks by paying lip service to the importance of fiscal discipline. Then they immediately endorsed a variety of policy ideas, each of which they believed clearly deserved funding by the minister of finance. Unfortunately, the ideas always required the expenditure of billions of dollars of public funds. No one ever suggested cuts to existing programs, or tradeoffs that might make some of their ideas affordable. There was a naive (unspoken) view that the minister of finance could liberally fund all good ideas while still maintaining rigorous fiscal discipline.

I could always discern from these discussions some broad philosophical preferences of ministers such as the need to deal with health care, child poverty, preparation for the knowledge economy, and unemployment among the many priorities identified around the Cabinet table. With considerable imagination, these broad philosophical preferences could sometimes be translated into overall general governmental priorities. Nevertheless, because Cabinet ministers were unable to make real tradeoffs collectively, Martin was always able to walk away from the meeting confident that he had complete freedom to recommend whatever he wanted to the prime minister for the next budget. Chrétien also understood that, like the minister of finance, he could rationalize to his colleagues any of his decisions on priorities by referring to what someone had said at the Cabinet retreat.

A New, Colourful Approach

BY 1999, AS budget surpluses were growing for the first time in decades, Chrétien tried a more innovative way to involve the whole Cabinet in setting spending priorities. He instructed the Cabinet to meet for a full evening, several weeks before the finance minister had to finalize a budget. The prime minister himself decided not to attend, so that his presence would not influence the discussion in any way, and he asked Martin to listen to his colleagues but not to reveal any of his own preferences. Chrétien had the Privy Council Office distribute to ministers a complete list of all of the priorities of each department that had been discussed and approved in principle – subject to the prime minister and the finance minister approving the funding – at one time or another during the course of the year in committees of Cabinet. He wanted ministers to study the entire list distributed by the Privy Council Office, to express their general views orally, and then, anonymously, list their top-five priorities on paper. The results would be compiled by the Privy Council Office and made available to the minister of finance and the prime minister. Chrétien hoped that this would be a way to get ministers to establish real priorities and have a collective input into the budget.

The Privy Council Office worked overtime to prepare a colour-coded book with all of the permutations and combinations that bureaucrats were sure would enable ministers to come to rational decisions.

I remember vividly the evening when the deputy secretary to the Cabinet, Samy Watson, was so proud of the book he had produced that he came into the Cabinet room early before the meeting started and approached Intergovernmental Affairs Minister Stéphane Dion, whom he considered to be particularly thoughtful, and asked him, "Minister, what do you think of this colour-coded book?" He was devastated when Dion, skeptical about the process, responded truthfully, "I am colour blind."

Dion was right to be skeptical. When my colleagues in the Privy Council Office and I first examined the compilation of the ministerial preferences, I realized that in choosing their five priorities from the long list in front of them, some ministers had voted for the last item on the agenda of the most recent Cabinet committee meeting they had attended as their overriding priority because it was the last thing they remembered – no matter how unimportant it was. Others had clearly decided in a more cynical manner that since the most important priorities of the government would obviously be funded anyway by the prime minister and minister of finance, they could choose less important items as priorities, in the hope that some of their own favourite projects might be funded. Many others, victims of the PIMBY syndrome, obviously voted for their own departmental priorities as top priorities for the government. Like the Cabinet retreats, the results of the voting for priorities were so scattered and inconclusive that they allowed the minister of finance and the prime minister to rationalize whatever priorities they chose for the budget as expressing the will of Cabinet.

You Scratch My Back and I'll Scratch Yours

ONE OF THE prime reasons that ministers are unable to make the tradeoffs and hard choices necessary to choose priorities is the unwritten rule of the Cabinet system, which is, "If you scratch my back, then I'll scratch yours." When he assumed office, Chrétien had wanted Cabinet committees to be where the real policy debates would take place. Committee meetings are less formal than full Cabinet itself; the prime minister is not present, so ministers feel less constrained in what they say, and senior officials sometimes sit at the table and, unlike at full Cabinet, even occasionally are invited to participate in the discussion. Chrétien had long before concluded that his predecessors had created too many committees. In what was a major innovation, he decided that there would be only two major permanent policy committees, which would meet most weeks when the House of Commons was sitting. The Social Policy Committee sat for two to three hours on Tuesday afternoons, and the Economic Policy Committee sat for two to three hours on Thursday mornings. Ministers brought their departmental policy proposals to these Cabinet committee meetings for debate and decision, subject to formal ratification by the full Cabinet.

Over ten years I attended almost all of those meetings. Looking back, I found that there were times when a proposal by a minister might not obtain the approval of his or her colleagues because it was not well explained, clearly needed more thought, or simply was antithetical to the views of certain ministers. Proposals dealing with issues that did not require the spending of much money, such as Criminal Code amendments, immigration policy, or changes to human rights legislation, often sparked intense and interesting policy debate. Generally speaking, however, from my vantage point, ministers showed excessive deference to their colleagues, and it was rare that a minister opposed the substance of a proposal of a colleague unless the proposal was seen to clash with the interest of the objecting minister's department. The reason for that deference was simple. Few ministers had any interest in criticizing another colleague's departmental proposals out of an unspoken fear that the colleague would object to the next proposal that particular minister brought to the table for his or her own department.

The rule "If you scratch my back, then I'll scratch yours" applied particularly where there were proposals for new spending programs or the expansion of existing programs. When ministers supported the general idea behind a proposal, there was rarely any discussion about the proposed cost. I sometimes thought that all ministers put three spending options to their colleagues for any proposed new initiative: option one, having not enough money to do the job properly; option two, having just enough money to do the job not very well; and option three, having the amount of money necessary to do a great job. There was no incentive for ministers to make hard choices or tradeoffs because all committee decisions on spending were simply approvals in principle, subject to the later approval of the finance minister and the prime minister. Not surprisingly, committees would usually agree in principle to option three (while the Department of Finance always chose option one!).

To illustrate that point: I attended many meetings of Cabinet committees at the time of agricultural crises – droughts, too much rain, early frosts, etc. Ministers always expressed great sympathy for the plight of the agricultural sector, and generally competed among themselves for how much more each wanted the government to allocate to unfortunate Canadian farmers. As a representative of the prime minister, my role in these meetings was to listen to the debate, give advice at times to ministers informally at the back of the room, or in the ante room, but rarely to intervene at the table. However, one time when an expensive support system was being considered for the grains and oilseed sector, I asked the chair of the committee if I could ask a question. "It's clear that everyone agrees with the minister of agriculture that we should spend a lot of new money to support these needy farmers and to deal with this crisis," I said. "If we do it, unfortunately, the finance minister will have to cut planned spending elsewhere in the government. Why don't we help him by suggesting what should be cut elsewhere in the government, or even in the budget of the Department of Agriculture, to allow us to spend more money to deal with this farm crisis?" The response was total silence. My point – as I expected – was completely ignored as the discussion progressed.

In the twenty-first century, governing successfully requires the ability, discipline, and backbone to be able to make specific choices, set spending priorities, and stick to them. Money is always at the root of the hard decisions that have to be made, and there is never enough to satisfy all interests. It is clear to me from all the failed attempts I witnessed at involving the whole Cabinet in setting priorities that ministers subconsciously, and sometimes very consciously, want to leave the really tough choices to the minister of finance and the prime minister. Over the years, this led me to the conclusion that, at least in terms of determining and setting overall government spending priorities, it is a simple fact of life that there can be wide consultation at the early stages, but at the end of the day, the alternative to "governing from the centre" is not governing effectively at all. It has nothing to do with dictatorship or "democratic deficits," and it is why the PMO has to be heavily involved in the government's priorities.

As such, the biggest issues Chaviva Hosek and I began to work on right from the beginning involved the minister and the Department of Finance.

Chapter 7

THE PMO AND THE DEPARTMENT OF FINANCE

"In any sphere of action, there can be no comparison between the positions of number one, and numbers two, three, or four."
– WINSTON CHURCHILL

All the resources of the public service become instantly available to a new government, and of course to the PMO, as soon as it assumes office. Professional public servants quickly bring a new government face to face with the constraints of governing, as opposed to what seemed easy and possible only a little while before in Opposition. I was given a quick lesson in the first weeks after the formation of the Chrétien government. David Dodge, the deputy minister of finance, invited Chaviva Hosek and me to dinner.

Dodge is an economist by training and an occasional university professor. With a very keen public policy mind and a deep belief in public service, he always focused on advising governments on the policies that have to be put in place in the short-term to meet the challenges facing the country ten, fifteen, or twenty years down the road. A voracious worker, oriented to problem solving, he could not care less about hierarchy and loves to debate ideas wherever they come from. Always careful in the way he spent public money (he had the lowest expense account of any deputy minister), Dodge could sometimes be too parsimonious for his own good. The first expenditure his successor as deputy minister of finance had to charge to the government was for badly needed new brakes on the deputy minister's government car, because David hadn't wanted to spend public money to repair them.

Chaviva and I met with him for several hours one evening in a small private room at Le Cercle Universitaire in Ottawa. Dodge wanted to prepare us early in the administration for the years ahead, take us through some of the hard facts of economic life, and (in the nicest way possible) make sure that we understood that governing is more than just focusing on the day-to-day.

He explained to us the consequences for the economy of the growing federal deficits and the continuing large increases in the public debt that we inherited from the Mulroney government. The national debt had more than doubled in nine years, and the federal deficit was at a record high. He was unambiguous: "The new government won't be able to focus on the jobs and growth agenda that it promised in its election platform without first putting Canada's public finances in order. You can't expect a weakened economy to create jobs, and it won't be possible to expand existing social programs or institute new ones as you wish to do, without healthy public finances."

Looking to the future, Dodge reminded us that heavy demands will be placed on the government when the baby-boom generation begins to retire during the second decade of the twenty-first century. He discussed the need to address the growth in health-care costs and, as well, the need to ensure the sustainability of the public pension system. "Now is when you have to make the difficult early decisions to prepare for that time. The first thing is serious action to address deficits as you promised in the Red Book. None of this will be easy or painless. But you have to do it." To hammer home his message, Dodge brought a document with him explaining the drastic and unpleasant measures the Labour Party government in New Zealand had recently imposed on that country because it had not addressed its public debt and deficit in time. He told us that Canada needed to take action on its own before the International Monetary Fund stepped in and forced our hand. Things were that bad.

It was a wake-up call from the highest level. Chaviva and I had come to dinner expecting Dodge to give us the usual talk from someone in his position about the financial cupboard being bare; we left dinner under no illusions that the country was facing a fiscal crisis, for which tough medicine was required. And the bottle of wine we shared that evening did nothing to dull the impact of the message.

Dodge stressed that he recognized that his prescription would be difficult politically for the government. He understood that governments operate on a four-year electoral cycle, and he sympathized with the political problems they face in having to make tough decisions where the pain is up front and the benefits are many years away. But he was equally critical about the private sector, talking about the irony of those loudly criticizing the relatively short-term nature of a government's political timetable without reflecting on the fact that too many corporations themselves focus their own strategies on quarterly earnings reports.

Chaviva and I recognized that evening that Liberals in the first days of the Chrétien administration in Canada were facing the same policy dilemma that had caused heated debate and great division among Democrats only a few months earlier in Washington in the first days of the Clinton Administration. The stark policy choice there for President Clinton was between deficit reduction or, after twelve years of Reagan and Bush, the introduction of expensive new social and economic programs that were very dear to the hearts of Democrats. Clinton took on the traditionalists in his own party and decided that reducing the U.S. budget deficit was not a repudiation of the ideals and values of the Democratic Party; rather, it was an essential prerequisite to achieving the long-term social and economic objectives of his administration. We were certainly aware that a similar decision in Canada by the new prime minister who, like Clinton, had campaigned on a message of hope and job creation much more than on deficit reduction, would be an equally hard sell for those elements of the Liberal Party who had spent years in Opposition confident that, once in government, they could almost immediately introduce new social programs and reverse some of the program cuts of the Tories.

Unexpected Advice from China

DAVID DODGE WASN'T the only one educating us about the facts of
economic life. The issues facing the new Chrétien government were
not unique to Canada, and it is useful to put them in a broader perspective. Too often, it seems to me, Canadian media and political commentators and even MPs focus exclusively on what the Canadian
government is doing on this or that issue without any reference to
similar circumstances in other countries. They scrutinize, as if under a
microscope, the domestic policies of a government, and the possible
internal machinations of the governing party, and draw conclusions
about decisions without accounting for the global context in which
those decisions are taken. Governments, however, have to take account
of the world beyond the borders of Canada.

For instance, when the Chrétien government assumed office, not
much time had elapsed since the Iron Curtain had come down; the
countries of Eastern Europe and the former Soviet Union were rapidly
becoming converts to the market economy. China – the sleeping giant
– had awakened. The new global economic realities and the changing
role of government everywhere came through to me loud and clear as
I listened to President Jiang Zemin of China during his first meeting
with Prime Minister Chrétien, less than a month after the election.
They met in a suite in a Seattle hotel in November 1993 at the time of
the first heads of government summit of the Asia-Pacific Economic
Co-operation Conference (APEC). The prime minister was there not
only to meet and establish relations with his Chinese counterpart, but
also to promote Canadian economic interests in China. He reminded
President Jiang that Nortel, a well-known Canadian company, was
bidding for a large contract in Shanghai. "I hope you can help them
get the contract. They are very good and it is important for Canada."

The response from the Chinese president was succinct: "I hope they
are competitive."

We learned a lot that day. If the president of China was preaching
the virtues of a competitive market place and questioning the established role of government in the economy, Canada should take note.

The new leader of the last remaining important communist-led country in the world understood and was comfortable with the forces of globalization. He spoke at some length about the new "socialist market economy" in China. During the conversation, his emphasis was on "market," not on "socialist." After that first encounter, it was less surprising to us when, at a meeting in Beijing a few years later, I listened to Jiang recount to Chrétien a recent trip he had taken to the United States where he had proudly rung the bell to open trading on the New York Stock Exchange. The irony of listening to this story in a room in the Great Hall of the People was not lost on us. As we left the building, we walked down the stairs facing Mao Zedong's tomb not many metres away, and I wondered whether the Great Helmsman would be surprised about the evolution of his country and the world.

China's new direction served as a dramatic illustration of the changing role of government in the world, and of the dramatic shift away from the type of direct government intervention in the economy that dominated the era from the end of the Second World War to the end of the Cold War, and towards a much greater role for market forces. Faced with the improbable alliance of David Dodge and Jiang Zemin, Jean Chrétien, like Bill Clinton, came squarely down on the side of tackling the public finances as his first economic priority.

The decisions required to bring the public finances of Canada under control would make or break the whole of the government's agenda. They would affect every department of government, impact on federal-provincial relations, and have national unity implications. Paul Martin and the Department of Finance would be central players; the relations between the Department of Finance and the PMO would be critical; and the prime minister expected me to manage those relations.

A Formative Moment for Chrétien

I ALREADY KNEW from my own experience about the importance of that relationship; I also knew that, regardless of the personalities involved, it could easily go wrong. The relationship between Jean Chrétien and his two ministers of finance, Paul Martin from 1993–2002 and John Manley in 2002–3, was shaped to a great degree by an event that occurred in the summer of 1978. The Trudeau government was then in considerable political difficulty. The public opinion polls were discouraging as the government entered the fifth year of its mandate. The PMO was desperate to find ways of increasing support for the government. Prime Minister Trudeau's principal secretary, Jim Coutts, convinced him to make a television address to the nation to announce radical new economic measures. Unfortunately, Coutts prepared the speech without any consultation at all with the finance minister, Jean Chrétien, and the Department of Finance. Jim did not keep them in the loop possibly because he thought they might disagree with him and perhaps convince the prime minister to abandon or amend his proposed course of action.

In any event, Trudeau went on television at 8 p.m. on August 1, 1978, to make his announcement. I was a young assistant to Jean Chrétien, the nation's first francophone minister of finance. I was in my office that day in Ottawa and had spoken to him on the telephone several times at his summer cottage where he was on vacation. He never once mentioned to me that the prime minister would be speaking on the economy on national television that evening. Driving home around 7:45 p.m., I was surprised to hear on my car radio that Trudeau was about to address the nation on the economy. I tried to phone Chrétien, but there was no answer at his cottage. Finally, more than two hours after I had seen the speech on television, I succeeded in reaching him. He had just returned from an evening with friends, and sounded slightly annoyed that I was calling late at night while he was on vacation. "What do you think about the prime minister's speech?" I asked.

"What speech? Why are you calling me this late? To whom was he speaking, and what was he talking about?"

"It was a national television address in which the prime minister announced new economic policies."

There was a long silence. Chrétien was stunned and almost speechless.

The minister of finance had been publicly humiliated by the prime minister and the PMO. Chrétien told me that he came close to resigning the next day. The only reason he stayed in the Cabinet was that he feared that the resignation of the first French-Canadian minister of finance in Canadian history could be beneficial to the Parti Québécois government of René Lévesque, which at that time was in the process of planning a referendum on the separation of Quebec. In the end, Trudeau's television address did no political good for his government, which continued to fall in the polls and lost the next election.

There were two lessons applicable to all governments coming out of that episode that both Chrétien and I never forgot. One is that it is essential at all times to maintain complete trust and communication between the prime minister and the finance minister. The other is that good economic policy, properly communicated, always trumps short-term political gimmicks.

Another example, less painful for me, happened a few years later in the Mulroney era. In the budget of 1985, Finance Minister Michael Wilson sought to bring the public finances into balance. To impose fiscal discipline, he proposed the partial de-indexing of old age security payments. This was part of a plan to reduce the growing federal budget deficit, and to make it work, Wilson needed total support from Prime Minister Mulroney. He did not count on the prime minister's reaction when a protest on Parliament Hill ensued, and an enraged senior citizen from Quebec, Solange Denis, pointed her finger at Mulroney as he walked out of his office towards his car and, in the full glare of television cameras, said, "So long, Charlie Brown." Mulroney took the advice of Madame Denis over that of his finance minister. Those famous words were enough to say "so long" to Wilson's plans for reducing the deficit. The larger impact of this incident was to undermine the effectiveness of the finance minister. They served another unintended purpose. They were a constant reminder to Brian Mulroney's successor of the importance of supporting the minister of finance at all times.

When the government was sworn in on November 4, 1993, Jean Chrétien and I had learned the hard way from our own experience in the 1970s that the prime minister and the PMO must always work hand in glove with the Department of Finance and the minister of finance. We knew that there are bound to be policy differences at times between them, because each have different functions that require them to approach issues in different ways. But we were determined that their relationship would be such that they would routinely keep their debates and disagreements private – even from other Cabinet colleagues – and always show a united face in public.

Prime Minister and Finance Minister: Two for the See-saw

PRIME MINISTERS AND finance ministers have to understand each other's responsibilities. The prime minister is ultimately responsible for the overall policies and the political success of the government. He has to balance a multitude of diverse interests and pressures, and has responsibilities that no minister, no matter how important, not even the minister of finance, can come close to matching. The prime minister must ensure not only smooth administration but also smooth politics. He has the delicate task of managing conflicting egos in the Cabinet and must also keep the government caucus united. In minority government situations, he must also take into account the particular needs of Opposition MPs. And he has to deal with provincial premiers and his counterparts in governments around the world.

As a result of his responsibilities, there are always some expenditures that a prime minister has to agree to that aren't necessarily on the list of priorities he and the minister of finance have put together at the beginning of a government's fiscal year, and the finance minister has to have the flexibility in his budgeting to be able to accommodate them. Examples of such pressures are almost infinite – in my experience they included building a four-lane highway from Ottawa to Highway 401, which connects to Montreal and Toronto, so as to satisfy Liberal caucus members from Eastern Ontario; adopting special measures for farmers suffering from the effects of drought as a result of representations from the premiers of Saskatchewan and Manitoba; providing funding for the decommissioning of Russian nuclear material as a result of an agreement by G-8 heads of government; and increasing transfer payments to the provinces in return for their agreement on a Social Union Framework.

On the other hand, the prime minister has to give the finance minister his complete and unwavering support so that he can manage the public finances of the country. Government in a modern society is complicated and expensive. From national parks to veterans' benefits, all the way to help for the disabled and to health care, to education and support for research, to public infrastructure, to national defence and foreign assistance, to support for the arts and culture, to the environment, and to providing a safety net for the elderly, and a good start in life for the very young, the demands on all levels of government are almost infinite. The spending pressures on any minister of finance from Cabinet colleagues are enormous, and very few spending ideas are completely without foundation. Almost all benefit some region or some interest in the country. The problem for a minister of finance is that all of these legitimate requests from colleagues, when assembled together, are simply not affordable. Inevitably, then, the minister of finance has to say no to many of them. He can only do so if he knows that the prime minister will back him up when he is faced with appeals from colleagues, provincial premiers, or outside interest groups.

It is particularly important in the early days of a new government for the prime minister to make his support for the finance minister very clear. Opposition parties often convince themselves that the elimination of "waste" is all that it takes to bring order to the public finances. "Eliminating waste" is good rhetoric in an election campaign and Opposition politicians love to denounce from the rooftops highly publicized examples of bad spending or waste of taxpayer dollars. In fact, the examples of waste tend always to be minuscule in terms of overall government expenditures. For example, the infamous sponsorship program cost $50 million a year out of a total federal government budget of $150 billion. The hard reality is that finance ministers need far more than the elimination of waste or misspending to put a dent into the demands on the federal budget. That is another reason why they need the full support of the prime minister when they have to take tough actions that will make an actual difference to the federal budget.

The symbiotic relationship between a prime minister and a finance minister is difficult at the best of times, as Michael Wilson – a great political ally of Brian Mulroney – found out. We recognized that the political rivalry between Chrétien and Martin could easily make it even more complicated.

Chrétien, Martin, and Winston Churchill

CHURCHILL, IN HIS *War Memoirs*, might very well have been describing the Chrétien government and the relationship between Chrétien and Paul Martin when he wrote:

> In any sphere of action there can be no comparison between the positions of number one and numbers two, three, or four. The duties and the problems of all persons other than number one are quite different and in many ways more difficult. It is always a misfortune when number two or three has to initiate a dominant plan or policy. He has to consider not only the merits of the policy, but the mind of his chief; not only what to advise, but what it is proper for him in his station to advise; not only what to do, but how to get it agreed, and how to get it done. Moreover, number two or three will have to reckon with numbers four, five and six, or maybe some bright outsider, number twenty. Ambition not so much for vulgar ends, but for fame, glints in every mind.

During our period in Opposition, Martin and his executive assistant, Terrie O'Leary, worked closely together with Peter Donolo, Chaviva Hosek, and me in building the Liberal Party platform for the 1993 election. Our collaboration served to put most of the divisions of the leadership campaign behind us. So we arrived in government with the makings of a strong working relationship between the new minister of finance, his office, and three of the most senior people in the new PMO. It was a relationship that lasted throughout Martin's tenure as minister of finance, and it was as crucial to the building of Martin's reputation as a successful finance minister as it was to the success of the Chrétien government. It was therefore surprising and seemingly out of character for Paul Martin ten years later – in an attempt to differentiate himself from the government in which he had for so long served as the most senior minister – to make the gratuitous remark that "Who you know in the PMO" is the problem with the way government works in Canada. Who Martin knew in the PMO and the absolute support he received over the years from his prime minister were key to the remarkable turnaround of the public finances of the nation during the tenure of the Chrétien government.

My Life as a Bridge

PERSONAL AND POLITICAL rivalries make for better media stories and more exciting books than the substance of policy. They are a factor that can complicate the normal management of a relationship between a prime minister and a minister of finance. But it is essential to put rivalries in perspective. Their impact on policy and on the workings of a government is usually blown out of all proportion by those who write about events they did not themselves witness. The conspiracy theories about how and why decisions are made simply do not take account of the fact that most decision makers lack the ability, the imagination, and especially the time to engage in them.

Nevertheless, I had to deal with a difficult relationship, which could easily have gone sour at any time (and eventually did), between two highly competitive men. One of my most onerous responsibilities was to be the bridge between Jean Chrétien and Paul Martin, two colleagues who were never really comfortable with each other, and often eyed each other warily. On one side stood an elected prime minister who wanted to remain prime minister, and on the other, a finance minister he had appointed, who wanted to become prime minister, and who had an active political organization in the Liberal Party and in the country throughout his whole time in the Cabinet that was intended to make that happen as quickly as possible.

The professional relationship between Chrétien and Martin had to be managed with great delicacy so that their personal animosity would not get in the way of good public policy. I never found any textbooks to give guidance on how to manage such a relationship. In some cases, direct contact is the best approach. In Great Britain, despite the notable rivalry between them and their supporters, Tony Blair and the Chancellor of the Exchequer, Gordon Brown, met alone several times a week for many hours to discuss the management of government policy. In Canada, it was different. Neither Chrétien nor Martin particularly looked forward to meetings with each other. When one requested a meeting, the other would often ask me, "What does 'he' want?" Martin was never completely comfortable at the beginning of any meeting with the prime minister. It was evident from his body language that he worried, in Churchill's words, about "not only the merits of the policy, but the mind of his chief; not only what to advise, but what it is proper for him in his station to advise." And it was evident from the body language of the prime minister that he worried about the "ambition that glints in every mind" and, in particular, in the mind of his minister of finance.

In the mid-1990s, Chrétien, Martin, and I were meeting in the prime minister's office on a Monday morning to prepare for the next budget. At the time, there was obvious tension between the two of them because of Martin's ambitions and Chrétien's concern about those ambitions. The prime minister opened the meeting by telling his finance minister that he had been golfing the day before with Mike Robinson, who had run Martin's first leadership bid. Robinson later worked hard and loyally on each of Chrétien's general elections, but it was well known that he was likely to organize Martin's next bid, whenever the time came. In the course of the game, a stray shot from Robinson sent the ball buzzing past the prime minister's head. Chrétien said, "Paul, I told Mike there are better ways to make Paul Martin prime minister." Martin laughed nervously, didn't find it very funny, and rapidly changed the subject.

In 1998, Martin hosted a dinner in Ottawa for the finance minister and deputy prime minister of Malaysia, Anwar Ibrahim, who had a reputation in the international community as a thoughtful, highly cultured, progressive leader with a deep understanding of the significance of international economic and political trends and a great future ahead of him; indeed, his counterparts saw in him the face of modern progressive Islam. Martin invited me to sit at his table with his Malaysian guest. During the course of the conversation, Ibrahim told us that he had spoken the day before on the telephone to his friend, BJ Habibie, who had just become the new president of Indonesia. Habibie, the long-time deputy to President Suharto, who had just been forced out of office, appeared to be a breath of fresh air. I expressed doubt that someone who had been number two for so long could be as different from his predecessor as the new president was pretending to be in his public statements. Ibrahim responded that he had been the number two in the Malaysian government for many years and that he would definitely be very different from his prime minister if ever he were to succeed him. I took the opportunity to jump in and ask, "Paul, does that apply to you as well?" He smiled sheepishly, looked embarrassed, said nothing, and moved on as fast as he could to something else. (Unfortunately, Ibrahim never got the opportunity to show how different he would have been, because Prime Minister Mahathir soon threw his overly ambitious finance minister into prison for the next six years on trumped-up charges. Fortunately for Paul Martin, Canada wasn't in the habit of treating overly ambitious finance ministers in the same way!)

Because of the wariness with which the two protagonists regarded each other, it was particularly important right from the beginning for me (and for Peter Donolo and Chaviva Hosek) to establish a relationship of confidence with Martin, his political staff, the deputy minister, and senior officials in the Department of Finance. The personal relations we established were such that hardly a day went by during ten

years without some contact between the PMO and the Department of
Finance or the minister's office. Sometimes it was simply a heads-up
about some matter; sometimes it was to seek advice on a specific issue;
sometimes there were lengthy meetings, sometimes it was a call to
bounce ideas off of one another, and sometimes it was just, "Hello,
what's new?" There was no hierarchy. We were in and out of one
another's offices depending solely on convenience. Deputy ministers
of finance got to know my boardroom very well, and I was equally
familiar with theirs. Their takeout food for lengthy dinner meetings
was much better than mine, so I preferred to work in their office at
those times. In the morning, they preferred my coffee. Our focus,
though, was not on food but on results. The more we worked together,
the better we got to know one another, and the easier it was to achieve
the objectives of the government.

Martin and I talked regularly – sometimes several times a day – on
the telephone, saw each other during and after Cabinet and Cabinet
Committee meetings, met in each other's office, and had many meals
together every year. Our policy towards each other was "no sur-
prises." We were open with each other and always shared information.
In that way, we made up for the infrequent contact between Chrétien
and Martin.

One of my responsibilities in the Prime Minister's Office, in consultation with the Privy Council Office, was the preparation of each
Speech from the Throne, opening a new session of Parliament. The
Throne Speech, which sets out the overall agenda and plans of the government, is strictly the prerogative of the prime minister. As such, I
always consulted Cabinet ministers and their deputies on their own
individual departmental agendas, but never on the whole speech. I
believed, however, that the role of the Department of Finance was so
fundamental to the overall agenda of the government that I sought its
input in a way that I did with no other department. I assumed the
responsibility on my own – without asking Chrétien for permission,
afraid of what his answer might be – to give early drafts both to Martin
and to the deputy minister of finance for their comments, even before

showing the prime minister a draft, and I would accommodate their comments in later drafts. As such, it was disconcerting after some Throne Speeches to read stories in the media – planted by Martin's political supporters – that the finance minister should have been consulted because he had reservations about some of the commitments in the Speech.

Another area of close collaboration between the PMO and Paul Martin was the orchestration of public speeches and statements. Prime ministers and finance ministers use major speeches to announce policies, to signal priorities, or, if necessary, to calm financial markets. The minister and the deputy minister of finance and I worked closely to coordinate speeches that the prime minister or the minister of finance would give. We would discuss whether particular economic circumstances required a speech or statement and, if so, who would be best suited to speak on a particular subject, what he should say, and when the most appropriate time would be to deliver it. We would then prepare and trade preliminary drafts and comment on them until we were satisfied with the final product.

Political Staff and the Public Service

THOSE WHO TRY to draw a sharp line between politics and policy, between the political staff and the permanent public service, don't understand how government works in practice, where there are few watertight compartments. My relationship with the Department of Finance illustrates how the public service and political staff work together to exchange views and opinions, share information, debate issues, and make recommendations to ministers.

Over ten years, I was fortunate to work with three outstanding deputy ministers of finance: David Dodge, Scott Clark, and Kevin Lynch. While respecting each other's roles, we worked very closely together. We established open and confidential relationships and, as a side benefit, lasting friendships. When we thought we had good ideas, we tried to figure out how to sell them to our respective principals. When we knew of problems, we tried to solve them ourselves if possible, because prime ministers and finance ministers are best served when they do not have to deal with issues that others can solve. When we could help each other, we did.

To illustrate the point, one day when the Canadian dollar was under considerable downward pressure in the foreign exchange markets, the governor of the Bank of Canada, Gordon Thiessen, made the difficult decision to increase interest rates by one hundred basis points. Scott Clark telephoned me at the end of the day: "Gordon is doing the right thing, but he needs moral support before he makes his announcement tomorrow morning. He has really agonized over this decision. It's tough to know that you're responsible for increases in mortgage rates and consumer loans. He's really feeling under a lot of stress. Could you call him and reassure him that it's the right decision and that he's not alone and will be fully supported after it is announced?" I knew that financial markets look for any sign of disagreements between governments – which, for political reasons, rarely like interest rate increases – and central bank governors, who for economic reasons, have to increase rates. So I called Thiessen right away and assured him that he had the full support of the prime minister and the PMO, and I know that he appreciated that support from our office.

Deputy ministers of finance and I spoke freely to each other about the positions of our respective bosses on issues. There were times I called to say, "The PM will raise something today with Paul that he won't like. It isn't that important in the overall scheme of things, but it is important to the prime minister. Try to get Paul to agree. Tell him not to make a federal case out of it." Or I would be on the receiving end of a call from the deputy minister: "Paul will raise something with the PM that he may not like. What do we do?" He would explain the issue and I would reply, "Put that way, the boss will never go for it. Put another way, it might be okay. Tell Paul to wait before he speaks to the PM, and let's you and I try to fix it." In many respects, we acted preventively. When we saw that personality problems risked getting in the way of good decision making, either between the prime minister and the minister of finance, or the minister of finance and some of his colleagues, we tried to act as intermediaries. More often than not, we were successful.

The PMO has a perspective of government that even the Department of Finance does not have. I attended all meetings between the prime minister and provincial premiers. Often only the premier, the prime minister, and I were in the room. I always informed Paul Martin, Terrie O'Leary, or the deputy minister immediately after the meeting about any financial requests any premier made of the prime minister, as well as his response, and we would decide together what followup was required.

When I knew that the prime minister might be lobbied by an MP or a provincial premier on a particular matter that would involve the expenditure of public monies, I would seek the views of the Department of Finance and then brief the prime minister before he made any decision. There was one particular incident where a Liberal MP got on his high horse and threatened to vote against the government in the House of Commons unless a project in his constituency was funded.

The MP was adamant: "Tell the prime minister I have a conscience to protect." The response of the prime minister was equally adamant: "Tell him I have a budget to protect." On the other hand, if Chrétien needed to satisfy a particular MP, a provincial premier, or even a foreign head of government seeking Canadian aid, it was my role to make sure that my colleagues in Finance understood why.

By the beginning of 1994, the outlines of the almost revolutionary steps that would be needed to bring order to the public finances were becoming clear to the new prime minister and the new minister of finance. No one could have predicted then, or after that first sobering meeting Chaviva Hosek and I had with David Dodge, that nine years later, the federal budget would have been in balance for six years, with the government running surpluses, and taxes and the national debt considerably reduced. Finance Minister John Manley's March 2003 budget made large investments in health, the National Child Benefit, support for post-secondary education and research, foreign aid, and arts and culture, and was still able to reduce the national debt by billions of dollars. David Dodge, at this point governor of the Bank of Canada, came up to me at a post-budget party with a large smile on his face and, with characteristic exuberance, proclaimed in a loud voice, "Wow, would you have ever thought this possible back in 1994 and 1995?" In fact, it was only possible because of the complete support Chrétien gave to his finance minister at all times, and because of the co-operative relationship between the PMO and the Department of Finance. That relationship made for smooth decision making in the preparation of budgets, and in the allocation of government spending priorities.

Chapter 8

BUDGET MAKING

"We have two classes of forecasters; those who don't know and those who know they don't know."

– JOHN KENNETH GALBRAITH

I was sitting in the House of Commons gallery beside former finance minister Mitchell Sharp when Paul Martin was reading his budget statement of February 1999. Sharp listened with amazement to the budget speech, when Martin, after spending a considerable amount of time announcing a variety of health policy and health research measures, turned his focus to post-secondary education, information technology, and other matters under the responsibility of the Department of Industry. Sharp (then eighty-six years old and with experience and institutional memory going back to his days in the 1940s in the Department of Finance when Mackenzie King was prime minister) turned to me and said, "I thought Martin was minister of finance. Is he also minister of health, and minister of industry, and what other portfolios does he have which might become evident in the rest of the budget?"

In that one question, he captured how government in Canada had changed over the years. Sharp had once explained to me that when he was minister of finance in the Pearson government from late 1965 to 1968, the prime minister and his office did not get involved in budgets.

Finance ministers traditionally presented budgets that focused entirely on taxes and tariffs, and fixed the overall spending limits for the year for the government, without establishing overall government program priorities. Budgets were prepared in secret without public consultation, and with only rudimentary consultation with other departments of government, including even the prime minister. The few copies of budget drafts that were available were closely guarded, and even within the Department of Finance not many people were involved. Prime Minister Diefenbaker's finance minister, Donald Fleming, in the days before computers and even Xerox machines, took personal control of the Finance Department's mimeograph machine, so he could know how many copies of budget drafts were available and to whom they were sent. Fleming, in stark contrast to his successors more than a quarter-century later, jealously and successfully protected his autonomy even from the prime minister of the day in preparing his budgets.

Times have changed since those days, and the budget has become the single most important policy document of the year for the government. (It not only establishes all the government's spending priorities, but it also uses the tax system as an important instrument of social policy.) This means that the prime minister and the PMO need to be heavily involved in budget making. The way in which a prime minister participates in the preparation of a budget is a matter of personal style. Some prime ministers want to get involved in detailed decision making and to be part of lengthy meetings with departmental officials and the minister of finance; others want trusted policy advisers to do that work for them, and to brief them on a regular basis.

The Chrétien Style

CHRÉTIEN DIDN'T WANT to get involved in the nitty-gritty of budget making. He believed that the role of the prime minister was to set out the overall priorities of the government and then let his ministers implement them. Before the election of 1993, he promised in the Red Book that any government he headed would reduce the federal deficit to 3 per cent of gross domestic product within three years of taking office, as a first step to achieving a balanced budget. Having set out his deficit-cutting priority, Chrétien's style was to delegate to Paul Martin the responsibility to carry out that commitment in his post-election budgets.

Similarly, Chrétien made certain decisions before the election of 1997 that would determine future budgets. His whole philosophy of governing was to provide what he saw as a balanced approach to public policy, leaning neither too far to the right or too far to the left. Chrétien called me at home on a Saturday morning in early 1997 to tell me that he had been reflecting on how to deal with balanced budgets. He had decided that the Liberal Party should commit in its 1997 election platform that 50 per cent of any future government surpluses be allocated to spending on social and economic priorities, and the other 50 per cent to tax and debt reduction. It was a formula that appealed to his sense of balance and had the additional advantage of being easy to communicate to the public. He asked me to inform the minister of finance and the chairs of the Liberal Party platform committee that he had made the decision, and that it was not open for debate.

At the beginning of the 1997 election campaign, Chrétien set out the spending priorities of his government for a second mandate – health, children, and knowledge, education, and innovation. Just as after the election of 1993, the prime minister expected his finance minister to fund those commitments in his post-election budgets, and having set out the parameters, he didn't have to be personally involved in budget making on a daily basis.

There were three other reasons why Chrétien didn't want to get involved in the day-to-day details of budget making. First – much as he wished it wasn't the case – he recognized that the presence of the prime minister in a room too often inhibits even senior officials and senior ministers from expressing their real views about policy when they contradict those of the prime minister. Second, Chrétien also understood there is a big difference between being prime minister and being minister of finance. The prime minister has a lot of decisions to make all the time, and must know how to delegate. While a finance minister has the crucial task at all times of inspiring confidence in the financial markets and the national and international financial community (something Martin did with extraordinary ability), this does not require pressure-cooker decision making on a daily basis. It means that the finance minister has the time to focus throughout the year on the next budget without the pressure of too many daily decisions. He has the luxury of time to weigh options, examine alternatives, look at details, and engage in policy seminars. He can throw around ideas, and still – as in the case of Finance Minister Martin – be very much the micro-manager in the Department of Finance.

Third, and above all, Chrétien had learned from Pearson and Trudeau that a prime minister should always keep himself in reserve to be the ultimate arbiter where necessary at the end of a process once ministers are ready to bring their recommendations to him, rather than to be part of the process from the beginning, and so be unable at the end to stand back with the perspective needed for ultimate decision making. It was an approach that served him in good stead.

The Senior Policy Adviser and the Budget

WHILE CHRÉTIEN DIDN'T want to be involved in the daily budget process, he expected me to be very much involved so that I could keep him fully informed of progress and problems. During the course of a year, I had many meetings, lunches, and dinners with Paul Martin (and in 2003 with John Manley), his executive assistant, and the deputy minister of finance. Sometimes we would all meet together, sometimes with one or more of them. Often Chaviva Hosek was present. At these meetings, particularly in the years after the elimination of the deficit, we would discuss various possible thematic options for the next budget, whether it be health, children in low-income families, university research, or, on the other side of the ledger, tax cuts and debt reduction. I would then have the opportunity to discuss with Chrétien the initial thinking about the next budget, and I would feed the prime minister's thoughts into the process.

Budgets were usually tabled in Parliament some time in February. Each of them was the product of many months of work. The finance minister and his department spent much of the year preparing options and recommendations, which only crystallized late in the fall when the economic forecasts for the following year are most up to date. The minister of finance was then ready to meet with the prime minister with broad outlines of a general budget approach. It is the type of meeting that in any circumstances needs to be well prepared in advance. It was particularly necessary to do so given the relations between Chrétien and Martin.

Managing a Tenuous Relationship

AS THE INTERMEDIARY between Chrétien and Martin, I tried to ensure as much agreement as possible in advance before the two men met. Before any meeting to plan a budget, Chrétien knew from me more or less what Martin was planning to say, what my own views were, and how the thinking going into the budget had evolved; and Martin knew from me more or less what the prime minister's response would be. When they met, it was normally either at the prime minister's residence or in his office in House of Commons. It was Bruce Hartley's job, as Chrétien's executive assistant, to schedule meetings at a time when Chrétien was as relaxed as possible, and as little preoccupied as possible with other matters. They were usually planned to go on as long as necessary, but it was rare that they lasted more than an hour. If a meeting took place at the end of the day at 24 Sussex, the prime minister always offered refreshments. The meetings, always cordial, usually began with light comments and, when appropriate, some reference to the latest international meetings that either of them had attended. There might then be some talk about the political situation of the government in the country. Before getting down to the business at hand, Chrétien often used the occasion, as he did in almost all of his meetings with any of his ministers, to talk in some detail about national unity – which was always his number-one preoccupation – and his plans

for handling Quebec issues, particularly in the period after the referendum of 1995. Martin would listen and say little, expressing neither
agreement or disagreement. (But it was wrong for him in February
2004, when the Auditor-General's report on the sponsorship program
was tabled, to suggest that he had been "out of the loop" and unaware
of the Quebec strategy of the Chrétien government.)

I am the only one who, for nine years, attended almost every one of
the meetings between Jean Chrétien and Paul Martin. Most often, only
the three of us were in the room. I can attest to the fact that it is wrong
to examine or judge the economic policies of the Chrétien government
primarily through the prism of the Chrétien-Martin rivalry. It was not
the focal point around which the day-to-day policy activity of the
Chrétien government gravitated, although it was pivotal (and destructive) in the internal politics of the Liberal Party. While there was clearly
great political rivalry between the two, it didn't get in the way of the
decisions made by the prime minister and the minister of finance.

In fact, the two men shared similar views. Chrétien was a strong
proponent of social programs, and had been in the House of Commons
when the Pearson government created many new such programs in the
1960s. But he recognized that while many Liberals in the 1990s looked
back upon that time as a golden age, Pearson was able to accomplish
his social agenda primarily because of many years of sustained economic growth that produced low budget deficits, and more often surpluses, a relatively low tax burden and a low public debt. Chrétien had
been parliamentary secretary to Mitchell Sharp and then a junior minister in the finance department when Sharp was the finance minister.
Sharp, who became his mentor for the next thirty-five years, was a prac-
titioner of fiscal responsibility, and as minister of finance in the Pearson
government delayed the introduction of medicare for one year until it
was fiscally affordable. Chrétien learned from him the imperatives of
a clean balance sheet. And Chrétien also understood from his experience as minister of finance under Pierre Trudeau, and also from his
observation of the difficulties between Pearson and his first finance

minister, Walter Gordon, in the early 1960s, how important it is for the prime minister always to support the finance minister.

Martin shared Chrétien's views even if the two men came to them from different life experiences. Martin did not have thirty years in Parliament to shape his thinking. But like many successful business-people, he was not a believer in deficit financing in the public sector, although, ironically, he had borrowed deeply to finance the purchase of his own company. (It has always been the case that while the private sector uses borrowed capital to finance growth and expansion, and while banks make their profits by providing loans, private sector bor-rowers and lenders are among those who preach the loudest against governments who finance their activities with borrowed money.) Unlike most of his business contemporaries, Martin was also a deep believer in an activist role for government, particularly in social pro-grams. No one had a more profound influence on him than his father, who as a postwar Cabinet minister was one of the prime architects of the Canadian social safety net.

The real story of the Chrétien-Martin relationship is not of a series of policy disagreements culminating in Martin's spectacular departure from the Cabinet on June 2, 2002. On the contrary, the professional – as opposed to the personal – relationship between Chrétien and Martin, much like the professional relationship in Great Britain between Tony Blair and Gordon Brown, is the best example of how prime ministers and finance ministers should support each other. They knew that they had to be in agreement publicly and privately in front of their colleagues, and they always were. For nine years it was a partnership between a prime minister and a minister of finance that turned around government finances, provided room for activist government, and left Canada with strong economic foundations. Sometimes the competi-tive nature of the two men even contributed to better public policy. For example, in 1997, when Chrétien proposed a scholarship program as a millennium project, it inspired Martin to focus the major elements of his next budget on accessibility to higher education.

Making Cool Decisions on Cold Pizza

AFTER THE DEFICIT had been eliminated in 1997, Chrétien and Martin always found it relatively easy in their initial pre-budget meeting in the late fall to agree on the broad budgetary approach. Chrétien and Martin (and Manley in 2003) wanted budgets to focus on the government's principal priorities – innovation and education, health, children, and tax and debt reduction. They rejected the notion of reducing spending on these priorities in order to spend more on other matters such as the military, which lobbied hard for its own interests. Chrétien would then leave me to represent him in working out the details of the budget with Martin. I became an essential go-between because I knew Chrétien's views and had his confidence, and also had the confidence of the minister and Department of Finance.

That first meeting between the minister of finance and the prime minister on the general themes of the budget was followed by long sessions that I would participate in over several weeks with Martin, his staff, the senior officers of the Finance department, and Chaviva Hosek from the PMO in order to translate the budget themes into a detailed final document. Our meetings often lasted many hours, sometimes ending well after midnight. We would have so much hot and (too often) cold pizza in boardrooms in the Finance department during budget time that none of us wanted to eat any more pizza for the rest of the year. As the protector of the public purse, the Department of Finance was always rightly extremely prudent, particularly at the early stages of budget making, in how it proposed to allocate fiscal resources. Entering those meetings, Chaviva and I knew we had to push Finance to get to its real bottom line. At a time of budget surpluses, we believed that our role was to test the outer limits of what is fiscally possible and responsible, and we usually tried (with some degree of success) to persuade Martin to agree to make more significant investments – in health, research, innovation, and education, and in children living in low-income families – than he was initially prepared to make. And we made clear Chrétien's instructions to devote increased resources to arts, culture, and foreign aid, something Martin always resisted.

One of my rules was that just as there should never be any public distance between the prime minister and minister of finance, the rest of the government has to see the PMO as totally supportive of the finance minister. Anything else can put in jeopardy the financial credibility of the government, and risks creating instability in currency markets in addition to creating political problems for the government. So, I would never contradict the finance minister or his officials in front of other departments and other ministers. That allowed us to have fierce debates among ourselves, often using language that is not taught in any school for diplomats, and we had plenty of those over the course of budget preparations. On more than one occasion, I slammed the telephone on Martin, and then we would call back to apologize to each other. It was as a result of the frankness of our internal discussions that Martin and I usually reached agreement on final recommendations to the prime minister.

Not all ministers agreed with my complete support of the Finance department. Once, David Dingwall stood in front of me beside the coffee machine in the Cabinet room two hours before Martin was to table one of his restraint budgets, wagging his finger and pointing at me, angrily referring to the budget as "Your budget." I was prepared to take it as a compliment, but since it was not intended that way, I reminded him about the principle of Cabinet solidarity, and how the budget is that of the whole government of which he was a part, as long as he chose to remain in the Cabinet.

Subjective Tradeoffs are Part of the Budget System

THE PRESSURES TO spend money on a wide range of issues and departments are almost infinite. Only some can be accommodated. In coming to final recommendations on the budget, it is always difficult to make tradeoffs that allow the best use of scarce resources. The role of human nature in the decision-making process should not be overlooked. Sometimes when we considered spending pressures put forward by different departments, and had to decide on which to accept and which to reject, we made our late-night decisions on the basis of how

co-operative certain ministers and their officials had been during the
year with the PMO and the Department of Finance. When a minister
had recognized the constraints of fiscal responsibility, and had tried to
reallocate spending within his or her own department rather than just
seeking new resources, there was more likelihood of that minister
getting satisfaction for his or her priority than another minister who
had been less willing to make tradeoffs, and more difficult to deal with
during the year. If some minister had suffered a series of political losses
over the year and needed to demonstrate some success in the interests
of the political image of the entire government, there might be help at
budget time.

The Role of Compromise

THE CHRÉTIEN GOVERNMENT was remarkably successful in putting
70 to 75 per cent of its new spending year after year into the priority
areas of health, children in poverty, and the knowledge-based economy,
despite enormous pressure to spend a lot in other areas. Nevertheless,
in establishing our final recommendations for the prime minister, the
Finance department and I understood that in addition to focusing on
overall priorities, a prime minister and a finance minister have to be
able to respond to some particular needs of Cabinet colleagues that are
important to their own departments, even if they are not key to overall
government priorities. All Cabinet ministers determine their own
success in part on how they meet the needs of their departmental
constituents. Members of Parliament rightly or wrongly judge their
success – and sometimes their enthusiasm for supporting the government during the course of a parliamentary session – on what they can
claim to have brought to their constituents.

While fiscal responsibility is an honoured principle for ministers
and MPs in the abstract, they don't necessarily consider the continued
cutting of their own favourite budgets and programs as the best path
to political success in practice. It is almost impossible for a prime minister to manage a Cabinet if he has to tell most of his ministers year
after year that none of their own priorities can be addressed for years

to come, not because the government has no money and is actually reducing expenditures across the board, but because the government has more important priorities elsewhere. Good political management of the government requires that there always be some hope held out for ministers and for caucus that some relief for their own priorities is not too far down the road, and that good news might be coming the next year, even if it doesn't come in the current year. The real test of leadership for a prime minister and a finance minister is to be able to set and enforce a few major priorities, without which a government cannot be successful, while still making the inevitable compromises required to maintain the unity of a Cabinet and a caucus.

Reaching Consensus

IT WAS ONLY when we had a consensus among ourselves, or when there were very few remaining items of difference between us, that Martin and I would go back to the prime minister with final budget recommendations. Chrétien already knew from my briefings that his own views had been incorporated in the budget recommendations, so he was usually comfortable before the meeting with Martin started. But he still sometimes asked certain questions or expressed views that differed in some respects from his minister. Before the budget of 1999, for example, Chrétien was prepared to make a $3 billion payment to the provinces for health. Martin was reluctant to go above $2.5 billion. Because it was not an issue of overriding principle, the prime minister's approach was to respect the wishes of the finance minister and not to insist on imposing his own will.

There were times when Chrétien and the PMO surprised Martin. For instance, Chrétien, Chaviva Hosek, and I had the reputation of being less comfortable with the so-called "corporate agenda" than Martin. Yet before the budget of February 2000 where Martin was planning to propose large personal income tax cuts, Chaviva and I, with the prior agreement of the prime minister, convened a meeting in my boardroom of Don Drummond, who was the associate deputy minister of finance, Munir Sheikh, the assistant deputy minister for tax policy, Kevin Lynch, then deputy minister of industry, Rob Fonberg, the deputy secretary to the Cabinet, and David Dodge, then deputy minister of health, to brainstorm as to whether cuts to corporate income tax and to the capital gains tax were also necessary to spur investment, productivity, and economic growth. Everyone in the room agreed they were important, although Drummond's pragmatic view was not to do anything that might jeopardize getting agreement from the prime minister to major personal income tax cuts. When Chaviva and I reported back to Chrétien, he instructed us to tell Martin to add corporate and capital gains tax reductions to his personal income tax proposals for his budget. When Martin and I met with Chrétien, Martin said that he agreed with the prime minister's economic rationale and would include his suggestions in his budget, but (obviously considering his future ambitions) hoped that "I won't be accused of bringing down a rich man's budget." I wondered silently which one was the "populist," and which one was "pro business."

The Surplus Debate

THE MOST INTERESTING part of all the budget preparation meetings between Chrétien and Martin after 1998 was the continuing debate between the two about the projected budgetary surplus of the government. Chrétien, who was always skeptical about the accuracy of the Finance department's conservative projections, enjoyed working with numbers. He loved going through revenue and expenditure projections, and forecasts of employment growth, interest rates, and economic growth. It became a standing joke for all of Chrétien's deputy ministers of finance, who had trouble containing their laughter as he explained his own very complicated formula (which only he understood) to predict the surplus. He would do his calculations on a scrap of paper, try to explain to Martin and me how he reached his conclusions, and then tell the minister of finance what the budget surplus would actually be. Martin and I would listen respectfully but skeptically. My notes from the meeting would say, "Surplus – same old stuff from PM." And each year, the prime minister and his finance minister bet $100 with each other on who was right. Invariably, at the end of every year, much to everyone's surprise each time, the formula on the scrap of paper produced results much closer to the actual outcome than all the sophisticated computer models of the Department of Finance. (Chrétien has never collected his winnings from Martin.)

The debate on the projected surplus between Chrétien and Martin, and in 2003 between Chrétien and Manley, was not so much a matter of pride between two men as one with profound implications for the country. The size of the projected government surplus determined what investments could be made in, for example, health, the National Child Benefit, research and innovation, and much else; it determined what new tax cuts were affordable, and what debt repayment would take place. Extra spending or tax cuts on the basis of too rosy projections risked putting the country back in fiscal deficit; on the other hand, decisions based on projections that were too conservative limited the ability of the government to spend more on its own priorities or to transfer more to the provinces, or to reduce taxes more. Chrétien always suspected – but couldn't prove – that Martin was being exceptionally conservative so that he could keep resources for his government to use after he became prime minister.

Forecasting the budgetary surplus isn't an exact science. Domestic and international economic circumstances change in the course of a year, so it is impossible to make completely accurate forecasts. With annual federal budgets of close to $200 billion, a small error in forecasting implies billions of dollars, in one direction or the other. The problem for the government is that federal budgets only operate in individual fiscal years. Accounting rules as enforced by the Auditor General require that surpluses at the end of the fiscal year must automatically be applied against the national debt. Extra money cannot be rolled over into the next fiscal year either for investments in programs that are priorities for Canadians or for tax cuts. Compounding the problem is the fact that it takes several months after the end of the fiscal year before the books are finally closed.

In almost every year since the budget was balanced in 1997, the actual federal surplus has turned out to be much higher than was projected in the budget, at a time when other decisions could have been made about the allocation of the surplus. This has meant that many billions of dollars have been automatically applied to reduce the national debt. While debt repayment may be good economic policy, it should be a considered choice rather than one imposed by accounting rules. I tried with no success to persuade the Department of Finance to find ways of providing flexibility for dealing with unanticipated surpluses. The Martin government actually introduced legislation to that effect in 2005 but was defeated before the bill was adopted.

Memorable Disagreements

THE BUDGET OF 1995 – with its massive cuts to government spending – was one of the most important in Canadian history. It turned around a quarter-century of deficit financing, and put Canada on the road to a decade of balanced budgets, sound financial health, and sustained economic growth. It did more than cut expenditures; it fundamentally changed the Canadian approach to the role of government in society. Such a change was difficult for Liberals in particular. Like Democrats in the United States, they had been very comfortable with spending programs that required ever more public borrowing. Chrétien, like his counterpart Clinton, who had to deal with the same issues at about the same time in his party, understood that the increasing burden of public debt charges was unsustainable and had to be reversed. The prime minister had to bring around a Liberal Cabinet and caucus that was already uncomfortable with the position he had taken on free trade. Now he was going to put forward a fundamental reform as significant to Canada's future as was Mulroney's free trade agreement of a few years earlier.

What made this tectonic shift possible was the complete co-operation of Chrétien and Martin, and their work on it proved to be the high watermark of their partnership. Each was determined to succeed, and each had his own role to play. For his part, Chrétien created a Cabinet committee (the Program Review Committee) to review all the programs of the government and recommend major cuts. He made sure that its membership would be broadly representative of the ideological spectrum of the Cabinet so that a unanimous committee would have great weight with colleagues who were not members of it. He appointed Marcel Massé to chair it and counted on his recognized expertise in government to drive the committee forward. Most important, he accorded his full support publicly and privately around the Cabinet table to his finance minister.

Martin's role was critical. He spent a good part of the year conditioning the Canadian public to the need for drastic action to restore the health of the country's finances. He arm-twisted his Cabinet colleagues and made sure that the members of the Massé Committee understood that the perilous state of the public finances required them to act boldly. Once the committee had made its recommendations on cuts to each department in a manner that satisfied Martin and the Department of Finance, Chrétien made it clear that he would not reverse any decisions recommended by Massé and approved by Martin. I tried one Saturday morning at 24 Sussex to persuade the prime minister that two of the cuts were wrong. His response was, "If I change anything, everything will unravel." Then Martin – working seven days a week, long into the nights – prepared the budget.

Chrétien – as was his style – didn't get involved in the details of the budget, and simply made it clear to his ministers that the finance minister had his full support. Yet he saw his role as prime minister as the ultimate decision maker responsible for the overall interests of the government. Rather than get distracted by details, he wanted to pass judgment on the budget document in its entirety. This led to a high-stakes drama in early February 1995.

Martin had made one proposal that had not been discussed by the Massé Committee. He had come to the conclusion that the budget should cut some government benefits for senior citizens. This concerned the prime minister deeply and resulted in a dramatic disagreement between the two of them that almost led to a government crisis.

Martin's argument was that the success of the budget would be determined by the reaction of financial markets who held billions of dollars in Canadian debt, and who influenced interest rates. He was convinced that they would not pass positive judgment on the budget unless it cut an "entitlement" program. Chrétien, on the other hand, was convinced that the rest of the cuts were more than deep enough to satisfy financial markets. His political instinct told him that any tampering with senior citizens' benefits would have catastrophic effects on the upcoming Quebec referendum. Martin's response was that an unsuccessful budget would also be catastrophic in Quebec.

Chaviva Hosek and I also debated the issue ourselves for weeks to determine how we would advise the prime minister. It was not easy. As we weighed the pros and cons, we kept changing our own minds in opposite directions. Then Chrétien, Martin, Hosek, and I met in the prime minister's House of Commons office. Chrétien said to Martin, "So, Paul, we have a tough issue here, what do you think?" Martin responded, "Prime minister, I think difficult issues are for ministers to decide; the impossible ones are for the prime minister to decide. This one is for you." And then he explained why he wanted to reform seniors' benefits.

What was fascinating was that both men had exactly the same objectives – a successful budget and a federalist victory in Quebec. They fundamentally disagreed, however, on what it would take.

In this case, their disagreement went to the core of the relationship between a prime minister and a finance minister. Martin expected – not without some reason – that the prime minister had to support his finance minister on a matter he considered fundamental to the success of a budget. The prime minister held – also not without some reason – that his overall responsibilities as head of government required him to pass final judgment on all significant government initiatives, even if it meant overriding his finance minister. Martin told me that he was prepared to resign on a matter of principle.

My reaction – based in large measure on the memory of the discussion Chaviva Hosek and I had with David Dodge in late 1993 about

Canada's fiscal situation – was that such a resignation would lead to chaos in financial markets and had to be avoided almost at all costs. At one point, Martin said to me, "If the prime minister doesn't agree with me, perhaps he would agree to meet with one of my advisers, who will explain why I want to tackle seniors benefits." It was a reasonable request, and I saw it as an opening. I arranged for his adviser, Peter Nicholson, a distinguished economic thinker, to meet with Chrétien on a Saturday afternoon at 24 Sussex. I hoped the chemistry between the two would be good. Nicholson's father was a former Nova Scotia finance minister and a friend of Chrétien, and Peter had made a major contribution to the Aylmer Conference when we were in Opposition. When the meeting was over, Nicholson called me and said, "I thought I had hit a home run, but the PM caught the ball as it was going over the fence. The bottom line is he will not change his mind."

Chrétien remained unconvinced that there was any need to touch entitlement programs for the budget to be a success, and was firmly of the view that doing so would be the straw that would break the camel's back in terms of the acceptance by Canadians of the budget. The prime minister – as he must in our system of government – had to have the last word. Therefore, there would be no change to seniors' benefits in the budget. I then helped broker a compromise to save some face for the finance minister. At my suggestion, there would be wording in the budget documents that the government would study the structure of those benefits over the next year. It was enough to satisfy a reluctant Martin, although it was another wound in their relationship that never healed. Chrétien turned out to be right. The Martin budget was a remarkable success, and the finance minister agreed a year later that there was no need to tamper with seniors' benefits.

The other occasions where there were disagreements between the two men were less dramatic but also important. Martin always argued vigorously – even at a time of budget surpluses – against the prime minister's support for a substantial increase in foreign aid. One day as we sat in the living room at 24 Sussex, Martin – to our astonishment – told the prime minister in all seriousness that because many aboriginal

Canadians live in Third World conditions, federal spending on aboriginals should be counted as the equivalent of foreign aid! But when
Chrétien then suggested increasing the budget for aboriginals, the
finance minister argued that enough was already being spent.

Regardless of the proposal, Martin's instinctive response was always
that of a prudent finance minister. He would warn that any new spending might put the federal government back into deficit. Martin was
usually far more fixated on the long-term fiscal implications of a proposal than on its substance, and would almost always eventually agree
to a proposal when he was convinced that the fiscal situation of the
government allowed for it. Even so, he fiercely resisted provincial
pressures for increases in equalization payments; and in particular, he
opposed any changes to the formula for calculating equalization for
the province of Newfoundland to allow it to keep more benefits from
its offshore resource revenues; and he was always reluctant to agree to
large increases in transfer payments to the provinces for health care. In
those days, he also blocked all attempts by Human Resources Development Minister Jane Stewart to put federal money into a national childcare program. Chrétien insisted on increasing spending on foreign aid,
culture, and aboriginal people, but went along with his finance minister
on other matters, including the Newfoundland equalization formula.

Conflicts Between Ministers: A Case Study

THERE ARE MANY large egos in politics and with them go fierce ambitions that can get in the way of governing. It wasn't only the prime
minister and the finance minister who were political rivals within the
same party. I found that I sometimes had to step in to help manage
relationships between the finance minister and other ministers who
were in competition with him. For example, the focus of the budget
of February 1999 was to be health. The two ministers principally
involved were Allan Rock, the minister of health, and Paul Martin, the
finance minister. Both saw themselves as potential successors to the
prime minister. There was no question in each of their minds about
the "glint of ambition" in the eyes of the other. Mostly for that reason,

by the beginning of the second term in office of the Chrétien government, neither minister got along particularly well with the other, and their political staff only exacerbated the competition between the two.

In the fall of 1998, well before the budget decisions were to be made, Rock and Martin, their executive assistants, and their deputy ministers met for dinner one evening in an Ottawa restaurant. The meeting was a disaster. They agreed to nothing. And Martin, who was in a particularly bad mood that evening, made it very clear that he had little money to allocate, and definitely much less than the minimum Rock believed was required for a credible health budget. The two ministers were at loggerheads and were political adversaries within the same party. The stakes were high because the government needed a successful budget to deal with an issue as important for Canadians and for federal-provincial relations as health care. I was in the middle and worked hard to find a management solution that would keep the two ministers apart during the whole process of preparing the budget.

Their deputy ministers, as well as Chaviva Hosek and I, worked separately with Rock and Martin and acted as mediators and intermediaries between them. We thought we knew what it would take to have a successful budget without creating a crisis in the Cabinet. David Dodge, who had recently been deputy minister of finance, was by then the deputy minister of health. He understood the constraints the department of Finance worked under, and he also knew what the health minister needed. Dodge was highly respected in the Finance department, where his views carried a lot of weight. It soon became clear to me that while Martin didn't want "to give in" directly to his colleague in Cabinet, he was prepared to do what was necessary as long as it was seen to be his decision and not forced upon him by a colleague.

I had many discussions with Allan Rock to understand fully his position on the fiscal resources required to meet health policy needs. Rock had little confidence that Martin would agree to what he thought he needed, and often told me he wanted to meet with the prime minister to plead his case. I discouraged him from having any such meeting on the grounds that if a prime minister is put in a position of having to choose at budget time between the position of a finance minister and the contrary position of another minister, he always has to support the finance minister. Rock listened to me and, to his credit, did not insist on a meeting. But I could sense his reluctance, and I was quite certain that he thought I was setting him up for failure, when in fact I was telling Martin that an unsatisfactory health budget would be a political disaster for both of them.

As long as no crisis was brewing, I would keep the prime minister generally informed about progress in the development of the budget without going into details of the issues in dispute. One day as the Martin-Rock controversy continued, Chrétien complained to me, "We're getting close to the budget and I don't feel that I'm doing anything about this very important issue." "You're very much involved, even if you don't realize it," I said. "I have told both ministers that if they don't agree on a common approach and a joint recommendation to you, you will be the final arbiter and you will likely make a decision that neither likes. I've told Allan that you have to support the finance minister, and I've told Paul that you can't let Allan down. This has focused their minds, and I am sure we will soon have a common recommendation. So you don't have to do anything more right now to be fully involved."

It is exactly what happened. At the end of the day, through intermediaries, a compromise was reached. I know that Rock thought I always argued the Finance case, while Martin was sure I was a big spender who wanted to give everything to Rock. In the end, both Martin and Rock were happy with the outcome. As soon as both the minister of health and the minister of finance brought a joint recommendation to the prime minister, he was pleased to agree. The final decision was undoubtedly better than it might have been if there had been a major battle between the two ministers in front of the prime minister, who would then have had to play Solomon.

My conclusion from that experience is that the Cabinet system works best when the prime minister doesn't have to impose decisions on ministers unless it is absolutely necessary. It is much better for ministers to work things out wherever possible between themselves rather than to have a top-down approach where the prime minister gets involved too early in the details of too many policy decisions.

Tobin versus Martin

MY CONCLUSION WAS reinforced in light of a more difficult conflict, with a less happy result, at the time of the budget of December 2001. This time the opponents were Brian Tobin and Paul Martin. I was in the middle of it as well. Tobin was industry minister and intent on being a leadership candidate whenever Chrétien stepped down. Tobin was an instinctive risk taker, and sometimes in the course of his career he had gambled big and won big. Martin was so far ahead in the putative leadership race that Tobin felt that he needed to do something dramatic. He decided on setting up and winning a confrontation with Martin. The 2001 budget would be the moment. Tobin counted on what he thought was a particularly close political relationship he had with the prime minister, and gambled that his relationship with Chrétien was such that the prime minister would support him in any confrontation against his erstwhile rival, Paul Martin.

As industry minister, Tobin had made a large number of proposals to Martin to include in the budget to promote the knowledge-based economy. In particular, he advocated large-scale funding for a rural broadband access initiative. Martin agreed to each and every one of them except for the broadband proposal, which Department of Finance analysts had concluded was not well considered, needed a lot more work, and should not be funded in the budget. (Martin also thought Tobin wanted to use the program to fund political organizers throughout rural Canada.) Tobin had a choice: he could demonstrate his clout to his colleagues by trumpeting that the budget gave him more than almost any other minister, even if he didn't get everything he wanted, or he could go for broke, and appeal directly to the prime minister to overrule Martin on broadband. He decided to appeal to the prime minister. It was clear to me that the issue had nothing to do with broadband; it was Tobin versus Martin. There is no doubt in my mind that if it had just been Tobin versus Martin, Chrétien would have been sorely tempted to come down on Tobin's side. But it was also Tobin versus the minister of finance.

Here, Tobin made a fundamental error. He underestimated Chrétien's longstanding position that in the end, and particularly at the time of a budget, a prime minister has to support the minister of finance against any other minister. Chrétien had never forgotten being let down by Trudeau in 1978, and wasn't going to let down his finance minister – even despite Martin's by then open campaign to replace him. But he didn't want a confrontation and hoped that Kevin Lynch, the deputy minister of finance, and I could find a compromise acceptable to both ministers, and he asked me to try. He was asking for a miracle. It was clear to me that Tobin wanted nothing less than the humiliation of the finance minister, and Martin had the same wish in reverse for Tobin.

Late one night, however, Lynch and I came up with wording that provided limited funding in the budget for a pilot project for rural broadband access, with more money for further study, and an opening to do more in future budgets. It took us several hours of persuasion and careful rewriting until well past midnight, when Martin reluctantly agreed to our proposed wording, which was nothing more than a face-saver for Tobin.

Early the next morning, I reported back to the prime minister on the telephone. He liked Tobin, and was sympathetic to his opposition to Martin's ambitions, but he was clearly uncomfortable with the position Tobin had put him in with respect to the minister of finance. He asked me to brief Mel Cappe, the secretary to the Cabinet, about the situation. Cappe and I talked it over and then we called the prime minister from Cappe's office around 9:00 a.m. and asked him what he wanted us to do with the wording Martin had agreed to. Chrétien asked Cappe to call Peter Harder, Tobin's deputy minister, and ask him if it was acceptable to him. Cappe placed the call in my presence, read the wording to Harder, and asked him if he could accept it. Harder said, "It works for me."

We then called the prime minister back, informed him of what Harder had said, and Cappe asked, "Prime minister, do you want me to call Tobin and get his opinion?" I was surprised when Chrétien said that he didn't want to involve Tobin personally. "It's good enough that you have spoken to the deputy minister. We'll go with that wording." It was clear to us that no matter how much he might have wanted to help Tobin, the institutional relationship between a prime minister and a finance minister at budget time was far more important to Chrétien than internal Liberal Party politics. Chrétien simply wasn't going to jeopardize a budget process that, from the time of the elimination of the federal deficit in 1997, had been the most important instrument in rebuilding the federal government in the lives of Canadians. Tobin, deeply hurt, and feeling let down by the prime minister, shortly afterwards resigned from Cabinet.

But rebuilding the importance of the government of Canada in the lives of Canadians took more than budgets. It was only possible in the context of a united country.

Chapter 9

QUEBEC: SETTING THE CONTEXT

"They were the two poles of Quebec politics. Lévesque is what we are;
Trudeau is what we would like to be."

– CLAUDE CHARRON, 1986

The most important priority for any Canadian government has always been the unity of the country. It was certainly front and centre on the agenda of the Chrétien government when it assumed office in 1993 and faced the prospect of a second Quebec referendum on independence. It remains the case for Prime Minister Stephen Harper, as the possibility of a third referendum looms on his political horizon. An understanding of the referendum campaigns of 1980 and 1995 and their aftermath – and, more importantly, planning for another one – requires some historical perspective, because Trudeau, Chrétien, and Harper are not the only prime ministers for whom combatting the forces of separation has been a principal preoccupation.

Ever since the time of Sir John A. Macdonald, there have been crises that have threatened the very existence of the country. As early as 1869, the Nova Scotia legislature voted for separation from Canada on the grounds that the new province had been hard done by in Confederation. The dispute with Nova Scotia could have been catastrophic for the two-year-old country, but Sir John A. handled it in his own inimitable way. He ignored the vote, promised some more federal money to

Nova Scotia in transfer payments (the dispute actually was primarily over money), and soon succeeded in recruiting the separatist leader, the great orator Joseph Howe, into his Cabinet, where he was able to keep Howe on side and turn him into a supporter of a united country.

While federal-provincial disputes, particularly over money, have been endemic since the founding of the country, it has been the place of French Canada and of the province of Quebec that has created the greatest threats to national unity, and has therefore preoccupied Canadian prime ministers since Confederation. Throughout Canadian history, two strands of French-Canadian leaders from Quebec have engaged in a great democratic struggle for the hearts and minds of Quebeckers. Those with a pan-Canadian vision come from the school of Louis-Hippolyte LaFontaine, George-Étienne Cartier, Henri Bourassa, Wilfrid Laurier, Ernest Lapointe, Louis St. Laurent, and later Pierre Elliott Trudeau and Jean Chrétien. They stand in contrast to the provincial school of Louis-Joseph Papineau, Honoré Mercier, Abbé Lionel Groulx, Maurice Duplessis, and, later, René Lévesque, Jacques Parizeau, Lucien Bouchard, Bernard Landry, and now André Boisclair.

The First Choice

IN THE 1990s, when we faced crises and problems of national unity, we knew that history showed that when forced to choose, Quebeckers had always chosen Canada, and that they had done so when federal representatives from Quebec had not been afraid to take clear and sometimes even initially unpopular stands in that province. The first time the people of Quebec had to decide on an issue of the gravest consequence is now largely forgotten. It was in the fall of 1939, shortly after war had been declared against Nazi Germany. Premier Maurice Duplessis called a snap election, pledging to keep Quebec out of the war as much as possible. It was far more than a challenge to the legitimacy of the federal government; his success would have rent the country apart, creating bitter anti-Quebec sentiments from coast to coast and a national unity crisis of immense proportions. Mackenzie King's federal Liberal Cabinet ministers from Quebec, under the leadership of Ernest Lapointe and Chubby Power, then confronted the provincial government head-on in a remarkable display of political courage. They told Quebeckers that they would consider a victory for Duplessis to be a repudiation of their legitimacy in Ottawa, and that they would resign from Cabinet if he won the election. Their resignation would have left Quebec without any representation in the federal government at a time of war. Despite their profound anti-war sentiments, Quebeckers still chose to support their federal representatives, and defeated Duplessis in the election. King's extremely skilful political manoeuvring during the rest of the war managed to prevent the fissures between English and French Canada from widening irreparably, and he succeeded in keeping the country united.

The Quiet Revolution and the Evolution of Canada

THE ELECTION OF the provincial Liberals under Jean Lesage in 1960 had a profound impact on the evolution of Canada over the next forty years and still resonates in the twenty-first century. The new Lesage government stood for an activist role for the state in education, in the economy, and in social policy. At a time when the economy of Quebec was primarily in the hands of a very closed English Protestant business establishment, the new government looked upon the Quebec State as one of the very few important instruments of power that French-speaking Quebeckers could control, providing a stimulating environment for young, bright, innovative, and dynamic francophones to pursue careers. The Lesage government itself was composed of energetic, socially progressive, and nationalist-leaning young ministers, including René Lévesque. It called and won a snap election in the fall of 1962 on a platform of nationalizing privately owned hydro-electric companies in the province, under the tantalizing slogan, "Maîtres Chez Nous," "Masters in Our Own House." As French-speaking Quebeckers developed more confidence in their abilities to run an active and progressive government, the independence movement in Quebec, previously marginal, became more mainstream and had a particular emotional appeal to young people excited by the prospect of building a new country.

In the midst of the excitement generated by what had become known as the Quiet Revolution in Quebec, a new federal Liberal government under Lester Pearson was elected in 1963 with an activist social policy agenda of its own. Pearson greatly expanded the Canadian social safety net with new social programs such as medicare, but the activism of the new Pearson government ran straight up against the activism of the Quebec government. The Lesage administration wanted to control and manage social policy itself in Quebec. To do so, it needed some of the tax revenues being collected by the federal government. As the growing separatist movement loomed in the background, there were a number of occasions where a crisis atmosphere prevailed between Quebec and Ottawa during high-stakes negotiations on matters of jurisdiction. Pearson solved problems with the Lesage government in an innovative way, which sometimes resulted in the creation of parallel but portable federal and Quebec social programs. In some cases, the federal government reduced the taxes it collected in Quebec so as to allow the Quebec government to collect those taxes for itself and spend the revenues on comparable programs. Some historians rate the Pearson government as one of the most activist, progressive, and successful governments in Canadian history. But its early compromises and doctrine of "co-operative federalism" soon gave rise to concerns about the role, relevance, and visibility of the Government of Canada in Quebec. These same concerns remain very much part of the political debate in Canada, as the Harper government tries to define its approach to Canadian federalism.

Enter Trudeau

ONE OF PIERRE Elliott Trudeau's reasons for agreeing to run for office as a Liberal in 1965 was his alarm about the weakening of the federal government in Quebec. I heard him speak about it at the press conference when he announced his candidacy in September 1965. He feared the long-term consequences for Canada if the federal government continued to create programs that applied in nine provinces while Quebec opted out and established its own programs. He predicted that there would soon be a debate on the role of MPs from Quebec in Ottawa, and whether they should be able to vote on matters relating to such federal programs. Trudeau saw this as a slippery slope towards separation, and quickly influenced the Pearson government in its second term to move away from the "co-operative federalism" of its first term.

Constructive Engagement in Havana

IN THE SUMMER of 1967, the president of France, General Charles de Gaulle, gave the separatist movement in Quebec instant international legitimacy when he famously proclaimed from the balcony of Montreal City Hall, "Vive le Québec libre!" The next day, after an emergency Cabinet meeting in Ottawa, Prime Minister Pearson called the statement "unacceptable," and the French president immediately cut short his visit, returned to France, and left Canada to deal with the immense controversy he had stirred up. Some thirty years later, de Gaulle's speech was still remembered in the most unlikely places, most notably when Prime Minister Chrétien was on an official visit to Cuba in April 1998. The trip itself was controversial in some circles in Canada, where critics accused the prime minister of giving comfort to the Cuban dictatorship by making a state visit to Cuba. Chrétien's standard answer, similar to that of other Western leaders when asked how they justify meeting dictators with abysmal human rights records, was that the best policy to bring about change is one of "constructive engagement."

President Fidel Castro hosted a small dinner for the prime minister and five Canadians, including me, in a very nondescript dining room on the second floor of the Palace of the Revolution in Havana. Castro was famous for spending many hours talking, mainly in monologue, and he did not let us down. Dinner began at 9:00 p.m. After Castro had discussed Margaret Thatcher, whom he disliked, President Clinton, whom he greatly admired, the stock market, about which he was curious, the more than two hundred assassination attempts on his life, which he had survived, the conditions of the Third World, with which he identified, the shooting down of two airplanes flown by Cuban exiles, which he said was best explained in an article in the *New Yorker*, capitalism, which the old Marxist said was doomed to fail, and much else, the clock had reached 3:00 a.m.

At that point, Castro asked Chrétien about the situation in Quebec. The prime minister gave his host some standard answer about how Quebeckers had twice rejected separation in referendums in 1980 and 1995. Castro responded, "At least you do not have to worry about General de Gaulle any more." The Canadians in the room, bleary-eyed from more than six hours of listening with some fascination to Castro's monologue, looked at one another, wondering whether the old revolutionary had finally lost it. We had no idea what he was talking about. After all, de Gaulle had been dead for almost thirty years and was totally irrelevant to the circumstances of the late 1990s in Canada. Then with perfect timing and a twinkle in his eyes, Castro deadpanned, "When de Gaulle spoke in Montreal, did you consider it an example of 'constructive engagement'?"

Trudeau and Lévesque

DE GAULLE'S SPEECH may not have been an example of constructive engagement for Canadians, but it certainly was a wake-up call. In 1967, René Lévesque – a contemporary and rival of Trudeau – left the Quebec Liberal Party, renounced federalism, and formed Le Mouvement souveraineté-association, which soon became the Parti Québécois. Less than one year later, Pierre Elliott Trudeau became leader of the Liberal Party, captured the imagination of Canadians, and won an overwhelming victory in the general election of June 1968. He campaigned for a strong national government, a major role for French-speaking Canadians everywhere in Canada and not only in Quebec, and implacable opposition to the separation of Quebec. He was not afraid of proclaiming that his Cabinet in Ottawa was one of "French power."

On November 15, 1976, the Parti Québécois, under the leadership of René Lévesque, swept into office in Quebec, defeating the Bourassa

Liberal government. The stage was set for an epic confrontation that would last for decades, and is not over yet. The centuries-old struggle for the hearts and minds of Quebeckers would be fought in national and provincial election campaigns and in two Quebec referendum campaigns. It would be the centrepiece of many federal-provincial negotiations, and would take centre stage in the House of Commons. It would be the cause of great debates and profound divisions within all Canadian political parties. I observed and participated in much of it.

Lessons for Mulroney

BY 1976, TRUDEAU had already been in office in Ottawa more than eight years. He had tried without success several times to bring about constitutional change in Canada. There were no fewer than seven First Ministers' Conferences held between February 1968 and the one in Victoria in June 1971. At that conference, Trudeau and the ten premiers – including Bourassa – finally reached an agreement on a constitutional amending formula and a limited Charter of Rights. It was not to last. Once the conference was over, the tentative agreement produced great controversy in Quebec. Influential elements in Quebec's Cabinet, public service, and intelligentsia wanted more powers for the Quebec government. They had discussed for years in books, conferences, articles, and speeches all sorts of concepts for Quebec in and out of Canada, including "special status" or "particular status" or "associate statehood." The agreement in Victoria fell far short of their desires and Bourassa, as a result of immense pressure at home, soon withdrew his consent to what was called the Victoria Charter. His Liberal predecessor Jean Lesage had done exactly the same thing six years earlier after Prime Minister Pearson thought he had reached a unanimous agreement with the provincial premiers on another constitutional amending formula, known as the Fulton-Favreau formula. Then Lesage backed out.

Thus it was two Quebec premiers, Jean Lesage and Robert Bourassa himself, who set the precedent of provincial governments later withdrawing their consent to agreements on constitutional change that they had previously reached at First Ministers' Meetings. There is a clear lesson in all this that Prime Minister Mulroney should have remembered before the Meech Lake Accord fell apart in 1990 after Newfoundland and Manitoba withdrew their prior consent. The lesson, of course, is that public debate and public opinion have an important role to play before constitutional amendments can be finally ratified, even after First Ministers have agreed.

The Provinces Turn Up the Heat: Lessons for Chrétien

BY THE TIME of the election of the Parti Québécois government in November 1976, constitutional reform had still eluded Trudeau. After the failure in Victoria, Trudeau had tried again – albeit with little enthusiasm – in 1975 and 1976. Because the provinces asked for new powers for themselves and for the restriction of certain federal powers as the price for agreement to the patriation of the Constitution, Trudeau would not accept. He was prepared again to try to achieve constitutional reform after Lévesque's victory, now saying that all options were open. And he appointed a commission (called the Pépin-Robarts Commission) to travel the country and make recommendations on constitutional change. But by 1978, Trudeau was aware that this time it would be even more difficult, since he was clearly in a weaker political position. After so many years in office, the barnacles were starting to attach to his government, as tends to happen to all long-term governments. The next federal election was looming, and he was well behind in the polls.

For some reason – and not for the last time – the presence of a separatist government in Quebec had not served as a wake-up call to the other provinces. On the contrary, they saw Trudeau's precarious political situation as an opportunity to make jurisdictional demands of their own. The most stunning example occurred in the summer of 1978. Premier Allan Blakeney of Saskatchewan chaired a conference of provincial premiers that set out a lengthy list of federal powers to be restricted or transferred to the provinces in return for provincial agreement on a Charter of Rights and a new amending formula for the

Constitution. The list was presented to Trudeau, who despite his reputation as an unyielding centralist, was prepared to make major compromises. But the provinces were in no mood for compromise, and would not agree to the patriation of the Constitution and a new constitutional amending formula unless the federal government agreed to strip itself of many important functions.

Jean Chrétien was finance minister at the time, and he and I watched with considerable disgust the proceedings of these federal-provincial meetings, with all the provinces lined up on one side of the table taking on the federal government, which was alone on the other side. Sometimes he talked with me on how such meetings should be conducted in the future. He applied what he had learned in the 1970s twenty years later, when he conducted federal-provincial relations as prime minister.

Enter Joe Clark: Not Very Visible

ALTHOUGH HE WAS behind in the polls everywhere except in Quebec, Trudeau had no choice but to call an election for late May 1979, shortly before the expiry of his five-year term. Joe Clark won a minority government with only two seats from Quebec in his caucus and his Cabinet. This placed the Parti Québécois government under the leadership of the charismatic René Lévesque in an advantageous situation to call and win a referendum on the separation of Quebec. Lévesque was able to point to the two Quebec seats and to make a powerful argument that Quebec, as the homeland of French Canada, should not be part of a country that does not provide it with proper representation at the most senior decision-making levels of the federal government. More than a quarter-century later in 2006, Prime Minister Martin began his election campaign, making the argument that the election of a Conservative government with no representation from Quebec could have disastrous consequences in another Quebec referendum. Quebeckers agreed with him. But instead of voting Liberal, as Martin wanted, they gave Stephen Harper's Conservatives ten seats in Quebec.

In 1979 and 1980, the separatist forces must have been substantially encouraged by the attitude and actions of Joe Clark's new government in Ottawa. For Clark, who later became Mulroney's minister of inter- governmental affairs, did not approve of any type of confrontation with provinces either when he was prime minister or later as a minis- ter. Clark's policy with respect to Quebec – even as a referendum approached – was one of benign neglect. Any sort of confrontation, it seemed, was to be avoided at all costs. He applied that policy to a small group of senior officials that Pierre Trudeau had brought together to prepare the federal government for a possible referendum in Quebec. The group was headed by Paul Tellier, then a young civil servant (who later had a brilliant career in both the public service as a deputy minis- ter in several departments and finally as secretary to the Cabinet, and in the private sector as chief executive officer of the CNR and of Bombardier). On taking office, however, Clark disbanded most of the federal team. Tellier told me in 1980 that Clark had reluctantly agreed to the presence of billboards in the province of Quebec promoting fed- eralism, "only as long as they were not very visible."

Before Lévesque had the opportunity to call a referendum, the Clark government bungled its way to defeat in the House of Commons after only a few months in office, and Trudeau unexpectedly returned as prime minister after the election of February 1980. Jean Chrétien became minister of justice and minister responsible for federal govern- ment activities in preparation for a Quebec referendum. He asked me to coordinate his referendum responsibilities.

The Referendum of 1980

WE WORKED ALMOST nonstop from the beginning of March, when the new Trudeau government was sworn in, and were soon faced with a referendum, which was officially called in early April for May 20. Like the referendum question fifteen years later, the question in 1980 was very unclear. It was nothing like, "Do you want Quebec to sepa- rate from Canada and become an independent country?" It was:

The Government of Quebec has made public its proposal to negotiate a new agreement with the rest of Canada, based on the equality of
nations; this agreement would enable Quebec to acquire the exclusive
power to make its laws, levy its taxes and establish relations abroad
– in other words, sovereignty – and at the same time to maintain
with Canada an economic association including a common currency;
any change in political status resulting from these negotiations will
be effected with approval by the people through another referendum; on these terms, do you give the Government of Quebec the
mandate to negotiate the proposed agreement between Quebec
and Canada?

An Active Federal Role

CHRÉTIEN'S POLICY, with the full support of Prime Minister Trudeau,
was the polar opposite of Clark's benign neglect. He worked closely
with the Leader of the Opposition in the Quebec National Assembly,
Claude Ryan, who, by Quebec law, headed the No Committee, which
was there to persuade voters to say no to the referendum question.
Chrétien and I met frequently with Ryan, and I was in daily contact
with his organizers. Both Trudeau and Chrétien were of the view in
1980 – as Chrétien was again in 1995 and in following years – that a
referendum on the separation of a province from Canada is not the
same as a referendum on a matter like municipal restructuring that is
solely within provincial jurisdiction. Therefore, they held that no
provincial law, including the Quebec law regulating provincial referendums, can restrict the federal government, elected by all Canadians,
from determining how it would fulfill its responsibility to preserve the
integrity of the nation.

Chrétien believed in 1980, as he did twenty years later, that it was
vital for the presence of the federal government to be well known in
Quebec. He had watched disgustedly as the Parti Québécois government
used subliminal messaging in its government advertising almost from the
moment it assumed office. One example was a campaign to promote
seatbelt usage with the catch line "on s'attache au Québec" – a clever

pun meaning both "In Quebec we buckle up" and also "We belong to Quebec." He wanted to counter it with similar federal messaging.

The federal strategy for confronting the separatist challenge in Quebec after the closeness of the referendum in 1995 – and particularly the federal sponsorship program, whose mismanagement later became so controversial – can best be understood in the context of what happened in 1980. At that time, Chrétien orchestrated a massive federal campaign to increase the visibility of Canada in Quebec. As justice minister, he was prepared to use all the tools at the disposal of the federal government, as he later did when he was prime minister. He authorized and encouraged federal departments and Crown corporations to advertise heavily, as described by L. Ian MacDonald in his book, *From Bourassa to Bourassa*:

> If you wanted arguments as to the presence of the federal government in Montreal, why you just had to turn on the television between periods of the Stanley Cup playoffs and look at the Good Works of Transport Canada, which had built and paid for half the cost of the Trans Canada Highway, not to mention 33 airports, 44 ports and the St. Lawrence Seaway. All of which was brought you courtesy of Canada, in letters that lit up the screen. As for the proprietary sense of the North, they arranged, in the year of the Arctic Centennial, for a teenager in the Northwest Territories to write a pen pal in Québec, describing the life of the territory. 'I'm a Canadian of the North,' the letter concluded, 'and I love my country.' That was not all, the Department of Health and Welfare reminded viewers that they meant pension cheques and family allowance cheques and New Horizons programs. And the Secretary of State merely went on the air and played the national anthem, a shorter version of the 84 second hymn produced by the National Film Board that ends with a couple of blond kids kissing. It was evidence of how hard the feds were prepared to fight. Altogether, it was pretty powerful stuff. All of this was quite systematic, and the federal propaganda blitz got under the skin of the Yes forces.

Playing Hardball

DURING THE 1980 referendum battle, federal ministers from Quebec and I met under Chrétien's chairmanship once a week to plan and co-ordinate their activities. I attended one meeting where Health Minister Monique Bégin informed her colleagues that her department had plans for an anti-alcohol campaign with the slogan, "Non merci, ca se dit bien." ("No thanks is a great thing to say.") Chrétien's eyes lit up; he relished the anticipated reaction of the Parti Québécois. Feeling certain that the advertising would be effective and would provoke the anger of the separatist opposition, Chrétien told Bégin to speed up the campaign, put coloured inserts in all federal mailings to Quebeckers from her department, and buy space on billboards throughout the province. With an overturned glass of alcohol barely visible, and the slogan prominent in large letters, it was a powerful campaign tool; yet its ostensible purpose was so legitimate that the Provincial Court in Quebec rejected an injunction request from the outraged separatist side.

Advertising by federal departments was only part of the federal involvement. The federal forces worked in large part out of the Canadian Unity Information Office, which had been created by the Tellier Group, and which Clark had fortunately not got around to abolishing before his defeat. It reported directly to Chrétien, and provided an enormous amount of polling data, facts and arguments, advertising copy, draft brochures, buttons, and other necessary elements of a political campaign that we gave to the provincial organizers of the No committee.

Mistakenly, in my view, the lessons of the campaign of 1980 were ignored in 1995, and these successful strategies and tactics were not repeated.

Managing Trudeau's Impact

CANADIANS HAVE FORGOTTEN that during the 1980 referendum, the polls oscillated between victory and defeat several times during the campaign. In the earlier and darker days of the campaign, Liberal MPs and some of Trudeau's advisers in Ottawa urged him to be far more involved on a daily basis than he had planned. There is always a tendency – particularly when campaigns are not going well – for campaign advisers to want to multiply the interventions of leaders in the hope that frenetic activity by a leader will turn the campaign around. Sometimes it works. More often than not overexposure harms the impact, and the more a leader speaks, the more it appears to be out of desperation. The media then tends for good reason to focus on the tactics of the campaign, and the message is often lost in the confusion of stories about why speeches are being given, rather than about what is being said. Good, unreported speeches to small audiences may give great comfort to the campaign strategists in attendance; unfortunately, they have no more impact in a political campaign than the noise of the proverbial tree falling in the forest when no one is around.

During the ups and downs of a political campaign, it takes great discipline to be strategic in planning the participation of a leader and in resisting pressures to act in "quick-fix" ways that invariably prove to be counter-productive. Just as Franklin Roosevelt's famous fireside chats were few and far between, and highly effective, Trudeau agreed with the proposition that his impact as prime minister would be far more dramatic if he made a few measured interventions than if he were to campaign every day. In the end, Trudeau made only three major speeches in Quebec and one in the House of Commons during the entire course of the 1980 referendum campaign. Each was a passionate defence of Canada and a vibrant appeal to Quebeckers to be part of a larger whole. Trudeau was also extremely effective when he set out the logical impossibility inherent in the referendum question. His speeches received maximum press coverage and made a major impact on voters. Fifteen years later in the second referendum campaign, it was to be more difficult to convince Chrétien of the wisdom of a strategy of only a few measured interventions.

Promising Change: More Lessons for Chrétien

DURING HIS CAMPAIGN appearances, and particularly in his famous speech at the Paul Sauvé Arena in Montreal a few days before the referendum, Trudeau promised constitutional change if the No forces won the referendum. Trudeau was clear in all of his speeches that his idea of "change" included the patriation of the Constitution, a constitutional Charter of Rights and Freedoms that would include protections for the two official languages across the country, a federal government strong enough to redistribute income and equalize opportunity among the regions of Canada, and a willingness to negotiate the distribution of powers in a way that ensured that the federal government's role of serving all Canadians was not threatened. These were the principles he had advocated all his life. Unfortunately, the vehemence and the eloquence by which Trudeau promised "change" led some in Quebec, well after the fact, to claim that Trudeau had somehow deceived Quebeckers by not delivering the change advocated by the nationalists, which he had fought against all his life.

As a result of Trudeau's experience, Prime Minister Chrétien was very conscious of the lessons of 1980 in the preparation of his speeches during the referendum campaign of 1995. Despite enormous pressure from his Quebec allies to make promises of major change in the event of a No vote, he was very reluctant to risk creating expectations that could later be twisted out of context.

An Historic Meeting

JEAN CHRÉTIEN AND I watched the results of the 1980 referendum in a suite in the Bonaventure Hotel in Montreal. With 60 per cent of the vote for the No forces, the extent of the victory was much greater than we had anticipated. Because we had both seen up close during the campaign the divisions that referendums create in a society, our feeling that night when the results were known was much less one of celebration than simply of relief that it was over and that it had ended well. We left early the next morning to drive to Ottawa and go directly to the first meeting held in Prime Minister Trudeau's office on Wednesday, May 21, 1980, the morning after the Quebec referendum.

It is rare to walk into a meeting knowing that it will be historic. I knew this one would be, and was excited to be a privileged participant.

There were about ten people in the room on the third floor of the Centre Block, including Jim Coutts, principal secretary to the prime minister; Michael Pitfield, secretary to the Cabinet; Michael Kirby, secretary to the Cabinet for federal-provincial relations; some other PMO staffers; Jean Chrétien, and me. Trudeau did not waste any time in self-congratulation or even in talking about the results of the night before. He was ready to seize the moment, and had already decided to move quickly and decisively to achieve the constitutional changes he had been advocating all his life. After referring to Napoleon's strategy at Austerlitz, and quoting words that he attributed to General de Gaulle, "Maintenant, il faut attaquer à tous azimuts" (Now we have to attack everywhere), Trudeau instructed Chrétien to leave that very day on a whirlwind tour across the country to meet the provincial premiers. The plan was that this would launch a new decisive round of constitutional negotiations. When we set out, we were far from certain that it would lead, as it did, to the patriation of the Constitution in 1982 and the proclamation of the Charter of Rights and Freedoms – and all the controversy that followed.

The period of constitutional negotiations that began immediately after the referendum was a time of high-drama, high-stakes political poker and great accomplishment that profoundly marked the history of Canada and shaped much of the political debate into the twenty-first century. What happened between 1980 and 1982 set the tone for how the Mulroney and Chrétien governments handled Quebec-related issues in particular, and federal-provincial relations in general, between 1984 and 2003. Those years sowed the seeds for future political controversy, particularly with respect to Quebec's place in Canada, and they were filled with lessons for the future conduct of federal-provincial relations.

Towards a Charter of Rights

THAT VERY AFTERNOON, May 21, 1980, Chrétien and I and a small group of senior officials (including Deputy Minister of Justice Roger Tasse and Secretary to the Cabinet for Federal Provincial Relations

Michael Kirby) climbed aboard a government jet with Toronto as our first stop. Our objective was to convince the provincial premiers of the need to enter into immediate negotiations to achieve a constitutional amending formula and a Charter of Rights and Freedoms for Canada.

Despite our fatigue from the referendum campaign, we still had some adrenalin left. We were to need every ounce of it. We had dinner with Premier Bill Davis in Toronto, and then flew on to sleep that night in Winnipeg. The next morning we had breakfast with Premier Sterling Lyon of Manitoba, left for Regina, where we had lunch with Premier Allan Blakeney, then rushed back to the airplane to make a meeting over coffee in the afternoon with Premier Peter Lougheed in Edmonton, and finished our day with a dinner meeting in Victoria with Premier Bill Bennett. On Friday, we flew from Victoria to Charlottetown, where we met with Angus Maclean, the premier of Prince Edward Island, and then flew to Halifax, where we spent the night. On Saturday morning, we began with a meeting with John Buchanan, the premier of Nova Scotia, left for Newfoundland to have lunch with Premier Brian Peckford, and spent time in the afternoon in Fredericton with Premier Richard Hatfield. We returned late that day to Ottawa. Immediately after the referendum we were not expecting the Parti Québécois premier of Quebec to be prepared to join in an effort to modernize the Canadian Constitution, and were not surprised when René Lévesque refused to see us.

In those hectic few days, we established a general consensus among the premiers that negotiations for constitutional reform should begin in an intensive way over the summer. Over the course of the next eighteen months, there were many ups and downs and tense moments. At the very beginning of the negotiations in the summer of 1980, Chrétien decided to approach things differently than the federal government used to do. At the outset, he instructed his team (of which I was a member) to prepare a federal position paper proposing to strengthen the Canadian economic union by guaranteeing in the Constitution the mobility of people, goods, and capital across provincial borders as well as clarifying and expanding federal jurisdiction over the regulation of trade and commerce. The dynamic of the negotiation changed as soon as the federal document, entitled "Securing the Canadian Economic Union," was put on the negotiating table and released to the media. The document was clear, well written, easy to understand, and presented an appealing public case. The provinces were dumbfounded that for the first time in living memory the federal government had its own jurisdictional agenda. They had fond memories of the one-way negotiations of 1976 and 1978. Now, by contrast, negotiations over the powers of federal and provincial governments had just become a two-way street. As prime minister years later, Chrétien followed the precedent he had set in 1980 and never entered into one-way negotiations with the provinces.

The summer of intense negotiations on constitutional reform between Chrétien and his provincial counterparts did not produce a constitutional agreement. But they were not a failure. The issues that were discussed, particularly the proposed Chàrter of Rights and Freedoms, captured the public imagination. Substantive discussions on every issue paved the way for later agreements. The specific areas of disagreement in many instances were narrow and might have been bridged if there had been a willingness to come to an overall agreement. In early September 1980, the First Ministers met in Ottawa and agreed on nothing. It turned out that the deepest and unbridgeable chasm was the lack of willingness on the part of provincial premiers – except for the premiers of New Brunswick and Ontario – to allow Trudeau to claim any sort of victory because their personal distaste for him was so great. Chrétien was almost literally sickened at the First Ministers' Meeting when Newfoundland premier Brian Peckford expressed his disagreement with the prime minister by saying that he preferred the Canada of René Lévesque to the Canada of Pierre Trudeau. It was something Chrétien never forgot, and it affected his later approach to the conduct of federal-provincial relations.

Breaking the Logjam

THE FAILURE OF the September Conference turned out to be a way station on the road, not the end of the road. Unable to achieve provincial agreement to constitutional reform, Trudeau threatened to take advantage of a relic of colonialism whereby the Constitution of Canada, still being an Act of the British Parliament, could only be amended in Westminister. He indicated his intention to seek a constitutional amendment in Great Britain patriating the Constitution, providing a new Canadian amending formula, and incorporating a Charter of Rights and Freedoms in the Constitution. The provinces vigorously objected and three of them – Quebec, Manitoba, and Newfoundland – went to court to try to block the federal action. Trudeau wanted to act quickly with little public debate, but he was forced by Joe Clark's skilful use of House of Commons rules to refer his constitutional proposals to a parliamentary committee, which engaged in a lengthy and massive public consultation.

The committee sat for 56 days, held 267 hours of hearings, and received representations from more than 1,200 groups and individuals. The hearings of the committee were an education for all of those who attended or participated (as a constitutional adviser to the minister of justice, I was one of them). In 1980 and 1981, Canadians including Quebeckers were interested in substance. They saw through the process arguments of their elites just as they did twenty years later when the Clarity Act was introduced over the loud objections of the Quebec government. Aboriginal Canadians, women's groups, representatives of people with disabilities, and the multicultural communities made powerful and often emotional representations that resulted in a draft Charter of Rights and Freedoms that emerged from the committee that Canadians strongly supported, and that Trudeau accepted. The Joint Parliamentary Committee on the Constitution is a textbook example of the importance and usefulness of well-structured public participation in achieving constitutional reform.

After hearing vigorous provincial government challenges to the legitimacy of unilateral action at the same time as the parliamentary committee was proceeding, the Supreme Court of Canada ruled that it was technically legal to go to Westminister to seek a constitutional amendment, but that doing so violated the conventions of the Constitution. Within two months from the Supreme Court decision, Trudeau convened another First Ministers' Conference in Ottawa to try one more time to reach agreement on constitutional reform.

He was immediately faced with the implacable opposition of eight provinces – all except Ontario and New Brunswick – who worked together to block the federal proposals. After three days of stalemate, for reasons best known to himself, René Lévesque decided to march to his own drummer and, to their consternation, broke away from his colleagues in the so-called "Group of Eight" to oppose Trudeau in his own way. By so doing, he unwittingly opened the door to constitutional reform.

In the ensuing confusion, Jean Chrétien, Roy Romanow, then Saskatchewan's justice minister, and Ontario's Attorney General, Roy McMurtry, got together to try to break the deadlock. As a group, they proved how important personal relations are to successful negotiations. These three pragmatic politicians of three different political parties, respectively Liberal, New Democratic, and Progressive Conservative, had become good friends during the intensive constitutional negotiations of the summer of 1980. They trusted one another, knew one another's bottom lines, and were so familiar with the positions of all the provinces that they understood which compromises could be acceptable to the provinces as well as to the federal government. None was a technician in the intricacies of constitutional law, although Romanow was much more a details person than either Chrétien or McMurtry.

I was a member of the federal team at that conference in Ottawa and was present on the afternoon of November 5, 1981, in the fifth-floor windowless kitchen of the Ottawa Conference Centre – an unlikely venue for such an historic moment – when the three justice ministers put the finishing touches to an agreement in principle, which Romanow carefully wrote down on a pad of yellow lined legal paper that was to serve as the basis of the next day's formal agreement.

Where Was Quebec?

THE GOVERNMENT OF Quebec was not a party to the agreement. More than a quarter-century later, there are still a lot of myths about what happened that November day in Ottawa. There is plenty of room for legitimate debate about whether it was good or bad politics, or good or bad for Canadian unity, to have made changes to the Constitution without the consent of the government of Quebec. There is no doubt that it created a deep and lasting scar in the psyche of Quebec and set the stage for further confrontations. But there is no basis in fact for the claim about an alleged "Night of the Long Knives" where Quebec was deliberately left out, stabbed in the back, and humiliated.

After the way Lévesque had acted at the conference that morning, all of the other premiers understood that a government committed to the separation of Quebec from Canada would never betray its principles and agree to a reformed Canadian Constitution. Claude Morin, the chief Quebec negotiator and minister of intergovernmental affairs in the Parti Québécois government, admitted as much when he later wrote in his memoirs that Quebec's sole purpose at the November First Ministers' Conference was "to block the federal project."

It still did not take long for the constitutional agreement to create a political storm in Quebec. Separatists, nationalists, many federalists, the media, intellectuals, commentators, and much, but not all, of the Liberal Opposition caucus in the National Assembly united to attack the legitimacy of a Constitution that had not received the approval of the government and National Assembly of Quebec. The Quebec government even went to the Supreme Court of Canada and argued its right to veto the new Constitution. I was a member of the federal legal team that fought that case. We won a unanimous judgment that held that there was no constitutional veto in law for Quebec or any other single province.

Nevertheless, the proponents of separation continued to use the constitutional agreement reached by the federal government and nine provinces to create a rallying point for their cause and worked hard to develop a sense of grievance and "humiliation." In the short run, they failed. By the time Trudeau left office in 1984, the federal Liberal Party was well ahead in the polls in the province of Quebec, support for separation was below where it was at the time of the referendum in 1980, support for the Charter of Rights in Quebec was very high, and the Parti Québécois was on the verge of serious internal turmoil. The time seemed right to turn the national agenda away from constitutional issues. Then came Brian Mulroney and ten years of national unity turmoil, with Canada at times on the edge of the abyss.

Chapter 10

"WITH HONOUR AND ENTHUSIASM": MULRONEY AND THE CONSTITUTION

"A constitution should be short and obscure."

– NAPOLEON

I n 1983, Brian Mulroney was elected leader of the Progressive Conservative Party of Canada. Born in Baie-Comeau on the north shore of the St. Lawrence River, he was the first leader of his party from Quebec, and the first who was fluently bilingual, steeped in the culture of Quebec, and deeply comfortable in his home province. He never failed to remind his party that its inability to form the national government over most of the twentieth century resulted from its failure to appeal to French Canada, and would repeat over and over again to them that it was simply not possible for a party to form a government in a House of Commons of 283 seats if it was not competitive in any of the 100 seats in Canada where the francophone vote made the difference. Mulroney came to its leadership determined to change the Progressive Conservative Party.

As soon as he entered the House of Commons, he made it clear that as long as he was leader, there would no longer be any room in his party for opposition to the official language policies of the Trudeau government. His performance in the French-language television debate during the 1984 election campaign wowed Quebeckers, many of whom had previously known little about him. He soon overcame a huge Liberal lead in the polls in Quebec. In some respects, despite his political party affiliation, Brian Mulroney appeared to Quebeckers to be much more the real successor of Pierre Elliott Trudeau than John Turner. Quebec rewarded him with fifty-eight seats, compared to seventeen for Turner, the worst showing for the Liberal Party in the province of Quebec in the twentieth century until then.

However, the election campaign of 1984 sowed the seeds of years of political turmoil on the national unity front, and of bitter division in the Liberal Party, and it also led to the destruction within a decade of the Progressive Conservative Party and almost to the destruction of Canada itself. For like an earlier Conservative leader, Sir Robert Borden, in the election of 1911, Mulroney had decided to make a political alliance with the nationalists in Quebec. As with Borden, the alliance was electorally successful, and like Borden's, it lasted only for a few years. Unfortunately for Canada, Mulroney concluded that the best way to cement his relationship with the nationalists was to campaign vigorously on the issue that the signing of the constitutional accord of November 1981 without the signature of Quebec was a grave injustice to that province. He promised to bring Quebec into the Constitution "with honour and enthusiasm." He made that promise in a speech written for him by his old friend and law-school classmate Lucien Bouchard, who carried a membership card of the Parti Québécois in his pocket at the same time as he was helping his friend Mulroney develop his constitutional position as the leader of the Progressive Conservative Party of Canada. It was the first step on the fateful road to Meech Lake.

After becoming prime minister, Mulroney convinced himself that his immense personal charm and persuasive abilities would be sufficient to turn separatists into federalists. He truly believed that he could co-opt some of the best-known leaders of the separatist movement, and in so doing that he could unite Canada with the support of Quebec in a way that Trudeau could not. For a while, it seemed to be working. He even persuaded René Lévesque to give up, at least for a while, the separatist option of the Parti Québécois and try, in Lévesque's words, the "beautiful risk" of a reformed federalism. The result in a short time was a schism within the separatist party, Lévesque's resignation as premier, and the return to office in the provincial election of 1985 of the federalist provincial Liberal Party once again under the leadership of Robert Bourassa.

If necessary, Mulroney was prepared to make pacts with the devil. For example, he appointed Lucien Bouchard as Canada's ambassador to France, and later brought him into his Cabinet. He named separatists from previous Parti Québécois Cabinets to federal agencies, such as Yves Duhaime to the board of directors of the Bank of Canada and Louise Beaudoin to the board of directors of Telefilm. His Cabinet members from Quebec in 1984 included some who had voted yes in the 1980 referendum. No prime minister before Mulroney had tried to co-opt separatists since Sir John A. Macdonald brought Joseph Howe into his Cabinet. But Mulroney thought the combination of his charm with the lure of government appointments would trump their separatist principles. Within a few short years, however, his sincere and bold efforts almost destroyed Canada, and he must be held responsible for their spectacular failure. It turned out that Brian Mulroney was no Sir John A., and Lucien Bouchard was no Joseph Howe. Mulroney's failure holds important lessons for his successors.

Mulroney was successful in reinforcing Quebeckers in their conviction that they had been left out of the Constitutional Accord of 1981 and had thereby been humiliated by the federal government. He presumed that the more he blamed the previous Liberal government, the more he would strengthen support for the Conservative Party in Quebec. In the short term, he was very successful. Demonizing the Liberal Party as having humiliated Quebec consolidated the support of his own party at least through the election of 1988. Unfortunately, the by-product of his political rhetoric was the demonization not only of the Liberal Party – which was fair political game on his part – but of Canadian federalism itself. Up to then, it was only the rhetoric of the separatist movement that had appealed to the sense of grievance and humiliation of Quebeckers, and it would always be neutralized, more or less successfully, by the positive rhetoric from Quebec federalists. This time the rhetoric about grievance and humiliation came as much from the government in Ottawa as it did from the separatists in Quebec. Unwittingly, Mulroney, with the help of his close ally Lucien Bouchard, helped to create the general belief in Quebec that federalism itself had not worked. Mulroney proved the adage that if you tell the people often enough that they have been humiliated, they are going to believe it.

Meech Lake

THEN MULRONEY DECIDED to perform a high-wire constitutional act with no safety net. If he failed to achieve his objective to bring Quebec into the Constitution "with honour and enthusiasm," he would set the conditions for a major national unity crisis. In 1987, Mulroney convened a First Ministers' Conference at a government-owned country estate overlooking Meech Lake, a twenty-minute drive north of Ottawa in the Gatineau Hills. At the end of a marathon negotiation that lasted all day and well into the night – a strategy he had learned from his days as a labour lawyer in tough negotiations – the prime minister emerged to announce that he had achieved the unanimous agreement of all provincial premiers including the premier of Quebec to constitutional amendments. For a brief moment it seemed that he had succeeded in obtaining the support of all provinces for the government of Quebec to agree to the Constitution "with honour and enthusiasm." It soon became evident, however, that constitutional negotiations between governments that have long-term consequences for a country are very different from labour negotiations that provide for short-term collective agreements.

Before long, the provisions of the Meech Lake constitutional agreement – including the recognition of Quebec as a "distinct society" – created profound division and aroused great passions in the country. It was soon clear that there was no national consensus. Many Canadians interpreted the accord as decentralizing too much federal jurisdiction to the provinces and particularly to Quebec. Jean Chrétien's first

comment to me after studying the agreement was, "Who spoke for
Canada in the negotiating room?" Pierre Trudeau emerged from
retirement to denounce the Meech Lake Accord as contrary to his
vision of Canada. On the other hand, the Parti Québécois Opposition
in Quebec denounced the accord as an abject surrender by Robert
Bourassa to the rest of Canada.

The Vital Business of Building Consensus

MANY GOVERNMENTS TEND to talk about the importance of public
consultation and participation. Despite their rhetoric, public consultation is usually not welcome once a decision is made, particularly in the
case of a decision that is the product of lengthy, difficult, and fragile
negotiations. Governments fear, sometimes quite legitimately, that as
a result of public consultation, they will lose what they have so
painstakingly achieved. The Mulroney government was so preoccupied with achieving its objective in Quebec and, in its view, securing
national unity for a long time to come, that, for it, support for the
Meech Lake Accord became the litmus test of support for Quebec's
place in Confederation.

It quickly became apparent that the government did not want any
debate. Mulroney wanted speedy ratification of the Meech Lake
Accord, and would not brook any changes. Lowell Murray, the minister of intergovernmental affairs, proclaimed that only "egregious
errors" could be changed if they were found. Opponents of the accord
found themselves tarred with the brush of giving aid and comfort to
the separatist movement. It was as though their patriotism was being
called into question.

The period 1980 to 1982 had provided lessons about constitutional
change that Mulroney did not heed. He had not learned, as he should
have, that public participation is essential for a satisfactory outcome.
Trudeau, despite all of his attempts over many years, had been unable
to succeed in achieving constitutional reform until there was a substantial consensus in the country. Joe Clark had forced him in 1980 to
refer his proposed Charter of Rights to a parliamentary committee,

which listened to the public and recommended major changes to the original proposals. Instead, Mulroney, by refusing public participation in the process, was responsible for an unparalleled crisis in Canada.

Supporting all the provisions of the accord became a question of honour for Quebec. Rational discussion was difficult because of the extent to which passions had been inflamed. I learned that one day when I spoke about Canadian affairs at the School of Public Administration at Cornell University in upstate New York. During the question-and-answer session, a student from Quebec asked me about Meech Lake. He prefaced his question with an emotional statement to his classmates about the fact that there were five conditions in the Meech Lake Accord that constituted the absolute minimum requirements for Quebec to remain in Canada. I began my answer by saying that I understood how important the five conditions were to him, so perhaps he might want to explain them to the class before I gave my own views.

There was an embarrassed silence as he confessed – as I expected – that he did know what they were.

Whether the substance of the Meech Lake Accord was as fragmenting as its detractors claimed, or as benign as its supporters argued, became almost irrelevant. Perception and psychology are as important as reality when it comes to proposed changes to the fundamental law of the land. Mulroney learned too late one of the most important lessons from the constitutional debates of the 1960s, 1970s, and early 1980s, which is that constitutional reform is not something to be entered into lightly or often. And when you start the process, the stakes should be downplayed rather than exaggerated. Reform is very difficult to achieve, takes a long time, dominates the national debate, arouses great passions, and is successful only when there is a substantial national consensus. That consensus, in my opinion, simply was never there for the Meech Lake Accord.

Meech Lake and the Liberals

THE DEBATE AROUND the Meech Lake Accord not only tested the unity of the country, it created divisions and internal wounds in the

Liberal Party that never completely healed throughout the Chrétien leadership and during the Martin years. It produced two branches of the party, the Trudeau-Chrétien faction, of which I have been very much a part, and the Turner-Martin faction.

Quebec had been a stronghold of the party since the time of Laurier, with the sole exception of the Diefenbaker election of 1958. The loss of seats in the 1984 election in Quebec had been traumatic for the Liberal Party. John Turner and his Quebec lieutenant, Raymond Garneau, whose political career had been in the Quebec provincial Liberal Party until he was elected to the House of Commons in 1984, were desperately afraid that Liberal opposition to the Meech Lake Accord would allow Mulroney to paint the Liberal Party as anti-Quebec and further consolidate the Tory party in Quebec for a long time to come. It was not Turner's only consideration. For reasons that can only be explained by the longstanding rivalry between Trudeau and Turner that went all the way back to the leadership convention of 1968 where Turner lost to Trudeau, the Turner Liberals were also trying to distance themselves from Trudeau's heritage. Meech Lake gave them that opportunity.

It was a classic political error. An old lesson teaches us that when political parties simply try to imitate their opponents on issues where they are clearly uncomfortable doing so, they never do very well. The electorate almost invariably supports the real thing. In this case, the leadership of the Liberal Party abandoned its political base and its deepest principles out of fear that it had been politically outmanoeuvred by its adversaries. John Turner's decision to give his immediate support to the Meech Lake Accord in the House of Commons split the caucus and threatened his leadership. And his support for the Meech Lake Accord did not even help the Liberal Party in Quebec, where it won only twelve seats in the 1988 election. Turner may have succeeded in differentiating himself from Trudeau, but Trudeau had been the most successful Liberal leader since Mackenzie King, and had been particularly successful in Quebec. Later, Paul Martin, like Turner, succeeded (as he clearly wished to do) in differentiating himself from Jean

Chrétien. In both cases, the results they achieved were definitely different than those of their predecessors – they both lost many dozens of seats that their predecessors had won, and ended up in Opposition. In 2000 in the United States, Al Gore tried so hard to differentiate himself from Bill Clinton that George W. Bush won the presidency. A lesson for party leaders is that being different from popular predecessors in their own party, simply for the sake of being different, does not always make them more successful.

The death of the Meech Lake Accord set the scene for some dramatic political theatre with serious consequences for the whole country. The failure of the accord was portrayed in Quebec as a rejection of renewed federalism by the rest of Canada, arousing passions that, in the short term, revived the separatist movement. By coincidence, the Meech Lake Accord died on June 23, 1990, the day Jean Chrétien won the leadership of the Liberal Party. At the same time, Lucien Bouchard was in the process of forming the Bloc Québécois, the first separatist party in the House of Commons. Much like the Irish under Charles Parnell a century earlier, who used the House of Commons in Westminister to promote Home Rule for Ireland, Bouchard would use his position in Ottawa to fight for the independence of Quebec. His first MPs were disillusioned Conservatives who crossed the floor with him, as well as two Liberal supporters of Paul Martin who, in a well-staged move, dramatically left the Liberal Party the moment Chrétien won the leadership. Then Gilles Duceppe won a by-election in what had been a long-standing Liberal seat in the Montreal riding of Laurier Ste. Marie within two months of Chrétien's election as Liberal leader and became the first elected member of the Bloc.

Charlottetown and Allaire

FOLLOWING THE DEMISE of the Meech Lake Accord, Brian Mulroney made one last attempt at constitutional reform. This time he welcomed public participation, created a parliamentary committee that held lengthy public hearings, and appointed Joe Clark as minister of intergovernmental affairs to negotiate with the provinces and aboriginal groups, while agreeing to hold a national referendum to ratify any federal-provincial agreement on constitutional change.

An agreement was reached at a federal-provincial conference held at the end of August 1992 in Charlottetown, the "cradle of Confederation." The so-called Charlottetown Accord was much more comprehensive than Meech Lake and won the support of the federal Liberal Party and the New Democrats. But if the fatal flaw in the Meech Lake Accord was the lack of public input, ironically the fatal flaw in the Charlottetown Accord was too much public input. The final product tried to satisfy too many interests and read more like an Income Tax Act than a solemn constitutional document. While it satisfied many interests, it aroused the ire of many others and was resoundingly defeated in a Canada-wide referendum at the end of October 1992.

The defeat of the Charlottetown Accord following the failure of the Meech Lake Accord allowed the separatist movement in Quebec (which itself had opposed both Meech Lake and Charlottetown) to make the argument that the rest of Canada would never agree to any constitutional changes that even slightly favoured Quebec. Taken alone, this argument might have been dismissed as mere separatist rhetoric. But the Bourassa government had been deeply wounded by the failure of its attempts at constitutional reform. The Quebec Liberal Party appointed an internal committee (the Allaire Committee) to recommend a new constitutional position for the party. It was not long before it produced the Allaire Report, advocating a massive transfer of powers from the federal government to Quebec.

It was ominously clear as the federal election of 1993 approached that national unity and Quebec's place in Canada would be centre stage in Canadian politics in the years ahead.

Chapter 11

PREPARING FOR THE 1995 REFERENDUM

"All we want is an independent Quebec within a strong and united Canada."

– YVON DESCHAMPS, 1978

The Setting

IN THE GENERAL election of October 25, 1993, Chrétien won a healthy majority, and 177 seats – but only 20 from Quebec – in a Parliament the likes of which had never been seen before in Canada. The Progressive Conservative Party, which had formed the government for the previous nine years, was essentially wiped out and won only two seats; the New Democrats retained nine seats, not enough for official party status in the House of Commons; a new Western Canadian–based populist right-wing party, the Reform Party, won fifty-two seats and became the third largest party in the House of Commons. But it was the Bloc Québécois, with fifty-four of Quebec's seventy-five seats, that to everyone's surprise formed the Official Opposition in Ottawa. The defeated Conservative government – assisted by the Paul Martin Liberals in 1990 with their shouts of *"traitre"* and *"vendu"* – had successfully portrayed Jean Chrétien as one of the "undertakers" of the Meech Lake Accord who had humiliated Quebec. The beneficiary was Lucien Bouchard and the separatist movement.

Our new government took office facing a gigantic national unity crisis of unparalleled proportions, combined with a rapidly deteriorating fiscal situation in Ottawa – inherited from the Mulroney government – that required politically painful surgery, with potentially harmful national unity implications.

In Quebec, Premier Robert Bourassa chose to retire due to ill health and was succeeded by Daniel Johnson in January 1994 as leader of the provincial Liberals and the new premier of Quebec. It had been more than forty years since any Quebec government had been re-elected for a third mandate, and the Quebec provincial Liberal government was coming to the end of its second one. Johnson was in a difficult position as the underdog in a rapidly approaching election. His Liberals faced a reinvigorated separatist Opposition under Jacques Parizeau, who promised to hold a referendum on separation within eight to ten months of taking office. Johnson had to show Quebeckers that he could work co-operatively with the federal government for the benefit of Quebec in a way that the Parti Québécois could never do. But he would be destroyed politically if the Parti Québécois could paint him as the puppet of the Chrétien administration.

Chrétien and Johnson: The Politics of Quebec

CHRÉTIEN WANTED TO do whatever he could to help the prospects of Johnson's re-election, and certainly to avoid doing anything that would hurt. He and Johnson agreed to work together and decided that Jean Pelletier, the prime minister's chief of staff, and I would meet weekly with the two most senior members of Johnson's office, Pierre Anctil and John Parisella. Pelletier was highly respected in Quebec. He was thoughtful, courteous, diplomatic, tough as nails, able to get things done, and could serve as a link between Chrétien and Johnson in a way that no one else could. It was not an easy task for any of us, because the complex politics of Quebec are so delicate that a too supportive federal government can be as politically counter-productive for a provincial Quebec leader as a federal government that appears insensitive and even hostile; we felt as if we were walking on eggshells.

A historic photograph. Seen celebrating the patriation of the
Constitution in 1982 are (left to right) my father, Carl Goldenberg,
Minister of Justice Jean Chrétien, Prime Minister Pierre Trudeau, and
me. The inscription reads "Dear Eddie, It was a great story! Thanks for
your help in telling it. Pierre E.T."

Jean-Marc Carisse

Dear Eddie: It was a great story! Thanks for your
help in telling it... *Pierre E.T.*

Replaying the kitchen cabinet's role in reaching a constitutional deal in 1981: Chrétien, me, Roy Romanow, and Roy McMurtry.

Generations of Liberals. Paul Martin, his father, Paul Martin Sr., Jean Chrétien, Carl Goldenberg, and me, at the Aylmer Conference, November 1991.

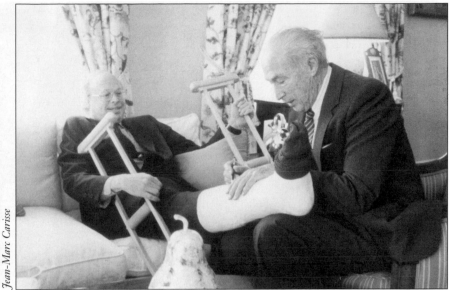

The famous broken leg attracts a signature from another well-known skier.

Another legend, Mitchell Sharp, along with his colleague Allan Lutfy, shares a joke with me and my colleague Chaviva Hosek, senior policy adviser to the leader of the Opposition, who became director of policy and research in our PMO team.

In the PMO, demonstrating Chrétien's well-known "clean desk" policy

Part of the PMO team. (Left to right) Peter Donolo, Jean Pelletier, m
Patrick Parisot, and David MacInnis stand behind the prime minister.

An informal meeting at 24 Sussex Drive involving David Dodge, dep
minister of finance, then of health, and Allan Rock, Chrétien's minist
of justice 1993–1997 and minister of health 1997–2002.

Three scenes from the fight to keep Quebec part of Canada. (Top) Chrétien meets with Daniel Johnson, leader of the No forces in Quebec, and his lieutenants in the course of the 1995 referendum battle. From the left, Serge Joyal, Jean Chrétien, Jacques Lamoureux, Daniel Johnson, Pierre Anctil (beside him), Geoffrey Chambers, Aline Chrétien, Eric Maldoff, and John Parisella. (Middle) Stéphane Dion, brought into politics by Chrétien to bring clarity to the issues, makes his point in a meeting. (Bottom) Meeting the opposition. I greet Quebec premier Bernard Landry at 24 Sussex Drive.

Jean-Marc Caris

Finance Minister Paul Martin pays a visit to the Prime Minister's Office, as my life as a bridge continues. So far, so good . . .

The very fact that we were meeting frequently would have been used against Johnson by the Parti Québécois; so we kept our meetings secret, and met in hotel boardrooms in Montreal rather than take the chance of being seen in each other's offices. Pelletier and I wanted to avoid any public disagreements between the Chrétien and Johnson governments that could give Parizeau the opportunity to argue that, see, even the federalist Johnson cannot accomplish anything with Ottawa. We made sure – with the help of the Privy Council Office as the administrative coordination centre, and the Prime Minister's Press Office as the political coordination centre – that we were aware of all planned federal government announcements or decisions with respect to Quebec, so that we could consult the prime minister and give our input both to avoid political problems and to maximize the political benefit. We tried where we could to give our Quebec friends a heads-up in advance about what the federal government was doing, and to seek their reaction, and they tried to do the same for us. If there were areas where they thought we could help by acting (or sometimes by not acting), we did our best to be accommodating. By and large it worked well, but it was not always easy or trouble-free.

Tobacco – An Interesting Dilemma

WE WERE SOON faced with a high-profile issue of considerable complexity. Federal and provincial governments had imposed high taxes on cigarettes with the dual objective of raising revenue as well as discouraging smoking. With the appalling complicity of Canadian tobacco companies, this produced a huge smuggling operation of cigarettes from the United States into Canada, much of it into Quebec through aboriginal reserves on the Quebec–New York border, and to a lesser but still serious extent into Ontario as well. Police authorities seemed unable to do anything about this lawlessness. If it spun out of control, as it was threatening to do, the first political casualty would have been the Johnson government. Provincial police departments as well as the RCMP told governments that the price differential of cigarettes between Canada and the United States was such a great incentive to smugglers that they simply could not be stopped. The police (who, I found, were always very reluctant to operate on aboriginal reserves) argued that the law was unenforceable, other than with immensely increased resources.

The government was faced with a dilemma. Giving in to tobacco interests – especially to manufacturers who were happily, if secretly, supplying the smugglers – was not very palatable to the government, nor was reducing the price of cigarettes, which would inevitably lead to increased consumption, particularly by young people. On the other hand, laws that are unenforceable and are openly flouted lead to disrespect for the law in general.

Chrétien struck a special Cabinet committee to examine the issue and make recommendations. I attended many committee meetings where the discomfort of federal ministers was palpable. They knew that they had not been elected to reduce the price of cigarettes, and were viscerally reluctant to do so. They listened with equal amounts of skepticism and frustration to Philip Murray, the commissioner of the RCMP, who briefed them for several weeks almost on a daily basis about what his forces could not accomplish. In the end, the Cabinet reluctantly concluded that the high taxes were not discouraging smoking because young people were now buying their cigarettes anyway at a much lower price from smugglers. So in conjunction with the Quebec government and other provincial governments, the federal government and several provinces reduced their taxes on tobacco products to bring them more in line with the prices in American border states and thereby put the smugglers out of business. It was not a decision we were particularly happy with, but it was necessary to avert a political crisis in Quebec, which no one wanted in the circumstances, and we succeeded in our objective of not doing any harm politically to Daniel Johnson.

Closing St. Jean

THE TOBACCO ISSUE was one that was resolved to the comparative satisfaction of both governments, and there were other issues of far less import where good communication between our two offices enabled us to resolve potential problems ahead of time. But it was far from a perfect scenario. There were major decisions that had to be made by the federal government in the interests of the whole country that could not be avoided. While we could do our best to avoid unnecessary political problems for the Quebec government, we could not govern only in the interests of the next Quebec provincial election. Obviously we could not negotiate the next federal budget with the Johnson government. Paul Martin's budget of February 1994 took the first steps to bring the finances of the country under control, by making substantial cuts to the budget of the Department of National Defence. It provided for the closure of Defence installations in every part of the country. Fairness required that Quebec not be exempt from any cutbacks. This meant the closing of the military training college in the town of St. Jean.

A controversy immediately flared up, fuelled by Quebec nationalists who argued that the predominantly English-speaking Royal Military College in Kingston should not be the only staff college available to French-speaking members of the Canadian Armed Forces. Despite repeated entreaties from the Johnson government to revoke the closure in St. Jean, the federal government had to stand its ground, making the case that every community across the country that faced a base closure also had special reasons to fight against it. Giving in to one would require giving in to all, and would be the best way to ensure that no cuts would be made to government spending anywhere. Johnson sometimes blamed his later electoral defeat on the St. Jean decision. It would have been more accurate to blame the loss of the St. Jean constituency, but not the whole province on that one federal decision.

Enter Parizeau

ON SEPTEMBER 12, 1994, in what would become almost a ritual for Quebec provincial elections and referendums, I was at 24 Sussex Drive with other senior advisers to watch the results of the Quebec provincial election. We were under no illusions. We knew that a victory that night by the Parti Québécois would plunge the country into another referendum on the separation of Quebec. The strength of the Bloc Québécois and particularly of its leader, Lucien Bouchard, in the House of Commons would make matters even more difficult for the federalist cause. The good news that night was that there was no tidal wave for separation. The popular vote was very close; only a few thousand votes in the whole province separated the losing Liberals from the victorious and openly separatist Parti Québécois. But the bad news was that the PQ had won a comfortable majority of the seats in the National Assembly.

Jacques Parizeau became premier of Quebec in September 1994. He never had any interest in running a mere provincial government. He had a longstanding and very clear agenda, the separation of Quebec from Canada, and he was going to do whatever it took to achieve his goal. During his election campaign, he had promised a quick referendum on independence for Quebec and, despite the closeness of the popular vote, he had every intention of keeping his promise. With Jacques Parizeau, what you saw was what you got. There was nothing that was not out in the open, even if some did not want to see it.

Parizeau acted decisively. On December 6, 1994, he introduced draft legislation in the Quebec National Assembly on the independence of Quebec. Article one read: "Québec is a sovereign country," and Parizeau announced that the referendum would be to approve the law.

The prime minister was out of the country that day. I remember vividly that I was sitting in the Cabinet room at the weekly Tuesday-morning meeting, which in the absence of the prime minister usually dealt only with the most routine administrative matters, when Parizeau's action hit Ottawa like a bombshell. As the news of his draft legislation spread in the room, ministers were visibly shaken and some seemed almost panic-stricken. Until then, the reality of what Parizeau was up to had not yet fully sunk in for some federal ministers, especially for those from outside Quebec, many of whom were quietly unhappy with a seemingly perpetual focus by Chrétien on Quebec problems. Now they wanted to act immediately, but had no idea what to do. It did not help that many ministers were certain that the planned massive cuts to government spending – with which they were uncomfortable anyway, and which were coming in the next budget only two months away – would be politically disastrous for the government.

I left the Cabinet room and used a phone booth in the adjacent anteroom. Through the PMO switchboard, I reached the prime minister overseas. Chrétien's reaction was predictable: "Tell them not to panic and not to worry. This is just another one of Parizeau's tactics. We have beaten the separatists before and we will beat them again." This did not mean that Chrétien was not worried. On the contrary, he was immensely preoccupied with the Quebec situation. But his view of leadership – sometimes to the dismay of his own staff, who thought he downplayed problems too much, or did not show appropriate concern – was that prime ministers only exacerbate already difficult problems when they allow their own worry and concern to show.

Parizeau's planning was meticulous. The provincial government, from the time it took office, directed all of its energies – and spent large amounts of public money – on the promotion of the independence of Quebec. It was not long before committees of the Quebec National Assembly criss-crossed the province of Quebec at public expense to "consult" on the draft bill and on a referendum that would soon be held. Some of Parizeau's planning was obvious during the campaign; more became known after it was over, particularly how much he focused on persuading the government of France to quickly recognize the new country of Quebec in the event of a referendum victory.

Forming the No Coalition

AFTER JOHNSON'S DEFEAT, Jean Pelletier and I almost immediately took up where we had left off and began regular meetings with Pierre Anctil and John Parisella, who were now in the Opposition leader's office in Quebec City, to work out a co-operative approach so that none of our actions as a government in Ottawa or theirs as an Opposition in Quebec would hurt the referendum prospects. One day when the four of us were to meet in Ottawa, Pelletier and I decided that it would be helpful for our relationship if we took them to a good restaurant, and so we chose Le Metro, then a fine Ottawa French restaurant. The atmosphere was pleasant; the lights were low; the food and wine were very satisfactory. We had a lot to talk about but couldn't help noticing that we were much more serious in our conversation than those at other tables around us. Even though we disagreed and argued a bit that evening, we were pleased with our relationship. It would never be nearly as intimate, however, as the relationship of the couples who filled every other table that evening. We had forgotten that it was Valentine's Day.

Pelletier and I offered our full co-operation and assistance in any way that Daniel Johnson would need as he led the No forces in the upcoming referendum. As the Opposition party in Quebec, the provincial Liberals did not have access to the type of resources that the Parizeau government could devote to the promotion of its cause. The federal government, however, did have research facilities, communications facilities, manpower, and access to information, and we made them available to the No forces.

We began to put together a coalition of federalist forces in Quebec that would co-operate in coordinating strategy for the referendum. In addition to the provincial and federal Liberals, it was augmented by the Progressive Conservative Party under the leadership of Jean Charest, who had delegated his senior Quebec organizers, Senator Pierre Claude Nolin, and my old friend, former Senator Jean Bazin, as representatives to our meetings, and by representatives of the Council for Canadian Unity based in Montreal. As well as Jean Pelletier, Chrétien's press secretary and trusted Quebec adviser, Patrick Parisot, and myself, two key federal representatives were John Rae and Eric Maldoff. Rae had organized Chrétien's leadership and election victories and had been a close friend and confidant of the prime minister since the late 1960s. Maldoff, a Montreal lawyer, had been a key strategic, political, and constitutional adviser to Chrétien since the time of Meech Lake; he held strong views and was never shy to share them, and was a major advocate for us during all the debates on what the basic message of the campaign should be. The prime minister appointed Howard Balloch, an enterprising and highly strategic foreign affairs officer, who shared the views of the prime minister about the campaign of 1980, as coordinator of federal activities in the Privy Council Office. He was also part of the coalition.

Making Way for Lucienne Robillard

IN EARLY 1995, Chrétien decided to strengthen his representation in Cabinet from the province of Quebec by recruiting Lucienne Robillard, a former minister in the Bourassa and Johnson Cabinets, who had narrowly lost her seat in the September provincial election. He asked David Berger, the sitting member of the House of Commons from the constituency of Saint Henri-Westmount, to give up his seat so that Robillard could run in a by-election. Berger loved being in federal politics but agreed to make a career sacrifice. He was appointed ambassador to Israel, a job he held for a few years, but which he enjoyed much less than his role as a member of Parliament.

It is not easy for a prime minister to ask an MP representing a very safe constituency to give up a career he enjoys and in which he performs well. In the private sector, there are all sorts of attractive financial packages that can be offered as a way of moving executives out; those packages are not available in the public sector. In these circumstances, appointments to a government position are sometimes the only way to create vacancies in the House of Commons to achieve desired recruitment, something that is often neglected by commentators who rail against "political" appointments.

Bringing Robillard into the Cabinet as minister of labour and designating her as the federal minister responsible for coordinating referendum activities was intended as an olive branch to the provincial Liberals. She had been a good provincial Cabinet minister, with a reputation of being a solid performer who could be trusted not to make mistakes, and she was highly regarded by her former colleagues in the provincial Liberal Party.

Maximizing the Clinton Advantage

PREPARING FOR THE referendum meant more than just organizing a political campaign. It meant carefully managing all government actions across every ministry, avoiding problems, and demonstrating that Canada can work well.

The state visit to Ottawa of U.S. President Bill Clinton in February 1995 was both an opportunity for us as well as a potential problem to manage. We knew that Clinton was popular in Quebec and that whatever he said about the nature of Canada would be carefully scrutinized there, with potentially important consequences. Chrétien and the president had already developed a good relationship, which later turned into a lasting personal friendship. The American ambassador, Jim Blanchard, was a former Congressman and past governor of Michigan. Fortunately, Blanchard was a lively, outgoing, and energetic character who had formed friendships with many members of Cabinet and with the prime minister and me. Unlike most career diplomats, Blanchard talked and understood the language of politics, and would be proud to be described as a real political addict. He was an expert in political campaigns, and enjoyed sharing his expertise and advice and applying it to any political campaign anywhere. Most important, he was a close political ally of the president and was a strong supporter of a united Canada, and he was prepared to be helpful.

Blanchard wanted us to profit from the opportunity provided by the Clinton visit, and asked me to suggest words the president might use in his televised speech to the Canadian Parliament to demonstrate his strong commitment to a united Canada. It is not often that anyone has the chance to write words for the president of the United States. Apart from the responsibility it implied, the opportunity gave me a memorable rush of adrenalin. Blanchard and I worked together to find the right phrasing that Clinton could use about the success of Canada as a model for the world. He then had suggestions for Chrétien to use in his introductory remarks that might be politically helpful to the president, who was still recovering from the Democratic Party's crushing defeat in the November 1994 mid-term Congressional elections. I was happy to oblige. On the basis of Blanchard's research, on the day of Clinton's visit, the prime minister solemnly told the House of Commons that no American president who had ever addressed the House of Commons of Canada had ever lost a second-term election, while several who had never spoken to the Canadian Parliament were not re-elected. Clinton replied that he hoped that "the iron laws of history would continue to apply." The visit could not have been a greater success. Clinton demonstrated in all of his remarks during his day and a half in Ottawa that he and his government were true friends of Canada.

But there was one potential rain cloud hanging over the visit. When the U.S. president comes to Canada, he traditionally has a brief meeting with the Leader of the Opposition. This time the Leader of the Opposition, Lucien Bouchard, was committed to the breakup of the country. In the months before the referendum, Chrétien did not want to give Bouchard the opportunity to show publicly that he could work well with the president of the United States. However, Bouchard would have exploited for his own political purposes in Quebec a refusal on the part of the Canadian government to allow him to meet the president. The ever-resourceful Jim Blanchard helped to find a solution. The ambassador – with the agreement of the prime minister – invited Bouchard to his residence to meet Clinton for coffee. The residence of the American ambassador in Ottawa lies behind an imposing gate and up a very long driveway. It is inaccessible to the media. Blanchard made sure there would be no photographers present so that there could be no pictures in the media of a smiling separatist leader alongside the president of the United States.

In the presence only of the Canadian ambassador to the United States, Raymond Chrétien, the nephew of the prime minister and a career foreign service officer by profession, and the American ambassador to Canada, Bouchard had his meeting with President Clinton. It was short, pleasant, and totally uneventful. Surprisingly, Bouchard did not take advantage of the meeting to talk about the separation of

Quebec. To the bewilderment of the two ambassadors, and likely the president, and most certainly of his own colleagues (if they had known what he was going to do), Bouchard, whose wife was an American, spent most of his time asking the president about the cost of American universities, and West Point in particular, and wondering how he would be able to manage it if his young children eventually wanted to study in the United States.

Chrétien's Role

THE FEDERAL GOVERNMENT under Chrétien's leadership had an important role to play in the upcoming referendum, but it was not a simple one. Just as in 1980, the rules of the referendum were set by the Quebec National Assembly. Quebec law strictly limited the role of the Canadian government, even though the object of the referendum was the breakup of Canada. The premier of Quebec was by law the head of the Yes committee, and the head of the No committee was the Leader of the Opposition in the National Assembly. The prime minister of Canada would simply be one member of the No committee, along with leaders of other federal political parties who had seats from Quebec in the House of Commons. In this case, the other leader was Jean Charest, who held his party's only seat in Quebec.

In 1980, Trudeau had just been returned to office with all but one of the seats in the House of Commons from Quebec and had tremendous political legitimacy in Quebec. There was a lot of internal debate in the Trudeau government at the time as to whether the federal government should ignore the Quebec legislation on the grounds that it is illegitimate for provincial legislation to limit the role of the federal government when the future of the country is at stake, or even simply proclaim that it considered the referendum with its ambiguous question to be illegitimate and that it would not recognize a Yes vote. In the end, the Trudeau government decided to sidestep the issue of the legitimacy of the referendum legislation. It participated in the No committee, but never considered itself bound by the provincial law. Trudeau authorized unrestricted federal advertising in Quebec.

Unlike Trudeau fifteen years earlier, Chrétien in 1995 was not popular in Quebec. He had been demonized for years because of his role in the patriation of the Constitution and his position on the Meech Lake Accord. That demonization had come from all quarters: from Mulroney, for partisan Progressive Conservative Party political reasons; from the separatists, because they saw him as an effective and passionate adversary; from the Quebec media and intellectual elite, who for years never understood Jean Chrétien and were embarrassed by his populism and apparent lack of sophistication; and from the Martin Liberals, who were shortsighted enough in the 1990 leadership race to neglect the obvious political reality that what is said in a leadership race about an adversary who is certain to win will be used against him and his party by the Opposition after the leadership race is over. So Chrétien entered preparations for the referendum perceived almost as a pariah by the political class in Quebec. Many viewed any participation on his part as a drag on the chances of the federalist side.

Furthermore, the dalliance of the Mulroney government with the separatists had helped create an impression in Quebec that the federal government had consistently acted against the interests of Quebec between 1980 and 1982 and may even have acted improperly in the way it had campaigned in 1980. Rather than accept that the federal campaign in 1980 – led by Chrétien as minister of justice – had helped achieve a strong victory for the federalist forces, even the Clerk of the Privy Council, Jocelyn Bourgon (who had worked very closely with Joe Clark and Lowell Murray – and greatly admired them – when they were in government), had swallowed the separatist line about the perfidy of the federal campaign in the first referendum, and now argued that it would be a great mistake for the federal government to do in 1995 what had been so successful in 1980.

For his part, Chrétien had no regrets about the role he had played in 1980. He was proud of it and convinced that it would once again be the right approach in 1995. This time, although he was prime minister, because of his own political circumstances, his approach found a less receptive audience among provincial Quebec Liberals.

Differences between Partners

BY THE SPRING of 1995, the coalition that would later put together
the referendum campaign for the federalist forces was holding weekly
meetings. The selected political organizers from all parties, the people
who manage the nuts and bolts of an election campaign, worked well
together. They had common interests and experiences, even if they
had worked on opposite sides, as Liberals and Conservatives, in federal
elections. It was particularly important that they work together
because with only twenty seats in Quebec, the federal Liberal political
organization was very weak and would not have been able to operate
effectively on its own, even if it had wanted to. Our problem, however,
wasn't the nuts and bolts. It was far more fundamental. During the
spring and summer of 1995, we couldn't agree on what the basic
message of the campaign should be.

Profound ideological differences lay at the core of our differing
views on Quebec's place in Canada. For the federal Liberals – and for
the prime minister, in particular – Canada was much more than a
balance sheet. Like Trudeau before him, Chrétien was convinced that
Quebeckers shared his profound attachment to Canada and believed
that the best way to appeal to them in 1995, as in 1980, would be to
their hearts more than to their pocketbooks.

The Quebec Liberals, however, were disciples of Robert Bourassa,
who had always been a master of ambiguity. Throughout his long and
successful political career, he argued that the best reason for Quebec
to be part of Canada is that Quebec is better off economically in
Canada than it would be as a separate country. His was a doctrine of
"profitable federalism." It was very much a pragmatic "Quebec First"
point of view, with no sense of passionate or visceral attachment to
Canada. Bourassa always walked a successful political tightrope as a
federalist, but as one who somehow encouraged the speculation that if
anyone could one day lead Quebec to independence, he would be more
likely to do so than the Parti Québécois.

To complicate our mission, Mulroney had resurrected much of the
existential angst of past decades of constitutional debate. The failure

of both the Meech Lake and Charlottetown Accords had provided plenty of ammunition to the separatists. And many Quebec Liberals, including some members of our coalition, had never given up on the various concepts of the 1960s of "special status," "particular status," or some other status for Quebec within Canada different from just that of a province. Then came the Allaire Report, which was totally unacceptable to Chrétien. Things were so bad that by 1995, the word *Canada* was almost anathema to some of the Quebec Liberal members of the federalist coalition; they preferred to speak publicly about "the economic and social union to which we belong" rather than to use with pride the word *Canada*. The coalition held lengthy drafting sessions throughout the early part of 1995 to prepare a public manifesto to be sent by the No committee at the time of the referendum campaign to all Quebec households. It took all of Eric Maldoff's pit-bull-like tenacity representing the federal Liberals to get the word *Canada* into the document.

Naturally, given those views, the provincial Liberals wanted the campaign to be a "Quebec only" one. Chrétien's representatives would have preferred MPs, provincial premiers, and concerned Canadians to come to Quebec to tell Quebeckers that they were wanted in Canada. The Quebec Liberals argued that such participation would be counterproductive and would alienate Quebeckers. In hindsight, we were wrong to accept their reasoning.

Chapter 12

TENSE MOMENTS FOR CANADA: THE 1995 REFERENDUM CAMPAIGN

"Winning isn't everything; it is the only thing."

– VINCE LOMBARDI

Hindsight is always perfect after political campaigns. The strategy the federalist coalition had agreed on in the spring of 1995 was based on an expectation that it would produce the large victory that was our common objective. It was a time when the polls were very good for us, and there did not seem to be any reason why there would be any change before the referendum.

The separatist forces were divided as to what to do. Bernard Landry, the Parti Québécois deputy premier, read discouraging polls for his side and said he would not be part of a modern-day Charge of the Light Brigade. Lucien Bouchard – who for months had been at odds with Jacques Parizeau – insisted that he would only participate in the referendum campaign if the question on the ballot referred to a partnership with the rest of Canada. To get out of a dead end, Parizeau reluctantly agreed to ask Quebeckers to vote on a very ambiguous question rather than on the stark question on independence that he had always favoured. This fudging enabled the leader of the small Action Démocratique, Mario Dumont, to embark his party as well on the Yes side. But as long as Parizeau was leading the Yes forces, Quebeckers did not seem to give credence to any notion of "partnership." Parizeau and his separatist option seemed headed for a crushing defeat.

The referendum was finally called in the fall for October 30, 1995. As we seemed to be heading for a decisive victory, my federal colleagues and I didn't worry as much as we perhaps should have about campaign tactics, and we reluctantly agreed to a campaign strategy that was much closer to the preferred approach of the provincial Liberals than to that of the federal Liberals. But those of us representing the federal government still knew that we would have to cope with a very uncomfortable prime minister in Ottawa, whose every political instinct told him that the "Quebec only" strategy was a big mistake, but whose political standing in Quebec – whether he agreed or not – simply did not give him the clout to take on the rest of the coalition.

The Yes campaign appealed to the heartstrings and pride of Quebeckers in a positive way with slogans such as "Vote yes and everything will become possible," while the federalist campaign was based on cold economic logic, with no emotion about Canada. It was no way to convince people of the advantages of being Canadian. Even the cold logic didn't work the way we anticipated, because the separatists were able to turn around the economic argument for remaining in Canada, either by accusing us of using scare tactics or with a clever pitch that the federal deficit at the time was so large that Quebeckers could not afford to remain part of a bankrupt country like Canada.

A Strategic Debate

AS THE CAMPAIGN progressed and as we continued to have a substantial lead in the polls, one strategic issue split the federalist campaign strategists right down the middle. It was that of the possible partition of Quebec, if ever Quebec achieved independence from the rest of Canada. All of us in the No coalition agreed that it was important for Quebeckers to understand that breaking up Canada would not be simple, and that the separation of Quebec would be a plunge into the unknown. Those on the federal government side – and the prime minister, in particular – were eager to use the further logical argument that if Canada is divisible, then Quebec must be too. This meant that it would be necessary to contemplate in the event of a Yes vote that parts of Quebec might choose to remain in Canada. Our polling results showed that raising the possibility of the partition of Quebec in the event of independence would cause more than 6 per cent of Yes voters to move to the No side, and produce a massive federalist victory.

That idea led to serious differences of opinion in our campaign strategy sessions with the Johnson Liberals, who refused even to contemplate the theoretical possibility that Quebec itself could be divisible. Pierre Anctil absolutely refused to have anything to do with a campaign that used partition as an argument. If Chrétien – as he desperately wanted to do – had made the case about the possible partition of Quebec, the intransigence of Johnson's strategists meant that there was a good chance that the whole federalist coalition and campaign might have imploded. In the aftermath of Meech Lake and Charlottetown, and with the separatists making the argument that Canadian federalists could never get their act together, we knew that the unity of the No forces was absolutely essential to winning, and so Chrétien did not make the case about partition that he wanted to make, because we were not prepared to take the chance of a rupture of our coalition in the middle of the campaign.

The Bouchard Effect

UNTIL THE LAST part of the 1995 referendum campaign, the Yes campaign was in deep trouble. With only about three weeks to go before the referendum, the federalist forces – despite our internal debates – were more than fifteen points ahead in the polls. Parizeau as leader of the separatist forces was simply not scoring with voters. His campaign was going nowhere and the prospects of a resounding federalist win continued to look very good. It was at this point that the Yes forces made a dramatic change in their campaign strategy. They basically replaced Parizeau as their leader by announcing that Lucien Bouchard would be "the negotiator in chief" of independence.

Adopting a new strategy in the middle of a political campaign is a highly risky and delicate operation that is rarely successful. When it happens, it is seen as a sign of desperation and panic. Usually, it backfires, as in the federal election of 1984 when John Turner changed his senior advisers midway through the campaign, only to accelerate his downward spiral.

But the Yes forces were desperate when Bouchard took over the campaign three weeks before the referendum. He had recently made a miraculous recovery from a flesh-eating disease that claimed his leg and almost his life, and he had become a charismatic hero to Quebeckers, who watched in awe as he had almost literally risen from the dead. He could say almost anything and get away with it, whether it was a claim that independence would have the effect of a "magic wand" to improve the economy of Quebec, or that Quebec's demographic problems were caused in part because white francophone women do not have enough babies. If Jean Chrétien or Daniel Johnson had made similar statements, their political careers might have come to an inglorious and quick end. Not so Bouchard.

The genius of Bouchard's appointment as "negotiator in chief" was not apparent to us soon enough, but it turned out to be powerful. As long as Parizeau had led the Yes forces, Quebeckers understood his separatist objective and were ready to vote No in large numbers. Once Bouchard took over the leadership of the campaign, however, he was able to downplay the fundamental rupture of the country that separation would entail. In fact, Parizeau's concession to Bouchard and his reluctant acceptance of Bouchard's new role in the last weeks of the campaign was purely tactical; as far as he was concerned, a Yes vote on any question was a mandate to separate, not negotiate. Cleverly and dishonestly – given the subsequent revelation of Parizeau's plans to move quickly to achieve separation – Bouchard created the impression for many voters that the results of any negotiation he would lead for Quebec with the rest of Canada would be like most labour negotiations with which Quebeckers are very familiar: producing some change, some improvement in circumstances, but nothing particularly radical.

Desperate Days

IN THE FIRST week of Bouchard's leadership, the polls stayed basically
the same as they had been. Then the "Bouchard Effect" took hold and
there was a dramatic shift. Soon, there was near panic on the federalist side. With ten days to go, the Yes campaign was in the lead. On
Thursday, October 19, I left Ottawa early in the morning to drive to
Montreal to be part of a tense three-hour emergency meeting of the
No campaign strategists. Despite our disagreements during the spring
and summer, we were all in the same boat and understood that we all
had to pull together in the crucial days ahead. There was an air of desperation in the room, particularly among the provincial Liberals, and
nobody had any really good ideas about how to turn around a seemingly successful campaign that had gone sour so fast. Those closest to
Daniel Johnson, who had previously been very reluctant to give any
profile to the prime minister, now surprisingly wanted Chrétien to be
omnipresent all the next week at rallies and on television. It was the
equivalent of a Hail Mary pass in football at the end of a game when
the quarterback has no other options. Johnson's strategists were also
counting on Chrétien to make an important statement the following
Tuesday evening at a rally in Montreal at the Verdun Auditorium, where
Daniel Johnson and Jean Charest would also be present and speaking.

It was obvious to all of us that something more dramatic than just
more interviews and more rallies was necessary to connect with voters.
Some of the most passionate and eloquent speeches about Canada were
delivered many times a week throughout the province by Jean Charest;
his message and that of other federalist spokespersons resonated in the
room with their audiences, but they were hardly covered in the media.
On the other hand, Bouchard's message seemed to be winning support
throughout Quebec. Johnson's chief of staff, Pierre Anctil, suggested
that the prime minister ask for time on the main television channels to
deliver a direct, unfiltered message to Quebeckers. Anctil's reasoning
was that the very fact that the prime minister of Canada found it necessary to use the provisions of the Broadcast Act to require Radio-Canada
to give him airtime in the last few days of the referendum campaign

might be a sobering reminder to Quebeckers that the stakes in the referendum outcome were a lot greater than the soothing rhetoric of Lucien Bouchard had led them to believe. In retrospect, I have concluded that Anctil's proposal was the turning point of the last week of the campaign.

Bringing in Chrétien

THOSE OF US representing the prime minister at the Montreal meeting knew that he was chomping at the bit to get more involved. It would not be difficult to convince him to campaign hard. He was a born campaigner and had wanted to be much more visible in the campaign than he had been up till then. What would be much more difficult would be to agree on the message he should convey. Predictably, the provincial Liberals wanted him to appeal to so-called "soft federalists" who could be brought back into the federalist fold with promises of substantive changes, including constitutional change in Canada in the event of a victory of the No forces.

Patrick Parisot and I drove back to Ottawa from Montreal and went straight to 24 Sussex Drive around 3:30 p.m. As we hadn't eaten for hours, Parisot first went into the kitchen and asked the chef to make us a sandwich, and then we were ushered in to see the prime minister. Chrétien understood the gravity of the situation but was not panicked. He remained convinced that Quebeckers in the privacy of the ballot booth would never vote to leave Canada, as long as they understood the consequences of their vote. There was also no doubt in his mind that he would never recognize a positive response by Quebec voters to an ambiguous question as a mandate to separate.

Chrétien had always been uneasy about the low-key strategy of the coalition and now regretted that he had not insisted on participating much more in the campaign. While he had used his answers to Lucien Bouchard during question period in the House of Commons as a platform, he had only made two speeches up to this point in Quebec, one in Shawinigan on the same stage as Daniel Johnson and Jean Charest, and one in Quebec City to the Chamber of Commerce. Neither had been widely reported in a way that would make an impact on voters. As he was complaining about the campaign, I jumped in and recalled the arguments in Ottawa in 1980, when the polls were not very good, that Trudeau should be much more involved. "Trudeau's success," I reminded him, "was because he spoke sparingly, and always at the right time. If you had campaigned as much as you wanted at the beginning before Bouchard pushed out Parizeau, by now your currency would be depreciated and no one would be paying much attention to you. This is the time for you to make a difference."

He, too, recalled the campaign of 1980. "I will go on national television next week. But I won't make promises that I can't keep after the referendum. I won't promise constitutional change. I don't want to create the expectations that Trudeau, rightly or wrongly, created in 1980 at the Paul Sauvé Arena, and then find I'm not able to deliver. In the long run, that would be disastrous for the unity of the country."

Parisot and I were definitely not immediately concerned about the long run. We had to deal with the short run, and particularly with the preparation of these important speeches. The next day we were back in Montreal for good meetings with our provincial colleagues, reporting that the prime minister had agreed to the strategy and the plan for the next week. In political campaigns, there are frequent, sometimes inexplicable, mood swings. Now with something like the Stockholm Syndrome taking hold of all of us, we convinced ourselves that we could be moderately optimistic. The whole team even took a few minutes in the afternoon to cluster around a birthday cake to celebrate John Rae's fiftieth birthday. It was a morale booster, given the respect and affection that everyone had for Rae. Then we listened to a range of views on what the prime minister should say the following week. Not unexpectedly, the range of views was very wide indeed.

The Day from Hell

WHEN I LOOK back at all the political campaigns I have known, Saturday, October 21, 1995, only nine days before the vote, stands out for me as the day from hell. It began with an early-morning strategy meeting in the Quebec Liberal Party headquarters on St. Denis Street in Montreal. Gregoire Golin, the pollster for the No committee, told us the race was now tight, and our support was continuing to go down while support for the other side was continuing to increase. I could feel the nervousness in the room. When the meeting was over, Patrick Parisot and I moved to a small room to start to draft a text for the prime minister for the Tuesday-night Verdun speech. Soon we were joined by Daniel Johnson and a number of other members of our coalition. There were only two chairs in the room, so everyone stood. We had a free-ranging discussion from which Parisot and I drew the sense that the prime minister should talk about his openness to change in Canada after the referendum, but that a promise of constitutional change was not necessary. When Johnson left to attend some campaign events, we wished him luck.

Parisot and I soon asked the others to leave so that we could write. We had worked well together for several years on a lot of speeches, and had come up with a simple system. We first talked over the structure of the speech we would propose to the prime minister, and each of us then jotted down some of our own ideas. For English speeches, I would . prepare a draft; for French speeches, Parisot, an excellent writer with a style that the prime minister was comfortable with, would pull it all together. This time it was Parisot's turn. We worked hard for the rest of the day.

While we were writing, Johnson was campaigning when he was questioned by a journalist about the possibility of constitutional change in the future. Without thinking about the immediate consequences of what he was saying, Johnson responded vaguely that he hoped there could one day be constitutional change in Canada. The media pounced on his answer and interpreted it as Johnson wanting constitutional change in the event of a No vote.

Meanwhile, the prime minister was at the United Nations, where leaders of more than one hundred countries were celebrating the fiftieth anniversary of the world body. New York was the last place Chrétien wanted to be that weekend, but he feared that cancelling his trip would be interpreted in Quebec as a sign that the referendum was going badly. Morale is important in political campaigns and he did not want to damage the already-fragile morale of the No campaign. So he decided to demonstrate confidence by going ahead with his scheduled plans. Later that afternoon at the UN, the prime minister was unaware of Johnson's comments when a reporter asked him whether there would be constitutional change after the referendum. The trap was set and the prime minister fell in. "No," he replied.

The media frenzy was predictable. "NO FORCES IN DISARRAY." "CHRÉTIEN CONTRADICTS JOHNSON." The television news that evening was sensationalist and disastrous. And the screaming headline in the following morning's Quebec dailies was, "CHRÉTIEN SAYS NO TO JOHNSON." Around six o'clock that Saturday evening, I saw Daniel Johnson back in the headquarters. He was badly shaken. "Eddie, I screwed up. I want to call and apologize to the prime minister."

"No, Daniel," I replied. "You don't have to. These things happen in campaigns. The prime minister has also made mistakes in campaigns. Let's just move ahead."

Parisot and I continued to work on the speech until about eight o'clock. Then he suggested that since we had agreed on what the speech should say, I could go back to my hotel while he finished putting our thoughts into a text. That was fine with me. I went back to the Queen Elizabeth Hotel and had a quick bite to eat. But the day from hell wasn't over. When I went upstairs to my room, an urgent message was waiting for me from Parisot. I called him late in the evening at his Montreal home, and he told me, "I have very bad news." His tone was so grim that my immediate reaction was to ask about his family, "Are Carmen and the kids okay?"

"Yes" he said, "but." I couldn't imagine what the "but" could possibly be, given his tone of voice. "I have lost the speech in the computer and can't find it." My reaction was one of relief. At least nobody was dead. I said that we both needed a few hours' rest and at the worst we would rewrite it the next day from our notes.

The next morning I woke up to see the damaging headlines in the newspapers, but was relieved when the phone rang and Parisot told me that his wife had retrieved the speech in his computer. We finalized a draft and sought comments from our colleagues in the No coalition. At noon on Monday, October 23, we drove back to Ottawa with our draft speech. We took it straight to 24 Sussex. Chrétien said he needed a few hours to work on it and asked us to come back at eight o'clock that evening for a final drafting session, and to discuss what he should say on national television forty-eight hours later.

High Stakes

THE MEETING THAT evening in the prime minister's study at 24 Sussex Drive was one of the most important I ever attended. Chrétien, Parisot, and I knew just how high the stakes were. This was not just an election campaign where one party wins or loses, where individual careers are made or broken, and where the policy directions of a country are set for the next four years. No matter how gloomy a picture political parties paint of the Opposition during election campaigns, changes in government don't normally put the survival of a country in jeopardy. When a party is defeated in an election, there is obvious disappointment among its supporters, but always the hope that the results can be reversed the next time around.

This was not the same. We all knew that a defeat could lead to the irreversible breakup of Canada. Chrétien had strategic decisions of immense significance to make that night about what he would say in two speeches that could make or break the future of Canada. There was no time for long debates or lengthy meetings with dozens of advisers around the table. Even if there had been time, it was not his style. When he knew the issues, whatever they were, and understood the pros and cons, he was prepared to decide. He always said it was what he was paid to do.

The prime minister, who had spent a lifetime thinking about Quebec issues, was focused and calm that night. He generally liked the text we had given him, but suggested a number of changes and improvements. He expressed concern, as he had a few days earlier, about overpromising. Chrétien was not sure that certain phrases some of the No strategists wanted in the speech would be as significant or meaningful to average Quebeckers as the proponents thought, but, after some hesitation, he agreed to keep most of them. He was already pondering the tightrope he would be walking in the circumstances of a defeat. "I don't think some of this language will help much, but it probably won't hurt – as long as I don't create expectations we'll never be able to meet. If I take out some of what Johnson's people want, and we lose, they might blame us for the defeat. I don't want to alienate them now because we'll need them when we refuse to accept a Yes result to a crooked question as a mandate for separation."

As we were finalizing the speech, the telephone rang for me. It was Jim Blanchard. "Have you heard what French President Jacques Chirac just said on *Larry King Live* on CNN?"

"Jim, I'm really busy. I can't talk now. I'm with the prime minister and we're working on tomorrow's speech."

"Eddie, listen to me. He just said he would recognize the results of a Yes vote."

"Thanks, Jim. I'll tell the prime minister."

Chirac's comments, as Blanchard had reported them, did not surprise me at all. A few weeks earlier, I had an unforgettable lunch with the French ambassador to Canada, Alfred Siefer-Gaillardin, who was personally a strong proponent of a united Canada. I had been quite shaken when he told me gravely, "You will recall that France adhered to the Maastricht Treaty forming the European Union after a close referendum result of only 52 per cent in favour. You had better win, because in France we recognize as a victory any majority in a referendum of more than 50 per cent plus 1."

When I told Chrétien what Blanchard had told me, he grimaced, paused, and said, "We can't do anything about it now. We have work to do on the speech. Let's continue."

We finished discussing the Verdun speech and then began to talk about the general message the prime minister would use in his televised address the next evening. Since Bouchard seemed to have been able to convince Quebeckers that a Yes vote would not be overly risky, Chrétien had the task of explaining why a Yes vote involved incalculable risks. It would not be an easy sell, and the future of the country might ride on that one ten-minute speech.

It was a time to reflect on the famous line of Marshall McLuhan, "The medium is the message." The very fact of taking broadcast time on television was a powerful message. Now we had to decide on how to use the medium. It was not easy. The polls were pointing to a victory of the Yes forces. While Jean Chrétien had long before decided that he would never recognize the legitimacy of a Yes vote to what he considered was a trick question, he wanted to do everything in his power to assure a No victory. He was convinced that Quebeckers would never deliberately vote for separation. If they could be persuaded that the referendum was on whether Quebec should remain a part of Canada, the choice, as it had always been in the past, would be for Canada. But if they thought a Yes vote would simply mean a negotiation to improve the status quo, then the Yes forces were poised to win.

Chrétien's dilemma was that he might not be able at the last moment to persuade Quebeckers of the real intentions of the Yes forces. He had an awesome responsibility. If he raised the ante in his television address and stated bluntly that a Yes vote would mean the breakup of Canada and then the Yes side won, how could he argue the next week that the vote was illegitimate because the question was unclear? On the other hand, if he did not make the argument that a Yes vote would mean the breakup of Canada, then the Yes forces had a much better chance of winning, with all the political and economic uncertainty in the country we knew that would entail, regardless of how we interpreted the result after the fact. Chrétien, Parisot, and I discussed the dilemma, and then the prime minister said, "Let's do everything it takes to win this week. If we still lose, I won't be deterred from making the argument that the

question was too unclear to be taken as a mandate to separate. Prepare
me a speech saying that the issue of the referendum is to stay in Canada
or leave Canada. Put it into my speech for Verdun for tomorrow night
and I'll use it again on television the next night."

Around ten-thirty that evening, Chrétien asked Parisot and me to
go back to our office and make the changes he wanted to the Verdun
speech. As for him, he was going to bed, but he needed to work on the
speech as soon as he woke up in the morning. "Aline is in Montreal so
I will leave the front door unlocked, and you could put the text on my
desk later tonight when you are finished." Parisot and I left 24 Sussex.
We both had the same thought. If our homes were behind high gates
with twenty-four-hour-a day police protection and security cameras
everywhere on the grounds, we would not worry about leaving our
front doors unlocked at night.

The Verdun Speech

THE MORNING OF the Verdun speech started like all mornings in
Ottawa during the referendum campaign. A small group of senior
PMO advisers met in Jean Pelletier's boardroom and participated in a
conference call with our own representatives in the No committee
headquarters in Montreal. John Rae passed on the bad news. The
overnight polling put us seven points behind. We seemed to be in free
fall. The telephone rang and it was the prime minister for me. "I have
the speech. Thanks. Is there anything new this morning?" I took a deep
breath and decided that a bit of gallows humour might work. "We have
good news and bad news. The bad news is that we are seven points
behind. The good news is that everyone is counting on you to turn it
around tonight." There was nervous laughter, and the man who always
defended salaries of ministers and MPs by saying that they were hundreds of thousands of dollars a year less than what the worst player in
the National Hockey League was earning replied, "I guess that's why
we are paid the big bucks."

Chrétien delivered the speech that night to thousands of people –
waving Canadian flags – packed into an overheated hockey arena. "On

Monday," he said, "we will have to decide whether the Canada we Quebeckers have built together will continue to evolve or will be broken apart." The atmosphere was electric, but I was afraid that he was preaching to the converted, and wondered whether his speech would make an impact outside the arena. I was marginally relieved that night and the next morning when the press coverage was substantial and favourable, although it still seemed to me that it would be next to impossible to reverse the trend in public opinion.

After the rally was over, the prime minister and his staff got into his motorcade to come back to Ottawa. Because Chrétien had not eaten dinner and was hungry, as we were getting into Ottawa he asked his police driver to pull into the local Harvey's restaurant for a hamburger. The whole motorcade of about ten cars followed. It was after midnight and the restaurant was empty and locked. When we banged on the door, an unimpressed young employee took a brief look at the hungry customers outside, including the prime minister of Canada, and announced that he had just closed for the night. For anyone who was superstitious, it did not augur well for the campaign. Not being either superstitious or hungry at the time, I was glad to get home without stopping, in order to catch a few minutes more sleep. The next day would begin early. How it ended might determine the future of Canada.

The Speech to the Nation

PATRICK PARISOT AND I met as planned at seven o'clock in the morning in my boardroom in the Langevin Building. We were physically and emotionally drained, and hoped that we had not completely depleted our reserves of adrenalin, something that is essential in political campaigns. We had nothing written, and had only blank pads of yellow lined paper in front of us on which to craft that evening's televised address to the nation. On the large table, we had copies of different speeches that the prime minister and others had made in the past that might have been of some assistance. We would also use a lot of the Verdun speech from the night before.

We knew how much depended on what the prime minister would say that night. So did a lot of our colleagues who phoned or came into the boardroom with ideas. Jean Pelletier and Peter Donolo gave us many useful suggestions. We were prepared to listen and accept any good ideas, but we didn't have much time, and the prime minister had already given us instructions about the main theme. Committees can't write speeches. We had the responsibility to produce a text, and the prime minister had to see it, give his input, have changes made, and practise his delivery. The speech had to be taped in both languages, and sent to the networks ahead of time for broadcast. It was to be on the air in English and in French at seven o'clock in the evening. So we only had a few hours.

We made progress slowly. Every word seemed to take forever. Around eleven o'clock in the morning, Lucien Bouchard's chief of staff telephoned me. Since the networks had given Bouchard time to respond – Canadian fair play and democracy at work – he wanted a copy of the prime minister's speech on a confidential basis ahead of time to help him prepare his own remarks. I thought that was taking democracy a little far, but instead of getting into a philosophical debate, I told the truth. "The text isn't ready. Call me later if you want." He did call back a few times, but somehow I was always too busy to take the call, and never returned it until just before seven o'clock, when I knew I would not reach him.

I took the next call a few minutes after the one from Bouchard's office; it was more difficult. The prime minister wanted to see a draft of his own speech. I had to tell him that we only had a few paragraphs written. He was nervous and not pleased. He called back several times over the next few hours, only to be told we weren't ready, but to have faith that we would be ready. His anxiety was completely understand-able, but it only added to our stress. Chrétien's approach to leadership was usually one of "Don't worry, be happy," but that morning he could no longer hide his own fears about the likely outcome of the referen-dum, and tears streamed down his face during an emotional speech to the Liberal caucus. Fortunately for our own stress level, Parisot and

I only learned of what had happened in caucus much later in the day.

By three o'clock, we had shown a text to Donolo and Pelletier, incorporated their last-minute comments, and drove to 24 Sussex, where we delivered a draft to the prime minister. He made a few changes and told us to fax a copy to John Rae in Montreal for him to go over with Daniel Johnson's senior staff. Half an hour later, Rae called back. Pierre Anctil was insisting that one addition be made, to repeat something that had been said the night before in Verdun. Since the passage had been omitted only in the interests of time and space, it was easy to add. Chrétien then took some time to familiarize himself with all the words and the sentence structure in both languages. When he was ready, he drove to his office on Parliament Hill. There, with a Canadian flag behind his desk, he would deliver the most important speech of his career, and surely one of the most important any Canadian prime minister ever had to make.

The words could not have been clearer:

> For the first time in my mandate as Prime Minister, I have asked to speak directly to Canadians tonight. I do so because we are in an exceptional situation. Tonight in particular I want to speak to my fellow Quebeckers. Because at this moment, the future of our whole country is in their hands. . . .
>
> The decision that will be made is serious and irreversible. With deep, deep consequences. What is at stake is the future of our country. What is at stake is our heritage. To break up Canada or build Canada. To remain Canadian or no longer be Canadian. To stay or to leave. This is the issue of the referendum.

There are different theories about what factors make the difference in close political campaigns. Some will argue that the great Unity Rally in Montreal – the brainchild of Brian Tobin, Sheila Copps, Sergio Marchi, and other federal Cabinet ministers – on the Friday before the vote was what swung the result. That rally mobilized Canadians from one end of the country to the other, and it was later extraordinarily important psychologically for all Canadians to feel that their emotional participation at the end of the campaign made the difference. However, pollsters now agree that it did not make any difference to the vote.

Others might argue that the polls were simply wrong and the No forces would have won even if nothing dramatic had been done in the last week of the campaign. My conclusion is that the fact Chrétien took to the airwaves in the way he did focused the attention of Quebeckers on the consequence of their vote like nothing else in the campaign. I believe that the drama of a prime ministerial appearance on television was the most important factor that turned a seven-point deficit in the polls a few days earlier into a narrow victory.

Chapter 13

THE MORNING AFTER THE NIGHT BEFORE

"Those who cannot learn from history are doomed to repeat it."
– GEORGE SANTANYANA

O n the night of October 30, 1995, the people of Canada held their breath for two and a half hours while the votes were counted in the Quebec referendum. It was a see-saw battle from the time the polls closed at eight o'clock until ten-thirty when Radio-Canada, the French-language network of the CBC, finally announced a narrow victory for the No forces – 50.6 per cent to 49.4 per cent. I watched the results that night at 24 Sussex Drive, the house where a lot of Canadian history had been made in the years since the days of Louis St. Laurent, when it became the residence of Canada's prime ministers. The question all of us were silently asking ourselves – although no one was prepared to ask it out loud – was whether this night might be the beginning of the end of that history.

The prime minister was joined that evening by a small group of advisers, friends, and relatives who watched and bit their nails along with the millions of other Canadians who were also glued to their television sets. Chrétien watched intently and said little. Although he clearly understood the responsibility that would lie on his shoulders for the days and weeks and months ahead, he remained icily calm. I knew that a characteristic of Jean Chrétien was this calm in big storms, balanced by considerable fretting over smaller, less important matters. Some of us who were less calm left the family room from time to time and prowled nervously around the house in search of television sets in empty rooms.

Once the results were final, and the narrow victory was confirmed, the prime minister got into his car and, followed by some advisers in an RCMP staff van, went straight to his office on Parliament Hill. There, at close to midnight, he would address the people of Canada on national television. During the day, Patrick Parisot and I had prepared a speech in the event of a federalist victory. Because of the closeness of the result, we made some adjustments to the text from 24 Sussex during the vote counting. When we got to Parliament Hill, we arranged for the speech to be put on the Teleprompter immediately, to be ready for the prime minister to use as soon as the television networks told him to begin.

Money and The Ethnic Vote

WHILE CHRÉTIEN WAS waiting alone in his office behind his desk, studying his text and preparing to deliver his address on television, Jacques Parizeau made a bitter concession speech in which he blamed the separatist defeat on "money and the ethnic vote." I was standing watching it with several of my PMO colleagues in a small outer office. We were stunned by his remarks, and Jean Pelletier and I rushed to tell Chrétien what Parizeau had just said. In retrospect, it is clear to me that we should have insisted on taking an extra few minutes so that Chrétien could adjust his text to respond there and then. Instead, in the emotion, hurry, and plain exhaustion of the evening, we did nothing. We allowed ourselves to be prisoners of our original planning. The prime minister was comfortable with the speech that was already in the Teleprompter and we knew he would be reluctant to have changes made at the last minute; furthermore, it was close to midnight and the television networks wanted Chrétien to speak as soon as possible. As a result, on that emotional night we missed an opportunity for the prime minister to react immediately and speak to Quebeckers about the equality of all citizens, regardless of their ethnic origin. It served as a lesson that even in times of crisis, there is always an advantage in taking a little extra time for maximum reflection before speaking.

Foreshadowing the Clarity Act

AFTER HE FINISHED his television address, Chrétien asked me to accompany him in his car back to 24 Sussex Drive. I got into the back seat of the limousine while he stood outside shaking hands with a small group of flag-waving citizens, drawn to Parliament Hill on this historic night. As soon as he got into the car, he looked at me, visibly relieved, and said, "I prefer the speech I just gave to the other one you gave me this afternoon." He was referring to the speech that Patrick Parisot and I had written earlier that day at his request in case the results had gone the other way.

Advising a prime minister in times of crisis involves a type of stress that is hard to imagine. I always tried to project calmness and assurance and certainty to others, including the boss. That air of confidence, however, didn't stop me at times from worrying deep down – and sometimes not so deep down – that the advice I was giving could be wrong, and worse still, it might be wrong and accepted. When I was the senior adviser, and often the last person the prime minister would hear from before he made an ultimate decision, I always understood that I had to be more cautious and weigh all the pros and cons of my advice much more carefully than when I was only one of many whose advice could be discussed and debated before final decisions were taken. In this case, Parisot and I understood that any serious mistake in the message we proposed to the prime minister in the circumstances could have grave consequences for the country.

Obviously, it was no fun writing a speech to be delivered in the event of a loss in the referendum, and both Parisot and I had chills running down our spines at the thought of a Yes vote. We understood the chaos it would bring to Canada. We recognized the responsibility that we might all face the next day, and we were well aware that if the Yes forces won the referendum, the prime minister's first comments would be the opening salvo in an uncertain battle for the future of Canada.

The draft speech certainly put a brave face on the outcome. It recognized that Quebeckers wanted change in Canada, but it firmly rejected the interpretation of a close Yes vote – or even any Yes vote – on an ambiguous question as a genuine vote to separate Quebec from Canada. During many telephone calls on the weekend before the referendum, Chrétien had speculated with me on the political tightrope he would have to walk in case of a Yes vote. He knew that it would have created the worst crisis in Canadian history. What he did not know at the time and, like me, only learned years later, was that some of his English ministers led by Brian Tobin held a secret meeting in the week before the referendum to discuss whether Chrétien, as a Quebecker, would have the legitimacy to remain as prime minister in the event of a Yes victory.

Chrétien did not underestimate Parizeau's determination to take such a vote as a mandate to achieve the separation of Quebec, and he knew that France might provide some international respectability for any such breakaway. But he told me in no uncertain terms that he never would enter into negotiations to break up Canada based on the question on that referendum ballot. In the car, as we turned into 24 Sussex, Chrétien was still angry about the sham question on the ballot, and, foreshadowing the Clarity Act that he introduced in Parliament four years later, he said grimly to me, "I will never allow the country to be put through something like this again."

Aftermath

AFTER THE BATTLE of Waterloo, the Duke of Wellington remarked on how his victory was a "near run thing" that could easily have gone the other way. The result of the 1995 Quebec referendum was also a near run thing, but while the Duke of Wellington and his allies could ship Napoleon off to St. Helena, Lucien Bouchard was not going away. If anything, his shadow would now loom larger than ever, after his personal success in reviving the Yes campaign. It was one thing, on the night of the 1980 referendum, for René Lévesque to rally his troops after a crushing defeat with the words, "À la prochaine." (Until the next time.) They were brave words, but federalists were not worried. The next time, if ever, clearly would be a long time away. On the morning of October 31, 1995, however, "the next time" looked as if it could be very soon, and many federalists had the instinctive reaction that time was not on Canada's side.

The challenge of preserving the unity of Canada that faced the Chrétien government the morning after the referendum made attacking the deficit seem simple in comparison. The latter was not rocket science. What had to be done was clear, even if it was not easy. It just required the discipline and political courage to cut government expenditures. By contrast, dealing with the aftermath of the Quebec referendum meant navigating treacherous and uncharted rapids. There were a lot of sharp obstacles and dangerous obstructions, swirling waters and no clear route forward, since no one knew what lay around the sharp bends in the river. Certainly no one would have predicted that within five years the federal government would find itself in calm waters, having reclaimed the initiative in a number of areas, put the separatist movement on the defensive, and – despite the opposition of the government of Quebec, much of the federal Cabinet, the whole Quebec political elite, most political commentators, editorialists, and the majority of the business community – established in the Parliament of Canada a legal framework for judging the legitimacy of both the question and the result of any future Quebec referendum. Nor would anyone have predicted how that would be accomplished because no one knew the way it would work. It would take a mixture of calmness and steadfastness in rough waters, instinct and intuition, and trial and error, with some good management and good luck added to the mix.

Finally, no one would have predicted that after all this had been accomplished, Paul Martin's Liberal government would reignite at least temporarily the separatist movement by a colossal overreaction to unacceptable mismanagement of one government program designed to increase federal visibility in Quebec.

The morning after the referendum the country and the Cabinet were in shock. I remember that the Cabinet met in an atmosphere of gloom and doom, conveying the sense that although we had won, the victory might prove ephemeral. After a lot of handwringing and emotional outpourings around the table with no real sense of direction as to what to do next, another Parizeau bombshell hit us. This time the news was that he had announced his resignation as premier of Quebec. He had wanted to be president of the republic, not premier of a province. Perhaps surprisingly, this news added to the gloomy atmosphere. Everyone took it for granted that his successor would be the popular and charismatic Lucien Bouchard. The question on everyone's mind was whether Bouchard might use his immense popularity to call and win a snap referendum. Chrétien adjourned the Cabinet meeting early, saying we all needed time to think and reflect.

From the beginning, the prime minister himself had been unhappy with the strategy of the No campaign. He had felt unwanted in the referendum campaign until the last week, when it was almost too late. He was convinced that his political instincts, combined with his decades of experience and knowledge of Quebec politics, were far superior to the advice he had reluctantly accepted. So during the long hours while the ballots were being counted, he decided that he would take charge of the post-referendum agenda. He always said that the first duty of a prime minister is to ensure the unity of the country and he was going to assume that responsibility. For better or for worse in the weeks, months, and years ahead, he would act sometimes on advice, solicited and unsolicited, and sometimes all alone. He told me and others many times that he knew he might fail and be forced to give up the prime ministership, but any failure would not be from want of trying. The experience he had in 1980 and his belief in the crucial role of the federal government made him decide to act quickly.

No Help from Mike Harris

THE EVENING AFTER the referendum, the prime minister addressed almost two thousand people at the annual Liberal Party fundraising dinner in Toronto. He did not want to use a prepared text and delivered an emotional speech, in which his determination to act quickly and decisively came through loud and clear. The next morning, Chrétien and I met for breakfast with the premier of Ontario. After the 1980 referendum, we had made the same visit to Queen's Park seeking the support of Premier Bill Davis in a time of national crisis, and he had not failed us. But the current premier, Mike Harris, was no Bill Davis. When Chrétien explained the delicacy of the situation in the country and asked him to work with the federal government to reach out to Quebec and give effect to the general commitments he had made in the Verdun speech less than ten days earlier, the atmosphere in the premier's corner office became almost glacial. The coffee was all that was warm in the room. Harris made it clear that he was not the slightest bit interested in anything other than his agenda for Ontario. The deep concern expressed for the future of the country by all Canadians at the Unity Rally in Montreal (ironically attended by Mike Harris himself less than a week before) was nowhere to be found that day in the office of the premier of Ontario, despite that province's traditional role as a keystone of the federation. Chrétien and I left Queen's Park disappointed and badly shaken.

In the car as we moved south on University Avenue, Chrétien recalled the unacceptable list of constitutional demands prepared by the provincial premiers in 1978 for Pierre Trudeau after the first Parti Québécois election victory and before the first Quebec referendum. We thought back to the federal-provincial conference of September 1980 shortly after the referendum of May 1980 when Newfoundland premier Brian Peckford said that he preferred the Canada of René Lévesque to the Canada of Pierre Trudeau. Now, the meeting with Harris, *provincial* in every sense of the word, was enough for him. Premiers of Ontario had traditionally played a nation-building role in Canada; this time the prime minister of Canada could not count even on the support of Ontario.

Chrétien decided there and then that he was not going to spend much energy on the provincial premiers. It was clear to him that action to meet the unprecedented threat to the country arising from the referendum results would have to come from Ottawa, and directly from himself as prime minister. His actions after the referendum were those only a prime minister has the authority and responsibility to take. He decided on what measures to introduce in Parliament and when to do so; he created a Cabinet committee to make recommendations to him on an action plan for national unity; and he shuffled his Cabinet.

An Assassination and a Break-in

ON THE SATURDAY after the referendum, the world learned of the assassination of Prime Minister Yitzhak Rabin of Israel. Rabin was the first foreign head of government Chrétien received in Ottawa after becoming prime minister, and they had met several times since then. Chrétien was anxious to pay homage to him, and came early that evening to his Parliament Hill office to broadcast a tribute on behalf of the people of Canada. I was waiting for him in the office along with the foreign policy adviser, Jim Bartleman, who had helped draft a statement. Once the prime minister finished delivering his remarks, he asked me to come home with him. "I will leave tomorrow morning for Tel Aviv for Rabin's funeral, and will go from there to New Zealand for the meeting of Commonwealth prime ministers, and then to meetings in Australia, before heading to Indonesia to the APEC heads of government meeting. There are a few things I want to discuss with you about what I want you to do in Ottawa while I am away. Would you come with me now to the house, and then my driver will take you back to pick up your car on Parliament Hill."

We drove back to 24 Sussex at about nine o'clock. We were passing the Foreign Affairs Building on Sussex Drive, close to the prime minister's residence, when Chrétien turned to me and said, "You know, with all the emotion provoked in Quebec by the referendum, I could be next after Rabin."

I realized how emotionally draining the referendum had been for him and simply answered, "Jean, I'm glad that you and Aline will be out of the country for two weeks. It'll be good for both of you." Later, as I was being driven back to pick up my car, I asked the prime minister's RCMP driver, "Did you hear what the PM said? He seems worried about his safety."

"He really doesn't have to worry about his safety," the driver replied. "We give him maximum freedom inside his own house, but are very careful with him when he is outside."

That night I was sleeping very soundly when, for the first and only time in my ten years in the Prime Minister's Office, the telephone rang at three o'clock in the morning, just six hours after my last conversation with Chrétien. It was the PMO switchboard. "The prime minister wants to speak to you." I didn't know if I was dreaming, having a nightmare, or whether my bedside clock had stopped during the night, and it was actually early morning. "I have a problem," he began. He paused and then he said, "Someone has just tried to kill me with a knife." I wondered if I was in a dream or a very bad movie, but realized that I wasn't. After a few nervous words, he said that he would pass the phone to his wife, who would tell me what had happened.

Aline Chrétien, who was calmer, told me that she was wakened by a noise in the house, wondered what it could be as they were alone, and decided to get up to investigate. As she opened their bedroom door, she came face to face with a man with a knife, "who looked like Forrest Gump." She slammed the door shut and locked it. He had broken into the house undetected, and wandered around looking for the master bedroom. If he had made less noise and found the bedroom right away, he would have stabbed the sleeping prime minister. The police guards – fifty metres away – had obviously been asleep. They had heard and seen nothing and, even after being alerted by Madame Chrétien, incredibly took twenty minutes to come into the house and arrest the would-be assassin.

The next morning, the embarrassed RCMP issued a misleading public statement downplaying the seriousness of what had happened and suggesting only that there had been an intruder in the prime minister's residence, that the Chrétiens were unhurt, and that the intruder had been captured. The prime minister was not pleased, to say the least, and told the whole story to the media – including the fact that the intruder was distressed by the loss of the Yes side in the referendum. Chrétien recounted with some relish how, once he was fully awake, he brandished an Inuit carving, ready to club the intruder if he succeeded in opening the bedroom door. The media, and Canadians in general, focused on the Inuit carving, laughed with the cartoonists, and down-played the seriousness of the assassination attempt. I thought back to the evening a few days earlier when Patrick Parisot and I – thinking of the security around 24 Sussex – laughed at Chrétien's comment that he could leave the door unlocked for us because his wife wasn't home.

But Jean Chrétien and his family were more traumatized for a long time afterwards than most people knew by his near-death experience the day after Rabin's assassination, and by the fact that it was a direct result of the referendum. Once, weeks later, when he was dwelling on the assassination attempt to an extent that I thought was getting in the way of dealing with issues, I said, "With due respect, you have to get this behind you. You can't just keep talking about it all the time."

"That's easy for you to say," he retorted. "My wife wakes up in a cold sweat every morning at three o'clock."

Three months later, Chrétien was confronted by a protester at close enough range that the prime minister grabbed him by the throat and pushed him away, using the now-famous "Shawinigan Handshake." When I came over to 24 Sussex at the end of that day for a previously scheduled meeting, Chrétien was still upset by what had happened – as he would be for a long time to come – and invited me to stay for dinner with him and his wife. At one point when he left the dining room for a moment, Aline leaned forward and asked me, "Eddie, do you think someone will kill Jean some day?" It was a sober reminder to me that heads of government have families, and feelings like the rest of us, and are affected by them, just as anyone outside of public life would be.

Chapter 14

NEW BLOOD IN CABINET

"We have to realize that Canada is not immortal; but if it has to go, let it go with a bang rather than a whimper."
– PIERRE ELLIOTT TRUDEAU, 1988

Chrétien wanted to give effect as soon as possible to the under-takings he had made to Quebeckers in his Verdun speech in the week before the referendum. Before Christmas 1995, he introduced a resolution in the House of Commons on the distinctiveness of Quebec society. And he introduced legislation providing a veto for each region of Canada, including Quebec, on future constitutional change, to fulfill his referendum promise that in the future there could be no con-stitutional change without the consent of Quebec.

The legislation on constitutional vetoes created an uproar in British Columbia, which the prime minister did not anticipate, and which he handled badly. In this case, his grasp of history and too much institu-tional memory – which sometimes can be as bad as too little – caused the problem. He remembered that a constitutional conference in Victoria twenty-five years earlier had produced an ephemeral agree-ment on a constitutional amending formula that provided for vetoes for four regions of Canada: the Atlantic, Quebec, Ontario, and the West. He decided to reproduce that formula in his legislation. Chrétien may have remembered that short-lived constitutional agreement; few others did, and even fewer cared twenty-five years later. And it certainly did not persuade British Columbia, which argued that it had grown so much over the course of that quarter-century that it was now entitled to be considered a region of Canada on its own – an argument that touched an emotional chord in that province. Chrétien's historical rationalization left people completely cold.

Soon a storm was raging, with the entire province apparently furious with him. Alienating British Columbia or any other province was the last thing we needed as we were trying to reach out to Quebec. Much of the Cabinet, particularly the most politically astute ministers, and the whole British Columbia Liberal caucus, were pleading for a change. I walked out of a Cabinet committee meeting one morning with the mandate from a number of senior ministers – Brian Tobin, in particular – to go down the short corridor to the prime minister's office and tell him immediately that his colleagues wanted him to change his mind. I fully agreed with the message and told Chrétien exactly that. Chrétien was legendary for his stubbornness when he thought he was right, and he never liked to admit mistakes on anything. But this time he was particularly reluctant to be forced to make a change to one of his first post-referendum actions. He argued that there would be no end to pressure for more amendments once he agreed to make even one, and so he would not agree to anything that would set in place a process that could – at least in his mind – eventually derail the legislation entirely. It took less than thirty seconds for him to tell me to report back to his colleagues in the Cabinet room that he was not going to change his mind. I dutifully went back and reported to the Cabinet committee. Their response to my message was as blunt as his response to theirs. For a while, I was afraid that the only thing both the prime minister and the ministers would agree on that morning would be to shoot the messenger.

It is always hard for prime ministers to admit mistakes and backtrack. They don't like the inevitable accusations of flip-flopping. And, of course, pride too often gets in the way, despite the fact that the rest of us – who all make mistakes in our daily lives and in our workplaces

– often find an admission of error from leaders, and a willingness to correct it, to be refreshing. In this case, Chrétien soon relearned the lessons about the need to listen and to compromise where necessary whenever the Constitution in any form is affected, lessons that he had first learned from 1980 to 1982, and that he himself had served to Mulroney at the time of Meech Lake. While it did not take long for his stubbornness to give way to the irresistible pressure, it still took longer than it should have for him to agree to make changes. The whole affair left an unpleasant aftertaste in the mouths of British Columbians. Still, despite the problems in British Columbia, the actions in Parliament including passage of the resolution on the distinct society and the amended legislation on constitutional vetoes allowed Chrétien to argue to Quebeckers that he was delivering on the promises of the speech he made in Verdun before the referendum.

A Cabinet Shuffle

THE HOUSE OF Commons agenda was only one element of the prime minister's plans after the referendum. He also decided on a dramatic change to his Cabinet. Chrétien did not believe in undertaking Cabinet shuffles simply to create news. He had learned that unless the operation of the government requires a change in the Cabinet, shuffles are usually one-day media stories with no lasting public impact. On the other hand, he knew that all too often they can be politically and administratively counter-productive.

Cabinet shuffles are always difficult for a prime minister, and involve tough decisions that he cannot delegate or share with his colleagues. A prime minister begins the process of a shuffle knowing that it is rare for a minister to want to leave Cabinet. He also knows that it is equally rare to find a backbench member of Parliament who does not want to go into Cabinet, or who does not believe that he or she is better than any of the current ministers, and who will not be extremely disappointed if passed over. Furthermore, any shuffle involves a certain amount of musical chairs, and while moving ministers sometimes can give a useful burst of energy to a government, moving those who are doing a good job in their departments can be disruptive. Bringing in new ministers between elections from outside the caucus is even more of a gamble. Not only does it create jealousies among MPs who believe they are entitled to first consideration for Cabinet jobs, but those who have never been in Parliament before and have not been active in politics are not always successful.

The immediate post-referendum period was not a time of business as usual, however, and Chrétien was determined to act boldly. He appointed two new ministers from Quebec from outside Parliament to strengthen Quebec's representation and to give new focus to the promotion of federalism in Quebec. He did so knowing full well that prime ministers in the past have not always been successful in recruiting outsiders to the Cabinet. To defuse a crisis over conscription in 1945, Mackenzie King in a bold move appointed Chief of the Defence Staff General Andrew McNaughton as minister of defence; McNaughton was immediately defeated in the by-election that was called to bring him into Parliament and had to resign. In 1975, Pierre Trudeau named his old friend Pierre Juneau to the Cabinet to replace Gérard Pelletier, who was retiring as minister of communications; Juneau was promptly defeated in a by-election in Pelletier's seat and also had to resign. Brian Mulroney's recruitment into his Cabinet of his lifelong friend Lucien Bouchard turned out to be less than a roaring success when Bouchard two years later abandoned the Tories to create the Bloc Québécois.

Chrétien was prepared to take a chance. He had been particularly impressed by what he knew about a Quebec academic, Stéphane Dion, a professor of political science at the University of Montreal. Dion was a frequent commentator on French television during the referendum campaign. His analysis was incisive and his criticism of the logic behind the separatist approach was extremely powerful and very welcome to Chrétien. So, unbeknownst to anyone on his own staff, including Jean Pelletier and myself, Chrétien called Dion in December 1995 and invited him to meet one Saturday at 24 Sussex. They had several long discussions before the prime minister, still without telling anyone on his staff, invited him to join the federal Cabinet as minister of intergovernmental affairs, with particular responsibility for making the case for Canada in Quebec. Dion was to play a major role in the rest of the Chrétien administration.

Some History with the Dion Family

IT MUST HAVE been awkward for Jean Chrétien to approach Dion, and awkward for Dion to accept, for reasons that went back two decades. Dion's father was a leading Quebec intellectual, a professor of political science at Laval University, and was well known as the Quebec nationalist who had coined the phrase that Quebec needed "to keep a knife to Ottawa's throat." In 1976, Professor Leon Dion had made a speech arguing that because French Canadians had been discriminated against in the past in the public service of Canada, to compensate for this in the future, half of the federal public service should be French Canadian. At the time, Chrétien was president of the Treasury Board with responsibility for official language policy in the government of Canada. He feared that Professor Dion's speech would create a damaging public controversy, and provoke a backlash in English-speaking Canada against existing government policies promoting the French language and the participation of French-speaking Canadians in the federal public service. Therefore, Chrétien took the opportunity of an invitation to speak at Laval University, his own alma mater, to confront Leon Dion head-on.

At the time, I was a young assistant just out of university who enjoyed the opportunity of writing something provocative. I later learned there are sometimes great lines – which give the writer and the speaker enormous private satisfaction – that belong in the first draft of a speech but that are best left out of the final version. At the time I was too young to think that way. I convinced my boss to end his speech with a quote from George Bernard Shaw, "Those who can, do; those who cannot, teach." And then to add, "Professor Dion teaches."

Needless to say, Leon Dion was furious and wrote a lengthy and virulent attack on Chrétien, which was published in all of the newspapers in Quebec. No one, least of all Chrétien or me, ever expected then that twenty years later Chrétien would be prime minister of Canada and that he would invite Leon Dion's son to be the federal minister whose principal responsibility would be to take on the separatists. Fortunately, time heals most wounds and Leon Dion, to his great credit, encouraged his son to accept the prime minister's offer and was extremely proud to see him sworn into the federal cabinet.

Not a Conventional Minister

JUST AFTER NEW Year's in January 1996, the prime minister was leaving Ottawa for a two-week Team Canada trade mission to India and Pakistan. Chrétien asked me to stay behind to work on a number of Quebec-related issues. He told me of his intention to appoint Stéphane Dion to the Cabinet, and asked me to meet with him. I telephoned Dion and introduced myself. I said that I had often seen him on television and was impressed by his arguments. I did not mention the speech at Laval University and hoped that he wouldn't mention it to me, but in order to establish some bond, I did tell him that his father and my father had been friends and that when I was much younger, I had met his father many times at our home in Montreal. Dion replied, "I have also heard of you. Apparently you are an unreconstructed Trudeauite, a centralist, and completely inflexible."

I was taken aback but suggested that it might be a good idea for us to meet, and for him to be able to judge for himself that I was actually much more reasonable than he had been led to believe. When I put the phone down, the last thing on my mind was the famous line in the movie *Casablanca*: "This is the beginning of a beautiful friendship." But it actually turned out to be so over the next eight years.

We agreed to meet in Ottawa on a Sunday evening. He told me that he would arrive around seven o'clock and would call me at home when he got into town. We would go to a restaurant for dinner where we could have a quiet discussion. I was unsure whether to put on a tie and jacket to meet the prospective Cabinet minister or to dress casually. The telephone rang about fifteen minutes before seven o'clock. Dion was on the line: "The bus from Montreal has arrived early and I am at the bus station." I picked him up; he was wearing jeans and carrying the backpack he would later bring into the House of Commons. I was glad I hadn't put on a tie. Obviously, this would not be a conventional minister in many ways, even though he would soon have a government car and driver. We had a long, pleasant, and fascinating dinner.

I was struck by his deep commitment to principle, his sense of duty, and his absolute certainty about what had to be done. But I was equally struck, as well, by the naïveté of an academic who specialized in government, taught courses about it, and yet knew very little about how government actually works. The principle of Cabinet solidarity and the need to build alliances among Cabinet colleagues for what he wanted to accomplish seemed totally foreign to him. After all, he had a mandate from the prime minister, and surely that was good enough. What, I wondered, did he teach at university?

The prime minister telephoned me from Asia late that night to ask me how dinner had gone. I said, "Your choice will either be a spectacular success or a spectacular failure, and nothing in between. I cannot predict which it will be." (And I definitely would not have predicted that ten years later, at the time of publication of this book, that Dion would be a serious contender for the leadership of the Liberal Party.) I was still not sure a few months after Dion joined the Cabinet, when he complained to me bitterly one day that one of his Ontario colleagues did not understand a particular issue about Quebec. "Tell me, what's wrong with the minister of trade? I can't get anything through his head. And by the way, what is his name?"

"Art Eggleton," I informed him.

"Oh yes, I forgot."

Yet within a few years, no one had better learned the system of Cabinet government, no one knew better how to build alliances within the Cabinet, and no minister was more respected by his colleagues. No minister was better prepared for Cabinet discussions on a wide variety of issues far beyond national unity, so that when Stéphane

Dion spoke, his colleagues put down their coffees, stopped signing correspondence, and listened attentively. He had learned a lot about government, a lot about politics, and a lot about how to get things done. And he was recognized by even his fiercest adversaries as the perfect example for those who go into politics for principle, who serve selflessly, and who are prepared to take a lot of slings and arrows for doing what they think is right.

Dion remembered that when Pearson decided to invite the Quebec trade union leader Jean Marchand to run as a Liberal candidate in 1965, Marchand did not want to come into federal politics alone and insisted that Pearson also recruit Pierre Trudeau and Gérard Pelletier. Thirty years later, Dion said that he, too, did not want to come into politics alone and urged Chrétien to invite his friend, Pierre Pettigrew, to join the Cabinet as well. Pettigrew had served before as an executive assistant to André Ouellet in the 1970s, had been executive assistant to Claude Ryan when he was leader of the Liberal Party in Quebec, and was working as an international trade consultant at the time of the referendum. He had once run and been defeated as a federal Liberal candidate. The prime minister quickly agreed to recruit Pettigrew as well.

The day before they were sworn into the Cabinet, Dion and Pettigrew met with Jean Pelletier and myself in a small conference room beside Pelletier's office. We were there to tell them that the prime minister had identified constituencies for them. Shirley Maheu, the MP for the riding of Saint-Laurent–Cartierville in northwest Montreal, would be appointed to the Senate, and Dion would be designated the Liberal candidate in a by-election in that riding. André Ouellet was to leave the Cabinet and the House of Commons, and Pettigrew would run in his former boss's riding of Papineau–Saint-Michel in the northeast of Montreal. Dion, who knew nothing about the political landscape, asked where the riding of Saint-Laurent was. Pettigrew was much more political and knew that in the 1993 election, Maheu had won with a huge majority, while Ouellet had won a close race. He said, "Stéphane, if you want to know where Saint-Laurent is, just look on the map for the safest Liberal seat in the country. If you want to trade with me, I don't mind!"

On January 25, 1996, Pettigrew was sworn into the Cabinet as minister of international co-operation and Dion as president of the Privy Council and minister of intergovernmental affairs. Chrétien's plan for the Clarity Act was taking shape with Dion, the key man, in place.

The Massé Committee – An Action Plan

MARCEL MASSÉ WAS one of the "star" candidates Chrétien had recruited in 1993; he had previously served as a deputy minister in the most important departments of the government and entered the Cabinet in 1993 as minister of intergovernmental affairs. The prime minister had a high regard for him and used his abilities wherever they could be most helpful to the government. For example, in the fall of 1994, Chrétien, who preferred to use special committees rather than permanent Cabinet committees to address the most important issues facing the government, created the Program Review Committee of Cabinet, and asked Massé to chair it. Its role was to review all government expenditures and make the recommendations for the drastic cuts that were incorporated in Paul Martin's seminal budget of February 1995. The work of the Massé Committee was the first step towards the restoration of the fiscal health of the federal government. Massé's role after the referendum would be even more important. Chrétien turned to him to chair an ad hoc Cabinet committee of the most senior ministers from different parts of the country to make recommendations on an action plan to restore the unity of the country.

I sat on the committee as a representative of the Prime Minister's Office and was able to keep the prime minister informed of progress and of any problems, and eventually helped Massé draft his report, which he presented to the prime minister at the beginning of February 1996, at which time the committee was disbanded. Dion, on joining the Cabinet, had immediately become a member of the committee, but at a time when it was about to terminate its work. He made a number of useful interventions in its final deliberations, but had not been there long enough to play a major role in its recommendations. He agreed with the tenor of the report but would have liked to see more specific suggestions, and would play the key role in taking its general recommendations and turning them into bold action in the coming years.

There were three different elements to the recommendations of the Massé Committee. The first was a salutary reminder that an overall good government agenda in areas that have nothing to do with traditional national unity issues was, as always, essential for Quebeckers, to give them a sense of belonging to a country that works well. This also served, as a by-product, to give a sense of purpose to other ministers by showing them that their own agendas, whether economic, social, or foreign, could contribute directly to national unity. For example, Canada's leading role (largely as a result of the work of the Prime Minister and Foreign Minister Lloyd Axworthy) in achieving an international land mines treaty in 1997 created a real sense of pride in Quebec about being part of Canada. Yet Axworthy was not consciously promoting national unity when he was doing his work as foreign minister. Similarly, the decisions of Prime Minister Chrétien in 2002 to ratify the Kyoto Accord, and in 2003 not to go to war in Iraq, made Quebeckers proud to be Canadian.

The second element of the Massé Report touched on certain areas of jurisdiction where federal involvement was not necessary. It recommended that the federal government withdraw from its already-limited activities in a few areas such as mining and forestry. The recommendations were a relic of provisions in the failed Charlottetown Accord of 1992 and were, in my view, important only to those federal government officials who had spent time working on that deal and who had not yet got over its failure. It provided some fodder for speeches that few Canadians would actually listen to about the modernization of the country through the rebalancing of roles and responsibilities of both levels of government, and so on and so forth. None of it – except for labour market training – made much of a practical difference in the everyday lives of Canadian citizens.

Labour Market Training Was Different

JURISDICTION OVER labour market training had become symbolically important in Quebec. The federal government played a role in the area through its jurisdiction over unemployment insurance, and was spending considerable amounts of money to provide training for unemployed workers. In this case, Quebec made an argument that the federal role in training created duplication and precluded it from having its own seamless social policies. The issue became one of those all too frequent symbolic tests of whether Canadian federalism can adapt to the perceived needs of Quebeckers. The symbolism was far more important than the substance. In practice, studies showed that neither level of government performed well in that area, and most of the federal role was simply to issue cheques to pay for training that was provided by the private sector or in courses given by provincially run community colleges. Massé nevertheless recommended that we should hand over labour market training to Quebec. His Quebec colleagues in the Cabinet embraced the recommendation enthusiastically because they wanted to demonstrate to Quebeckers that their needs can be accommodated in Canada.

But it was not only a Quebec issue. Members of Parliament from Ontario, where the Liberals held all but one of the seats, did not want to see any weakening, real or symbolic, in the role the federal government plays in the country. They were involved in announcements of training grants and subsidies in their ridings, and they did not want to lose visibility with their electors. They knew that Chrétien opposed any special status for Quebec, and would treat all provinces equally. So they were vehemently against any Quebec-inspired precedent that would entail the federal government giving up a direct federal connection to citizens of Ontario and transferring jurisdiction and financial resources to their political enemy, the despised Harris government.

Chrétien had to decide how to handle this political hot potato at a time when Bouchard had just become premier of Quebec. He wanted to halt Bouchard's momentum by making sure that he did not have an issue to exploit as an excuse to call either an early election or an early referendum, or both. So Chrétien agreed to negotiate a transfer of jurisdiction to individual provinces. The negotiations started with Quebec and were successful, and at least removed one argument from the separatists. That was Step One. In Step Two, the prime minister allowed discussions to start with Ontario, but to placate the powerful Ontario caucus he told his negotiators to drag on negotiations indefinitely. Harris played right into his hands by making demands that would have been hard to accept in any circumstances. Eight years later, when Jean Chrétien left office, there were agreements on the delegation of manpower training reached with most other provinces, but to the relief of federal Liberal members from Ontario, somehow there was still no deal with the Government of Ontario, although there was a semblance of an offer on the table!

The Federal Presence in Quebec

THE THIRD PART of the Massé Committee recommendations dealt with promoting Quebeckers' attachment to Canada. This involved combatting separatist myths, supporting federalist spokespersons in Quebec, coordinating federal communications activities, as well as generally increasing the federal government's presence in Quebec.

In the years that followed, the government acted in a concerted manner on all of these recommendations. One part of the federal strategy was to be as visible in promoting attachment to Canada as the Parti Québécois government was in promoting attachment to Quebec. During and after the referendum campaign of 1980, Chrétien was a strong proponent of federal visibility in Quebec. He deplored its absence during the years of the Mulroney government and watched with growing concern as the Quebec government filled the vacuum. He believed that Quebeckers needed to be more aware of the role of the government of Canada in their lives. After the referendum of 1995, Chrétien expected the federal government to counter the subliminal messaging of the provincial government, whether through radio and television advertising, billboards, or by sponsoring community events.

Federal sponsorship of community events was therefore something that was important to the prime minister as part of a multi-pronged overall Quebec strategy.

Sponsorship

THE PURPOSE OF the now infamous sponsorship program was a legitimate desire to counter the separatists by increasing federal visibility in Quebec.

The cost of the program – administered by the Department of Public Works and Government Services – was some $50 million a year, which is a substantial amount of money in absolute terms, but is relatively small in the context of a department with thousands of employees, that manages over 80,000 contracts a year, and is responsible for billions of dollars of expenditures annually. The size and scope of that department makes it hard to discover immediately any abuse and fraud, otherwise the problems with the sponsorship program would have come to light much earlier. The abuse that occurred was eventually uncovered as a result of an internal audit (which is the way government departments discover irregularities in their management processes). When evidence of wrongdoing was uncovered and brought to his attention, Chrétien immediately ordered that it be referred to the Auditor General and the RCMP.

The fact that the prime minister was known to want urgent action to increase federal visibility in Quebec, and that the minister of public works was also the political minister for Quebec (which was and is a mistake) was taken as an opportunity by a few fraud artists to line their own pockets. They hoped that by promising to deliver the quick results the government wanted they would not be carefully scrutinized. And with what tuned out to be the criminal connivance of a senior public servant (Charles Guité) in the Department of Public Works who had the authority to issue contracts and sign off on accounts, they defrauded the Canadian taxpayer. The sponsorship program was unconscionably abused. According to the Auditor General, "All the rules in the book were broken."

When the new prime minister, Paul Martin, received the final report of the Auditor General in February 2004, he might have taken the approach simply of referring everything to the RCMP – as Chrétien had done – in the knowledge that justice would be done, and wrong-doers charged, and tried. (Which is exactly what happened. By June 2006, two advertising agency executives and Charles Guité had been sentenced to prison terms.) Instead, Martin decided in February 2004 that it would be in his political interests to separate himself from his predecessor by highlighting what in fact was an isolated case of un-acceptable greed, abuse, and wrongdoing by a few officials in govern-ment, a few advertising agency executives, and a few Liberal Party organizers in Quebec, all acting on their own behalf and in their own interests. He made speeches saying that the Liberal Party in Quebec was full of "cronyism and corruption," and then asked Quebeckers to vote Liberal because (after sixteen years as a Liberal MP and nine years as the most important member of the Cabinet) he was, of course, dif-ferent from all the others!

Martin appointed a Commission of Inquiry headed by Justice John Gomery to investigate what had gone wrong. Gomery examined under a microscope – and in full public view, to the delight of the media – the fraud that had already been referred by Chrétien to the police. In my view, Gomery might have reported accurately and undramatically that, human nature being what it is, there are always a few people in large organizations – public and private (including political parties) – who abuse positions of trust for their own financial gain. They should be caught – as they were by the routine internal audit – and then pun-ished (as they have been). Instead, while Gomery eventually found that the mismanagement in the Department of Public Works "was an aberration," the sensationalism surrounding the inquiry – and the incendiary language in the report – was such as to gravely damage public respect for the institution of government itself, and the cause of federalism in Quebec.

Nevertheless, governments have to take responsibility for what goes wrong in their administrations if they want to take credit for what goes right. Even though the day-to-day administration of the sponsorship program was not his responsibility or that of the PMO, and was far from his daily preoccupations, the mismanagement of the sponsorship program is a liability that must attach to the record of the Chrétien government.

I wish the sponsorship program – which had been created for good reasons in the aftermath of the Quebec referendum – had not gone so terribly wrong. But the media in Canada – which is essential in a democratic system – has its own responsibility to engage in some careful thinking and self-examination about the consequences of how it reports and interprets events. Ever since the abuses of the Nixon Administration in the United States were uncovered by the famous *Washington Post* reporters Bob Woodward and Carl Bernstein, media around the world have tried to find their own Watergates. The unfortunate by-product of that search – particularly where real Watergates don't exist – is the creation of understandable but unwarranted public cynicism about democracy and institutions of government. Cases of administrative mistakes that inevitably occur in large organizations are immediately described in the media as "scandals," rather than human error. When cases of fraud by a handful of unscrupulous individuals come to light (and the culprits are caught), the concept of individual responsibility is put aside, and much of the media covers the case as though corruption permeates whole governments and entire political (and sometimes corporate) cultures. The problems with the sponsorship program were, in my opinion, sensationalized out of all proportion, thereby casting discredit on the more than 99.9 per cent of Canadian politicians and public servants who are dedicated, hard-working, and honest.

Chapter 15

THE CLARITY ACT

"I see but one rule: to be clear. If I am not clear, all my world crumbles to nothing."

– STENDAHL

The question put to Quebeckers on October 30, 1995, was not: "Are you in favour of Quebec becoming an independent country?" It was:

> Do you agree that Quebec should become sovereign after having made a formal offer to Canada for a new economic and political partnership within the scope of the bill respecting the future of Quebec and of the agreement signed on June 12, 1995, Yes or No?

Quebec voters might have been forgiven for presuming that the agreement of June 12, 1995, was a solemn agreement with Canada when in fact it actually referred to an agreement between the Parti Québécois, the Bloc Québécois, and the Action Démocratique. Polling after the referendum found that 60 per cent of those who voted Yes expected to remain as part of Canada if their preferred option had won. Yet Parizeau, as he has since admitted, would have interpreted the narrowest majority in favour of the ambiguous question that was on the referendum ballot as a mandate to proceed full steam ahead to achieve the independence of Quebec.

Chrétien was determined to see that this could never happen again. Ever since the 1980 referendum, he had been wrestling with the issue of the legitimacy of a Yes response to an ambiguous question as well as with the issue of what margin of victory should be required to break up a country. Chrétien decided after the 1995 referendum to impose clear rules for the future.

Chrétien and Dion

CHRÉTIEN'S STYLE OF governing was to give overall direction on major issues, ensure that his ministers knew his priorities, and then leave them to do their jobs as they saw fit. It was rare that he would spend any time with individual ministers on the details of their work. Contrary to the belief that he was, in Jeffrey Simpson's phrase, a "friendly dictator," he gave his ministers a great deal of latitude, so much so that sometimes when his own staff raised with him their disagreement with what a particular minister was doing or not doing about a file, his response, to our great frustration, would invariably be that unless the issue was fundamental to the government, neither the prime minister nor the Prime Minister's Office should get involved. "Let them do their job. If they don't do it well, I'll shuffle them or fire them from Cabinet, but don't micro-manage them." His relationship with his ministers was extremely professional. While he personally felt closer to some than to others, he made a point of saying that a prime minister must not be friends with any of his ministers, because he must never forget that he might have to fire one at any time.

Stéphane Dion was the exception to the rule. Dion worked more closely with Chrétien than any other minister ever did. They worked together shoulder to shoulder to combat separatist myths and to establish the rules of the game in case of another Quebec referendum. Dion was bull-headed. He had come into federal politics to do a job. He was going to do it, and damn the torpedoes. He did not care how unpopular he would be with the separatists, and some editorial writers, and he never guessed how popular he would be with political cartoonists, even if they were sometimes cruel in return. While other Cabinet ministers rarely had one-on-one meetings with the prime minister, Dion and Chrétien spent a lot of time together in person and on the telephone. They looked at details in documents that were often written by Dion himself. One of Dion's deputy ministers once said to me, only partly in jest, "In the past, I usually prepared three or four drafts of a document before I was ready to give it to my minister, who would then give me his comments. Stéphane Dion prepares three or four drafts himself and then asks me for my comments!"

Dion and Chrétien were very much the odd couple. One was an academic, intellectually rigorous, the antithesis of a typical politician, always focused on all the details of an issue, extremely serious, and with a sense of humour that he rarely brought to the office. Dion acted as though the weight of the world was on his shoulders twenty-four hours a day. George Anderson, Dion's deputy minister, once asked him, "Until what time can I call you tonight?"

Dion's reply was, "The state never sleeps."

Anderson feared that his minister was not entirely joking and told him, "The state may not sleep, but the deputy minister goes to bed at eleven o'clock."

Chrétien took himself a lot less seriously than he took his responsibilities. He might have had the weight of the whole government on his shoulders, but he always tried not to show it. He was wary of losing sight of the forest for the trees. Details, he believed, were for ministers and officials, not for prime ministers; he would focus on the big picture. He always tried to put people at ease in his office by beginning a meeting with some stories and some humour. The first time Chrétien tried to do that with his new minister, Dion's stern response was, "Prime minister, this is a serious matter and we do not have time for joking around."

No other minister would have dared to say something like that to a prime minister. But Dion could get away with it.

Soon, the two formed a very close relationship, almost one of father and son. When Jean Chrétien became prime minister, he told me that he would do what Trudeau had done, and reserve for family any invitations to the beautiful rustic summer residence of prime ministers at Harrington Lake in the Gatineau Hills. It became a place where he could relax and reflect, fish, or walk in the woods and watch the sun set over the private lake. Unlike 24 Sussex Drive, which was almost an extension of the office and where he held meetings almost every day, there were to be no meetings at Harrington Lake. It was only on the rarest occasion that a non-family member or a minister would be invited for a meal (I was there twice in ten years). The one exception was Stéphane Dion, who almost became family. He would be invited alone to spend afternoons and evenings at Harrington Lake to discuss plans for avoiding, if possible, and dealing, if necessary, with a future Quebec referendum. Chrétien, who had his own scars from decades of fighting to keep Quebec in Canada, had tremendous admiration for his new minister's guts and determination in joining the Cabinet in the darkest days, and then in taking on the solidly hostile political class in Quebec and challenging conventional wisdom there.

Towards the Clarity Act

FROM THE TIME Stéphane Dion joined the Cabinet in January 1996 until the passage of the Clarity Act in the spring of 2000, he and Chrétien together took enormous risks in devising and implementing a policy designed to make sure that the legitimacy of a Yes vote in any future Quebec referendum would require a clear question and a clear majority. Their task was much more complicated than the tough budgetary decisions Chrétien and Martin made together. When the minister of finance and the prime minister agree on something, it is rare that the Cabinet will question it; other ministers may not like the decisions, but generally speaking they defer not only to the policy but to the political instincts of the two senior members of the government.

It was very different in the case of Dion and Chrétien. Their colleagues knew that they were both unpopular in Quebec, and often worried that their instincts were wrong and, if followed, could lead to serious difficulties for the government, and even for the country.

Ministers smiled nervously at Dion's obvious naïveté when he said at his first Cabinet meeting that the agenda he was bringing into politics with him would eventually make Jean Chrétien the most popular federal politician in Quebec. In December 2003 when Chrétien left office, the polls showed that Dion had helped to achieve the seemingly impossible.

Most observers would have said that it would require a miracle for the federal government to take on the government of Quebec and the whole Quebec political elite, commentators, editorial writers, and even the business community to establish a framework for judging the legitimacy of any future Quebec referendum. It did not matter to Dion and Chrétien that they were two of the least popular and most vilified politicians in Quebec at the time because they were convinced that Quebeckers would agree with them that the consequences of a referendum have to be crystal clear ahead of time. They fundamentally disagreed with those who held that their approach would fan the flames of separation, and they were prepared to act single-mindedly – and often against the advice and the instincts of much of the Cabinet and many of their advisers.

The context in which they operated was fraught with peril. At the end of January 1996, when he succeeded Jacques Parizeau as leader of the Parti Québécois and premier of Quebec, Lucien Bouchard rode a wave of enthusiasm into office. Not only was he personally popular in the polls, but more ominously for the Chrétien government, the Yes option that had been defeated so narrowly in the October referendum was now considerably ahead in popular support. The federalist forces, if not on the ropes, were at least on the defensive throughout 1996.

It was in this context that Chrétien, Dion, and Justice Minister Rock decided that the federal government should participate in a case that had been brought before the courts of Quebec by the well-known lawyer and former separatist Guy Bertrand to seek clarification about the legitimacy in international law of a unilateral declaration of independence by a province. The Quebec government argued that the courts had no jurisdiction in the matter and threatened all sorts of dire political consequences (including calling a provincial election, followed possibly by another referendum) if the federal government were to get involved in questioning in court the legitimacy of any possible declaration of independence. These threats in the political circumstances of the day made federal ministers from Quebec, other than Dion, very nervous.

Each time, as Chrétien predicted, the threats turned out to be empty rhetoric. Once, Bouchard held a lengthy Cabinet meeting to map out a strategy against Ottawa. The press waited with bated breath outside the room for hours until Bouchard came out to announce to the people of Quebec that he had cancelled a meeting he had originally asked for with the prime minister – no more and no less. It wasn't long before he sheepishly rescheduled the meeting. Chrétien was never impressed by grandstanding by anyone, including Bouchard or any other provincial premier. His response to a threatened election was simple and cutting. "If you call an election, there are two possible outcomes. If you lose, I am better off. If you win, you will be where you are now. I will be where I am now. I will still go to court." There was no election call.

When the Quebec court ruled that it had jurisdiction to hear the case, the government of Quebec refused to participate in any further legal actions about the legitimacy in international law of a unilateral declaration of independence. Chrétien – in one of the most important decisions of his political career – then decided on a move that was bound to infuriate the Bouchard government. At the end of September 1996, the government of Canada referred a series of questions, in what became known as the "Secession Reference," to the Supreme Court of Canada, to get a judicial determination on what is required in Canadian and international law to recognize the legality of the separation of a province from the rest of Canada. Bouchard protested the federal action, but did nothing about it.

Throughout 1997, Dion continued to press the federal case for clarity with a series of highly publicized, sharply worded, and rigorously logically argued letters to the premier of Quebec, the deputy premier, and the minister of intergovernmental affairs. Dion's letters won grudging respect in Quebec, and enthusiastic support in the rest of Canada (as well as in the Cabinet and the Liberal caucus) for finally taking the offensive against the separatists.

In August 1998, the Supreme Court of Canada held in the Secession Reference that there would be an obligation on the part of the federal government to enter into a negotiation about separation with a province only if a referendum had resulted in a clear majority in favour of a clear question, that such a negotiation would have to be in accordance with Canadian constitutional law, and that an attempt at unilateral secession by a province on the basis of an ambiguous question and an uncertain majority would be illegal, unconstitutional, and contrary to international law. The court set out very difficult and clear requirements that must be followed if ever the country were to be divided, and left it up to the political actors to determine what constitutes a clear majority and a clear question.

The Secession Reference served to illustrate the prime minister's style. The decision to go to court was a crucial strategic decision for the government and one that only a prime minister can finally make. It was strongly advocated by Stéphane Dion and by Justice Minister Allan Rock. It was opposed by many ministers, while others nervously sat on the fence. Chrétien listened to all the arguments, and decided to go to court. Then he left the rest to Dion and to the justice minister, so much so that when Rock one day asked to see the prime minister to take him through the final draft of the written arguments the federal government would submit to the court, the meeting (which I attended) was short. Chrétien said, "Allan, you are the minister with responsibility for preparing the case. I have confidence in you. If you and Stéphane are satisfied with it, go ahead. I don't have to go through the factum with you." Rock knew, like other ministers, that he had better do his job well, because he would be held accountable.

This incident helped me to answer a question Pierre Pettigrew put to me when we were sitting together on an airplane one day. "Who works harder, a minister or a prime minister?"

"It depends on what you mean by 'harder,'" I said. "Is it 'harder' work to decide to go to the Supreme Court of Canada with the Secession Reference with all the consequences the decision might imply for the country and the future of the government, or is it 'harder' work to spend many hours, days, and weeks on preparing a factum to be submitted to the court to set out the federal case? Ministers may work more hours, if that is what you mean by 'harder,' but a prime minister has infinitely more responsibility. He should spend fewer hours on paperwork and in meetings than ministers do, and more hours reflecting on how to handle the most important issues."

It was not long after the Supreme Court decision that the prime minister told Dion that he had decided to enshrine in law the principles enunciated by the court. In the greatest of secrecy, he instructed Dion to prepare draft legislation that would codify how the federal government would react in the case of a referendum on the separation of a province, what type of question would be considered legitimate, and what type of majority would be considered sufficient. Chrétien did not want any leaks of his intentions until the legislation was ready. The only ones in the government who were aware that this initiative was being planned and who participated in the initial drafting of possible legislation were Jean Pelletier, Patrick Parisot, and myself in the PMO, a few officials in the Privy Council Office, and George Anderson and a few other officials in Dion's ministry of intergovernmental affairs. By the fall of 1999, the preliminary work had been done, and the prime minister was ready to move forward. In November 1999, he began to foreshadow publicly what he wanted to do, in speeches he delivered in Halifax, St. John's, and Hull.

In Search of Clarity

FROM THE BEGINNING, Chrétien met with a great deal of resistance from ministers and advisers. None was opposed to the principle of clarity that the prime minister was so anxious to put into law, but many of his advisers, and I was one of them, were concerned that Chrétien would create a dangerous backlash in Quebec. They argued that it was better to let sleeping dogs lie, particularly since Bouchard had only narrowly won a general election in Quebec in November 1998 with a virtual tie in the popular vote, and had made clear after the election that there would be no early referendum and, in any event, no referendum until he was sure he had "winning conditions." I was among those who worried that the prime minister's confrontational approach might give Bouchard the "winning conditions" he was seeking for the next referendum. Jean Pelletier and Patrick Parisot, who were normally more cautious than me, this time were in full agreement with the prime minister's instincts. They were right and I was wrong.

Chrétien did not come to his decision lightly. He spent a great deal of time with close confidants talking over all the pros and cons, and a lot of time alone reflecting on what he considered to be the most important decision of his prime ministership. He knew that the stakes were very high, but his instincts told him that Quebeckers wanted to know clearly what a vote in a referendum would mean. On this, Chrétien, the instinctive politician, was joined by Dion, the professor, who prized rationality and logic above all else.

On November 23, 1999, the Cabinet held a two-hour session where, from the start, there was tension in the air. Normally, the Chrétien Cabinet meetings were very businesslike. Sometimes the agenda dealt with matters that were serious at the time they were discussed, but were not necessarily of long-term importance to the government, and were rarely of historical significance for the country. In fact, many important policy initiatives were the product of decisions taken by the prime minister and the minister of finance and then announced in budgets, without Cabinet discussion. This meeting was different, and everyone around the table knew it. Often ministers stand up during meetings and walk over to the table on one side of the room where there is coffee and refreshments. Others occasionally leave for a few minutes to return calls when the item under discussion does not concern them. No one budged from the table at this meeting.

The prime minister dispensed with ordinary business. He said that a decision to introduce legislation to set the rules for determining the legitimacy of a referendum in a province on secession was fundamental for the country. He stressed that he wanted to hear the views of all ministers, but that at the end of the day, he, and only he, would decide. At that point, he reminded ministers of the principle of Cabinet solidarity in support of whatever decision is made and said in a steely tone of voice, "We are all in the same boat and we will all row together or I will find different rowers." Then he turned to Dion to make the case for introducing legislation setting out the principles governing the conduct of a future referendum.

Dion began by acknowledging and then dismissing the concern he had heard about the timing of the initiative. He argued that Canada is a real country (Bouchard had once famously said that Canada is not a "real" country) and that no self-respecting country could accept the process of 1995. "Since 1995," he said, "we have celebrated the country and its values. Our strategy has been clarity, and it works because Quebeckers want to be Canadian. The Supreme Court of Canada says that clarity is for the political actors to determine and therefore it is our responsibility to enact a law that is reasonable, that fully respects the National Assembly of Quebec, that is normative, and is within the framework of the Supreme Court of Canada decision."

He then explained the content of the Clarity Bill he wished to introduce, stressing in particular that the Parliament of Canada would have to be satisfied as to the legitimacy of a referendum question and the clear nature of the majority required before the federal government could enter into any negotiations respecting the secession of a province. Dion noted that obviously the government would need a communications plan, and recognized that there were few immediate allies in the country, but mentioned the respected former premiers of Ontario and Alberta, Bob Rae and Peter Lougheed, as possible supporters. He said that while there were no allies in Quebec political circles, he was confident that the bill would be acceptable to Quebeckers.

The prime minister then sought the views of all the other ministers. "Speak your minds. Say what you believe, not what you think I want to hear." Almost every minister spoke, each from the heart and each candidly. Paul Martin, for example, began by saying that he believed that the principles made enormous sense and he supported them. Then, however, he shifted away from implementing them. His view was that the principles are really subject to political, not legal, interpretation. Therefore, he said that a law is not necessary and could be replaced by a prime ministerial declaration. Then he voiced concern about the timing even of a prime ministerial declaration, which he thought should not take place until after the Parti Québécois convention scheduled for the spring of 2000 so as not to provoke a possible backlash from the separatists. Most other ministers also supported the principle of ensuring clarity, but were leery about the mechanism Chrétien and Dion had proposed, and expressed great concern about the possible backlash in Quebec. Only a few ministers supported the legislation right away.

The prime minister summed up by saying that the issue for many ministers seemed to be process more than substance. He said that the advantage of a bill over a prime ministerial declaration is that a bill is much more difficult to repeal. He told his ministers that the easiest thing is to do nothing, and that the timing could never be perfect, but that he had a duty and a responsibility as prime minister and as a political leader. He recognized the advantages of letting sleeping dogs lie, but could not understand why it would be easier to act when the dogs were awake. Finally, he said that he would reflect on the discussion and decide later. In the meantime, he would tell the press that the Cabinet wants clarity, but that the mechanism is still not decided.

I walked out of the Cabinet room with Stéphane Dion, who had heard what he wanted to hear, which was approval of the principle of ensuring clarity in any future referendum. He dismissed the arguments about process as irrelevant. So, bull-headed as only he could be, Dion said to me, "Everyone agrees with the substance, the prime minister can deal with the politics, so the bill should be introduced in the House of Commons the day after tomorrow." To his genuine surprise, I replied that it would not be that easy, because there was no Cabinet consensus to move forward quickly. We went back to the prime minister's office along with Jean Pelletier, who also was a great proponent of moving ahead with legislation, but who understood that the formidable resistance in the Cabinet needed political management.

The prime minister had made up his mind. He told us that he wanted legislation, but that he recognized some additional work had to be done to bring more of the Cabinet on side. He decided to create a Cabinet committee to meet over a short period of time to go through a draft bill, make any recommendations for improvement, and, most important, to discuss and recommend how best to handle parliamentary strategy once the legislation was introduced. This was a good plan. Once the ministers on the committee understood that their role was to prepare a bill – and not to discuss whether there should be a bill – they worked quickly on parliamentary strategy. I participated in all the meetings of the committee; my role was to serve as a link between the committee and the prime minister.

Drafting the Bill: A Case Study

IT WAS VITAL that the language of the draft bill accurately reflected the intentions of the prime minister. I discovered that a Cabinet committee trying collectively to draft clarity legislation produced a legal mish-mash. Knowing the aphorism that a camel is the product of a committee trying to design a horse, I invited Allan Rock to come to my house on a Saturday morning to get his private suggestions on the draft bill. Even though by then Rock was minister of health and no longer minister of justice, the prime minister needed the best possible advice, regardless of where it came from. Rock was a member of the Cabinet committee, but what was more important, he possessed a fine legal mind. He gave excellent counsel, which was incorporated into the final bill.

Next, I convened a meeting in my office with the deputy minister of justice, Morris Rosenberg, and his associate deputy and chief draftsperson, Mary Dawson, along with two outside counsel from Montreal, Pierre Bienvenue, who had been one of the federal lawyers in the Secession Reference in the Supreme Court of Canada, and Eric

Maldoff, whom the prime minister had long counted on for advice on the most difficult constitutional matters. We met for several hours; I gave them Rock's comments, and Bienvenue and Maldoff made creative suggestions that had not been thought of earlier. They helped overcome some of Mary Dawson's innate caution, which was typical of many Department of Justice lawyers. Rosenberg was then able to finalize a draft and recommend the bill to the government, as the deputy minister of justice must do with all legislation. The Cabinet committee agreed with the draft and, in turn, recommended it to the prime minister. He asked me who had been consulted and, when I told him about Rock, Bienvenue, and Maldoff, he was satisfied.

The work of the committee was finished two weeks after it began. Then Chrétien brought the issue back to Cabinet. The atmosphere in the room was as electric as two weeks earlier, but now the conclusion was foregone. Discussion was short and to the point. Chrétien began by informing his colleagues that he had made the decision to proceed, and that he had a bill that was ready for introduction in the House of Commons. He said that he knew the risks, but was confident that it was the right thing to do. Then he tried to close the discussion, saying there would be no more debate. Stéphane Dion leaned down the table from his seat well to the right of the prime minister and asked to speak. Chrétien interjected, only half-jokingly, "Stéphane, I have said all that needs to be said – unless you can improve on what I have said." For Dion, the decision to proceed with the Clarity Bill was a moment of triumph. He really wanted to speak and said, "Mr. Prime Minister, I cannot improve on what you have said, but I can add to it." Everyone laughed and he continued for a few minutes. Then the discussion was over.

Chrétien's strategy was to introduce the bill immediately in the House of Commons. To those who wanted him to wait until he could build more public support, he had a ready response. "It is too cold in Montreal in December for demonstrations in the streets against the government. Why should we wait till spring when the weather will once again be conducive to demonstrations?" By the spring of 2000, the Clarity Bill was the law of the land.

Chrétien and Dion had won their gamble. Events soon proved that their instincts were better than those of all the so-called experts. No matter how unpopular the Clarity Act was in some circles, it fundamentally changed the context in which any future referendum could be held. The separatists, to their dismay, could not gather any traction for their opposition to the legislation. In the general election of November 2000, the federal Liberals gained a number of seats from the Bloc Québécois and for the first time in twenty years won more votes than any other party in Quebec. A few months later – and not many years since he had dismissed Stéphane Dion with the comment, "For me, he does not exist," – Lucien Bouchard announced his resignation as premier of Quebec, citing as one of the main reasons his disappointment with the results of the recent federal election.

The Clarity Act and the Supreme Court Reference Case had international ramifications of major significance as well. In 2006, in the face of a possible referendum in Montenegro on independence from Serbia, the European Union cited both the Clarity Act and the Canadian Supreme Court decision in setting a minimum requirement of a clear question and at least a 55 per cent majority of voters in order for the international community to recognize a new state based on the results of a referendum. And significantly for Canada, France – which in 1995 subscribed to a simple majority as sufficient – agreed in 2006 to the new international standard set by the European Union that a more substantial majority of voters is now necessary in international law to recognize the independence of a state that wishes to separate from another country. (On May 21, 2006, the people of Montenegro voted 55.5 per cent in favour of independence from Serbia.)

The Chrétien government had successfully managed the crisis resulting from the Quebec referendum of 1995, and even had an impact internationally. But there were also international crises with impacts on Canada to manage in the future.

Chapter 16

SEPTEMBER 11: "THE WORLD WILL BE A VERY DIFFERENT PLACE"

"There cannot be a crisis next week. My schedule is already full."

– HENRY KISSINGER, 1969

W hen I arrived at 24 Sussex Drive around 8:30 a.m. on September 11, 2001, for a meeting with Lorne Calvert, the new premier of Saskatchewan, crisis management was not a preoccupation for either the prime minister or myself. We had enjoyed a quiet summer. It was less than a year since the last election, and there were no particularly dark political clouds on the horizon. It was only in the very back of my mind that I was conscious of how the former British prime minister Harold MacMillan had responded to a young reporter who asked him what he had most worried about when he was in government. "Events, dear boy, events," said the old man. Little did we know that we were less than an hour away from an event that would shake the world, and have a profound effect on governments everywhere. No one can forget the drama of that day.

The Setting

AT ABOUT 8:45 a.m., Lorne Calvert and his deputy minister, Brent Cotter, arrived for their meeting with the prime minister. It was the first time Calvert had ever been to 24 Sussex Drive and, as his eyes roamed around the house, he was clearly excited to be there. The prime minister welcomed him, offered coffee or freshly squeezed orange juice, and suggested that we go into the living room where we could have a comfortable informal meeting. He asked Calvert how long he planned to be in Ottawa. "As soon as we finish our meeting, we're leaving for the financial district of Manhattan to see the province's bankers," the premier replied. He had actually wanted to meet the prime minister the day before so he could get to New York on the evening of September 10, but had graciously accommodated Jean Chrétien, who had promised Aline that he would take time off that day to celebrate their wedding anniversary. Years later, when I saw Calvert at a dinner party, he told all the guests that he would never forget the date of the Chrétien's wedding anniversary!

The meeting began with an exchange of pleasantries where the prime minister joked that Calvert bore a striking physical resemblance to his famous predecessor, Tommy Douglas. Calvert thanked his host for the compliment; he liked being compared to his political hero. And then he began discussing the lamentable state of the roads in rural Saskatchewan and their harmful effect on grain transportation. It was no surprise to us to discover that Lorne Calvert, like Roy Romanow before him, was seeking more federal money for roads in Saskatchewan. All provincial premiers always ask prime ministers for more federal money, and grain transportation by road and by rail is high on the agenda of all Saskatchewan premiers.

In the middle of this all too familiar discussion, the prime minister's executive assistant, Bruce Hartley, walked into the room to say that television news was reporting that a plane had crashed into the World Trade Center. We continued our meeting, thinking, as many others did, that it was probably an accident involving a small plane. And then Hartley was back, breathless and shaking, with news of the second attack, clearly no accident.

The five of us sat around for a few minutes trying to digest what we had just heard. Then Calvert said, "I am obviously not going to New York, but Brent and I will leave right away because you have a lot to do," and they left. There may have been a lot to do later, but in situations of breaking news involving disasters, leaders of governments – initially at least – don't have any more information than anyone else. Chrétien, Hartley, and I moved down the hall into the prime minister's study, where Hartley had already tuned a television set to CNN. It was quickly apparent to us that the peace and security of the post–Cold War era might have ended in the moments it took for those planes to fly into the Twin Towers in New York.

Early Decisions

LATER THAT MORNING, as the horror sank in, Chrétien said to me in a very quiet voice: "Everything all of us have fought for all our lives may be gone. The world will be a very different place." There were certainly no briefing notes to turn to for advice as to what to do if terrorists hijacked airplanes and flew them into the World Trade Center and the Pentagon. The immediate reaction of a head of government in totally unforeseen and dramatic circumstances is the product of experience, accumulated knowledge, and instinct. He has to hope that what he does will be more right than wrong, but there are no certainties. Chrétien himself always believed that leaders must project an aura of calm in crisis situations. His most immediate challenge was how to deal with unsubstantiated rumours that there might be further attacks, this time perhaps in Canada.

There were quick decisions to make in the next few hours, complicated by the fact that while the first requirement for good decision making is always good information, there was not much of it that morning. We had no facts other than what was on CNN and other media, all of which were trying to grasp the situation. At first, no one knew who the terrorists were, and Chrétien and I were aware that it was vitally important not to jump to hasty conclusions about who was responsible for the attacks. The bombing a few years earlier in Oklahoma City was fresh in everyone's mind because, in that case, initial suspicions of Islamic fundamentalist terrorists had been proven wrong, since the culprit turned out to be a former U.S. Marine by the name of Timothy McVeigh.

The prime minister decided to call General Ray Henault, the chief of the defence staff, hoping he might have more information than CNN. The general was at a conference overseas, and could not immediately be reached. Chrétien then tried both the deputy chief of the defence staff and the commissioner of the RCMP. Neither had any hard information, other than unsubstantiated rumours and speculation on television of more hijacked planes and more attacks. One of the rumours was of attacks on the Capitol Building in Washington, which is situated close to the Canadian embassy. Chrétien immediately called Ambassador Michael Kergin to ask about the safety of the embassy staff, and learned that there had not been any attack on the Capitol.

The prime minister then telephoned Minister of Transport David Collenette to find out what he knew. Collenette informed him that the Americans had closed the airspace over the United States, and that he had immediately agreed to an urgent American request that international flights destined for the United States be diverted to Canada, after which he would be closing Canada's airspace. Chrétien congratulated his minister for his quick action. While Chrétien called Collenette, Margaret Bloodworth, the deputy minister of transport, received a call from Washington from the Federal Aviation Administration (FAA) asking her if she could confirm a rumour that an Air Canada flight with a particular tail number had been hijacked. She had no idea and called Steve Markey, Air Canada's vice-president of public affairs, to see what he knew. Fortunately, he was able to tell her that all Air Canada flights were safe.

At a time when all sorts of rumours were circulating, Collenette had acted quickly and decisively without consulting the prime minister or anyone else. It was the right thing to do. This was a crisis situation where immediate decisions were required. The planes were in the air and they had to land somewhere, and there was no time for consultation, even with the prime minister. Ministers and other government departments – whether the intelligence services, the Department of Defence, the RCMP, the Department of Foreign Affairs, or, for example, the Department of Finance working with the Bank of Canada to avert a liquidity crisis – all sprang into action and did what they had to right away within their own areas of responsibility. On September 11, they acted as quickly as they could, often on their own, knowing that there would be time later to pull the whole apparatus of the government together. I was with the prime minister for most of the day, and focused on what he had to do. It is the part of the story of the unforgettable drama of the day at the centre of the government that I am able to tell because that is the part I know directly, but it leaves out all the other things that were taking place that day elsewhere in the Canadian government, which may have been equally or even more important.

After talking to the minister of transport, Chrétien thought about whether he should call the president of the United States to offer Canada's sympathy and support. He knew other world leaders undoubt-edly were placing such calls, and to reassure their own citizens that they were on top of matters, they were telling their media that they had spoken to President Bush. Always a pragmatist, Chrétien tried to put himself in the president's shoes. He told me that President Bush had far more important things to do in those early hours than to take phone calls of sympathy from those of America's friends who could do nothing more for him than commiserate; he would speak to the president later. Instead, Chrétien tried to call the U.S. ambassador to Canada, but Paul Cellucci was unreachable as he was on a plane between Calgary and Ottawa. Chrétien spoke instead to Steve Kelly, the deputy head of mission in the American embassy, to offer Canada's condolences and any support that our country could give to the United States.

The Parliament Hill Scare

DURING THE COURSE of the morning, the head of the House of Commons security staff, General Gus Cloutier, called the prime minister and told him that there was a car, with a package lying on the front seat, illegally parked on Parliament Hill. Cloutier didn't want to take any chances and recommended the immediate evacuation of the parliamentary precincts. Chrétien had a different reaction. He was skeptical that the package was dangerous and reasoned that if Parliament Hill were shut down, every office building in the country would soon follow, and this type of panicked reaction was not what Canada needed at the time. So he refused to accept Cloutier's recommendation. Fortunately, the car turned out to belong to a tourist who, early in the morning, had found a convenient, if illegal, parking spot. The decision not to evacuate Parliament Hill may seem insignificant in the context of the events of September 11 in the United States, but it serves as an example of a circumstance where decisions have to be made alone by a prime minister, on the basis of experience and instinct, with no time for meetings or consultation, and with the full understanding of where the responsibility would lie, if the decisions turned out to be wrong and resulted in serious harm.

The next day, Chrétien had another similar decision to make. He wanted to find a very public way for Canadians to demonstrate their sympathy for the United States, and liked the idea of holding a massive outdoor rally on Parliament Hill in Ottawa. Security officials told Chrétien in no uncertain terms that it would be far too dangerous in the circumstances to hold an outdoor rally. He disagreed, saying that he didn't want terrorists to dictate our agenda, and rejected the recommendations to stay inside. Three days after the attacks, the prime minister, accompanied by U.S. ambassador Paul Cellucci, the Governor General, and other dignitaries, led a massive outdoor rally of solidarity with the United States on Parliament Hill – televised live in the United States on CNN – where 100,000 people were able to join together in an emotional remembrance ceremony, expressing Canada's commitment to stand shoulder to shoulder with the United States.

Naturally, during the course of the morning of September 11, the PMO press office was deluged with requests for comments by the prime minister. Other world leaders were speaking to their citizens, and the prime minister's director of communications, Francie Ducros, wanted Chrétien to meet the media quickly. But while other leaders had spoken, the world was still waiting for the first comments from President Bush, who understandably took time to get as much intelligence as he could about what had happened before addressing not only his compatriots, but the whole world. Chrétien agreed with my recommendation to wait until Bush had spoken, and asked Ducros to tell the media that he would only comment after the president. He and I talked a little about what he might say, but he told me that he didn't need notes, he would listen carefully to the president and then go to Parliament Hill to meet the media in the foyer of the Centre Block. Shortly after 1:00 p.m., he expressed Canada's horror at what had happened, our sympathy for the victims, and our resolve to defeat the terrorists.

The Following Days

OUR DAILY PMO senior staff meetings had for years been quite routine. They were very different in the days after September 11. The fear of another attack anywhere in the world – and possibly even in Canada – was palpable, and there were unconfirmed rumours, which later turned out to be false, that some of the terrorists had entered the United States from Canada. At the meetings, we talked earnestly about what the prime minister's public profile should be. We knew the importance for Canadians, like citizens of any country, of political leadership in times of crisis. In Great Britain, Tony Blair was going on television several times a day. Should Chrétien do the same in Canada, and, if so, what should he say? Would too many public appearances be regarded as a cynical attempt to get political mileage out of a massive human tragedy? Would too few public appearances be perceived as an abdication of leadership?

While we were there to advise the prime minister, we were as emotionally affected ourselves by the attacks as all Canadians. None of us had the confidence we had in normal circumstances about giving advice as to the best way to handle issues, because in this case there was no apparent right way. Our discussions took much longer than usual and produced options for the prime minister to consider rather than our usual practice of giving him consensus recommendations. Francie Ducros, who two years earlier had succeeded Peter Donolo as director of communications, reported the gist of our discussions to the prime minister, and he decided to make one public appearance a day. Chrétien wanted to walk the fine line between showing enough empathy and understanding, and being accused of using one of the great tragedies of our times for political gain. Right or wrong, it was a carefully considered decision.

Demonstrating empathy in symbolic ways is an important element of political leadership, but is one that is hard to get right. Chrétien was always uncomfortable with public displays of emotion. On the evening of September 11, for instance, he went alone to a blood donor clinic to give blood to be used if needed in New York, because he thought it was the right thing for individuals to do. But he refused to let the PMO press office notify the media of what he was doing until after he was back home because he thought that it would be playing politics to be filmed at the blood donor clinic. In fact, I believe that it would have been seen as an act of leadership and an example for others. Similarly, despite the advice of his senior staff, he didn't want to visit Ground Zero in the days following the attacks, as many other world leaders were doing, because he was uncomfortable with the idea of drawing attention to himself in a place where so many people had recently died. It was only with great reluctance that the prime minister eventually agreed to go to New York. Chrétien could never be the great comforter of his nation like President Bill Clinton in the United States after the Oklahoma City bombing or the shootings of children at the high school in Colombine. Instead, by leaning too far the other way, he created the impression for some of not being caring enough.

Two days after the attacks, Chrétien was the first NATO leader to suggest publicly that, for the first time in the history of the Alliance, Article Five of the NATO Charter, which provides that an attack on one member state is an attack on all member states, should be invoked. Claude Laverdure and Michael Kergin immediately did their job of making sure that the National Security Council and the State

Department in Washington were aware of the remarks Chrétien had made in Ottawa.

But Chrétien was not only thinking about the role of NATO. He reflected on the unconscionable treatment of Japanese Canadians during the Second World War, and the possibility that it could be repeated in another way in 2001, this time with Canadians of Muslim faith as the victims. He wanted to make a strong symbolic public statement to that effect. At a PMO senior staff meeting a few days after the attacks, we decided to recommend to the prime minister that he make a well-publicized visit to a mosque in Ottawa to make clear that the struggle against terrorism was not a struggle against Islam or against Canadians of Arab background. He made that visit a few days later.

Addressing Priorities

THE EVENTS OF September 11 required the government to address with great urgency a number of now vital issues that had not even been on its radar on September 10. While the early rumours that some or all of the terrorists had entered the United States from Canada were not true, many Americans believed them; others were concerned that it could have been the case or, more worrying, that it might be the case in the future. The incident of the "millennium bomber" who was apprehended crossing the border from Canada to the United States in December 1999, where he intended to blow up the Los Angeles airport, took on renewed and expanded importance, and was something of which we were constantly reminded by the Americans. In the days immediately following September 11, border crossing points were clogged and lineups stretched for twenty kilometres as American customs agents carefully and slowly searched all cars and trucks. The largest trading relationship in the world and the economic security of Canada and the United States were at risk. Security had immediately become the single most important focus for the U.S. government. This had particular implications for Canada because of our shared and, for so long, proudly unguarded border. The Canadian government had to put in place – and fast – new ways to deal with our common security issues and to meet legitimate American security preoccupations. Otherwise, we would not be able to ensure the continued free flow of commerce between our countries.

It was clear that crisis management would have to continue for a long time, even if it became somewhat more orderly after the frenetic activity of the first few days. There were huge issues to deal with. Would the need to focus on security require a fundamental change in the management of our common undefended border with the United States? How would that affect overall relations between Canada and the United States? How much new government money would be needed for new security measures, and what effect would that have on other government priorities? How would a focus on security affect Canada's traditional immigration and multiculturalism policies? Chrétien's approach in those circumstances, the issues he reserved for his overall direction, and the ones he delegated to ministers are an illustration of a prime minister's management style, and of the way government works when it is forced by external events beyond its control to suddenly shift direction.

Establishing the Manley Committee
THE PRIME MINISTER wanted the advice of his colleagues in the Cabinet. But he felt that discussions in full Cabinet, with more than thirty people around the table, would be lengthy, inefficient, and likely inconclusive. Just as after the Quebec referendum he created a Cabinet committee of senior ministers to make recommendations on national unity, this time he set up a Cabinet committee to make recommendations on security matters, the Canada-U.S. border, and all other issues directly related to the consequences of September 11.

The stakes for Canada were very high, and Chrétien turned to the minister in whom he had over the years developed the greatest confidence. He had come to admire John Manley for his incisiveness, intellect, good judgment, and ability to deal with complex issues, and often sought his advice on a wide range of issues outside his own departmental responsibilities. Whenever Manley spoke in Cabinet meetings, his arguments often won the day. Chrétien now asked Manley – who had become foreign minister a year earlier, after Lloyd Axworthy's retirement from politics – to take responsibility for dealing with the United States on border issues, and put him in charge of coordinating the government's approach to meeting the myriad policy challenges arising from the events of September 11. As foreign minister, Manley had won the respect of the American administration, because unlike some of his colleagues, he never tried to score political points at home by comments designed to provoke the United States, and he had already established a particularly good working relationship with U.S. Secretary of State Colin Powell.

Chrétien instructed Manley and his colleagues to meet as often as needed, including breakfasts, lunches, and dinners, and to report to him as quickly as possible and as often as necessary. In addition to Manley as chair, the committee was composed of ministers whose departmental responsibilities were most in play, including Finance, Defence, Transport, Justice, the deputy prime minister, the Solicitor General, Immigration, Health, and Revenue. Each minister was accompanied at the meetings by a senior official only when necessary. The secretariat of the committee was staffed by senior Privy Council officials. I attended all the meetings in my capacity as senior policy adviser.

Manley soon asked all relevant departments of government to come before the committee to set out and justify urgent new security spending requirements to Martin so that he could be ready to bring down a budget before Christmas. As a result of the committee's deliberations, the budget of December 2001 provided close to $8 billion of new money for air travel security, intelligence and policing, emergency preparedness, screening of immigrants and refugees, and border infrastructure and security.

In retrospect, the government should have categorized all the new security spending – even though it was not traditional military spending – as "defence spending," rather than as new spending for the Departments of Transport, Immigration, the Solicitor General, and the like, because the enemy is no longer a state or a government, as in the days of the Cold War, but shadowy individuals who could be living anywhere, including in Canada, with the intent of doing damage here at home, or of crossing the border to attack the United States. As such, the needs of national defence against terrorists are different from the traditional measures against conventional armies. By failing to take into account the fundamental change in the meaning of "national defence," we left the door open for traditional defence contractors and the traditional defence establishment to disregard the massive new public security spending and continue to argue that the government was negligent in not increasing the traditional defence budget, which they did, and do, vociferously.

Security at the Expense of Freedom?

THE NEW SECURITY challenge posed by September 11 also raised a fundamental question for Canada and other democracies as to the balance between the needs of security and the protection of civil liberties. The prime minister decided that it was an issue where as head of government, he and only he should set the overall tone, while ministers, and particularly the justice minister, could later fine-tune details in new legislation if necessary. Chrétien was proud of his role in bringing about the Canadian Charter of Rights and Freedoms and did not want September 11 used as a pretext to introduce restrictive policies that were contrary to the values that his government had stood for over a long time. As early as September 13, he asked me to take charge of the preparation of a speech he would give in the House of Commons on September 17, less than a week after the attacks.

The prime minister's instructions were clear. He wanted the speech to address not only the horror of what had happened, and Canada's determination to do its part to ensure that it would not happen again, but also to say that the Canadian government did not believe that secure borders should be closed borders. As a young man, he had been a defence lawyer and was always wary of possibilities of abuse by police forces. Chrétien wanted to sound an alarm about how easy it is in the heat of the moment to put civil liberties and Canada's traditional open immigration and refugee policy at risk. He worried about the pressure for a substantial tightening of immigration policy that was coming from the principal Opposition party in the House of Commons, whether it called itself the Reform Party or, by then, the Canadian Alliance. He did not agree with the view that was being propagated by spokespersons for the business community and editorialists in the right-wing press that to maintain open borders for trade between Canada and the United States, there should be a common security perimeter around North America, which would require Canada to "harmonize" many of its laws with those of the United States. The prime minister saw that as a diminution of Canadian sovereignty, an idea he wanted to nip in the bud, and knew that in doing so, he would have the strong support of the Liberal caucus.

I asked our speechwriter, Ken Polk, to craft the words. Polk and I had worked on a lot of speeches together over the years. He was a quick writer and usually prepared the first draft, after which I would insert my own comments. We were ready to present a draft to the prime minister two days before he was to address Parliament. He gave us a few changes he wanted and, when he was satisfied with the final draft, Chrétien took time at home to practise his delivery. Then, in the House of Commons, after expressing horror at what had happened in New York and Washington and our determination to stand shoulder to shoulder with our American friends, the prime minister added words that Polk and I had drafted:

If laws need to be changed, they will be. If security has to be increased to protect Canadians it will be. We will remain vigilant. But we will not be giving in to the temptation, in a rush to increase security, to undermine the values that we cherish and which have made Canada a beacon of hope, freedom and tolerance to the world. Immigration is central to the Canadian experience and identity. We welcome people from all corners of the globe: all nationalities, colours and religions. This is who we are. And let there be no doubt:

we will allow no one to force us to sacrifice our values under the pressure of urgent circumstances.

Those words were crafted to reflect a balanced approach to policy making, something that Chrétien always tried to bring to government. Because of his belief that a balanced, centrist approach was critical to the success of Canadian governments, the prime minister had structured his Cabinet to reflect different views. His experience under Trudeau and Pearson was that balance in a Cabinet provides for good debate and better decisions. That is why he appointed some ministers who were more on the left of the political spectrum and others more on the right. Depending on the orientation he wanted to give to the government at any particular time, Chrétien was careful which ministers he placed in which departments. For example, Lloyd Axworthy came to Foreign Affairs with a different perspective than André Ouellet, and John Manley brought a very different approach to Canada-U.S. issues than Axworthy.

Chrétien instructed the Manley Committee to examine everything through both a security lens and a civil liberties lens. During the course of the committee meetings, it wasn't surprising that the minister of justice and the minister of immigration were more likely to make stronger cases for minimizing restrictions on traditional civil liberties, while the minister of defence and the Solicitor General were more open to increasing police powers.

I believed that in the days following September 11 there were more than enough advocates around of increased police powers, and that they didn't need any additional help from the PMO. So I worked quietly with Morris Rosenberg, the deputy minister of justice and a thoughtful advocate of civil liberties, to satisfy myself, and then to reassure the prime minister that the final draft of proposed tough new anti-terrorism legislation was in keeping with the Charter of Rights. The Manley Committee itself recognized that there were dangers in taking far-reaching and long-term decisions in the context of the immediate post–September 11 fear of new terrorist attacks anywhere in the world. It decided to recommend that the new legislation should provide for an obligatory three-year parliamentary review, at which time the legislation could be looked at again in a less emotional context. This helped achieve consensus between those who were more concerned with civil liberties and those who focused almost exclusively on security, which of course was a key issue in our relations with the United States.

Chapter 17

WHEN PRIME MINISTERS AND PRESIDENTS MEET

"At home you always have to be a politician. When you're abroad, you almost feel yourself a statesman."

– HAROLD MACMILLAN, 1958

Canada–U.S. watchers sometimes judge the relations between the two countries by how the prime minister and the president appear to get along. Perceptions about the relationship between the U.S. president and the Canadian prime minister have always been particularly important in domestic Canadian politics. In the 1963 general election, Lester Pearson benefited from the correct impression among Canadians that he would get along much better with the popular John F. Kennedy than did his rival, Prime Minister John Diefenbaker. On the other hand, Pierre Trudeau benefited in Canada from not having good relations with the unpopular Richard Nixon.

In April 1997, Chrétien made what was by all public appearances a highly successful state visit to Washington. State visits to the United States are full of pomp and ceremony, with marine bands and nineteen-gun salutes on the south lawn of the White House. There was a glittering state dinner with fine china, men in tuxedos and women in long dresses, impressive menus, and the most senior members of the administration scattered throughout the state dining room in the White House, along with, in the case of the Clinton Administration, leading

Democratic Party contributors and fundraisers and other political friends of the president. There was great entertainment and pure fun. None of us who were there will ever forget that President Clinton had invited a young African-American opera singer, Denyce Graves, to perform after dinner. After a few pieces, she took a break and expressed appreciation to the president for inviting her and particularly for inviting her mother to watch her perform in front of the Clintons. She then turned, looked at her mother, and very solemnly said, "Mom, without you, I would never have been able to perform in the White House." Then she paused, and everyone applauded her mother. When the applause stopped, she added with exquisite timing, "When I was a little girl, my mother warned me that if I did not improve my table manners, I would never be invited to the White House!"

The warmth of the visit produced favourable media coverage in Canada for the prime minister, who was only a few days away from calling an election. But little of substance was actually accomplished. I attended a meeting in the Cabinet room in the White House with the prime minister and several Canadian Cabinet ministers sitting on one side, facing the president, the vice-president, and several senior U.S. Cabinet officers on the other. The meeting actually ended well ahead of schedule because, at the time, there were few specific issues between the two countries that needed to be addressed at the highest levels.

State visits to Washington may be useful in developing personal relationships, but because of the formality not much business is accomplished. Working visits, on the other hand, are lacking in pomp and ceremony, which is all to the good. I accompanied Chrétien on three working visits to the White House to meet George W. Bush. Some Canadian commentators suggested that the president was somehow snubbing his guest because there were no bands, no nineteen-gun salutes, no formal welcoming party at the airport, no state dinner, just business. They were wrong. Such visits often accomplish much more than a formal state visit because there is time for real work to be done. We had two dinners and one lunch with President Bush in a room with only a few advisers on each side present. The dialogue was much more substantive than is possible during a glittering state dinner. There you can only talk to the person seated beside you, who, more often than not, turns out to be the spouse of a fundraiser.

Bush and Chrétien: Their First Meeting

JEAN CHRÉTIEN WAS the first foreign head of government to visit the White House in February 2001 shortly after George W. Bush became president. They first met alone in the Oval Office, accompanied only by Bush's national security adviser, Condoleezza Rice, and Chrétien's foreign policy adviser, Claude Laverdure. That meeting was friendly and businesslike. The president then hosted a dinner that included some of the most senior members of his new administration: Vice-President Dick Cheney, Secretary of State Colin Powell, U.S. Trade Representative Robert Zoellick, Chief of Staff Andy Card, and Condoleezza Rice. On the Canadian side were John Manley, Pierre Pettigrew, Jean Pelletier, Michael Kergin, Claude Laverdure, and myself.

The U.S. ambassador to Canada, Gordon Giffin, was also present. Unlike the case in Canada where political appointees are the exception to the rule, many American ambassadors are political and Giffin was no exception, having been a close ally of Bill Clinton. He knew that he would soon be replaced by a Republican, and discovered when we got to the White House that no one in the new administration knew him. Giffin and I joked about the fact that it was the prime minister of Canada who had to introduce the American ambassador to the president and his Cabinet.

Chrétien had a lot of experience meeting with other heads of government. He knew that conversation can sometimes be stilted and uncomfortable, so he broke the ice by recounting political war stories. Bush enjoyed a good laugh and reciprocated with his own anecdotes. Throughout the evening, Bush showed a determination that he was not then reputed to have, and a clarity and focus on what he wanted to achieve that is not always found in leaders of governments. Despite his inexperience in national and international affairs at the time, the president dominated the American side of the conversation, rarely turning to his colleagues for their views or support. The one time he did so was during a discussion of agricultural subsidies when, after agreeing with Prime Minister Chrétien that they should be radically reduced, he allowed Vice-President Cheney to interject a comment about the need to keep American subsidies high, to compete against those of the European Union.

When Chrétien asked the president whether he expected to be able to convince the Congress to approve "fast-track" authority that would allow him to enter into international trade deals, the response was surprising but demonstrated the Bush style of governing. The president did not equivocate, answering that he did not expect to receive Congressional authorization because he had identified his three most important priorities and was determined to deliver on them. "Fast-track" authority was not one of them. He told us that he would be spending a lot of political capital on education reform, tax changes, and reform of social security, and doubted that when he was finished with them he would have enough political capital left for the trade measure. (It later turned out that he did have enough capital left to persuade Congress to give him that "fast-track" authority.)

Both Chrétien and Bush shared and enjoyed the fact that they were often underestimated by their adversaries, and that they both sometimes mangled the English language. Something else that they had in common was their managerial style, where they delegated a great deal to their Cabinet ministers, but at the same time held them accountable. For example, in discussing his approach to abrogating the antiballistic missile treaty with Russia, President Bush pointed to Secretary of State Powell and said, "I don't want a new arms race, and that is why I have given Colin responsibility for this file." And then the president added, with a warm smile but a hint of steel in his voice, "If it doesn't work, Colin, you will have to pay the consequences."

Because President Bush was brand new to office, he had not met many of the heads of government around the world with whom he would be dealing. He wanted to learn as much as he could about them, and was interested in Chrétien's impressions of those he had known over the more than seven years he had already been in office. He asked pointed questions about Hugo Chavez of Venezuela, whom he had heard was "a pain in the ass." Chavez later confirmed that initial impression, and has been, to put it more discreetly, a thorn in Bush's side throughout his presidency. But Bush was particularly interested in hearing Chrétien's impressions of the leaders of the G-8 countries. At one point, when he asked the prime minister for his impressions of Russian president Vladimir Putin, Vice-President Dick Cheney interjected to say something uncomplimentary about Putin's becoming president of Russia after a career in the KGB. Bush chuckled and said, "Don't forget my father was director of the CIA before becoming president of the United States."

When the discussion turned to the issue of energy security, Chrétien talked at some length about the potential of the oil sands in Alberta and said that the recoverable reserves there were almost as great as those of Saudi Arabia. Interestingly, neither Bush nor Cheney, despite their previous careers in the energy sector, had heard of the oil sands. They listened politely, but were clearly skeptical as Chrétien waxed enthusiastic about the potential in Canada. Six years later, the possibilities inherent in the Alberta oil sands are in the forefront of discussions in the United States about future energy supply.

Once the substantive discussion was over, the two leaders began the process of getting to know each other in much the same way as any two people who meet for the first time go about it. Chrétien at one point mentioned to the president that he had some Texan friends who were close to the Bush family. George Bush was surprised and happy to learn about that connection and, in turn, obviously started trying to think of a Canadian he knew who might be a friend of the prime minister. Finally a light dawned, and the president asked Chrétien, "Do you know Conrad Black? I really like the guy. His newspaper in Chicago endorsed me, but I lost the state."

What Bush did not know was that Chrétien had just come through a huge public battle with Black, who had wanted to be appointed to the British House of Lords. Chrétien had intervened with the British government to block the appointment because Black was a Canadian citizen, and Black had then furiously renounced his Canadian citizenship and moved to England in order to become Lord Black of Crossharbour. At the mention of Conrad Black, the prime minister, who had also just won an election, replied with an impish grin on his face, "All his papers opposed me, but I swept the country. At any rate, he is no longer a Canadian." The Canadians at the table laughed at this exchange. Almost five years later, Black had not only lost control of his Chicago newspaper, but he had been indicted and was awaiting trial in Chicago on a variety of fraud counts.

Soon after September 11, Chrétien instructed Claude Laverdure to get in touch with his American counterpart, Condoleezza Rice, to arrange an early meeting with President Bush. They scheduled a lunch meeting at the White House between the two leaders for September 24. In the days preceding the meeting, the Opposition, some media, and some of the business community were critical of Chrétien for not demonstrating sufficient solidarity with and sympathy for the United States because of his remarks on the importance of preserving civil liberties and an open immigration policy. It didn't matter to his critics that the Americans appreciated both the quick action of the Canadian government in allowing flights destined for the United States to be diverted to Canada on September 11, and that Chrétien was the first NATO leader thereafter to publicly support the invocation of Article Five of the NATO treaty. The prime minister's critics pointed out that President Bush, in his first speech to Congress after September 11, thanked a great many countries by name from around the world for their great support, but did not mention Canada. They drew the conclusion from this omission that the American administration was angry with the Canadian government.

Having participated in the drafting of many speeches in circumstances of great stress and pressure, I was certain that omitting Canada from President Bush's speech was more likely the result of simple oversight than any deliberate slight on his part. I knew very well that there is a tendency to attribute far more cunning to speechwriters than they actually possess, and I often chuckled at the erroneous interpretation given by analysts to words that I had written. I also knew from experience that the U.S. administration, of whatever political stripe, rarely focuses on Canada. The controversy about what the prime minister had or hadn't said or done in Canada had passed totally unnoticed in Washington, but that didn't matter to some in Canada. Before Jean Chrétien went to Washington to meet President Bush at the White House, the *Toronto Sun* predicted, with absolutely no evidence to back up its assertion, that the U.S. administration was so angry with the Canadian government that the prime minister "would be taken out to the woodshed." Other Canadian media made similar, but less colourful, predictions.

A Somewhat Jaded View of Formal Meetings

I ATTENDED MANY meetings between Chrétien and leaders of governments from countries large and small from every continent, and observed the way it actually works. All too often meetings between heads of government are overly formal and staged. The two leaders sit beside each other, usually in very uncomfortable chairs, placed in such a way as to allow the best possible obligatory media photo opportunity before the actual meeting gets underway. At the meeting, advisers to each leader are lined up alongside their leader and face one another across the room. When the meeting starts, the heads of government obediently read from notes on file cards that have been carefully prepared for them by their advisers. Sometimes, but rarely, there are weighty discussions between the heads of government of two countries with important issues between them; much more often, there are vague discussions about the state of the world, no different than people may have around their dinner tables, and often with no more effect. The leaders, whether presidents or prime ministers, invariably express their satisfaction, either with the long-standing close friendship and close relations between their two countries or with the progress (that few others may have noticed) that is being made towards building such close relations. Then they enthusiastically invite their counterpart to pay a return visit to their country.

Leaders usually also express a fervent willingness to increase trade between their two countries. They really know that, except in the case of trade disputes involving their governments, or in the case of those countries with a large state sector, there is not much they can actually do about trade, which in the economy of the twenty-first century is primarily a matter for the private sector. All the while, ambassadors and foreign policy advisers take copious notes of what each leader has said to the other to relay back to their foreign ministries, who hope to find that their own advice as to what to say had been followed. The notes are then filed and disappear until they are made public twenty-five years later.

I attended one such bilateral meeting in Portugal in 1998 between Prime Minister Chrétien and the new Polish president of the day, Aleksander Kwasniewski, during the course of a conference of heads of government of the Organization for Security and Co-operation in Europe. The Polish president opened the meeting by casually asking his Canadian counterpart when he had arrived in Lisbon. Chrétien confessed that he was exhausted, having arrived the night before after flying almost twenty hours from Tokyo with a stop to refuel in Edmonton. President Kwasniewski understood that this was one of those meetings where momentous decisions are not made, and joked, "Let me help you, Jean. Today is Thursday. This is Lisbon. And this is your meeting with Poland!" Press secretaries have to use all their powers of imagination to brief their media afterwards on the significance of such meetings.

Yet these meetings – while often non-substantive – are important for other reasons. They give heads of government the opportunity to learn in general about each other's country and, in an era of globalization, to compare how each handles common problems. Leaders sometimes ratify work that has been done by their officials in preparation for the meeting. Most important, these meetings give them a chance to establish personal relationships and get to know each other, so that they are later able to deal with problems or opportunities arising between their own countries, and with wider issues in the United Nations or other multilateral forums when they arise. For this reason, Chrétien devoted a great deal of time to developing and cultivating an extensive network of colleagues around the globe.

Chrétien and Bush – 2001

THE LUNCH MEETING at the White House that Prime Minister Chrétien and President Bush held on September 24, 2001, was very different from the usual "getting to know you" meetings between heads of government. I was not surprised that what transpired between the president and the prime minister bore no resemblance whatsoever to the scenario predicted by Chrétien's Canadian critics. It was not, of course, the first meeting between the two. They had already met several times since Bush had assumed office and, despite the conventional wisdom that had been propagated in the Canadian press, they actually got along very well. This time there was something of great importance that needed to be discussed. Claude Laverdure, Michael Kergin, and I accompanied Chrétien. President Bush was joined by Paul Cellucci, the U.S. ambassador to Canada, Condoleezza Rice, the U.S. national security adviser, and John Maisto, one of Rice's deputies.

There was not a lot of formality. The eight of us sat around a small table in the Old Family Dining Room in the White House. We talked as lunch was served. The president's lack of formality was more than offset by his focus. What I found striking about Bush two weeks after September 11 was not only his strength and determination, but also how moderate, calm, reflective, and statesmanlike he was. There was no arrogance, no "You are with us or against us" rhetoric. He told us that he had learned how important it was to be careful in his vocabulary, to talk about "extremism," not "fundamentalism," and not to talk about "crusades." Chrétien was there to say that Canada would do whatever it could to help the United States, but he mainly wanted to listen to the president and learn about his plans.

Bush had obviously been briefed by Cellucci about the controversy north of the border caused by the omission of "Canada" from his speech in Congress. As I suspected, he had not been aware of the omission and assured us it was not intentional. In fact, at the beginning of the meeting, Bush told Chrétien how pleased he was with the Canadian reaction immediately after the attacks, and thanked the prime minister in particular for Canada's allowing so many planes destined for the United States to land in Newfoundland and Nova Scotia on September 11 when American airspace had been closed. He said that the events of that day had not been politicized in the United States and that it would be counterproductive for politicians in Canada or any other country to play partisan politics with what had happened. Chrétien, who had been subject to criticism in the House of Commons, welcomed this comment and was particularly pleased when President Bush repeated it in no uncertain terms to the assembled Canadian and American media in the Rose Garden.

The crisis management necessary in Canada (not to mention our petty partisan debates and media sniping) paled in comparison to what the president had on his mind. Bush was getting ready to meet later that afternoon with the families of the victims of the plane that had crashed in Pennsylvania, and was emotional when he said that he hoped he could maintain his composure. As we ate our first course (my menu says it was seared Chilean sea bass), Bush said that this was not a war to fight conventionally, because there was no conventional enemy. "I am not going to send a $1 million Cruise missile into a $40 tent." Then he said something deeply profound, which brought home to us the enormous responsibility on his shoulders: "I have to manage the bloodlust of the American people."

As if this wasn't enough, his greatest fear was that there could be another attack somewhere at any time.

Bush explained that as the United States had been attacked, under the Charter of the United Nations he could act in self-defence without having to seek authority from the Security Council of the United Nations, but he wanted to obtain the support of the international community for whatever actions he had to take. Unlike his position eighteen months later on Iraq, this time he stressed that he would act in a manner that added to American credibility in the rest of the world, noting that he would need a collaborative effort from the whole world to go after terrorist cells wherever they are. He didn't say anything explicit at our lunch about attacking Afghanistan, where al-Qaeda had its bases, but rather that when he was ready with more explicit plans, he would talk further to the prime minister and the leaders of other countries. He fulfilled that commitment to us a few weeks later.

An interesting piece of global politics came up when he mentioned that his first call from a foreign leader after the attacks had been from Russian president Vladimir Putin, who reassured the president that he fully understood why American troops had immediately been put on alert on September 11, and said that Russian troops would stand down. President Bush shook his head in relief. "Imagine," he said, "if this attack on the United States had happened twenty years ago – we would have had a nuclear crisis on our hands." But he expressed some concern to us that the Russians could use American actions in response to the attacks on the World Trade Center as a pretext for what they might do to respond to events in Chechnya and Georgia.

At home, he realized that he had too many agencies reporting directly to him to be able to manage security issues efficiently. He had decided to centralize responsibility and to appoint Governor Thomas Ridge of Pennsylvania as a new Homeland Security coordinator. Both the president and the prime minister agreed that Canada would work closely with him, and that John Manley would be his Canadian counterpart. In the months following, Manley worked with Ridge to negotiate a Shared Border Accord with the United States, which mitigated the impact on the flow of goods and services between the two countries caused by increased border security from what it had been before September 11.

Contrary to what Canadian critics of the prime minister expected, the president explicitly said that he was not asking Canada to harmonize any of its laws with those of the United States: "You have your

laws, and we have our laws, and we can work together." It was a statement that Chrétien welcomed, and in light of the debate at home over
harmonization of some of our laws and regulations, it was everything
we could have hoped the president would tell us. During discussions
about Homeland Security issues, the president and Condoleezza Rice
showed much more concern about the Mexican border, with which he
had more knowledge and experience as a former governor of Texas,
than about the Canadian border. When we learned this first-hand from
Bush, I couldn't help thinking that some Canadian pundits are wrong
when they assume that Americans are always likely to worry most
about Canada.

During the rest of the lunch there was little more discussion about
September 11 because there was no disagreement whatsoever between
the two leaders.

The Leaders Club of Political Junkies

THE PRESIDENT AND the prime minister also talked more generally
about politics. Leaders of democracies are proud to belong to a very
exclusive club. Only a few people in the world are elected to lead their
countries, and when they get together, they love to talk politics,
regardless of the circumstances. Political discussions are almost always
unscripted and are the part of bilateral meetings that heads of government enjoy the most. It is always fascinating to be a part of these discussions, and I learned that government leaders are the ultimate
political junkies. To my surprise, Bush was even well informed about
personalities in Canadian politics. He asked Chrétien about his various
potential successors in the Liberal Party as well as about the Leader of
the Opposition, Stockwell Day, whom Bush had met in Quebec City a
few months earlier at a reception. Recalling the encounter, he asked,
"Who is that religious guy I met in Quebec City?"

When the prime minister mentioned with some relish that the two
right-wing parties in Canada were divided, the president said, "The
successful politics of incumbency are to marginalize the opposition."
His analysis of what is required to be successful in office explains in

part why – against the opposition of conservative Republicans with whom he was usually aligned – he was such a strong proponent of a new prescription drug plan under Medicare. It allowed him in his second election to appeal in some measure to the centre of the political spectrum, even though he had governed from the right during his first term.

Months before the September Bush-Chrétien meeting, Joe Clark, the leader of the Progressive Conservative Party in the House of Commons, planned to visit Washington and wanted to see the president of the United States. Clark had briefly been prime minister, and had been foreign minister under Brian Mulroney, but in 2001, he had fallen on hard times and led a party of only twelve members in the House of Commons. He tried to use Mulroney's connections to the Bush family, instead of the Canadian embassy, to set up his meeting. As soon as he learned that Clark was trying to see President Bush, Michael Kergin informed me and I told the prime minister. Chrétien considered Joe Clark's request itself to be insignificant, but he never wanted to give any opportunity to those whose objective was to break up Canada to claim legitimacy in their ability to deal internationally. He worried about Clark's meeting setting a precedent whereby leaders of small Opposition parties, including the separatist Bloc Québécois, could meet with the president of the United States in Washington. So the prime minister asked me to make sure that the Canadian ambassador in Washington knew his point of view. Ambassador Kergin duly passed on the message to the White House.

At our lunch on September 24, George W. Bush smiled and said to Jean Chrétien, "You know the guy who wanted to see me, what's his name?" "Joe Clark," the prime minister replied. "Yes, that's the name," said the president. "You should know I didn't see him."

I could not help thinking that twenty-five years earlier, an almost unknown Joe Clark had first won the leadership of his party, to be greeted the next day by a screaming headline in the *Toronto Star*, "JOE WHO?" It was a moniker that stuck to him for his whole political career. Poor Joe Clark, I thought. Now after a twenty-five-year career in politics, he had gone from "Joe Who" in Canada to "What's His Name" in the White House.

Afghanistan

BUSH WAS NOT yet sure – or at least did not tell us – how he would respond to the terrorist attacks, but it wasn't long before he decided to attack their bases in Afghanistan and overthrow the Taliban regime that supported them. To do so, he decided to put together an international coalition. With the approval of the United Nations, he sought the active support of many countries including Canada, which was a willing participant. The last details of our participation, including the final approval of the prime minister, were worked out over the Canadian Thanksgiving weekend in October 2001 in meetings in the Langevin Block chaired by Mel Cappe, then Clerk of the Privy Council. I was present along with, among others, Jim Judd, the deputy minister of national defence, Ward Elcock, the director of the Canadian Security and Intelligence Service (CSIS), General Ray Henault, chief of the defence staff, and some of his most senior officers. We talked in general terms about the resources Canada could provide, and then Henault went alone to 24 Sussex to make his recommendation to the prime minister. On Thanksgiving Day, Chrétien and Bush spoke, and later that morning the president announced to the world the composition of a multilateral coalition including Canada that would fight in Afghanistan.

I was with Chrétien when he met President Bush again in the White House in the Oval Office in March 2002, six months after the September 11 attacks and just over a year after he had become president. Our meeting was devoted primarily to the softwood lumber dispute between Canada and the United States, and to preparing for the Group of Eight Summit that Chrétien would be chairing later that year in Canada. Those parts of the meeting went well, with the president knowledgeable and well briefed as usual on the issues. But we also briefly saw another side of the president, one more in line with his public image. This time he was less the moderate statesman we had seen in February and September of 2001, and more the president who deserved the public reputation of the George W. Bush who had chosen years earlier to live in West Texas, the land of the Texas cowboys.

The initial war in Afghanistan had gone very well. Canadian troops were present on the ground, so it was perhaps understandable that the president – who had been under enormous strain over the previous six months – jovially greeted the prime minister by saying, "Jean, together, we've been kicking some real ass in Afghanistan."

Later in the discussion, however, he made one offhand remark that showed his strain, but that I found troubling. This time, when the two leaders were talking about their dislike of those who leak to the press – a dislike shared by all heads of government, regardless of party, ideology, or country – the president said, with a smirk on his face, "If I catch anyone who leaks in my government, I would like to string them up by the thumbs." He paused for a few seconds and added, "The same way we do with the prisoners in Guantanamo!" Then the president laughed at his own joke.

It certainly would not have been funny at all three years later to the top White House officials who were being investigated for leaking secret information about the identity of a CIA agent. Nor was it funny to me when I recalled those words after the revelations in the media of the abuses in the Abu Ghraib prison in Iraq, the allegations of abuse in Guantanamo, and the allegations of torture being condoned if not practised by the CIA. Despite the poor taste of the president's joke in March, it was still the recollection of the friendly meeting with the president in the White House right after September 11 and the trauma of the attacks in the United States that made the final Canadian decision on participating in the war in Iraq so difficult.

Chapter 18

IRAQ AND CANADA–U.S. RELATIONS

"One more such victory and we are lost."

– KING PYRRHUS (ON DEFEATING THE ROMANS AT ASCULUM), 279 B.C.

Prime Minister Chrétien and President Bush met once again, this time in Detroit in September 2002. They were there for a joint announcement on border security and co-operation between the two countries. But by then, the situation in Iraq was the principal foreign policy preoccupation of the American administration. Bush was beginning to link the regime of Saddam Hussein directly to al-Qaeda and support for terrorism. The president wanted to talk to Chrétien about Iraq, and asked to meet the prime minister alone with no advisers present.

Senior diplomatic advisers to heads of government always hate one-on-one meetings between two heads of government, and they usually couch their objections on the grounds that note-takers are required to provide followup. (All domestic advisers also feel the same way about any meeting involving their boss.) They never admit the real reason, which is, of course, that they are afraid that their bosses might actually make decisions on their own, as Reagan and Gorbachev famously did in their summit in Iceland. Worse, those decisions might be contrary to the presumably wise advice that would otherwise be given by those who have years of diplomatic training, in other words, themselves. It is probably for this very reason that heads of government often prefer to have candid discussions without their advisers and note-takers present. They sometimes reluctantly compromise, and meet together alone for some time, before calling in their advisers to debrief them as to what has already happened in the private discussions. In practice, this is important, because their advisers are right that heads of government are usually notoriously bad at precise followup.

In Detroit, the private meeting between Bush and Chrétien ended without note-takers ever being called in. Condoleezza Rice, then the national security adviser to the president, normally attended all meetings between George W. Bush and other heads of government. For some reason, she could not be in Detroit that day, and when she found out that the meeting had taken place without note-takers, she called Claude Laverdure to ask him how on earth he could have allowed such a thing to happen! It didn't matter because, as it happened, no irreversible decisions were made at the meeting.

As soon as it was over, Chrétien told Mike Kergin – as they rode together in a car to the next event of the day – that he had told the president that without evidence of weapons of mass destruction, it would be impossible to convince the international community to support an invasion of Iraq, and that Canada would only participate in military action that had the support of the international community. Later in the morning, he repeated to Laverdure and me that he had made it clear to the president that Canada's participation in a war with Iraq would depend on the support of the United Nations. Then he told us that he had not heard anything convincing from Bush about Iraqi weapons of mass destruction. The prime minister shrugged and said, "I started my career as a small-town lawyer, and I heard nothing today from the president that would convince any judge in a rural courthouse." But Chrétien also said that he was encouraged to hear that Bush was about to address the United Nations, and intended to seek a resolution of support from the Security Council before taking military action in Iraq.

Canada soon faced a difficult decision. On the one hand, the government did not want to go to war in Iraq without the sanction of the United Nations; on the other hand, it was acutely sensitive to the impact of September 11 on the United States, Canada's closest ally, and hoped it wouldn't have to make a decision that would appear insensitive to the trauma caused by the attacks on the World Trade Center. Our preference was to be as supportive as possible of the United States. In making its decision, however, the government also had to consider whether participating in a war declared by non-Islamic western countries, without the support of the United Nations, against the government of an Islamic country, no matter how abhorrent the regime, would in the end bring about more democracy in the Middle East, or whether it would be responsible for provoking more terrorism in the world. It was this same dilemma that the caucus, the Cabinet, Parliament, the media, and individual Canadians struggled with for many months. Throughout the fall of 2002, the American and British military buildup in the Persian Gulf continued. By early 2003, it was becoming clear that the UN Security Council was not likely to support direct military intervention in Iraq without concrete findings by weapons inspectors of evidence of weapons of mass destruction in Iraq.

Caucus and Cabinet

THE ROLE OF caucus in government decision making is often underestimated by outsiders who focus on the highly visible party discipline usually on display in the House of Commons. Because caucus does not meet in public, and is therefore not visible, its role in the process is not often given the significance it deserves. It is in the government caucus – which in the Chrétien years met with no PMO advisers or other staff present – that MPs speak their minds to ministers and the prime minister. Jean Chrétien had never forgotten his first four years in Parliament as a backbencher in the 1960s, and like his predecessors Pearson and Trudeau, he rarely missed the weekly Wednesday caucus meeting. There he measured the mood of his MPs, and was much influenced by it.

He expected his staff and the Privy Council Office to understand the preoccupations of caucus. Chrétien instructed his parliamentary secretary to take notes of what was said in caucus, to brief the senior staff meeting in the prime minister's office in detail the next morning, but to preserve confidentiality and, above all, not to reveal the names of who had said what. This was standard practice for ten years after every caucus meeting. The prime minister himself always raised the concerns that MPs had expressed in caucus at his regular morning meeting the next day with the Clerk of the Privy Council. In this case, throughout the fall of 2002 and the early winter of 2003, Chrétien's parliamentary secretary, Rodger Cuzner from Nova Scotia, reported on Thursday mornings to the PMO senior staff meeting that, with few exceptions, the Liberal caucus was against Canada's participating in any military action in Iraq unless it was sanctioned by the United Nations. The views of caucus were a significant factor in the final decision.

Cabinet also discussed the issue of Iraq a number of times during that same time period. Chrétien had read with great interest a report to the Department of Foreign Affairs by the respected Canadian ambassador to the United Nations, Paul Heinbecker, describing the radical new approach to unilateral military intervention in other countries that had recently been promulgated by the Bush Administration. This doctrine of pre-emption profoundly troubled the prime minister and his Cabinet colleagues. It was clear to me from all the Cabinet discussions that while the government shared the view of the United States that September 11 had profoundly and unalterably changed the world, it rejected unilateralism as the best way to respond, except in the most extreme circumstances of direct and obvious threat.

At one Cabinet meeting, I listened as the prime minister referred to Canadian history, as he often liked to do, recalling that in 1956 Canada's relationship with Great Britain was somewhat analogous to the closeness of its relationship a half-century later with the United States. Chrétien didn't need to remind his colleagues that he had been a protegé of Lester Pearson, as he had often talked about what he had learned from him. This time he recalled that as a young MP in the

1960s, he had asked Pearson about how difficult it was in 1956 for Canada not to take the side of the United Kingdom when it invaded the Suez Canal. Pearson, who had been external affairs minister in 1956, had acknowledged that it was a challenging decision, even though it was the right one. Chrétien – a keen observer of prime ministers during his time in Parliament – went on to tell his Cabinet colleagues of the debates he remembered in Parliament and in Cabinet in the 1960s over the war in Vietnam. He also referred to the great disagreement between Diefenbaker and Kennedy over Cuba, and to the fact that Trudeau and Nixon were not part of a mutual admiration society.

Clearly then, in slowly developing the Canadian position on Iraq, Chrétien and his Cabinet had reflected on our history with the United States, and on the fact that, despite the closeness of relationships and friendships, our two countries do not always take the same position in international affairs. They were all well aware that the management of a sometimes ambivalent political relationship between Canada and the United States has been a principal preoccupation of Canadian governments since Confederation. It has never been easy to manage because Canadian governments have to be conscious both of the importance Canadians place on their independence and also of the constraints imposed by the size and influence of the United States. They hardly had to be reminded that the single most important economic and cultural relationship Canada has in the world is with the United States, and that Canadians recognize and admire the fact that the United States – despite its faults – has been a great force for peace, freedom, democracy, and economic progress in the world for two hundred years.

For Canada to say no to the United States – the world's only superpower, our next-door neighbour, our very close ally and friend, and the destination of 87 per cent of our exports – was not a decision to be taken lightly. It was one thing to have different views on the International Campaign to Ban Landmines, which was signed in Ottawa and is sometimes called "The Ottawa Treaty," or on the creation of the International Criminal Court, both of which were strongly opposed by the Bush Administration. Iraq was much more important to the

United States, and saying no was particularly difficult because the Bush Administration, conscious of the difficulty of intervening in Iraq in a unilateral way, was seeking moral support much more than extensive military resources from Canada or from other countries. It was keen to have the names of as many countries as possible on a list of the "coalition of the willing" against the brutal dictatorship of Saddam Hussein. Nevertheless, after lengthy discussions, it was clear that, as in the case of the caucus, and despite inaccurate media speculation about divisions among ministers, there was no support in Cabinet for participating in an American-led war in Iraq without the sanction of the United Nations.

Setting Out the Canadian Position in Chicago: A Case Study

HEADS OF GOVERNMENT sometimes use speeches to prestigious audiences abroad to make important foreign policy statements, just as they choose particular audiences at home to announce major domestic policy initiatives. Prime Minister Chrétien decided to take advantage of a long-scheduled speaking engagement in Chicago to the Council on Foreign Relations on February 13, 2003, at a time when the situation in Iraq dominated world attention, to set out the Canadian position. I had the responsibility to coordinate the preparation of the Chicago speech.

Claude Laverdure and I first talked to the prime minister about the speech before we prepared a draft. We presented our own ideas in general terms and he provided us with his feedback, so we felt we knew what he wanted when we started the process. Chrétien decided he should enunciate very clearly the basic principles of Canadian foreign policy. He wanted first to express his strong belief in the value of a multilateral approach to global problems; second, to set out that the use of force is most legitimate when sanctioned by the United Nations; and third, to warn the United States explicitly about the dangers of proceeding unilaterally in Iraq. Based on this, I asked Michael Kergin, our ambassador in Washington, to have the Canadian embassy prepare a first draft.

Kergin and I had become good friends during the course of long trips overseas when he was foreign policy adviser to the prime minister, serving his country with great distinction. We always worked well together. Low-key and self-effacing, Kergin had strong, cogent, and informed views that he was always prepared to share. He had become an outstanding ambassador, and was highly respected in Washington. In this case, he easily grasped what the prime minister required and was particularly helpful with the preparation of all the drafts of the speech. Kergin told me that it was especially important for the prime minister of Canada to recognize the closeness and the importance of our relationship with the United States in the first part of the speech, before setting out our differences. The first draft prepared by officials in the embassy was well done with respect to the relationship between Canada and the United States, but it did not define a firm position on Iraq. I knew that this was characteristic of embassies everywhere, because they are understandably loath to draft critical speeches about the country in which they are located. By contrast, I thought it important to present a draft with a firm position on Iraq to the prime minister for his consideration.

Once I had received a first draft, I sought comments from Claude Laverdure and Paul Heinbecker, and asked Kevin Lynch, the deputy minister of finance, for his comments on the section of the speech dealing with economic issues. I collected all of the comments and prepared a new draft, incorporating my own views as well, which I circulated back to Mike Kergin, Alex Himelfarb, the secretary to the Cabinet, and others, including Paul Genest, who had succeeded Chaviva Hosek as director of policy in the PMO, for one more round of input. They provided me with extensive revisions. I then tried to incorporate their comments in another new draft, at which point I went to see John McCallum, the minister of national defence, and Bill Graham, the minister of foreign affairs. I gave them copies and told them to consult their officials if they wished, but not to circulate drafts in their departments to avoid leaks. Instead, I wanted them to return the draft to me, with their own handwritten comments on it. When I received a last set of comments from those I had been consulting, including handwritten notes from both ministers, I then coordinated pulling all the comments together and prepared a final draft for the consideration of the prime minister.

It took several weeks to prepare the speech, and the process I have outlined reflects the way we prepared the most important speeches given by the prime minister. Chrétien preferred to avoid large speechwriting meetings and lengthy debates about precise wording or "wordsmithing." He was much more concerned about the general substance of a speech than about the rhetoric. He did not like delivering long written texts, and always looked immediately at the number of pages we presented to him, then invariably he told me it was too long. When I objected to shortening it, he would tell me that I worried too much about words no one else would notice. (There were many times I found it disagreeable to strike out paragraphs we had painstakingly worked on, so we would try to reduce the number of pages to present to him by adjusting the typeface and the margins. Unfortunately, no matter how hard we tried, he wasn't easily fooled!)

Chrétien liked the text I presented to him, but suggested a few changes of his own, which we immediately incorporated. Then the day before he was to deliver the speech, he made a few more changes to the text to ensure clarity in his expression of Canada's position, at which point he approved the speech as final. But on the day of the speech just before we were leaving Ottawa for Chicago, Michael Kergin called me and said that on reflection, he found that a few paragraphs of the proposed wording could unintentionally create unnecessary difficulties for Canada-U.S. relations. I suggested a few revisions that improved the text, satisfied Kergin, and that were approved by Chrétien. The PMO press office then printed a final version in English and French, and provided us with copies to bring to Chicago to be distributed to the media as soon as the prime minister began to speak.

Consequences

CHRÉTIEN HAD NO doubts about the consequences of what he was going to say. In the government's Challenger jet on the way to Chicago to deliver this speech critical of any unilateral American military intervention in Iraq, he mused about having told both President Clinton and President Bush in his first meetings with both of them that Canada could actually be more useful to the United States over time in the international community if it were not seen as always automatically agreeing with the United States on everything. President Clinton understood what it would take for Canada to act as an honest broker in the international community. But we knew that President Bush at the time was not very interested in honest brokers. Chrétien reminded me that presidents from Texas are not known for their subtlety. After Prime Minister Pearson had gone to Temple University in Philadelphia in 1965 to criticize American policy in Vietnam, President Johnson's reaction to Pearson was, "You pissed on my rug." So a negative reaction to this speech from the current Texan in the White House would be neither unprecedented nor unexpected.

The Chicago Council on Foreign Relations is a prestigious audience. Rod Blagojevich, the young governor of Illinois, was present, as well as Chicago Mayor Richard Daley, a scion of the legendary Chicago political family. The room in the downtown hotel was filled primarily with leaders of the American business community as well as a few Canadians. As the prime minister began his speech, the room was quiet and the audience was listening intently. The times were serious and so was the speech. Measuring his words carefully, after talking about the close relationship between Canada and the United States, and between Canadians and Americans, Chrétien said:

> The price of being the world's only superpower is that its motives are sometimes questioned by others. Great strength is not always perceived by others as benign. Not everyone around the world is prepared to take the word of the United States on faith. Canada firmly supports the objectives of the United States. We have been close friends and allies for a long, long time. It is essential that the United States can count on support from around the world.

And then, using words that had been handwritten by John McCallum, the minister of national defence, he added, "Therefore it is imperative to avoid the perception of a clash of civilizations. Maximum use of the United Nations will minimize that risk." The prime minister finished his speech and, to our surprise, was met by a lengthy standing ovation from an audience that may not have entirely agreed with everything he said, but that clearly respected the thoughtfulness of his argument.

The Role of Honest Broker

OVER THE COURSE of the next month, Chrétien tried to be an honest broker between the United States and Great Britain on one side, and France and Germany on the other. Although Canada was not a member of the Security Council, he discussed with Ambassador Heinbecker what it would take to achieve a unanimous resolution. They hoped that Great Britain and the United States could be persuaded to agree to an extension of time for UN weapons inspections, in return for an agreement by France and Germany to accept military intervention in Iraq if the weapons inspectors reported that Iraq was in violation of UN resolutions. The ambassador worked with representatives of other countries at the UN, and the prime minister worked the telephone. It is at times like this that all of the "get to know you" bilateral meetings that take place between heads of government over the years prove useful. At times of crisis, leaders who know one another can talk easily and frankly. Chrétien knew and was in constant contact with the leaders of all of the countries on the Security Council. He worked particularly closely with his friends, the presidents of Chile and Mexico, Ricardo Lagos and Vicente Fox. Their countries were non-permanent members of the Council, and Chrétien believed that they might have the credibility that the United States and Great Britain lacked to bring about a compromise. At the end of the day, Canada's attempts to find a compromise did not work. There was absolutely no consensus in the Security Council; incredibly, there was not even a simple majority to support the American and British positions.

Canada had been clear from the beginning that it would not participate in a war against Iraq without the approval of the UN Security
Council. Chrétien always left the door slightly open, however, to how
he would interpret the meaning of *approval*; having discussed with
his advisers what Canada should do in a situation where a resolution
authorizing military intervention in Iraq passed with an overwhelming
majority on the Security Council but was vetoed by just one member.
In 1999, Canada had agreed to participate in a multilateral military
intervention in Kosovo under the auspices of NATO, and with the
full support of the European Union, instead of the United Nations,
because Russia had made it clear that it would veto any UN resolution
authorizing outside military intervention in a Slavic nation.

The circumstances with respect to Kosovo were very different in
1999 than they were in Iraq in 2003. Then the Clinton Administration
was not pursuing a unilateralist foreign policy; it insisted on the serious
participation of Europe and NATO in any military operation, and it
even refused to commit its own ground troops. Clearly, those circumstances did not arise in the case of Iraq. Indeed, the world now knows
that the United States had decided long before to overthrow the regime
of Saddam Hussein, and was not interested in a compromise that might
avert war. In the end, the war began without so much as a vote in the
Security Council. Chrétien's speech in Chicago a month earlier provided the framework for the decision he announced on March 17 in
the House of Commons.

The Fallout

AROUND 6:30 P.M. on March 17, after the announcement that Canada
would not join the Iraq War, the prime minister phoned me at my
office. "What do you think?" he asked. I told him that there had been
a lot of initial support in Canada. He was under no illusions. "Yes," he
said, "but it will be very rough. You know that with Bush on matters
like this, you are with him or against him. He will be very vindictive."
I listened to what he said and then told him that I had received a call a
few minutes earlier from a mutual friend of ours, the leading Canadian

historian John English. "John says the decision to stay out of the war has averted a potential major national unity crisis."

Chrétien asked me to elaborate. English had reminded me of how national unity is never far from the surface in Canada. Canadian participation in the war, he said, would have been extremely unpopular in Quebec. With a provincial election campaign underway, the Parti Québécois would have used a decision to participate in the war to argue that Quebec has no place in Canada because Quebec's values are so different from those of the rest of the country. In English's mind, the decision of the Chrétien government meant that the issue of the Iraq War would not be a part of the provincial election campaign. In fact, there had never been any reference to Quebec in all the discussions on Iraq in Cabinet or in any of my own talks with the prime minister. In this case, a positive contribution to national unity was the happy by-product of a decision taken for very different reasons, as was a substantial rise in Chrétien's personal popularity in Quebec.

The decision not to go to war in Iraq was immediately popular in Canada but, surprising as it may seem from a perspective of a few years later, there was certainly no unanimity at the time. Those who purported to speak for the business community were fearful that the Canadian position on the war could have a damaging effect on Canadian trade with the United States. But it wasn't just the business community that questioned the decision of the government. When the statue of Saddam Hussein fell in Baghdad, and the war seemed to have ended with an easy American victory, Stephen Harper, then the Leader of the Opposition in Parliament, who from the beginning had wanted Canada "to stand shoulder to shoulder" with the United States, was particularly critical of the government position. Some Liberal MPs, who had initially stood in the House of Commons and applauded the government's principled position on March 17, began to have different principles a few weeks later when they saw potential for a change in public opinion. When the situation in Iraq later became much more difficult for the Americans, they not surprisingly rediscovered their original principles. By the time of the election campaign of 2004,

Stephen Harper was suggesting that he had never really wanted Canadian troops sent to Iraq in the first place; and by the campaign of 2006, he was pledging never to send Canadian troops to Iraq.

Only history will judge whether the war in Iraq was a colossal mistake, or whether it was an extraordinary act of boldness by a brave American president. Whatever the judgment of history on the war, there can be no doubt that the decision of the Canadian government not to participate in Iraq was a seminal event in Canadian foreign policy. I later attended bilateral meetings with leaders of many other countries who went out of their way to congratulate Chrétien for his courage, saying that while they had come to the same conclusion as we did about Iraq, they were not pressured by the same history, trading relationship, and proximity to the United States.

Those who are cynical about politics and who sometimes glibly say that all politicians are the same, and that it does not matter who is in office, should see the decision of the Canadian government not to participate in the war in Iraq as a lesson in the importance and relevance of the democratic process. Voting does matter. A different government with a different prime minister might have made a very different decision, and Canada's reputation in the world would also be very different.

Canada-U.S. Trade Relations

SHORTLY AFTER CHRÉTIEN announced to Parliament that Canada would not join the American-led coalition, the Canadian Council of Chief Executives under Thomas d'Aquino sent a delegation to Washington, with the clear but obviously unstated intent to apologize to their counterparts in the United States for the Canadian policy. It didn't seem to matter to them that the United States had not been able to find support for the war from many of its other major trading partners, including Mexico, the other member of NAFTA. The embarrassingly obsequious reaction of some members of the Canadian business community to the decision to stay out of the war in Iraq caused me to reflect on the nature of the Canada-U.S. relationship and the management of issues between the two countries.

The first major issue on my desk after the 1993 election concerned the ratification of the North American Free Trade Agreement. Ten years later, when the Chrétien government left office at the end of 2003, the last major file on my desk concerned the long-standing trade dispute between Canada and the United States over softwood lumber. In between, I had participated in ten bilateral meetings between the Canadian prime minister and the U.S. president, dealt with three American ambassadors to Canada, met with numerous members of Congress and their staffs, and negotiated with American Cabinet secretaries and White House staff on issues as diverse as West Coast salmon stocks and Canadian cultural protections, wheat exports and land mines treaties, air transportation and softwood lumber, North American security after September 11, and G-8 support for Africa.

I learned certain lessons in my dealings with the Americans over those years. First, Canadians often wrongly assume that the American government focuses as carefully on issues involving Canada as Canadians do on issues involving the relationship with the United States. In fact, it is difficult for anyone to meet the intense competition in Washington to get the serious sustained attention of decision makers in the capital of the world's only superpower, and Canada is a relatively small country, even if it is the largest trading partner of the United States. While meetings between the president and the prime minister are always front-page news in Canada, in the United States, coverage (if any) is restricted to answers the president gives at press conferences to questions from American media about domestic American issues. When Canadian ambassadors speak in the United States, their speeches are far better covered in Canada than in the places where their message is directed. A small article about Canada in the *New York Times* or the *Wall Street Journal* is sometimes the subject of debate in the Canadian Parliament, but every word spoken, every article written in Canada about Canadian-American issues is not pored over in the White House.

While Canadian Cabinets regularly discuss the state of Canada-U.S. relations, and the progress of every file affecting the two countries, the

converse is not true. Those relations are put under the media microscope far less in the United States than in Canada where they are sub-
jected to the twenty-four-hour news cycle, to the focus on winners and
losers, to the instant commentators. In a meeting I had in his White
House office in September 2002, John Maisto, deputy national security adviser to George W. Bush, told me, "Your press would be devastated to know that we don't read them very much!" He was kinder than
Bush, who, after taking questions from Canadian media accompanying
Chrétien on a visit to the White House, commented to the prime minister, "While our media is bad, yours is goddamn impossible!" Not surprisingly, Chrétien did not express any disagreement!

The U.S. president meets a great number of foreign leaders during
the course of a year, sometimes more than one on the same day. The
relationships that receive the most time and attention in the White
House are those where important American domestic or security interests are at stake – such as persuading the president of China to enforce
an intellectual property regime, attempting to broker peace in the
Middle East between the prime minister of Israel and the leader of an
Arab country, dealing with illegal immigration into the United States
from Mexico. Canadian issues fortunately are not in that league in
Washington; and meetings between the president and the prime minister are, in my experience, far more routine, even though they can
sometimes serve to advance the solution of irritants between the two
countries, and the relations between a prime minister and a president
are important because they do set a tone.

Jean Chrétien used to his political advantage a perception among
many Canadians that his predecessor, Brian Mulroney, was too close
to Ronald Reagan and George H.W. Bush. Chrétien found that political rhetoric such as "My ambition in life is not to go fishing with the
President of the United States, because I do not want to end up as
the fish," and, in particular, "Friendship is friendship, but business is
business," resonated with the Canadian electorate.

The latter was good rhetoric, but I concluded, from my involvement in a number of trade disputes between us, that it is the Americans

who are the real masters at separating business from friendship and at putting internal domestic political considerations ahead of what some might argue would be their broader national interest. I learned that those in Canada who try to interpret trade disputes between Canada and the United States in the context of the relationship between the two governments, and sometimes even the personal relationship between the heads of the two governments, make a fundamental error. When the American administration gets involved in the economic relationship between American industry and that of other countries, foreign policy is rarely the primary consideration. What really counts more than any international relationships is the almost permanent electoral cycle in the United States, which makes it difficult to reconcile longer-term national interests with immediate domestic political interests. The result is that other countries, including Canada, get sideswiped in the process. That is simply the way it works.

For example, I was involved in years of negotiations over softwood lumber with both the Clinton and the Bush Administrations, and was part of discussions on the issue with both presidents and senior White House staff, the U.S. trade representative, the secretary and the under-secretary of commerce, U.S. ambassadors to Canada, and congressmen and senators. In all the discussions I participated in on softwood lumber, both formal and informal, regardless of whether Democrats or Republicans were in office, no one ever mentioned or alluded directly or indirectly to the Canadian position on any issues of foreign policy. What I experienced was not unique to Canada. Other countries who have trade disputes with the United States have also found that agreeing or disagreeing with the foreign policy objectives of the U.S. administration just isn't relevant to the resolution of those disputes. In those circumstances, it is domestic politics and interests, even when they are very shortsighted, that almost always predominate.

Another example: at the same time as some Canadian commentators were speculating that the allegedly strained relations between Chrétien and Bush were contributing to the deadlock over softwood lumber, the Bush Administration was refusing to lift protectionist measures against Pakistani textiles. This decision was made while Osama bin Laden was probably hiding out in Pakistan or on the Afghanistan side of the Pakistan border, and while the United States desperately needed the active support of Pakistan, an Islamic state whose president was under great pressure not to help the "Great Satan" in the war against terror. Even in that case, with a textile industry that was of huge importance to the Pakistani economy and of little importance to the overall American economy, it was clear that the White House didn't want to do anything that might possibly hurt the political chances of the president in the 2004 election in North and South Carolina, and a few other states, where the textile industry is somewhat important. Domestic politics trumped the apparently vital relationship with Pakistan.

Likewise, when the United States needed the support of countries of Europe in the period leading up to the war in Iraq, it still preferred to impose punitive tariffs on European steel exports to the United States to protect domestic steel producers in the states of West Virginia, Pennsylvania, Ohio, and Michigan, which were all crucial states to the re-election prospects of the president. And despite the close relationship between President Bush and Prime Minister Blair of Great Britain, the United States did not exempt Great Britain from the punishing tariffs. But the U.S. did exempt Canada and Mexico (both of whom later opposed the war in Iraq) because of the highly integrated nature of the North American steel industry.

In the American political system, the president and the administration are dependent on the Congress in a way that no Canadian prime minister is, even in minority government situations in the House of Commons. Congress itself operates with a number of almost independent power centres, coupled with the influence of special-interest groups, in a way that would be unthinkable in Canada. Senate and House of Representatives committee chairs are independent of the administration, are extraordinarily powerful, and can sometimes alone determine whether certain legislation will pass or fail. Consequently, there is far more logrolling and linkage between issues in the American political system than there is in Canada. This means that when the president has to rely on certain individual senators to move ahead on the priorities of his administration, he has to take full account – even if he fundamentally disagrees with them – of some of their particular interests in matters that are less important to the administration.

Softwood Lumber and Logrolling

THE CANADA-U.S. SOFTWOOD lumber dispute is a good case in point. For decades, the U.S. softwood lumber industry has complained about imports from Canada. The American industry alleges that the Canadian industry is unfairly subsidized and violates those American trade laws that define subsidies and dumping. The allegations of unfair subsidies have been referred over the years to international panels, which have almost invariably ruled in Canada's favour. But none of these decisions matter to the American industry. When they lose a case, they simply enlist allies in the U.S. Senate to change the rules of the game. Invariably the next step in Canada is for the prime minister to tell Parliament and the media that he will raise the matter on an urgent basis with the president of the United States. Prime Ministers Mulroney and Chrétien each negotiated on softwood lumber with Presidents Reagan, Clinton, and both Bushes. The prime ministers discovered that when the administration has to choose between its relations with powerful senators and a powerful American industry on the one hand, and the Canadian prime minister representing the Canadian industry on the other, it always chooses the powerful senators and the powerful American industry.

During the years I spent on the Canadian side of the softwood lumber issue, I saw first-hand raw domestic American politics under the influence of powerful special interests. First, in 2001–2, President Bush needed Congress to approve "fast-track authority" to authorize the administration to negotiate free trade deals with other countries and also to enter into multilateral trade discussions. At the time, Senator Max Baucus of Montana, who chaired the Senate Finance Committee, was responsible for the fast-track legislation, and he could

make it or break it. He was also the principal supporter in the Senate
of the U.S. softwood lumber industry, and made it clear to the Bush
Administration that he would not allow fast-track legislation to be
approved if the administration negotiated a softwood lumber accord
with Canada that wasn't completely to the liking of the American
industry. Not surprisingly, the result was that while no one could have
been more sympathetic on the surface to achieving an agreement with
Canada than President Bush, no one was less likely than the president
to press his administration to solve the softwood lumber problem in a
way that might have meant a confrontation with a powerful senator on
other issues of far greater importance to the administration.

President Bush and Prime Minister Chrétien often discussed the
softwood lumber dispute on the telephone and in person. In the
summer of 2001, they agreed that Condoleezza Rice would quarterback the issue for the president, and I would do the same for the prime
minister. Shortly thereafter, September 11 intervened and we had to
put any negotiations on the back burner as the administration had infinitely more important issues to deal with. In March 2002, with three
weeks to go before a legal deadline for the U.S. Commerce Department to impose duties on Canadian softwood lumber, I attended a
meeting between Chrétien and Bush in the Oval Office in the White
House. In preparing for the meeting, our team recommended to
Chrétien that he ask Bush to agree that both of them publicly request
their negotiators to reach an agreement within three weeks, and I suggested that he bring to the meeting some words that he would propose
that the president use in speaking to the media at the conclusion of
their meeting.

We knew full well that it is almost unheard of to put words in front
of the president of the United States that have not previously been discussed with his advisers, but we didn't want to take the chance that the
president's advisers would reject the proposed statement. The surprise
and dismay on the faces of Condoleezza Rice and Gary Edson, an economic adviser in the National Security Council who dealt with the
softwood lumber file, were a delight to behold when Chrétien gave

Bush a piece of paper that they hadn't seen. I reached into my brief-case, took out two copies, and handed one to each of them as they almost literally lunged for it. Edson immediately sprinted through a doorway into the small anteroom off the Oval Office, made famous by Monica Lewinsky, to make a phone call to get advice. By the time he came back, the president, smiling and totally nonplussed, had already agreed with Chrétien to use the words we proposed. As soon as the meeting was over, Chrétien and Bush walked outside from the Oval Office into the Rose Garden and told the assembled media that they were instructing their negotiators to reach a softwood lumber agreement within three weeks. We thought we had finally broken the logjam.

Negotiations began almost immediately. But the president's public exhortation to reach an agreement seemed to have no impact at all on his own negotiators, who refused any compromises whatsoever. To my disgust, at the negotiating table in the Madison Hotel in Washington, they literally read aloud from the printed position paper of the American softwood lumber lobby. A few days after the meeting in the Oval Office, I was part of a Canadian negotiating team that met with U.S. Secretary of Commerce Don Evans. Pierre Pettigrew, the minister of international trade, the Canadian ambassador Michael Kergin, and I sat down in Secretary Evans's large office in the Department of Commerce. Evans, who had been President Bush's campaign manager in 2000, was a tough, uncompromising Texan who wouldn't budge on anything, and made it quite clear that we were wasting his time and ours. As the meeting went on, I couldn't help focusing on the large fish tank standing near his desk, wondering whether he had piranhas swimming in it and whether he was getting ready to feed us to them. The meeting with Evans demonstrated to me beyond any doubt that the power of special interests and domestic political considerations were far more important in Washington than the president's genuine desire to remove a trade irritant between Canada and the United States.

When a tentative agreement on softwood lumber was finally reached in April 2006, it had far less to do with the good personal relations Prime Minister Harper had established with George W. Bush than with the fact that the new Canadian government had concluded that accepting half a loaf was better than no loaf at all. Prime Minister Harper came to the view that the Americans would continue to impose punitive trade sanctions regardless of the judgments of international trade tribunals, and decided therefore, to the consternation of some of the Canadian industry, to accept a "managed trade" agreement.

The American position on farm subsidies was no different. The first time Chrétien met Bush in the White House on February 5, 2001, less than three weeks after Bush had assumed office, the new president seemed quite genuine when he said that he would try to reduce and eliminate American agricultural subsidies as much as possible. At a meeting in the White House approximately one year later, I found that he had become a great defender of American agricultural subsidies. It was clear that the president had learned quickly about the political importance in the Congress of the special interests in the American farm belt. That is simply the way the American system works.

I concluded that if Canada had supported the war in Iraq, or taken other actions such as increasing defence expenditures in line with the public urging of the American ambassador to Canada, the American position on softwood lumber and agricultural subsidies would not have changed one iota.

Relations Post-Iraq

THERE HAD BEEN no real problems in the relationship between Chrétien and Bush until after the decision by Canada on Iraq. Not surprisingly, it resulted in the cancellation of a state visit by Bush to Ottawa scheduled for May 2003. The cancellation was actually a relief to the Canadian government, because anti-war feelings were so strong in Canada that there was a great likelihood of large anti-Bush demonstrations in Ottawa, which would have been carried live on U.S. television. A poor public reception in Canada for the president would not have sat well in the White House and might very well have damaged relations far more than the decision not to participate in the war.

But at the end of May 2003, Prime Minister Chrétien spoke candidly to reporters at the back of an airplane on the way to Greece for a Canada-European Union Summit. He was months away from retirement and was in an expansive mood. He reminisced about meetings he had with his friend President Clinton, and he explained the differences between his position as a Liberal, and that of President Bush as a conservative Republican, on issues such as gun control, capital punishment, abortion, and climate change. Then he expressed his serious concerns about the effect on the international economy of the U.S. budget deficit. The Canadian media treated the story in different ways. The *Toronto Star* reported his comments as the philosophical reflections of a retiring prime minister. The *National Post* sensationalized them as an all-out attack on the policies of the American administration and President Bush in particular. The article in the *National Post* was drawn to the attention of the White House, whether by the U.S. embassy in Ottawa or, as some suspected, by former prime minister Brian Mulroney.

The White House always reacted more strongly to any personal attacks on the president than to attacks on his policies. The administration was upset months earlier by unfortunate comments about President Bush attributed to Chrétien's director of communications, Francie Ducros, and by a statement by Natural Resources Minister Herb Dhaliwal after the beginning of the Iraq War that Bush had demonstrated a failure of statesmanship. In May 2003, the president was subject to much criticism at home and abroad, and appeared vulnerable as the G-8 Summit approached, and the White House was particularly defensive.

The result was a telephone call from Air Force One from Condoleezza Rice to Claude Laverdure to tell him that the relationship between Chrétien and Bush was "irreparably broken." What was fascinating was that she was not angry at all about foreign policy differences. Her objection was to perceived interference in domestic American politics by the prime minister's comments about the U.S. budget deficit and about "his friend Clinton" (who was Bush's political adversary).

Laverdure was very concerned. That was his job. We were in St. Petersburg for the three-hundredth anniversary celebrations of the city when the call came. Laverdure and I met the prime minister at one of the elaborately decorated dachas that President Putin had built on the Gulf of Finland for his foreign guests (even though the guests were only staying for a few days). The prime minister was less concerned. He was prepared to explain the context of his remarks to the president whom he would see that evening in St. Petersburg. He did so, and both leaders agreed that everything they read in the press should be taken with a grain of salt.

Chapter 19

TEAM CANADA: MORE THAN A TRADE MISSION

"We are all mere petty provincial politicians at present; perhaps, by and by, some of us will rise to the level of national statesmen."

– SIR JOHN A. MACDONALD

Students of federal-provincial relations in Canada, who are accustomed to acrimonious public posturing at televised meetings between the federal prime minister and provincial premiers, would be surprised to learn that crucial talks in 1997 between the federal government and Ontario about ensuring the solvency of Canada's public pension system took place in a hotel lobby in Seoul, South Korea; that early decisions on the amount of money to invest in the National Child Benefit were the product of discussions with provincial premiers on a sightseeing boat on the Chao Phraya River in Bangkok, Thailand; and that the Romanow Commission on Health Care first saw the light of day in conversations on a bus in Beijing, China. This was not the result of globalization creeping into federal-provincial relations; instead it was the product of a deliberate policy not to conduct federal-provincial relations in formal high-stakes settings in Ottawa.

Chrétien came to office in 1993 after decades of very public confrontations between prime ministers and provincial premiers over constitutional issues, energy policy, and, most often, money. The nation watched Pierre Trudeau's epic disputes with strong provincial premiers like Peter Lougheed of Alberta, Brian Peckford of Newfoundland, and René Lévesque of Quebec in the 1970s and 1980s, and then there was Brian Mulroney's famous rolling of the dice in his failed attempts at constitutional reform. The public nature of these confrontations – aided and abetted by media – may have created a heightened sense of drama and crisis in the country, but they were also the continuation of long-standing historical differences between the two levels of government that went back to the time of Confederation.

In 1887, the Liberal premiers of Quebec and Ontario, Honoré Mercier and Oliver Mowat, had formed an alliance to take on Sir John A. Macdonald's federal government. They convened a conference of provincial premiers in Quebec City without the presence of the prime minister. The premiers who attended duly demanded Senate reform in the interests of the provinces, a large increase in what were then called subsidies from the federal government to the provinces, as well as changes to the Constitution to increase provincial powers. Just as Macdonald had to face an alliance of Mowat and Mercier in the 1880s, Mackenzie King was confronted by an alliance of Quebec and Ontario under Premiers Maurice Duplessis and Mitchell Hepburn in the late 1930s, and again under Premiers Duplessis and George Drew after the Second World War.

In those days, Parliament did not sit for very long. There was no television news coverage, and there was no such thing as a news cycle that demanded instantaneous reaction from politicians. The prime minister had much more time then to reflect on what to do. Macdonald, for his part, received the provincial demands, studied them, put them in his desk drawer, and went on with his agenda of governing. While not having to meet his political adversaries on television every night probably made it easier for him to say no than it would be for a prime minister in the twenty-first century, Macdonald also had his own clear vision of Canada as well as the political backbone that enabled him to stand up to the demands of the provincial premiers. It is certain that if Macdonald, Mowat, and Mercier were to come back to life today more than one hundred years later, while they certainly would not recognize the world of technology around them, they would have little trouble recognizing the world of federal-provincial relations.

A Setting for Posturing, not Progress

CHRÉTIEN'S APPROACH to federal-provincial relations when he became prime minister was much influenced by his earlier days in government. During the thirty years from when he was first elected to the House of Commons in 1963 until he became prime minister, he had witnessed and participated in some of the highly publicized confrontations that pitted the federal government on one side of the negotiating table, resisting, as best it could, as all the provinces loudly clamoured on the other side of the table for more jurisdiction and more federal money. Inevitably, the public impression of ten articulate people on one side, and one stubborn unreasonable person on the other side – rather than of two orders of government with differing but legitimate points of view – always heightened the appearance of crisis and confrontation. The main story in the media was usually about who apparently "won" and who apparently "lost" rather than about the real issues under debate.

Chrétien often reflected with me on the lessons he drew from those experiences. He and I were both convinced that unless those representing the federal government have an unusual strength of purpose, a commitment to principle, a very strong backbone, and a very thick skin when it comes to media criticism, they will inevitably be worn down by incessant "fed-bashing" by the provinces.

We were both particularly influenced by two lessons we had learned from our participation in the federal-provincial constitutional negotiations of the summer of 1980. One is that when ministers and officials from federal and provincial governments spend time together informally, as they did for months in 1980, they establish the personal relationships that are later indispensable in finding practical solutions to problems. A second is that the federal government should never enter into a one-way negotiation with the provinces doing all the asking, and the feds doing all the giving; instead, as in 1980, the federal government should come to the table with its own list of what it wants from the provinces. His government applied those lessons in a variety of ways.

Chrétien's objective – particularly with the prospect of another Quebec referendum looming in the not too distant future – was to avoid the public posturing that had become endemic to federal-provincial relations since the early 1960s. He wanted to find ways to demonstrate that the country's governments could work together co-operatively. Having repeated over and over during the 1993 election campaign that if he were asked to list his one hundred priorities, constitutional reform would be priority number one hundred and one, Chrétien was determined to focus on achieving meaningful co-operation between both levels of government on matters of primary concern to Canadians, such as job creation, rather than quarrelling over esoteric constitutional issues. Accordingly, the first decision he made as a result of his decades of experience and reflection was to convene First Ministers' Meetings – like international summit meetings – only in order to formalize or put the finishing touches to agreements already reached in advance by ministers or officials, and to do so without television cameras in the meeting room.

Team Canada – At Home and Abroad

CHRÉTIEN HAD CAMPAIGNED in 1993 on a promise to establish, as a job-creating measure, a $6 billion federal-provincial-municipal infrastructure program, funded equally by the three levels of government. Upon forming his government, he named Art Eggleton, because of his experience as the former mayor of Toronto, as the minister responsible for infrastructure in addition to being president of the Treasury Board, and charged him with the task of negotiating an agreement with each of the provinces, to be ratified at an early meeting between the prime minister and the premiers. Eggleton moved quickly and soon reached an agreement in principle with his provincial counterparts. Needing only to formalize Eggleton's work, Chrétien took the opportunity in December 1993 to call the premiers together for the first time in his administration. They met in Ottawa in closed session – without the forum that television cameras normally provided for grandstanding – and with no other ministers or officials except for two note-takers in the room. In good spirits they quickly ratified the agreement on infrastructure that had been negotiated in advance, and then took advantage of the atmosphere of co-operation in the conference room to agree to a suggestion that the prime minister and all the premiers join together the following year to lead a Team Canada trade mission overseas to demonstrate how the different levels of government can work together. Chrétien, who wanted to establish the same type of informal rapport with provincial premiers as he had established with provincial ministers and officials during constitutional negotiations in the summer of 1980, sensed that even more important than trade promotion, Team Canada would be an innovative way to establish good personal relationships.

In November 1994, the prime minister and Aline Chrétien, and all the provincial premiers – with the exception of Jacques Parizeau, the newly elected separatist premier of Quebec – accompanied by their spouses and officials, along with some federal officials (myself included), hundreds of business people, and a large media contingent embarked on an airplane in Ottawa bound for ten days in China. The long flight included refuelling stops in Anchorage, and again in Tokyo, before finally arriving in Beijing almost twenty-four hours after leaving home. Almost from the moment of takeoff, there was a sense of adventure, excitement, and camaraderie, which was also nurtured by the generous hospitality provided en route by the Canadian Airlines crew.

The mission to Beijing, Shanghai, and Hong Kong produced much more than a number of business deals, signed contracts, and memoranda of intent that would lead to later contracts. It gave everyone the chance to work together, enjoy one another's company, and have fun together visiting the Forbidden City and the Great Wall, and it gave us the chance to get to know one another on a first-name basis in a way that would not have been possible if we had only seen one another during formal meetings in Canada.

The annual ten-day Team Canada trade missions produced results that, as Chrétien had hoped, were far better than formal annual First Ministers' Meetings in Canada. Being overseas and away from the grind of daily domestic issues and domestic media enabled everyone to put Canada's problems in proper perspective. We discovered that our own problems and so called crises paled into insignificance when compared with what other countries face. Perhaps more important, the prime minister and all the premiers were reinforced in their need to work together, avoiding petty quarrels and internal divisions as they came face to face with the fact that Canada is itself a small country on a world scale.

We had the opportunity during long airplane or bus rides together, over drinks and meals, and sometimes while sightseeing on a rare day off, or simply between meetings, to discuss issues of domestic concern to each government in a pleasantly relaxed way. The relationships we established with one another on our trips overseas enabled us to cut some seemingly intractable Gordian knots during the course of the trade missions themselves. For example, the Team Canada trade mission to Korea, Thailand, and the Philippines in January 1997 was the improbable venue for Prime Minister Chrétien and Ontario premier Mike Harris to address the sustainability of Canada's public pension system, and for Chrétien, Saskatchewan premier Roy Romanow, and Premier Glen Clark of British Columbia to make significant progress on the funding of the National Child Benefit.

The Canada Pension Plan

IN 1997, WHILE other countries in the industrialized world – no matter how hard they were trying – had still been unable to guarantee that their public pension plans would not go bankrupt before they could meet the expectations of an aging baby-boom generation, federal and provincial governments succeeded in reforming Canada's public pension system to make it sustainable well into the second half of the twenty-first century. The successful reform of the Canada Pension Plan was a singular achievement of long-term significance. In true

My life as the prime minister's adviser took me around the world, meeting many world leaders. Here Jean Chrétien and I confer privately at the Commonwealth conference in Edinburgh in October 1997.

Diana Murphy

Meeting Russia's current president, Vladimir Putin.

Diana Murphy

. . . and Chinese president Jiang Zemin.

Jean-Marc Carisse

. . . and Cuban president Fidel Castro. The scene reminded Peter
Donolo, to my right, of Fredericton, New Brunswick.

Jean-Marc Carisse

Fidel Castro expounds on a theory, while the Canadian delegation,
including his old friend James Bartleman, beside him, listens with
interest.

A gathering of family and PMO staff watches the highly satisfactory results of the 2000 election at the Chrétiens' home in Shawinigan.

The prime minister and I pose with the man who ran the campaign, my old friend John Rae.

A moment of triumph shows Chrétien in a jubilant mood.

Jean Chrétien and his staff demonstrate their keen interest as Paul Martin reacts on television to the news that Chrétien will be stepping down – but not yet.

Jean-Marc Carisse

At 24 Sussex Drive with Jean and Aline Chrétien.

Diana Murphy

A much more typical Ottawa shot – trudging back from the House wit[
Chrétien and Bruce Hartley in the snowy twilight.

Canadian style, it passed almost completely unnoticed in Canada, even though it was noted with considerable envy by governments of other countries. Without Team Canada, it may not have happened.

The Canada Pension Plan (CPP) was the product of difficult federal-provincial negotiations in the early 1960s, and was one of the most important achievements of the Pearson government. The law creating the CPP provided that any changes to the plan would require the approval of the federal government and two-thirds of participating provinces (Quebec has its own parallel but fully portable plan) representing two-thirds of the total population of those provinces. It also provided for a mandatory federal-provincial review every ten years so that the federal and provincial governments could agree to make appropriate changes to modernize the CPP structure. The federal minister responsible for overseeing the review of the CPP is the finance minister, and as a result, the ten-year review that was to take place in 1996 gave Paul Martin, and his deputy David Dodge, the opportunity to address the looming problem of how to ensure that there would still be public pensions for the baby-boom generation as it approached retirement. Chrétien gave Martin and Dodge the broad negotiating mandate they requested for their negotiations with the provinces, and, in particular, he authorized them to seek provincial agreement to a substantial increase in annual premiums paid by employees and employers to finance the CPP.

Dodge and Martin kept their negotiations with the provinces low-key and off the public radar. Working groups of officials and experts from the federal government and all the provinces met first and prepared options and recommendations for their finance ministers. Then ministers met in closed session. While Martin was unable to achieve unanimity among his provincial colleagues, he was successful in reaching an agreement in principle with enough provinces, including Ontario and Alberta, to obtain the two-thirds support legally necessary to accomplish a reform that would put the Canada Pension Plan on an actuarially sound basis for the next seventy-five years. But Martin soon discovered that the consensus he had achieved with his provincial finance colleagues was so fragile that it could fall apart before provincial governments had done the paperwork required for the necessary formal approvals.

Martin called me in early January 1997 shortly before I was to leave on the Team Canada trade mission to Korea, Thailand, and the Philippines: "Eddie, we have a problem with the agreement finance ministers reached to deal with the long-term viability of the Canada Pension Plan. Ontario represents more than one-third of the population, which makes its consent essential. Mike Harris apparently doesn't want to move on it now, and unless Ontario moves quickly, Alberta could drop out. As you know, because there wasn't unanimity among all the provinces, without Alberta, we won't have the requisite number of provinces on side even if Ontario later signs on."

"Paul, what's your problem with Alberta?" I asked. "You keep telling me you have great relations with its finance minister."

"I do," Martin answered. "The problem is that my friend Jim Dinning, who is the current minister, is about to leave politics. He'll probably be replaced by Stockwell Day, who, unlike Dinning, apparently opposes the increase in employer and employee premiums that are fundamental to the reform package. With Day as finance minister, Alberta might withdraw its consent to the whole deal. So we need Ontario to move quickly before Dinning retires. Can you and the prime minister do something with Harris on your trip?"

I felt then – as I often did in different files that were handed to me over the years – that my role was like that of a relief pitcher in baseball who is brought in late in the game with his team slightly ahead, but with the other side at bat, and the winning runs on base. Our team had done the hard work to get us this far, but now the prime minister and I were responsible for the final outs. It was the bottom of the ninth inning and there were two batters left to retire, Mike Harris and his finance minister, Ernie Eves. Harris was well known for his virulent opposition to tax increases of any sort. I was sure that it would have been counterproductive to organize a formal meeting with him – where he might very well have cast a veto – to seek his approval of a reform that provided for large-scale tax increases. On the other hand, the informality of the Team Canada format provided the perfect setting to raise issues.

When I saw Harris in the lobby of a hotel in Seoul one morning after breakfast, I took the opportunity to button-hole him and ask if we could talk for a few minutes. I quickly outlined what Martin had told me, and urged him not to block a crucial reform for Canadians. He listened, took a deep breath, and finally said, "Look, Eddie, you know I personally don't agree with any reform that increases any tax whatsoever, but you can tell Martin that I am prepared to leave the case of the CPP in the hands of Ernie Eves. If he agrees, I'll go along with it. I won't overrule him. When you get home, speak to my chief of staff, David Lindsay."

I was immensely relieved, but wanted Harris to confirm with Chrétien what he had told me. I immediately went to see the prime minister, who was in his hotel suite preparing for his next meeting, reported what I had just done, and suggested that he find an early occasion to speak to Premier Harris to confirm my conversation. Later that morning, Chrétien told me that as they were walking together into a meeting with Korean government leaders, Harris had confirmed with him that he would not be an obstacle to CPP reform. Their conversation took all of thirty seconds. That was one batter out.

I phoned Martin from Korea, told him what we had done, and undertook to call Lindsay as soon as I got back to Canada. Martin was relieved because he knew that Eves agreed in principle with the proposed CPP reforms. However, federal-provincial relations are not that simple. Eves and the Ontario government wanted to use any leverage they had in the pension negotiations to solve unresolved issues of their own with the federal government that had nothing to do with the Canada Pension Plan. Eves was the next batter we faced at the plate.

When I returned from Asia, I called David Lindsay. He and I had established a good personal relationship, having worked constructively together on several files between the two governments over the previous year. I told him about the progress we had made in Asia and suggested that we meet as soon as possible to finalize an agreement.

Lindsay suggested a meeting in Ottawa between the two of us and the deputy ministers of finance of Ontario and Canada, Michael Gourley and David Dodge. The four of us met for more than seven hours in my boardroom in the Langevin Building beginning just before lunch on a Friday afternoon in early February 1997. Shortly after we sat down, my assistant brought us some takeout Lebanese food on plastic plates with plastic cutlery for lunch. The prospect of something similar for dinner ensured that we would either reach an agreement or break off negotiations before the next meal. It was a harsh way of negotiating.

In the United States, logrolling takes place primarily in the Congress. With little party discipline, individual congressmen and senators unashamedly use their power over legislation to make tradeoffs to obtain what they want for their districts or states, or for the special-interest groups to which many of them are beholden. In Canada there is much less logrolling than in the United States in large part because of party discipline in Parliament and provincial legislatures. What logrolling there is takes place primarily between the federal and provincial governments. The negotiation in my boardroom was a classic case of Canadian logrolling. The Ontario representatives brought to the table a smorgasbord of issues that had nothing to do with the public pension system. They included matters relating to student loans, the collection of the retail sales tax at the border, infrastructure, employment insurance premium rates, and federal spending on immigration in Ontario. It was irritating for David Dodge and me to contemplate that critical reforms relating to the sustainability of Canada's public pension system required reaching agreement on such totally irrelevant matters. Dodge didn't hide his disgust and impatience and, at one point, was ready to walk away, but we both understood that if we wanted Ontario to agree to the pension plan reform, the nature of federal-provincial relations is such that we had little choice but to deal with the issues our counterparts had put on the table. Dealing with the issues, however, didn't mean agreeing to everything Ontario wanted. Dodge and I refused to agree to anything that would create precedents that might apply to other provinces, and we refused to tie our hands on matters strictly within federal jurisdiction, such as employment insurance premium rates, but we agreed to discuss those issues on the list that were specific to Ontario

Dodge and I had deliberately not sought a negotiating mandate in advance from the minister of finance and the prime minister because we wanted to have the maximum flexibility to achieve the government's objective. We knew that our bosses had enough confidence in us that they would not second-guess how we handled the negotiations. If we were unsuccessful, it would be our responsibility and not theirs, and they might then have another chance themselves to do it another way.

At around seven o'clock in the evening as dinner time and the prospect of more of what we ate for lunch loomed large, we finally came to an agreement on enough of the issues specific to Ontario to satisfy our Ontario counterparts, and to allow Eves to ratify the social security reform before the imminent Cabinet shuffle in Alberta. The last batter was out and the game was over.

Dodge and I walked out of the boardroom into my own office and looked at each other with both relief and some apprehension. I reminded him that in the first meeting we had in 1993, he had briefed Chaviva Hosek and me on the urgency of taking action to ensure the long-term safety of public pension plans, and now we finally had an agreement that would make the Canada Pension Plan sustainable for the next seventy-five years. Nevertheless, the political timing, as he had warned us back then, was potentially more problematic. The government would have to explain to the Canadian people shortly before an expected election that there would be a large increase in Canada Pension Plan premiums deducted immediately from paycheques in order to provide for pensions fifteen to twenty years or more in the future. It would be a test of whether good long-term public policy actually makes good short-term politics. For a moment we wondered whether our bosses would agree that we had done the right thing. With a big grin on his face, Dodge laughed and said to me, "Who will tell the finance minister what we just agreed to?" I upped the ante, "Maybe if I agree to tell the minister of finance, I could convince you to tell the prime minister." We both chuckled and then decided that we would each call our own boss. He called Martin and I called Chrétien. Both were unreservedly pleased.

The reform of the CPP illustrates the Chrétien government's approach to successful federal-provincial negotiations. Chrétien didn't like to raise the ante about a proposed major government initiative ahead of time, and say publicly that it was crucial to the success of the government as a whole. His considered view was that with few exceptions, important policy initiatives such as CPP reform are more likely to succeed if the prime minister approves the negotiating mandate, delegates to his ministers, such as Paul Martin in this case, the responsibility to carry the ball publicly, and reserves his own involvement to those strategic interventions, such as his and mine with Harris in Seoul, where only the prime minister and his office can make a positive difference. According to Chrétien, a day or two of good headlines for a prime minister sometimes simply serves to set a target for Opposition parties to shoot at to weaken the overall credibility of the government. This is exactly what later happened in the United States when President George W. Bush announced that social security reform would be the centrepiece of his second term agenda. The Democrats duly seized on the Bush plan as the centrepiece of their opposition strategy, and eventually succeeded in derailing it.

Reshaping the Role of the Federal Government

THE REFORM OF the Canada Pension Plan was one of two major federal-provincial initiatives that resulted in part from the Team Canada mission to Asia in 1997. Combatting child poverty had long been a goal of governments regardless of their ideological stripe. Low-income families often found themselves worse off in low-paying jobs compared with welfare because as soon as they moved off of social assistance they lost valuable benefits, including health, dental, and prescription drugs. By 1997, the Caledon Institute, a social policy non-governmental organization, and Western Canadian provincial premiers had developed and endorsed a plan to help low-income parents to clamber over the barriers they faced moving from social assistance into a paying job. The plan was for the federal government to create a National Child Benefit with monthly payments to low-income families with children, and give the provinces the ability to adjust their social assistance to ensure that enhanced benefits and services would continue when parents on welfare found full employment. It would, however, require considerable new federal financial resources. Team Canada provided the opportunity to talk about it.

The idea of the National Child Benefit found particular support from two NDP premiers, Glen Clark of British Columbia and Roy Romanow of Saskatchewan. They took every opportunity they could find, including a sightseeing cruise on the Chao Phraya River through Bangkok, to urge Chrétien to endorse the plan and build its funding over future years. The prime minister listened to their arguments, came back to Ottawa, and, within a month, delivered a major policy speech in which he committed the government to the idea of the National Child Benefit as a critical element in any concerted effort to reduce child poverty. It then took a year of federal-provincial negotiations, led on the federal side by Human Resources Minister Pierre Pettigrew, to turn the plan into reality and into what some have described as the most significant new Canadian social program since medicare.

Chrétien saw the National Child Benefit as a building block in reshaping the role of the federal government to make it more relevant to Canadians. When he came to office, many Liberals were nostalgic for the years between 1968 and 1984 when Trudeau's magnetic personality and the strength, vigour, and dynamism he projected were such that Canadians identified his tenure in office with a strong national government. Ironically, Trudeau had actually been responsible for strengthening the role of provincial governments at the expense of the federal government by ending conditional grants and providing a dramatic shift in taxation resources from the federal government to the provinces. Chrétien, who had always spoken out for a strong and highly visible federal government, wanted to vigorously reassert the federal role.

The early years of the Chrétien administration, however, had been dominated by a looming fiscal crisis as well as a Quebec referendum. There was no possibility of significant new federal initiatives until the country's finances were under control; instead the government had to make drastic cuts to programs that had a direct impact on citizens as well as to transfer payments to the provinces. Furthermore, the fallout from the Quebec referendum and the 1995 budget resulted in the delegation of some federal jurisdiction to the provinces. While these federal withdrawals, except for manpower training, were relatively symbolic, the symbolism itself was significant and worrying for some members of the Cabinet and the Liberal caucus, who were openly concerned that the federal government would soon be less and less relevant to individual Canadians.

By 1997, however, the imminent prospect of budget surpluses for the first time in more than a quarter-century presented the government with new opportunities. Chrétien decided to devote these newfound federal fiscal resources to health, the condition of children in low-income families, and the promotion of the knowledge economy. He wanted to do so in co-operation with the provinces, but in a way that would rebuild and reshape the role of the federal government in the lives of Canadians. His style, as always, was not to trumpet grand visions in advance, but simply to act. Within seven years, the federal role in each of those priority areas had become much larger, and the federal government's direct relations to citizens were stronger than they had been for a long time. The National Child Benefit came first; soon there was more money for health and the first Health Accord with the provinces, and throughout, there were major new initiatives to build the research and teaching infrastructure of Canadian universities. Each was accomplished in different ways, and provide different examples of how things get done.

Chapter 20

A HEALTHY DEBATE

"I came to believe that health services ought not to have a price tag on them, and that people should be able to get whatever health services they required irrespective of their ability to pay."

– TOMMY DOUGLAS

Ever since medicare came into effect in 1968, health-care funding has been a critical public policy issue in Canada for both levels of government. Medicare was originally created as a joint federal-provincial shared-cost program. Subject to certain conditions, the federal government undertook to fund the provinces for 50 per cent of the health costs that patients before medicare would otherwise have had to pay to doctors and hospitals, while the provinces paid the other half. In 1977, the federal government replaced this funding arrangement with a complex formula where the federal government paid half of its estimated share in cash and the other half in "tax points," that is by reducing the personal and corporate income taxes it collected and allowing the provinces to raise theirs by the same amount. This new formula made it difficult to calculate how much the federal government contributed to provincial medicare costs. However, whatever the calculation might have been, as a deficit-reduction measure, the Mulroney government began freezing cash transfers to the provinces, and then the Chrétien government made significant cuts to these transfer payments in its deficit-slashing budget of February 1995.

Unfortunately, these freezes and cuts were happening at the same time as provincial health-care costs were growing rapidly. People were living longer and needing more expensive care in the last years of life; there was an explosion in costly new medical treatments, technology, and equipment; and there was enormous pressure for increases in salaries for health professionals. While medicare had originally been designed to pay for doctors and hospitals, new drugs and the needs of home care had become essential components of a modern health-care system and were putting new strains on resources. Growing health-care costs were taking up ever-increasing portions of provincial budgets just as aging baby boomers were getting ready to place potentially heavy new demands on the system.

Provincial governments complained about the cuts to transfer payments when they were made in 1995, but they grudgingly understood the federal fiscal situation in the early Chrétien years. After the elimination of the deficit and the emergence of growing federal budget surpluses, they began in earnest to press for a significant increase in federal transfers for health. The federal government increased provincial transfer payments in 1997 and again in 1999, but the demand from the provinces for more health-care dollars continued to grow. In 2000, at a time when public opinion polling put health care at the top of the list of Canadians' concerns and priorities, provincial pressures on the federal government for substantial new increases in its funding of medicare increased almost daily. The Liberal caucus expected the government to act, and both the Cabinet and the prime minister were willing to do so.

By the summer of 2000, Chrétien was ready to hold a First Ministers' Meeting to discuss the financing of health care in Canada, but only in accordance with his stand that such meetings must be well prepared in advance. At stake was the expenditure of billions of dollars of taxpayers' money, the role of the federal government, and, most important, the health care of Canadians. The critical question for the government was not simply how much money to transfer to the provinces, but how to transfer it. For almost a quarter-century since Trudeau did away with conditional grants in 1977, other than the important principle that provinces respect the conditions of the Canada Health Act, which protect the public nature of Canadian medicare, the federal government had not tied new health-care funding to provincial agreement on how the money should be spent. However in 2000, as the demands for new health-care dollars were seemingly insatiable, there was a reluctance in the caucus, the Cabinet, the Finance department, and the Health department for Ottawa to simply issue more blank cheques to the provinces, without some understanding as to how the money would be spent.

Chrétien himself was never inclined to sign blank cheques to the provinces. He had always viewed the constitutional role of the federal government as much more than just that of a simple tax collector that turns its revenues over unconditionally to other levels of government and then gets out of the way. Ten years earlier, in a speech Eric Maldoff and I helped prepare that he delivered at the University of Ottawa, a week before he announced his candidacy for the Liberal leadership, he had set out his thinking about the role of the federal government: "The government of Canada has a crucial responsibility to provide leadership at the national level. Elected by all Canadians and endowed with the legitimacy that this bestows, the federal government must identify the challenges the country faces, set goals, and chart a course to equip Canadians to meet those goals." Identifying challenges, setting goals, and charting courses were not compatible in Chrétien's mind with simply signing blank cheques to the provinces.

Preparing for a First Ministers' Meeting

I SPENT A lot of my time in 2000 at the request of the prime minister preparing for the First Ministers' Meeting, which eventually took place on September 11. My own role was to help put together the federal team, work on the development of a federal position and a negotiating strategy, consult with outside advisers, keep the prime minister informed, and ensure that others on our team knew where the prime minister stood on the issues. Our task was to prepare recommendations for Chrétien on a federal position and a strategy for achieving our objectives, as well as to engage where appropriate in preliminary discussions with some of the provinces. The team was made up of those who could best get the job done regardless of their official capacities, or whether they were public servants or political advisers. They were all good people. There was Kevin Lynch, deputy minister of finance; David Dodge, deputy minister of health, and his assistant deputy minister, Ian Shugart; Paul Genest, senior policy adviser in the office of the minister of health; George Anderson, deputy minister of intergovernmental affairs; Mel Cappe, the Clerk of the Privy Council, as well as Ian Green and Ruth Dantzer from the PCO; Alex Himelfarb, deputy minister of Canadian heritage, in his capacity as a strategic thinker and an experienced federal provincial negotiator; and Chaviva Hosek and myself from the PMO.

We had to determine how much new money the federal government should commit to put into health, whether the money should be tied to certain specific provincial expenditures, what role the federal government should assume, and finally, how best to achieve our objectives. I prepared a strategy paper for initial discussion among our team. We met throughout the summer of 2000 at least weekly, and sometimes daily and even twice daily. One of the purposes of our frequent meetings was to report to each other on our activities so as to be well informed of what each of us was doing, and avoid being put inadvertently in a position where provincial governments could play one or more of us off against the other.

In Praise of Ad Hoc Committees

AS WELL AS the team of officials, Chrétien also created an ad hoc Cabinet committee to make recommendations on a federal approach to health care. In 2000, the Cabinet by happy chance included three former provincial ministers of health: Bernard Boudreau of Nova Scotia, Elinor Caplan of Ontario, and Lucienne Robillard of Quebec. Chrétien wanted the benefit of their expertise and appointed them to the ad hoc committee along with Health Minister Allan Rock,

Finance Minister Paul Martin, and Intergovernmental Affairs Minister Stéphane Dion. Chaviva Hosek and I attended all the meetings on behalf of the prime minister.

As would be expected, the committee spent considerable time listening to and debating the views and recommendations of Allan Rock. But in one respect it operated in a refreshing and creative way unlike normal Cabinet and Cabinet committees, which tend to debate papers prepared by officials and signed by ministers, and rarely seek advice from anyone outside the Cabinet or the public service. This committee invited a number of health-care experts – academics, researchers, hospital administrators – from different parts of the country to spend five hours one afternoon and evening to advise and help ministers draw conclusions. I came out of that session wondering why we had not done more of that in the past, and hoping that future Cabinets would spend more time seeking that type of outside advice.

Setting the Stage for the Meeting

BOTH THE COMMITTEE of Cabinet and the team of officials (many of whom attended the Cabinet committee meetings) concluded that there should not be a new unconditional injection of federal funds to the provinces. Instead, the federal government should make new money conditional on the provinces' using it for certain particular purposes, and accounting publicly to their citizens on its use. We agreed on a recommendation to the prime minister that he should negotiate a health accord with the provinces in return for new federal money. To reach a health accord, Chrétien counted a great deal on the work Allan Rock and his deputy, David Dodge, were doing with their provincial counterparts. I worked closely with them as part of the federal team, since they wanted to use my experience in federal-provincial relations, my contacts from Team Canada, and the knowledge I had acquired from my attendance at all meetings between the prime minister and provincial premiers over the previous seven years.

During the summer of 2000, I participated in federal-provincial conferences, first of deputy ministers of health presided by David

Dodge and then of health ministers presided by Allan Rock. It was fascinating to hear provincial health ministers say privately in one-on-one conversations with federal officials that ideally they would find it in their interests to be "forced" by Ottawa to agree on how to spend new federal money. They didn't want to go on pouring more money into the existing system, and confessed their fears that pressure from unions and professional associations would mean that new monies would go mostly to increased salaries for doctors and nurses rather than to new investments in the health-care system. They preferred to have an agreement with the federal government that they could use as a lever with the entrenched interests in their provinces, even blaming the federal government for their not being able to spend the money according to the wishes of the special interests.

There was little disagreement among health ministers as to the best approaches for using new resources to improve the health-care system in Canada. They all agreed – depending on the amount of the increased federal monies – on the need to create a system of primary care to improve access to family physicians, expand home care, deal with the increasing cost of new drugs, purchase new equipment, and create a system of electronic health records. They understood that an agreement with the federal government would "force" them to do what they wanted to do in the first place, but only if they could overcome the vested interests in their own provinces. Everyone agreed on the need for efficiency in health-care spending. To reach that objective and to encourage the development of best practices across the country, the federal government wanted the provinces to report publicly to their citizens on the results of investments in their health-care systems. No one disagreed with the principle of reporting and accountability, but there was little enthusiasm for it, as some provincial ministers and officials feared what the public reaction would be when their citizens (and electors) learned that their health-care system was not as good as elsewhere in Canada. However, they all understood that it would be hard to go on the record and argue publicly against transparency. So we were pleased when federal and provincial health ministers agreed in early August that David Dodge would prepare the first discussion draft of a potential First Ministers Health Accord. This was very important because in any negotiation, the person holding the drafting pen plays a crucial role in providing the desired shades of meaning, and usually has the upper hand in the outcome. We were determined that the federal government "hold the pen" and were relieved that everyone agreed. The federal team then held lengthy sessions with Dodge on the drafting of the accord.

Our federal team devoted a lot of time to discussing who should speak to whom in each province. It depended primarily on personal relationships, because federal-provincial negotiations, like private-sector negotiations, are most successful when there are pre-existing relationships of trust. It is another reason why Team Canada was so important. In the case of some provinces, I used my relationships; in others, it was Dodge or Lynch or Himelfarb. Sometimes I spoke to premiers, other times we spoke to ministers, deputy ministers, or chiefs of staff to premiers. And sometimes we asked the prime minister to place a call to a particular premier or find a reason to meet one. In those cases, I briefed the prime minister in advance, attended the meetings, or listened in the prime minister's office as he spoke on the telephone and then reported back to the federal team.

If our target audience had just been federal and provincial health ministers, it would have been relatively easy to reach an agreement on a federal-provincial health accord to present to First Ministers for ratification. But there were two major obstacles in the way. First, I learned in a conversation with Saskatchewan premier Roy Romanow that provincial health ministers did not necessarily speak for their premiers. Romanow and I had known each other since the constitutional negotiations of 1980, and had developed a friendship over the years that was nurtured on Team Canada trips, and that allowed us to share confidences, work together sometimes on issues involving only Saskatchewan and the federal government, and sometimes on general federal-provincial relations issues where Romanow's behind-the-scenes work was often crucial to successful outcomes. I called him several times to get his views as we were preparing for the First Ministers' Meeting on health. Romanow warned me to be careful of relying on the word of provincial health ministers, saying that his fellow premiers were wary that left to their own devices, their ministers would make commitments that would eat up most of the entire budget of each province. As a result, while Chrétien had complete trust in Rock and Dodge, through no fault of their own, they could not be the only ones negotiating in advance with the provinces, since the premiers were going to be involved down the line.

Rule One – Avoid Intergovernmental Affairs

THE SECOND OBSTACLE was that while health ministers saw that entering into a health accord with the federal government would be in the interests of achieving the reforms they wanted in their health-care systems, Intergovernmental Affairs officials in their provinces had a different view. They jealously guarded their own bailiwicks from any change to the status quo. Intergovernmental Affairs officials in many of the provinces had been around for a long time, were almost entirely process-oriented, focused on arcane trivia from past negotiations, and spent many years of their careers refighting old federal-provincial battles. I learned that the best way to achieve concrete results in federal-provincial negotiations is to keep most Intergovernmental Affairs departments at a great distance.

I relearned that lesson in July 2000, when I sat through a joint meeting in Ottawa of deputy ministers of health and of intergovernmental affairs where David Dodge had asked me to be part of his delegation. The meeting began with Kathy Bouey, the deputy minister of intergovernmental affairs in Ontario, challenging my right to be in the room. Dodge quickly told her that he wasn't choosing her delegation and she wasn't choosing his. I was quite certain that it wasn't personal and that she was acting under instructions (as she later confirmed to me during a coffee break), and was probably quite uncomfortable doing what she had to do.

Kathy Bouey and I had worked together in the past when she had been in the federal government. She also knew how much, as a young assistant to Finance Minister Chrétien, I admired and learned from her father, Gerald Bouey, who was the governor of the Bank of Canada; so I didn't take her challenge to my presence personally but saw it rather more ominously as a warning shot across the bows that Ontario would not easily agree to anything the federal government proposed.

The federal team throughout the summer knew that the prime minister had no interest in convening a First Ministers' Meeting that would end in deadlock with federal and provincial governments exchanging angry words. He would be very reluctant to convene such a meeting without being confident of a reasonable prospect of success.

By the end of August 2000 as a result of a period of intense informal discussions with different provincial governments – including Ontario – the federal team was ready to recommend to the prime minister that he convene a First Ministers' Meeting, even though we could not guarantee the outcome in a way he would have preferred. But we had come to the conclusion that in exchange for the right amount of new federal money, the provinces would agree to a robust health accord.

We had a difficult internal negotiation as well. We had to convince the Department of Finance to agree on the amount of money necessary for the prime minister to put on the negotiating table to reach an agreement with the provinces. The breakthrough with Finance came on the Labour Day weekend. Kevin Lynch, who is a fierce protector of the federal purse, had left Ottawa for forty-eight hours to drive his daughter to university in New Brunswick. He later jokingly told me that the trip with his daughter cost the federal Treasury $5 billion over five years! On the other hand, Erin Lynch can take credit for getting her father out of town at the right moment so as to allow us in his absence to make the compromises necessary to reach a final federal-provincial deal on health care!

Advance Strategy for the Meeting

CHRÉTIEN UNDERSTOOD that he was entering the crucial First Ministers' Meeting of September 11, 2000, without an agreement in principle that only required ratification. He developed a clear strategy ahead of time for achieving his objectives. First, he believed that the more people there are in the negotiating room, the more there is an opportunity for grandstanding. Political leaders have a tendency to play to the galleries, and particularly want their own officials to go back home and report on how hard their premier fought for the interests of their province. So he decided to keep officials and ministers away from the negotiating table. They could stay in anterooms and be available to give advice during adjournments. The negotiating room would be restricted to the prime minister, the provincial premiers, territorial government leaders, and one note-taker for the federal side and one note-taker for the provincial side. Second, he was not going to get involved in a long, drawn-out negotiation. He said that he had no intention of bargaining "like a rug merchant." He had a bottom line that he would make clear, and from which he would not be moved.

The first part of Chrétien's plan was to hold a dinner meeting with the premiers the evening before the conference began where he would tell them that he would only agree to increase the federal transfer payments for health care in return for their agreement to the health accord that federal and provincial health ministers had agreed to in principle during the summer. In particular, the prime minister would insist on provincial agreement to report publicly to their citizens on progress made in achieving their undertakings in the accord. At dinner, he decided to give the premiers some broad indication of how much he was prepared to increase the transfer payments in return for the health accord, but he wouldn't give them full details until the next day in the negotiating room. Chrétien didn't want the premiers – and particularly their advisers – to have the night to put together a strategy for extracting more federal money.

The prime minister had learned from years of federal-provincial negotiating that the only way to avoid a bad deal is to be ready to walk away from the table. So at the dinner table that night (I was not present), he made it clear to the premiers that he didn't need a deal at any price. He let it be known, apparently with a Cheshire cat grin, that as he was in the fourth year of his mandate, he might not be able to resist the temptation to call a federal election over a provincial refusal to agree to provisions for public accountability. As soon as the dinner was over, Chrétien asked me and some of the federal team to meet him at 24 Sussex. He told us that the dinner had gone well, and that he was particularly encouraged by the reaction of Ralph Klein, who said, "Let's sign now and go home." He expected the next day to go well.

It almost didn't.

"Eddie, Find Me Some Words. I Need the Money"

THE FIRST MINISTERS' Meeting started at 9:00 a.m. on Monday, September 11, on the top floor of the Pearson Building. It almost came apart near the start. Chrétien offered to increase federal transfer payments by $21.5 billion over five years, on condition that the provinces sign a health accord; but he made it clear that there would be no new money for any province that wouldn't sign the accord.

His position was critically important because many premiers entered the meeting believing that at the end of the day, Chrétien would not be able to resist the political pressure simply to give the provinces more money, even without an accord, or with a meaningless one.

They clearly didn't know Jean Chrétien very well. After the dinner the evening before, Bernard Lord of New Brunswick, John Hamm of Nova Scotia, Pat Binns of Prince Edward Island, Lucien Bouchard of Quebec, Mike Harris of Ontario, and Gary Doer of Manitoba had concocted a new version of the draft health accord, with little teeth and no role for the federal government. They didn't tell Brian Tobin of Newfoundland, Roy Romanow of Saskatchewan, Ralph Klein of Alberta, and Ujjal Dosanjh of British Columbia, whom they rightly considered to be allies of Chrétien. At least for that day! To the surprise of Chrétien, and the anger of Tobin, Romanow, Klein, and Dosanjh, they put it on the table as a take-it or leave-it proposition.

Chrétien adjourned the meeting and came downstairs to an eighth-floor office to be joined by myself, David Dodge, Mel Cappe, a few other officials, and soon the four premiers who were left out by their colleagues. Chrétien was livid and the other premiers were furious at their colleagues. Klein was ready to sign the accord, take the federal money, and go home. Romanow and Tobin were seething at the other premiers, to the extent that Romanow encouraged the prime minister to use their action as an excuse to call an election. Chrétien said that he would go back into the room, tell the rest of the premiers that what they had done was unacceptable to him and that he would rather have no agreement at all and leave it in the hands of the people of Canada to choose. He duly went in and when some provincial premiers asked for the money unconditionally, the prime minister said that he was not negotiating, and that he would put the share of any province that refused to sign the accord into a trust account in the bank until they signed. Then he adjourned the meeting, for a second time, saying he would think things over and call them back to order later in the morning.

Michael Harris came out of the closed-door meeting into a large waiting area, pulled one of his officials aside, and said, "What do we do now? He's serious that he won't give us the money." Harris then took the elevator to the garage of the Pearson Building and sat for a long time in his car contemplating what to do. There were a number of caucuses all over the Pearson Building; as provincial groupings conferred here and there, different officials from different governments met informally. The general mood was downcast, and it appeared that an agreement would not be possible. The provinces were caught between a rock and a hard place; they wanted the money; their health ministers all agreed with the principles that had been hammered out over the summer, and they knew that Canadians would not be sympathetic to the argument that the federal government had no role in health other than signing cheques to the provinces.

Chrétien came back to the office on the eighth floor. I told him that I was as angry as he was, but that I had read the provincial document, and while there was much in it that was unacceptable, it included a few clauses that were the same as in the original document, and others that just required the reinsertion of a role for the federal government.

I suggested that David Dodge and I take the provincial proposal, prepare marginal notes as to what was acceptable, what was totally unacceptable and why, and what could be made acceptable with some word changes. At first, Chrétien was reluctant. He seemed ready to end the meeting, denounce the premiers, and maybe call a snap election, but he finally agreed to let us try. Within half an hour and with the invaluable assistance of David Dodge, I had a handwritten annotated version of the provincial paper available for the prime minister. We went over it together, he made a few notes of his own, made jokes to others that I had heard countless times before about my lousy handwriting, and agreed to reconvene the conference. Then he used the marginal notes that Dodge and I had prepared for him to set out his bottom line to the premiers. Bouchard – desperate for more federal money – surprisingly spoke up and pronounced it as a good faith effort and the basis for an agreement. But there was still work to be done. Chrétien adjourned just before lunch and said that he needed to hear soon whether there was an agreement or not. An hour and a half passed with no word back from the premiers. It seemed like there was no deal. Then I received a phone call.

Michael Harris, Brian Tobin, and Lucien Bouchard had been meeting in a small office on the first floor of the Pearson Building. Tobin tried to be a consensus builder and a mediator, and he was very good at it. He had established good relations with a number of provincial premiers of different political stripes and formed friendships with them of a lasting nature. His connections and friendship with the prime minister and myself – even though he and I often disagreed on issues and strategy – were strong and long-standing. Yet when he reached me on my cellphone at two o'clock and said, "How fast can you get down here? I'm with Lucien and Mike and we can make a deal," I was skeptical. I knew Tobin very well – he had an Irish gift for blarney – and I was far from sure that he could actually deliver the two most difficult premiers.

"Where are you, Brian?" I asked.

"We're on the first floor. Someone will meet you at the elevator."

There was nothing to lose, so I said, "I'll be right there, but we have very little time. Some of the premiers are getting ready to go home, and the prime minister is angry, and has no intention of continuing a charade."

When I got to the windowless little room where the three premiers were meeting, I was shown to an empty chair beside Bouchard. Tobin was on the other side of him, and Harris was glowering, standing at the back, leaning against a wall. He had formed an unlikely alliance with Lucien Bouchard, and now would not agree to any federal proposal unless Bouchard first agreed. History was repeating itself; it was Mowat and Mercier, Drew and Duplessis against the federal government all over again, although this time Harris was aligned with a separatist premier. I wondered if he really spoke for the people of Ontario in the circumstances. Unlike Harris, Bouchard that day was reasonable and charming. We knew each other from Team Canada trips, and although there was an unbridgeable difference between us on Quebec's place in Canada, we could work together on other issues unrelated to that fundamental one.

With his left hand, Bouchard grasped my right arm just below the elbow and said, "Eddie, find me some words. I need the money." This, I thought, is what federal-provincial relations had always been about – words versus money. We wanted the words to be meaningful, and the provinces, who didn't much care about the words, wanted the money to be meaningful.

I asked him, "What are the problems you have with the draft agreement that the prime minister has proposed?"

Bouchard said that he didn't have problems with any of the principles, but that some of the wording was problematic for him. "You know what my party is like," he said, referring to the Parti Québécois.

I resisted the temptation to say something I might regret and responded matter of factly, "Let's go through it, but we don't have much time, and I don't have a mandate to make changes – although if we come up with something that I believe I can sell to the prime minister, I will try."

It was clear to me right away that all he needed were some face-savers. He wanted a clear statement that nothing in the health accord changed the division of powers between the federal and provincial governments. That was easy to deal with, because no agreement could change the Constitution. I agreed, and he wrote down some wording. When he raised another issue that was more problematic for the federal government, I told him that I could not agree. He said that the words in the agreement would only serve to help Allan Rock, and looking directly at Brian Tobin, Bouchard joked, "Eddie, surely you aren't supporting Rock as the next leader." Tobin laughed; Harris continued to scowl. I smiled, and thought for an instant that I would joke and say that my candidate was Stéphane Dion, the avowed enemy of the separatists, but didn't go down that road, fearing it might jeopardize an agreement.

Once again, Bouchard grabbed my arm and said, "Find me some words. I need the money." Once again, we found face-savers, which Bouchard wrote down. On one issue, technically outside the health accord, where the federal government was insisting that the provinces allocate specific resources to the purchase of new medical equipment, Bouchard said, "I can't agree to that today here in Ottawa. You understand my constraints with my Party. But I will announce in Quebec City when I get home that I will spend the money for new equipment. That way it will be my decision and will not look as though it was imposed on me." I thought that if that was all it takes, I could tell the three premiers I would report back to the prime minister and make a favourable recommendation. Bouchard then gave me his handwritten notes.

I went back upstairs and interrupted the prime minister, who was sitting in the negotiating room with the other seven premiers, waiting and wondering where Tobin, Harris, and Bouchard were. Chrétien came out into the corridor and I rounded up David Dodge and Mel Cappe. When I reported that all Bouchard needed were innocuous face-savers, Chrétien asked to see them. Then he smiled, knowing that he had won, and asked me to get them typed up while he informed the other premiers that a deal was at hand. Our last crisis was finding a typist who could read Bouchard's handwriting, which was even worse than mine. When she finished typing the changes and made copies, I brought them upstairs to the prime minister and the deal was done.

The health accord that was reached on September 11, 2000, was not perfect. Some of the provinces were less than enthusiastic after the fact about fulfilling all the provisions, particularly those respecting public accountability. But it was a beginning, and has been built on in further First Ministers' Meetings under Chrétien in February 2003, and Martin in September 2004. One of Prime Minister Harper's election commitments in 2006 was to negotiate an agreement with the provinces for patient wait-time guarantees for critical medical procedures. The role of the federal government has come a long way from just signing blank cheques to the provinces. It is now involved – as Chrétien hoped back in 1990 – in identifying challenges, setting goals, and charting courses in health care, while fully respecting provincial authority to run their health-care systems.

The next Team Canada mission in February 2001, a few months after the September 2000 First Ministers' Meeting, was once again to China. It was Roy Romanow's last as premier of Saskatchewan, as he was days away from retirement. Romanow took advantage of bus rides during our time in Beijing to speak to me about his idea for a Royal Commission on Health to make recommendations going beyond the September Accord. We found some quiet time in China to discuss the idea with the prime minister. It was not long after we returned to Canada that Chrétien appointed the Romanow Royal Commission on Health Care Reform – another product of Team Canada.

Chapter 21

PREPARING CANADA FOR THE 21ST CENTURY

"If Canadian universities are underfunded so badly that they can no longer function effectively, Canada would disappear overnight from modern history, and become what it was at first, a blank area of natural resources to be exploited by more advanced cultures."

– NORTHROP FRYE, 1984

In the early 1990s, new technology and the information revolution were literally changing the way the world worked. The challenge for governments everywhere was to prepare their countries for the knowledge-based economy. Throughout the forty-seven days of the 1993 election campaign, in speech after speech, three or four and sometimes five times a day, Jean Chrétien's rhetoric – inspired by the Aylmer Conference of the Liberal Party two years earlier – was the same: "We must prepare Canada for the twenty-first century." But he was vague as to how to do so. Chrétien's style was to commit to the general principles he wanted his government to focus on, then put the right people in place to get the job done, and finally leave the details to his ministers and his staff to recommend and implement. He believed that significant change is usually best achieved by proceeding incrementally, taking advantage of changing circumstances, developing concrete initiatives over time, and using each success to breed further successes. It was a style that served him and the country well as the government worked out the steps needed to prepare Canada for this rapidly changing world.

At the time Chrétien became prime minister in 1993, advances in information technology were proceeding at such a pace that it would have been very difficult for any incoming government to foresee and plan for all the detailed initiatives that would be most appropriate over succeeding years to meet the needs of the knowledge-based economy. It is hard to realize more than a decade later – when the Internet is taken for granted and "Googling" is second nature to a young child – that at the time the Chrétien government took office, the potential of the Internet was unfathomable to everyone other than a few research scientists. There were only some fifty Web sites in the world, and they were used for military purposes. On the rare occasion when some policy wonk in the Liberal caucus actually spoke about the Internet, George Baker, a colourful Newfoundland MP, would bring his colleague back to earth by joking that the only important nets were those used in the fishing industry.

Chrétien traced his personal commitment to promote, encourage, and support innovation, research, and post-secondary education to his own background. He came from a working-class family, where his parents inculcated in him and his siblings a belief that education was a key to success in life. His many brothers and sisters all became successful professionals in different fields of endeavour. As a result, he was unwavering in his support of the education initiatives of his government over ten years.

As the fiscal situation of the federal government improved over his years in office, Chrétien focused new spending initiatives on three major priorities, of which the knowledge-based economy was a critical one. Chrétien did so while telling his Cabinet and caucus to recognize that he was committing the government to long-term investments for which there would likely be little or no political return during the course of a normal electoral cycle. Beginning in 1997, the Chrétien government developed an agenda for research, innovation, and post-secondary education that within seven years – almost unnoticed by the general public – radically transformed Canadian universities, reversed a brain drain from Canada, became an example emulated by other countries, made Canadian campuses much sought after by outstanding students and faculty from around the world, and carved out a new role for the federal government at the forefront of support for research and innovation in Canada.

With investments of more than $11 billion over that period, the government duly created the Canada Foundation for Innovation, the Canadian Institutes of Health Research, the Canada Millennium Scholarship Foundation, the Canada Graduate Scholarships, and two thousand Canada Research Chairs in Canadian universities; it substantially increased the budgets of the Granting Councils, provided funding to universities for the indirect costs of research, established Canada Education Savings Grants, and made Canada the leading country in the Group of Eight leading industrialized nations (the G-8) and the fourth in the world in terms of public-sector research and development expenditures as a percentage of GDP. Many of these initiatives had not even been contemplated by anyone inside or outside of government until shortly before they were implemented. The way it happened is a story of how important policies develop and evolve – practically and politically – in the context of a rapidly changing world.

Putting the Right People in the Right Place

I LEARNED AN important lesson that was critical to advancing the research and innovation agenda, and other policy priorities of the Chrétien government, at a lecture I attended at Harvard University by Robert Reich on the day President Clinton was first elected in November 1992. Reich, a respected Harvard professor, was soon to become secretary of labour in the Clinton Administration. He explained his theory that the boxes in an organization chart are far less important than the people who are actually in them. The right boxes, he said, with the wrong people in them, no matter how good the management theory might be, are a recipe for disaster; but the right people, creatively used, can produce great results, regardless of what box they are in. The success of the Chrétien government's policies to promote the knowledge economy is directly attributable, I believe, to the creative use of personal and working relationships, and is a lesson that putting personal networks to good use is as important to achieving results in the public sector as it is in the private sector.

The minister of industry, John Manley, and his deputy minister, Kevin Lynch, were forward-looking, imaginative, and eager to search inside and outside of government for new ideas. The minister of finance, Paul Martin, and his most senior officials, David Dodge, Scott Clark, and Don Drummond, were committed to finding the necessary financial resources for federal initiatives. Peter Adams, the MP for Peterborough, took the initiative to create a special committee of the Liberal caucus that helped develop a consensus in the caucus to support the promotion of the knowledge-based economy as a major priority of the government. In the PMO, Chaviva Hosek and I were personally and professionally committed to coordinating and promoting the research agenda. All of us in government were fortunate to be able to rely on strong leadership from university presidents across the country, as well as from Robert Giroux, the president of the Association of Universities and Colleges of Canada. Their ideas and support were critical.

School Net: The Power of a Presentation

AS INTERNET USE became more widespread and its potential as a learning tool became apparent, Manley and Lynch, during the first Chrétien term in office, set as an objective that Canada become the most connected country in the world. They developed School Net – an innovative program, which no other country had – to provide computers and Internet connection to every school and library in the country. It was the first initiative of the Chrétien government with respect to the new economy. Manley even presented School Net to the Cabinet in a novel way. Normally, much of the time of Cabinet meetings was often taken up by ministers reading boring speaking notes, which had been prepared for them in advance by their departmental officials, and which, of course, had also been vetted by the Privy Council Office (to fulfill what I sometimes thought was its unstated role of ensuring an absolute minimum of spontaneity in Cabinet).

By contrast, Manley could sometimes be refreshingly different. He once came to Cabinet with a video of Inuit children in Nunavut communicating with children in Australia through the power of the Internet. Another time he showed a video of three wide-eyed children – making up the entire student body – excitedly learning how to use the Internet in their one-room schoolhouse – the last school to be connected in Canada – on Pictou Island, a remote island off the coast of Nova Scotia. These visuals by themselves did a lot to convince his Cabinet colleagues that School Net was not only good public policy, it might even be good politics. While PowerPoint presentations are now commonplace, Manley was one of the first ministers to use them in Cabinet; and he actually so impressed his colleagues with his early use of technology that it helped win their support for an innovation agenda. It was not long before Paul Martin and Manley competed, to the amusement of their colleagues, for who made the best PowerPoint presentations to the Cabinet.

The Canada Foundation for Innovation

BY 1997, AS the Chrétien government entered the fourth year of its first mandate, the bitter fiscal medicine of the 1995 budget was producing its desired effect, and in fact, the federal deficit was falling much faster than first anticipated. The result was that some additional fiscal resources were suddenly available for significant new investments in important priorities. The world of research was becoming increasingly competitive, and other countries were investing heavily in knowledge capacity. But for fifteen years, the research infrastructure of Canada had been underfunded. In the budget of February 1997, the government committed $800 million to create the Canada Foundation for Innovation (CFI), as an independent arm's-length corporation, free of political interference, to fund research infrastructure, and strengthen the capacity of Canadian universities, colleges, research hospitals, and non-profit research institutions to carry out world-class research and technology development.

The development of the CFI, like much of the research and innovation agenda of the Chrétien government, is a good illustration of the way the public policy process works. When key policy announcements are made by a prime minister or a finance minister, they are well covered in the media. When the public at large learns about new government initiatives, what is usually apparent is equivalent to no more than the tip of an iceberg. Because no one has the role of describing the 90 per cent of the iceberg that is below the water level, citizens have an understandable tendency to ask themselves what all those public servants paid with taxpayers money actually do all day long. The answer is that they translate concepts into reality, and they do that work quietly and usually out of the public limelight. The process of developing a policy or program and then putting into place the mechanisms to implement it takes much time, effort, imagination, and continuous hard work of public servants, in co-operation with ministers and their staff, and often in consultation with interested parties outside of the government.

The CFI was to a large extent the brainchild of Scott Clark, then the associate deputy minister of finance. He put together an informal task force of some university presidents, leaders of the Canadian research community, senior public servants including Kevin Lynch, and creative thinkers from the business community to work with the government to develop the idea of the CFI. When he was ready with a concrete proposal, Clark got enthusiastic support from Paul Martin, Chaviva Hosek, and myself, after which the four of us presented the idea to Chrétien, who received it with equal enthusiasm and who agreed that it should be part of the 1997 budget.

Over the next few years, the CFI's initial budget was increased by $2.85 billion. But the money wasn't simply used to subsidize university professors. It was also used for labs, equipment, and computer systems. Within a few years some of the largest construction projects in Montreal, Toronto, and Vancouver were to be found in universities.

In visiting different campuses, I was struck by the employment opportunities the CFI created for painters and plasterers, plumbers and day labourers. The most common sight on campuses across Canada were cranes and construction crews, often working overtime to provide state-of-the-art facilities needed to attract to Canada some of the best researchers from around the world, and to retain in Canada star researchers, who often receive attractive offers for employment at universities outside the country. The early successes of the CFI under the visionary leadership of David Strangway, a former UBC president, made future progress on an education agenda easier, as did some of the lessons the government learned in the election campaign of 1997.

The 1997 Election: Campaigning in Prose

THE CHRÉTIEN GOVERNMENT went into the campaign for the June 2, 1997, election with all the signs pointing to an easy victory. The Opposition parties were divided. The governing party was united. The polls were good. Jean Chrétien was proud of his first term, and particularly of how the government had managed the finances of the nation. The campaign actually turned out to be much more difficult than the prime minister and his team had imagined going into it. By campaigning far too much as good managers, we neglected an important political lesson taught by the former governor of New York, Mario Cuomo, who said that it is important to campaign in poetry, while governing in prose. Pierre Trudeau, who campaigned in lyrical poetry in 1968, almost lost what he also expected to be an easy election in 1972 with the prosaic slogan, "The land is strong." We almost made the same mistake in 1997. I attended with growing unease the many campaign rallies across the country where Chrétien was boasting about the government's record of good financial management, while the crowd seemed completely uninterested. The noise level from the talking in the room would grow alarmingly as the speech carried on. Canadians had expected their government to get the fiscal house in order, and would have punished it for not having done so, but now they wanted to know more about its plans for the future than about the past.

Successful election campaigns for incumbent governments have to be more about hope for the future than about self-congratulation for the past. The record of an incumbent government needs to be emphasized, but only as something to be built on, and as a guarantor for the future. In 1997, as in 1993, the Liberal Party's Red Book made a number of concrete commitments, including a promise to invest portions of any fiscal surpluses in knowledge and education. Other than to speak in generalities about health, knowledge, and children as his overall priorities for another term in office, however, Chrétien rarely used the platform as a centrepiece of his campaign speeches. It was almost as though he found Canada's new fiscal circumstances too good to be true. He liked to think of himself as a competent manager, and knowing how difficult it had been to get the public finances under control, the prime minister wanted to stress prudence as well as optimism for the future, and so he focused his campaign too much on the government's record. He failed to strike the difficult balance between creating hope and still being responsible. Nevertheless, after a rather joyless campaign, the government was re-elected, even though it came back with a reduced majority. After the campaign, the Cabinet and the caucus desperately wanted some new policies that could reconnect the federal government with Canadians.

Time for Action: Budget Surpluses and Millennium Scholarships

BY THE END of the summer of 1997, the Department of Finance had some really good news for the prime minister – for the first time in a quarter-century, Canada's budget would be balanced. The deficit was eliminated, and the country's fiscal straitjacket could finally be loosened. Chrétien understood, however, that a budget surplus didn't bring only good political news for a government. It brought with it political headaches that could be even more difficult to manage than deficits. He talked to me about a conversation he once had with a former prime minister of Norway, who had told him that he had lost an election because he had been unable to manage the expectations of Norwegians as government revenues from offshore oil mounted in that country.

Chrétien didn't want to suffer the same fate. As soon as the financial situation of the government allowed it, he was ready to bring forward innovative new policies. As a symbolic first step after the elimination of the deficit, he wanted to do something to make government more relevant to young people, and to show them that their concerns mattered. He expected me as his senior policy adviser to bring ideas and proposals to him.

One day in early September 1997, I called a lunch meeting with Chaviva Hosek and two of her staff: Liz Mulholland, who was responsible for social policy in Chaviva's office, and Marjorie Loveys, who had responsibility in her office for economic policy. We met over sandwiches in my boardroom, and I sought their views on an idea of mine that the government should invest between $2.5 billion and $3 billion from the anticipated financial surplus in the 1997–8 fiscal year, to create the Canadian Millennium Scholarship Foundation to provide 100,000 undergraduate scholarships to Canadian university students of $3,000 each, every year for ten years, starting in the year 2000. I said that the excitement in Canada – and around the world – about the coming millennium provided an opportunity to do something both innovative and symbolic. The British government had announced the construction of a Millennium Dome in London as a national project for Great Britain. We could have a Canadian millennium project that, instead of being in bricks and mortar, would be designed to improve access to post-secondary education for young Canadians, to help deal with the growing problem of student debt, and also to encourage more low-income students to consider going to university. I made the point that this wouldn't be an interference in provincial jurisdiction over education, because the federal government, through the exercise of its constitutional spending power, had been involved since the Second World War in providing income assistance to post-secondary students.

As our discussion continued around the table, Hosek, Mulholland, Loveys, and I agreed that, as in the case of the CFI, creating an independent foundation to operate at arm's-length from the government met two important requirements. First, it ensured that the government's fiscal hands would not be tied in any way in the future because all the money would be transferred at once to the foundation entirely out of the surplus of the fiscal year 1997–8. The foundation could disburse the scholarships out of its own account over the next ten years without further charges on future federal budgets. Second, the creation of an arm's-length foundation to administer the scholarships would ensure that they would not be subject to political interference from, say, MPs with exceptionally bright and needy young constituents, who thought they deserved special treatment.

The Auditor General has subsequently been critical of the creation of foundations. It is a surprising criticism because one of their purposes is to remove the kind of political interference Auditors General usually – rightly – deplore.

Timing and Presentation

MY COLLEAGUES WERE enthusiastic about the scholarship idea and urged me to propose it to the prime minister, but suggested that we first talk it over with Peter Donolo, Chrétien's communications adviser, so that I could give Chrétien the benefit of Donolo's communications advice as well. Hosek and I met Donolo later that afternoon. He, too, was enthusiastic and, right away, had some thoughts on the best communications approach to recommend to the prime minister.

Parliament was scheduled to open on September 23 for the first time after the election, at which time the Governor General would read the Speech from the Throne, setting out the agenda of the government for the new Parliament. The prime minister traditionally speaks in the House of Commons the following day and repeats and amplifies the messages in the Throne Speech. To give Chrétien news coverage that he might not otherwise have had, Donolo always advocated highlighting one particularly important initiative by keeping it out of the Throne Speech and saving it for the prime minister's remarks the following day. The day after we had met in my boardroom, Hosek and I went to see the prime minister in his office in the House of Commons and explained the idea of the millennium scholarships.

Then I said, "Peter's advice is that in your speech the day after the Throne Speech, you should make a dramatic announcement in the House of Commons that the first dividend from the elimination of the deficit will be the creation of a scholarship program for young Canadians for university education."

Chrétien was in full agreement with both the substance of our suggestion and Donolo's communications approach. He asked me to discuss the proposal with Paul Martin and Scott Clark to make sure that it was affordable, and then report back to him. They were both enthusiastic, although like any finance minister, Martin was concerned about the amount of money involved. He became a fervent proponent as soon as his officials were able to assure him that the Millennium Scholarship idea would not put the finances of the country back into deficit. I was ready to report to the prime minister on a day he and I were leaving on the government's nine-passenger Challenger jet for some meetings in Vancouver. Aline Chrétien was with us, and at one point during the flight, after I reported that the Department of Finance could find the money, the prime minister explained the idea of the millennium scholarships to his wife. "What do you think, Aline?" She looked at him and said, "Jean, if there had been something like that when I was young, I would have been able to afford to go to university." He looked at Aline and me and said, "I've just made my decision. We'll do it."

Implementing the Plan

CHRÉTIEN WAS CERTAIN that a new initiative that created a direct link between the federal government and young people would be popular with Liberal MPs. He was determined to move forward quickly. But he had learned from his Norwegian friend about the perils of managing surpluses, and knew that the competing demands from individual ministers in the Cabinet for the first fiscal dividend arising from the elimination of the deficit would be very great. In this case, he suspected that it would be impossible to achieve consensus amongst his colleagues, and decided that instead of a wrenching, divisive, and inconclusive debate, Cabinet management would be better served with no debate at all. As the final decision on the allocation of overall government priorities is the sole prerogative of the prime minister, Chrétien decided that he would exercise his prerogative by keeping the decision to himself until he spoke in the House of Commons.

On September 24, 1997, I sat with Jean Pelletier in the House of Commons Gallery overlooking the government benches to listen to the prime minister's speech. As Chrétien began the section of the speech about the Millennium Scholarships, Pelletier – knowing that Cabinet and caucus would be hearing about it for the first time – whispered to me, "They better applaud!" When the prime minister announced a $2.5 billion foundation to provide 100,000 scholarships a year of $3,000 each for young Canadians, there was an instant of silence, which seemed like an eternity to me. Then we watched as the Liberal members rose in a prolonged, loud standing ovation.

The prime minister's decision in the fall of 1997 to create the Canada Millennium Scholarships prompted Paul Martin, with Chrétien's enthusiastic agreement, to propose that learning be the theme of the 1998 budget. The budget of February 24, 1998, was a product of the positive side of the long-running competition between Chrétien and Martin. If Chrétien could propose millennium scholarships, then Martin had to come up with something more. The result was a budget that not only provided the funding for the millennium scholarships, but also described a new "Canadian Opportunities Strategy," aimed at preparing Canadians over the longer term for the new economy. It included an expansion of the School Net program, a variety of new scholarships, study grants, and tax and debt relief for both full-time and part-time university students, increased support to the federal granting councils for advanced research, and significant tax and cash help to parents to save for their children's university education through a new Canada Education Savings Grants program. The Canadian Opportunities Strategy in conjunction with the millennium scholarships helped create a new and highly visible role in post-secondary education for the federal government.

From my vantage point, I knew that the budget would not have been focused on a learning strategy if its priorities had been determined by preference votes in Cabinet. Its focus on the knowledge-based economy required the absolute determination and discipline of a prime minister prepared to say no to the wish lists of many other colleagues. Furthermore, it was clear to me that an ambitious minister of finance – faced with a variety of pressures from colleagues and MPs who might one day vote in a future leadership convention – had his spine stiffened by the absolute backing he received from the prime minister. The creation of the Canada Foundation for Innovation in the 1997 budget, followed by the Canadian Opportunities Strategy of 1998, prepared the groundwork for more to come in the budget of 1999.

The Next Step: Healthy Funding for Health Research

IN THE LATE summer of 1998, sitting on a warm sunny day on the outside patio of the National Arts Centre overlooking the Rideau Canal, I had lunch with Dr. Henry Friesen, a highly distinguished medical researcher from Winnipeg who was the president of the Medical Research Council of Canada. I soon discovered Friesen's abilities as one of the world's great salesmen, who could surely sell refrigerators to Inuit in the depths of winter. That day he wanted to sell me on a concept he was developing to wean the Medical Research Council away from its traditional centralized approach to medical research and transform it into a truly modern multidisciplinary body by creating a number of different research institutes that would work together in a new organization, the Canadian Institutes of Health Research.

Friesen proved to be a great example of what a combination of intellect, determination, and sheer willpower can achieve in moving an entire government. He was convinced that implementing his idea – along with, of course, a significant increase in federal funding – would propel Canada to a leading role internationally in health research and, most important, would help Canada attract and retain top medical researchers. He had already won support for his idea from the academic and medical research community, and he wanted the government to act quickly. I listened intently as he spoke, but when I asked him if he had something in writing that I could look at in my office, he said that he didn't have any paper to give me. I looked at the scrap of paper in front of him with a few scratched notes on it, and wondered to myself whether I was looking at everything ever written about the concept. So I said, as judiciously as I could, "Henry, this sounds interesting and innovative. You should really talk to David Dodge, the new deputy minister of health. His views would be very important."

Friesen replied eagerly, "I had lunch with David yesterday and he is completely supportive."

"Well, Henry, that is terrific. David is well respected in town. It sounds like a good idea," I said, "but of course I will need to know a lot more about it."

I went back to my office and picked up the telephone. "David, I just had lunch with Henry Friesen, who has what might be an interesting idea. He tells me you are fully in support."

"No, Eddie, I am not fully in support. I only heard about it yesterday, and I said that it sounds interesting, but I need to know a lot more about it."

"Good, David. That is exactly what I said – but we really should look at it."

"Of course we will, Eddie."

Meanwhile, Friesen was already telling everyone that he had the full support of first the deputy minister of health and now of the senior policy adviser to the prime minister. His list of supporters both inside and outside of government grew rapidly as more and more people said to him, "Henry, it sounds like an interesting idea." In fact, it was an interesting and highly innovative idea, but it took quite a selling job on his part to almost single-handedly transform how the federal government supported health research in Canada. Friesen mobilized his impressive support in the academic and medical research community outside of government to make his case, and they soon convinced some of us in senior positions in government to become his advocates with the Department of Finance.

Friesen was relatively new to the Ottawa system, so not everything went smoothly. We had one particularly difficult and almost fatal meeting in the Department of Finance one evening in January 1999, as we were preparing the budget that would be presented to Parliament only a few weeks later. Friesen came to the boardroom of the deputy minister of finance to make his case. He was accompanied by only one young assistant, who took notes for him, but said nothing all evening. He sat with his back to the wall where the photographs of all the past deputy ministers of finance hung. In their day, each had turned down many expensive half-baked ideas, and I always thought that some of their ghosts hovered constantly in the room. But Friesen had to confront more than the ghosts of past deputies; he found himself facing all of the senior present-day officials of the Finance Department, plus David Dodge from Health Canada and myself from the PMO. There was no way we could recommend the expenditure of hundreds of millions of taxpayer dollars in the coming years without something concrete and precise from Friesen about the concept he was promoting. Unfortunately, he had little in writing to give us. We asked a lot of difficult questions that even a great salesman couldn't answer on the spot. He was almost evangelical in his faith, but vague in his answers. As the hours passed, his chances – at least for the 1999 budget – seemed more and more precarious.

I didn't like the turn of events because I had become convinced that his idea made a lot of sense, and would be another significant step forward in the government's commitment to research and innovation, and I didn't want the meeting to end in failure. At one particularly heated moment, when he was about to be told that he was too late for the budget, I suggested that instead of taking an immediate decision, we should give Friesen a few days to come back with answers to the questions he had been asked. Scott Clark, who was chairing the meeting, agreed with me and joked, "We have been unfair to you,

Henry. We forgot to tell you that tonight was your thesis defence. We will reschedule it for next week."

Sure enough, Henry Friesen came back the following week so well prepared that everyone agreed to recommend to Martin and Chrétien the creation of the Canadian Institutes of Health Research (CIHR), with of course, considerably increased funding from that of the Medical Research Council of Canada. It became the centrepiece of the innovation section of the 1999 budget.

The announcement of the government's intention to create the CIHR was followed by intense consultations inside and outside of government, the creation of an outside advisory board, the production of organizational studies by the Public Policy Forum, the naming of an interim board of directors, followed by a permanent board, and then a search for a chief executive officer. Legislation creating the Canadian Institutes of Health Research was approved by Parliament in 2000, and a distinguished medical researcher, Dr. Allan Bernstein, became its first president. Within five years it was funding more than 8,500 researchers in universities, teaching hospitals, and research institutes in Canada to do more ground-breaking and world-class inter-disciplinary research in health sciences than ever before.

Establishing a Culture of Excellence

IT WAS CUSTOMARY in the days following its presentation for the prime minister to lead a government-wide communications effort to promote the budget to Canadians. In 1999, Chrétien decided to highlight the government's intentions with respect to the Canadian Institutes of Health Research. He chose to do so at the Institute of Clinical Research in Montreal where his brother, Dr. Michel Chrétien, a leading Canadian medical researcher, had once been the director. (The prime minister liked to say that Michel was more effective than anyone in pleading the case for government support of research.) On February 18, 1999, two days after the budget presentation in Parliament, I accompanied the prime minister to the institute. There I met, for the first time, Robert Lacroix, the rector of the University of

Montreal, one of Canada's largest research universities. He was present because the institute is affiliated with his university. It was a brief but fortunate meeting. Lacroix invited me to call on him if I ever had some free time in Montreal, and I said I would.

That chance meeting led directly to the creation of two thousand endowed chairs in Canadian universities, called the Canada Research Chairs. The initiative, one of the most important contributions the federal government has ever made to the university system in Canada, was the product of the imagination of two university presidents – and arguably and surprisingly, as these pages will show – the accumulated frustration of tens of thousands of Montreal Expos baseball fans, led by the prime minister himself. How it came to pass is a story of decision making in government, the role of outside consultation, the formation of ad hoc working teams, and the challenges of promoting a culture of excellence rather than one of entitlement.

Ideas from Vancouver

ONE OF MY functions was to seek out ideas and put them forward to be considered for the government agenda. In March 1999, I went to British Columbia (as I had done for many years every March) for a short skiing holiday at the Silver Star Resort in Vernon in the Okanagan Valley. This time, after only four and a half runs and less than two hours of skiing, my holiday ended painfully and abruptly with a broken leg. After surgery, I was driven to Vancouver, and told to stay there for a few days until I was allowed to take a plane home. With time on my hands, I decided to call Dr. Martha Piper, president of the University of British Columbia. I had come to know her because she had advised the government on the creation of the Canada Foundation for Innovation, the Canada Millennium Scholarships, and the Canadian Institutes of Health Research. Through our collaboration on these initiatives, we had become friends and often had a meal together in Vancouver or in Ottawa. In only her third year as a university president, Piper had already established a reputation for herself as one of the most innovative thinkers and ideas persons in the university community, and as one of the outstanding university presidents in Canada. She invited me for lunch at the university.

I had a personal ulterior motive in calling on her. Years before, she had been in charge of the department of physiotherapy at McGill University, and I was hoping that she remembered something about broken legs. To my dismay, she didn't; so I changed the subject and asked her whether she had any ideas for innovative policies that the government could consider as Canada entered the millennium year. She certainly did. She began by telling me about the problems Canadian universities were facing in competing with universities in the United States and Europe to recruit the best faculty. Large numbers of professors who had begun their careers in the 1960s would be retiring in both Canada and the United States over the next decade. The competition to attract the best new faculty to replace them would be fierce, and Canada started from behind. She explained to me that the Americans had a tremendous head start on Canadian universities because the best American universities have access to substantial financial resources from large permanent private endowments that, even taking into account the relative size of our two countries, hardly exist in Canada. She argued that the problem was made worse by the fact that provincial governments had not only been strapped for cash over many years, but that, in comparison to their funding of health care, they had not adequately funded universities, even with the resources available to them. While Piper was able to clearly identify the recruitment problem and had some general ideas about fixing it, she had no specific suggestions for me about what the federal government could do. I asked her to get back to me with any further thoughts she might have.

Ideas from Montreal

IN JUNE 1999 on a trip to Montreal, I took up Robert Lacroix's earlier invitation to me and made an appointment to meet him at the university. Still on crutches, I hobbled along a long corridor to reach his office. I sat down and enjoyed a superb painting by the famous artist Jean Paul Lemieux on the wall behind him and a stunning view of

Montreal through the window in front of him. I told Lacroix that I had a sentimental attachment to his university, as my father had received an honourary degree there some thirty-six years earlier. Then I asked him the same question I had raised with Piper a few months earlier: "Do you have any innovative ideas for a national project to mark the millennium?" Lacroix immediately made a bold proposal to me, much more specific than Piper's, but obviously inspired by the same concerns.

He said that the federal government should act dramatically to establish endowed research chairs in Canadian universities to meet the competition from American universities. I was surprised to hear it from him. "Surely in French-speaking universities like yours," I objected, "the competition from the United States is not nearly as stiff as it is in English-Canadian universities?"

"No," he responded. "You are not right. Our faculty are bilingual, very mobile, and are often tempted by good offers from the United States." Then he said, "The occasion of the millennium is an opportunity for the government of Canada to do something that will make a lasting difference to the welfare of the country. The federal government should create two thousand new research chairs in Canadian universities for the year 2000 and call them Canada Research Chairs." This was breathtaking. I quickly grasped the magnitude of his proposal. Given the relative size of Canada to the United States, it would be equivalent to 20,000 new endowed research chairs in universities in the United States. Not only did I find the idea itself breathtaking in scope, but in the context of the politics of Quebec, I was impressed that the rector of a Quebec university – dependent for almost all of his budget on a Parti Québécois government that had a reputation for vindictiveness – would propose "Canada Chairs."

After trying to digest his proposal, I told him about my conversation with Martha Piper and said that his idea was along the same lines as what she had suggested to me but was much more precise. I suggested that he call her and explore the idea in more depth and then get back to me so that the three of us could speak. Within two weeks they called me back with a well-thought-out proposal. I was excited by the possibilities and undertook to promote it within the federal government.

A Test Case: A Proposal from Outside

THE PROPOSAL FOR Canada Research Chairs, like the idea for the Canadian Institutes of Health Research, came from outside of the government and was made directly to the PMO. It could only move forward if it had a champion within the government, and I knew that as the proposal transcended different departments, the champion wouldn't likely be found in any box in the organization chart of the Canadian federal government. But since one of the prime minister's principal priorities was the promotion of the innovation agenda of the government, and as it was something I was also personally interested in and deeply committed to, I decided to take the initiative to champion the idea myself. I didn't even have to raise it with the prime minister at that early stage, because Chrétien expected his advisers to take initiatives, search for good ideas, and bring them to his attention only when they were well enough developed that he could pass judgment on them.

I began to put together the best possible team I could find. Given my experience with the Canada Foundation for Innovation, the Canada Opportunities Strategy, and the Canadian Institutes of Health Research, it was not hard for me to identify the team that came from both the political and the public service side of government. All that mattered was their ability and creativity. The PMO itself was easy. Chaviva Hosek, a former academic who understood the needs of the university community, would be a key member of the team. Kevin Lynch, the deputy minister of industry, who a few months later became deputy minister of finance, was a creative policy thinker and a tremendously hard worker, whose enthusiasm was infectious. He was a master at motivating a team and at getting results. Lynch was a very strong proponent of the need for Canada to be a leader in the knowledge economy; he believed that strategic investments by government in that area were very important for the future productivity of the Canadian economy, and also always made the point that government should focus its resources on doing a few big things well, rather than frittering away a lot of public money in so many areas that none made a real difference. (In 2006, Prime Minister Harper made him Clerk of the Privy Council and Secretary of the Cabinet.) David Dodge was one of the great strategic thinkers in the government of Canada and it did not matter that his current responsibilities in Health Canada had nothing to do with a proposal to endow research chairs in Canadian universities. He understood the challenges facing Canadian universities. The deputy minister of intergovernmental affairs and later of natural resources, George Anderson, was on the board of trustees of Queen's University. Anderson also had a lot to contribute. Then there was Alex Himelfarb, the deputy minister of Canadian heritage, a former university professor, well known in the federal government as a champion of progressive social policy, a strategic thinker, and someone who also could get things done; he later became Secretary of the Cabinet. The deputy minister of finance, Scott Clark, an economist and a former professor, was a crucial player, because he was the one who could recommend to the minister of finance that the idea was not only good but that it was affordable. Clark was a great believer in the importance of investment in post-secondary education.

While Clark never took personal credit for anything, and was self-effacing almost to the extreme, he had been responsible for much innovative thinking in the Department of Finance, and was the brains behind both the Canada Foundation for Innovation and the Registered Education Savings Plans.

With a team in place, I organized a conference call for them with Dr. Piper, Dr. Lacroix, and Dr. Robert Giroux, the president of the Association of Universities and Colleges of Canada (AUCC). We spoke for nearly two hours on the telephone at the beginning of September 1999. We all agreed that I should put the idea of the Canada Research Chairs forward to the prime minister. We also agreed that if the prime minister gave the green light, Kevin Lynch would coordinate turning the concept into reality.

The next morning, I went to see the prime minister in his office to tell him about the proposal and who was behind it. His immediate reaction was very positive but, in the post-referendum period, he had to concern himself with the possible reaction of the government of Quebec, which guards its prerogatives over education very jealously. He told me that it would be important to convince Stéphane Dion, who, despite the fact that he was vilified by nationalist circles in Quebec, always spoke vociferously in Cabinet against any perceived federal intrusions in provincial jurisdiction.

I let Robert Lacroix know how the prime minister had reacted, and he undertook to speak to Dion. They then had many hours and days of discussion before Lacroix finally called me at home late one night to say that Dion was onside. Lacroix promised Dion that he would defend the idea of the Canada Research Chairs publicly, if necessary, against any attacks from the Quebec government. That assurance, coupled with Lacroix's reputation in Quebec and a careful explanation of why Canadian universities needed such a program, was good enough for Dion, himself a former university professor. Then it was a question of convincing the prime minister to move forward.

Judging Proposals, the Chrétien Way

CHRÉTIEN'S REPUTATION for prudence and caution was legendary, even though his career as a minister over many years, and then as prime minister, was marked by a series of bold initiatives. Among them was doubling the number of national parks in Canada when he was a young minister responsible for national parks; a major relocation of federal government departments and services out of Ottawa into small communities across the country when he was president of the Treasury Board; the Charter of Rights and Freedoms; and the appointment of the first woman to the Supreme Court of Canada when he was minister of justice. As prime minister, he demonstrated that he could be bold in, for example, eliminating the deficit, passing the Clarity Act, deciding not to participate in the Iraq War, ratifying the Kyoto Accord, and reforming political party financing.

Chrétien had his own style and approach when new ideas were put before him. He understood that it is difficult to put the brakes on a bad idea that has been endorsed by the prime minister and, as a result, was always very cautious before embracing a new idea. He was never impressed by an argument that an idea should be endorsed because it was new or bold, saying that it is too easy to get carried away with something new without making sure that it is also something good. He was prudent for good reason. In his many years in government, he had seen numerous ideas that had been rejected in the past, repackaged, and presented as something new and different. He would tell his staff and his Cabinet that bad new ideas are a dime a dozen; new and good is rare.

I was certain, however, that he would move forward boldly if he could be convinced that the proposal for Canada Research Chairs was a good idea that would transform Canadian universities for the better. To present it in the most advantageous way possible, I arranged a meeting between Chrétien, me, and Robert Lacroix at 24 Sussex Drive on a September afternoon only a few weeks before the planned October 12 Throne Speech opening a new session of Parliament. The prime minister welcomed his guest, brought him into the living room, offered some refreshments, made some small talk to put him at ease, sought his views about the political situation in Quebec, and then said, "What have you come to propose to me?"

Lacroix began by congratulating the prime minister for everything the government had already done for innovation and research in Canadian universities. Then he said that creating two thousand endowed research chairs in Canadian universities to meet competition from abroad, reverse the brain drain, and prepare Canada for the knowledge economy would be the crown jewel in the government's research and innovation agenda. I had briefed the prime minister; he knew what was coming, but he kept a poker face, listened carefully, appeared skeptical, and then asked a question: "Robert, do you mean to tell me that your university does not have enough professors and does not have the ability to recruit faculty?" While Lacroix and I had prepared for the meeting, we had not rehearsed his answer. His response was far more persuasive than he could ever have imagined. He replied, "It's like the Expos. The Expos always have enough pitchers. Their problem is that they cannot retain their star pitchers like Pedro Martinez," who had recently left the Expos to sign with the Boston Red Sox. It took Lacroix some time to realize that he had just hit a grand-slam home run. He didn't know that Prime Minister Chrétien had always been a great fan of the Montreal Expos.

The prime minister smiled, reflected on the inability of the Expos over the years to retain their star players, and commented, "Now I understand exactly what you mean and what you are proposing for Canadian universities. I cannot promise you anything, but let me think about it." Knowing Chrétien the way I did, I understood that it was as close as he would ever come to saying yes, without having the opportunity to reflect overnight, or even to test the idea further with someone else. He never wanted to show his hand to someone outside of government until a final decision had been made. But I was certain that Chrétien had been convinced. Lacroix and I left 24 Sussex Drive and stood outside the house on the circular driveway for several minutes. He looked concerned. He said that he felt he had not connected in the way he had hoped. "Did we get anywhere?"

"Robert, this was a complete success," I replied. "I know the prime minister well. Just be patient. I'm certain we will have good news very soon." He shook his head, looked unconvinced, and remained skeptical.

The next day, the prime minister called me. "Eddie, that was a great meeting we had yesterday. Lacroix really impressed me. We will go ahead." He told me that he wanted to announce a program endowing two thousand research chairs in Canadian universities to encourage the best and the brightest Canadian researchers to stay in Canada, and to attract academic stars from around the world. With a Throne Speech only a few weeks away, Chrétien said, "Let's do it the way we did two years ago with the Millennium Scholarships. We won't put it in the Throne Speech, and I'll make the Canada Research Chairs the centrepiece of my own speech in the House of Commons the next day" – which is exactly what he did on October 13, 1999.

Entitlement versus Merit

ONCE THE POLICY had been announced, there were a lot of issues to hammer out. Kevin Lynch and I formed a team from inside and outside government and took responsibility for making recommendations to the prime minister. Some issues were relatively technical and involved the preparation of the appropriate documentation required for formal ratification by the Cabinet and the Treasury Board. By contrast, there was one issue – how to decide on the allocation of the research chairs to different universities across the country – that went right to the core of one of the most complex and fundamental issues of public policy and politics in Canada – entitlement as opposed to merit.

Which universities would get the research chairs? Who would choose them? Should there be differentiation between research-intense universities and small universities that excel in undergraduate education but do not do much research? What about the proportion of endowed chairs in the social sciences as opposed to medicine and the natural sciences? Would the politicians have any role? What about the role of the granting councils? How would it be possible to ensure that universities would only seek to choose the best and brightest? Over how many years should the two thousand chairs be identified? Answering these questions required first resolving the basic issue of whether each province and each university should get a so-called proportional or "fair" share of the pie, or whether the pie should be allocated according to strict criteria where the principal factor is merit, however that is defined.

It is hard to govern effectively, and certainly it is impossible to govern well, if all government policies and programs have to be designed so that they can be implemented in relatively equal proportions in all ten provinces, three territories, and 309 electoral districts. In Canada, all parts of the country are represented in the Cabinet room. This undoubtedly makes for more sensitive government than the alternative, but it leads to problems when ministers around the Cabinet table adopt the adage of Tip O'Neill, the well-known former Speaker of the United States House of Representatives, that "all politics is local," and feel obliged to fight primarily for their own province, constituency, city, or university. This Please In My Back Yard (PIMBY) mentality is found in Cabinets and caucuses at both the federal and provincial levels, no matter which party forms the government.

All members of Parliament want to have a direct relationship with their constituents. When facing re-election, they like to be able to campaign on their own record of achievement in their own constituencies, as much as on their party's overall platform. Historically, the direct relationship between MPs and their constituents involved government grants of one sort or another, preferably with ribbon-cutting ceremonies and speeches. Roads and sewers, wharves and bridges are things politicians have bragged about for generations. In the twenty-first century, in large urban constituencies in particular, not only is the role of government less given to ribbon cuttings, but technology that enables citizens to obtain information about government programs and entitlements online has made it less necessary for them to get in touch with their MP, as they used to have to do. As a result, regardless of how hard they work, MPs tend to have less and less direct connection with their constituents and tend to become almost invisible to them. As a result, they legitimately worry about losing touch and becoming irrelevant, about being, as Pierre Trudeau cruelly described them, "nobodies fifty yards from Parliament Hill." And so, understandably, they do all they can to make sure that no government programs pass their constituencies by. But their success doesn't always make for good public policy.

The way the Chrétien government dealt with some of its public infrastructure programs is an example of how good public policy intentions can be badly implemented because of political pressures from the caucus. Instead of targeting and allocating resources to the priority needs of the Canadian economy as it ideally should have, the government tended to distribute its public infrastructure spending equally between large cities, towns, villages, and hamlets. I often argued with Chrétien that the infrastructure money was spread too thinly across the country to have any real economic impact. He replied wistfully that to be able to govern well, a prime minister needs the co-operation and support of the caucus. Political reality within the caucus meant that on some matters like infrastructure, he had to be flexible and bow to the wishes of his MPs, if he expected to have their support for priorities that were particularly important to the government. Fortunately, the research chairs concept was one of those particularly important priorities.

Decision Making

THE DEBATE WITHIN the government over the allocation of the proposed Canada Research Chairs was instructive. The purpose of the initiative was to promote excellence in Canada by attracting the best and brightest faculty from all over the world to the best Canadian universities: it was to reward merit and not mediocrity. The decision Chrétien finally made was shaped in part by a breakfast he hosted at 24 Sussex Drive in late November 1993, just after he assumed office. It was in honour of Dr. Michael Smith, of the University of British Columbia, who had just won the Nobel Prize in chemistry. Chrétien had invited other distinguished Canadian scientists, including some Canadian Nobel laureates.

Dr. John Polanyi, a Nobel Prize winner from the University of Toronto, led a discussion around the breakfast table about the danger of a culture of perceived entitlement and false equality in Canada's universities. Polanyi and his colleagues were forceful in making the case that the only way for a country to move ahead in a very competitive, global knowledge-based economy is to foster a culture of excellence. We remembered that discussion years later in dealing with the allocation of Canada Research Chairs.

The ultimate decision to place a strict focus on excellence instead of "fair share" took political courage in the management of Cabinet and caucus. Those who made the case for equal distribution of funding couldn't get around the fact that unfortunately excellence is not equally distributed in Canada any more than anywhere else. But we found that universities, which cherish academic freedom and decry political intervention in principle, often have no compunction in practice from going to their political representatives to claim what they see as their entitlement.

For example, when the Canada Foundation for Innovation turned down grant applications for certain projects on the grounds that the projects did not meet objective criteria, some universities – such as the University of Windsor and the University of Winnipeg – then complained to their MP, who pressured the foundation to have the grants awarded. When the foundation rightly refused to bow to political representations, MPs who were admirers of Tip O'Neill, such as Herb Gray, the deputy prime minister who represented Windsor in the House of Commons for forty years, and Reg Alcock from Winnipeg, who became a minister in the Martin government, became ardent opponents not only of the CFI but of all arm's-length foundations, which had been expressly created to minimize the possibility of political interference. They preferred treating all universities equally, regardless of individual excellence, and supported criteria for allocation of research chairs on the basis of geography and equality amongst all universities. They lost that battle because of the prime minister's unswerving commitment in this case to individual excellence.

Capping the Agenda

BY 2000, A WHOLE edifice was now almost in place, from Millennium Scholarships, to the Canada Foundation for Innovation, to the Canadian Institutes of Health Research, and the Canada Research Chairs, and vastly increased funding of the two Granting Councils, namely the Social Sciences and Humanities Research Council, and the Natural Sciences and Engineering Research Council. But there was still work left to be done. Our trusted advisers Martha Piper and Robert Lacroix and many other university presidents soon told Kevin

Lynch, Alex Himelfarb, and me that the universities were having trouble finding the financial resources to accommodate researchers who were being funded by the new federal largesse. The costs of offices and facilities that the researchers needed to function were not covered in the federal funding, and these indirect costs were imposing a burden on the universities that might inadvertently keep us from reaching some of our common objectives. Funding the indirect costs of research became the next matter of great importance to Canadian universities. After much discussion and with the agreement of the prime minister, John Manley as minister of finance decided to announce in his budget of 2003 that the government would make permanent contributions to the indirect costs of research.

The final piece of Chrétien's education agenda was also part of the 2003 budget. Canadian universities were now well placed as a result of earlier government initiatives to meet the competition from abroad for outstanding faculty. But competition for the best graduate students was also fierce internationally, and Canada was falling behind. The risk for Canada was that when the best students go abroad, they may never come back. I was struck by what I learned at a meeting I had in his office in Toronto with Dr. Robert Birgeneau, then president of the University of Toronto, and his vice-president, Dr. Heather Munroe-Blum, who soon after became principal of McGill University. They told me that it was in a graduate student's economic interests to study at Harvard rather than at the University of Toronto. "Of course," I said, "with all due respect to the University of Toronto, with Harvard's reputation, the income expectations of a Harvard graduate are probably a lot higher than of a graduate from Toronto."

Birgeneau set me straight. "No, that is not what I meant. I'm talking about the years at graduate school. The scholarships and fellowships are such at American universities that it is in their overwhelming financial interests for good graduate students to study at American universities."

I came back to Ottawa and shortly afterwards talked to Kevin Lynch and Alex Himelfarb, now the secretary to the Cabinet, about my conversation in Toronto. We agreed to pursue it with Martha Piper and Robert Lacroix. They helped convince us – although we needed little convincing – that what was missing from the education agenda was a major initiative to support graduate students in Canada. The new finance minister, John Manley, was enthusiastic, and so was the prime minister. In the budget of March 2003, Manley announced the creation of two thousand permanent Canada Graduate Scholarships at the masters level at $15,000 per year per student, and two thousand more at the doctoral level at $35,000 per year per student. The education agenda of the Chrétien government was now complete.

Chapter 22

GETTING READY TO LEAVE

"It ain't over until it's over."

– YOGI BERRA

The morning of Wednesday, September 13, 2000, is unforgettable for me. I had spent most of the summer chairing meetings to prepare for the First Ministers' Conference on health and had not taken any holiday. We were a relatively small team that had worked extremely hard, and the adrenalin that kept us going had in my case run out once the First Ministers' Meeting was over. I spent the next day at the morning Cabinet meeting, and then returned phone calls and dealt with paper that had piled up on my desk. I decided to take it easy the following day. Rather than go into the office as I normally did around 8:15 a.m., I made myself a cup of coffee at home with the intention of relaxing for a while. I called my office and said that I would not come in until after an appointment at 10:30 a.m. with the physiotherapist who was helping me recover from my broken leg.

About 8:45 a.m., the telephone rang. The PMO switchboard operator said that the prime minister was on the line. "What are you doing now, are you busy?" he asked.

"No. I'm a bit tired and am just relaxing."

He said, "Could you come over now and have a cup of coffee? There's something I want to talk to you about."

"I'll get dressed and will be right over."

I could not imagine what he wanted to talk about so urgently. When I rang the doorbell at 24 Sussex, I was ushered into the wood-panelled study where Chrétien kept his personal library and his favourite photos of his family and of some world leaders. He offered me a coffee and some fresh squeezed orange juice. He was sitting behind his desk looking relaxed and wearing an open-necked golf shirt, and I sat on a chair opposite him. I almost fell off my chair when he told me why he had summoned me.

"I have decided to call a quick election. I have just spoken to Paul Martin and without telling him about an election, I have said that we should consider an early budget. I'm asking you to call your friend, the deputy minister of finance, and tell him that I want a budget within two or three weeks at the latest."

The decision to call an election came as a complete surprise to me. I knew all about the difficulties both of putting together a budget and of organizing an election campaign, and I also knew that the prime minister often tended to dismiss the time and effort that are needed to implement big decisions. My immediate thoughts were: how on earth are we going to get this done – and why are we doing it?

The two loneliest decisions any prime minister makes are about who goes into the Cabinet and when to call an election. Calling an election at the wrong time can lead to the defeat of a government, with the responsibility lying squarely on the head of the prime minister. Snap elections don't always produce happy outcomes for leaders. For example, Premier David Peterson of Ontario called an early election in 1990 when his Liberal Party was far ahead in the polls. He was never able to justify why he needed an election with two years to go in his mandate, and consequently the people of the province threw his government out, and he even lost his own seat. The Peterson precedent was fresh in the minds of Canadian politicians. But there were other precedents in Canada where a prime minister had gambled and won big. In 1940, Mackenzie King had promised not to call an election before holding a new session of Parliament. The Opposition did not expect that King would define a session of Parliament as the time necessary for the Governor General to read a Throne Speech. Instead, immediately after the Throne Speech, King surprised the Opposition, saying that he had kept his promise and dissolved Parliament. King swept the country in the ensuing election. Would it be King or Peterson for Chrétien?

Some had speculated that an election might be necessary if the First Ministers' Conference had failed. But the spectacular success of two days earlier did not seem to provide any reason to go to the polls early. So I asked the prime minister, "How can you justify calling an election now?" It was clear from Chrétien's response that he had carefully thought out why he wanted to call an election.

He gave me three reasons for an election in the fall of 2000. First, he told me that Stockwell Day, the new leader of the Canadian Alliance Party, the successor to Preston Manning's Reform Party, was not yet well organized, but that he might very well be by the spring of 2001. The prime minister could not believe his luck a few weeks later in the House of Commons when Day, in a burst of oratory, challenged Chrétien to call an immediate election; in that moment, any argument by the Opposition that an election was opportunistic and unfair went up in smoke. Chrétien's second reason was that Tony Blair in Great Britain appeared to be in some difficulty in the polls because of a rapid increase in natural gas prices in his country. Chrétien did not want a cold winter in Canada to produce increases in home heating costs that could add to voter discontent with his government in the run-up to a spring or early summer election. Third, he told me that he had polling data showing real strength for the Liberal Party in the province of Quebec. Winning a number of new seats in Quebec would reduce the possibility of Bouchard calling another referendum on separation. I was skeptical about Chrétien's friendly private pollster in Quebec, Marcel Giner, because his numbers were a lot more optimistic than anything I had seen elsewhere. (I readily admitted on election night in November that I was very happy to have been wrong.)

By the time Chrétien finished telling me why he wanted to call an election, I knew his decision was made, and that he was not asking for advice. I said, "Okay, if that's what you want to do, let's get it done right. To put a campaign together and produce a budget might take a few weeks. You'll have to be a little flexible on the date." He said he understood, but he wanted to move quickly.

I went off to my physiotherapist appointment and then hobbled back to the office as fast as I could. I had two important calls to make. First, I tracked down Kevin Lynch, the deputy minister of finance, who was at a meeting in Charlottetown. I greeted him with: "Kevin, are you sitting down?"

"Yes," he said. "What is it?"

"How fast can you prepare a budget?" I asked.

"What are you talking about?" he replied quite loudly.

"Look," I said, "this is highly confidential as you'll understand when I finish, but let me tell you about a meeting I just had with the prime minister." I then led him through Chrétien's thinking. Lynch was as surprised as I was, but he was a real professional. As a public servant, his job had nothing to do with politics, but if the prime minister wanted a budget, then it was his job to prepare one. Lynch said, "We'll get it done, but we can't do it in two or three weeks. Try to buy some time." I was in full agreement, not only because he was right in terms of preparing a budget, but because I knew the election team needed time to prepare a campaign. My next call was to John Rae, my good friend and colleague, and my companion in arms in many campaigns. He would have a big job ahead of him. I wondered what his reaction would be. I didn't have to worry. Rae was not surprised, because the prime minister had already called him.

An Attempted Coup

COMING ONLY THREE and a half years after the election of June 2, 1997, the timing of the election of November 27, 2000, took many observers by surprise. The massive Chrétien majority also surprised a lot of prognosticators, but the real surprise was that Chrétien sought a third term in office. He had often told friends and family – and never hidden from Cabinet and caucus – that he planned to retire after two terms as prime minister. His plans changed dramatically in March 2000 at the time of the regular biennial Liberal Party of Canada Convention in Ottawa. Here is what happened.

It was a time when the government and the Liberal Party had every reason to celebrate. The Clarity Act was about to become the law of the land; the budget was balanced; the National Child Benefit was in place; Canada had been instrumental in achieving an international land mines treaty; innovative policies to support the knowledge-based economy were widely admired; a large tax cut had just been introduced; the national debt was being paid down; and the political Opposition was dispirited and divided. But instead of celebrating six and a half years of achievements, the convention reopened old Chrétien-Martin wounds.

A day before the convention was to begin, the press got wind of a secret meeting at a Toronto airport hotel of more than two dozen Martin loyalists in the Liberal caucus, along with most of his putative leadership organizers. The media caught up to Martin in Ottawa on the first morning of the convention and tried to ask questions about the purpose of the gathering of the MPs. Instead of responding, Martin, who was at the top of an escalator ramp, turned and ran down the stairs. It was not long before the list of participants became known, and when each was asked about what they had been doing in Toronto, they gave a wide range of contradictory responses. Martin finally realized he had to say something and put out the story that it was just a meeting of MPs who wanted to discuss his most recent budget. Much later, the truth came out that the purpose of the meeting, chaired by Martin's closest political adviser, David Herle, had nothing to do with the budget. It was to discuss what to do if Chrétien tried to stay in office.

As far as Chrétien was concerned, the gathering at the Regal Constellation Hotel was nothing less than a botched coup attempt

against his leadership. Because he had always planned to retire at the
end of his second term, Chrétien and his staff had neglected to keep
firm control of the Liberal Party apparatus. (It was a mistake that
haunted him during his third term.) We knew that some members of
caucus slowly, and almost imperceptibly, had begun to turn their hopes
and aspirations towards the succession. But Chrétien expected to be
treated with respect until he decided when he was leaving. The meeting
of the Martin forces in Toronto infuriated him. He started to reflect on
what he saw as ten years of a concerted campaign to undermine him,
and in the end decided that rather than be pushed out, he would run for
another term in office (if he could convince his wife to make the family
sacrifices that another four years of public service entailed).

On March 17, Chrétien delivered the keynote address to the convention. He was warmly received, with shouts from the crowd of "Four
More Years. Four More Years." After finishing his speech, he went
downstairs in the Ottawa Congress Centre to a small holding room
reserved for the PMO. There, he relaxed with PMO staff and some old
friends and campaign organizers. Then the door opened, and in walked
Aline Chrétien with a smile on her face, "Four more years, four more
years," she cried out. The prime minister did not ask her whether she
was joking. A small smile creased his lips, and he said, "Okay, Aline,
four more years." The only obstacle to running again had disappeared.

In the aftermath of the Liberal Convention, Chrétien ruminated
with Jean Pelletier and me about shuffling his Cabinet and moving
Martin out of the Finance portfolio. We told him that it might result
in Martin's leaving the Cabinet altogether and further splitting the
party, neither of which in our view would be good for the government
and the country, given the confidence Martin deservedly inspired in
financial markets. Chrétien was far less concerned than Pelletier and
me about the consequences of a Martin departure, but eventually he
took our advice. He shouldn't have. Over the course of the next two
years, it became clear that Pelletier and I were wrong, and that
Chrétien's political instinct to lance the boil immediately was the
right one.

Martin Leaves the Cabinet

BY THE END of May 2002, the impatience of the Martin forces for Chrétien's retirement knew no bounds. It did not matter that Chrétien had several times indicated privately to Martin his intention of retiring from public life on April 8, 2003, the fortieth anniversary of his first election to Parliament. Martin and his organizers simply did not believe Chrétien would ever go voluntarily, and suspected he was planning to run for a fourth term. They were determined to push him out.

The last week of May was filled with drama. Chrétien by then was fed up with the jockeying for position by putative leadership candidates. He told his Cabinet that he wanted all underground campaigning to stop. His message was directed as much at Allan Rock as at Martin, but Martin took it as a dressing-down in front of colleagues, and turned white with rage. The week got worse. Several ministers, including Martin, were scheduled to speak in Hamilton at the annual meeting of the Federation of Canadian Mayors and Municipalities. The PMO policy unit asked to see all the speeches to ensure a co-ordinated government message. When asked to make a few changes to his text, Martin exploded that he would not be dictated to. He then decided to listen to his political advisers, and throw down the gauntlet.

The prime minister had a speech scheduled for the evening of May 31, 2002, in Toronto at the annual meeting of the Federal Liberal Party of Ontario. Without informing the PMO of his schedule (as all ministers were supposed to do, and as he had done for his morning speech in Hamilton), Martin had planned a speech for the same time that night in a different location in Toronto to some provincial Liberals. His obvious objective was to upstage the prime minister. Percy Downe, who was then chief of staff in the PMO, asked Martin to postpone his speech for a couple of hours and, instead, in a show of unity, to begin the evening by introducing Chrétien to the Liberal Party annual meeting. Martin – as he had done all those years before in Montreal – again refused to introduce his leader.

He went ahead with his speech, and then in a carefully orchestrated press scrum after the speech – with no warning to the PMO or any one else – the finance minister said that he was not sure he could stay in Cabinet and that he "would review his options." It was to all intents and purposes a public resignation from the government. In the Canadian parliamentary system, no minister – least of all the minister of finance, whose job it is to ensure the confidence of financial markets – can publicly question whether he has enough confidence in the prime minister to stay in office without violating all the principles and conventions of Cabinet solidarity, and no prime minister can retain such a minister without abdicating all of his authority.

The next day, Saturday, June 1, the phone rang at home around 10:30 a.m.

"Hi, Eddie, it's Paul. What's new?"

I could scarcely believe my ears. "What do you mean, 'What's new?' You went on television last night. You tell me what's going on."

"Well, Eddie, you know, ever since March 2000, the confidence that is necessary between a finance minister and a prime minister just isn't there any more."

"So, Paul, are you resigning from the Cabinet?"

"I don't know. I'll decide in a couple of weeks after a G-8 Finance Ministers meeting, which I am chairing."

"Paul," I said, wondering if he had thought out the consequences of what he had done the night before, "that doesn't work. How are you going to answer on Monday in the House when the Opposition asks whether you have confidence in the prime minister? What about financial markets when they open on Monday? You have to be in or out by the end of the weekend. You better talk to the prime minister right away."

"No. I don't want to talk to him now."

"What if he calls you?" I suggested.

"That won't be helpful," Martin answered.

We talked a little more and then I said to him, "Brutus was successful in stabbing Caesar, but you should remember that it badly hurt his reputation for the next two thousand years."

He laughed nervously and assured me that he didn't want to be Brutus.

I spoke twice more that day to Martin, who kept repeating that the link of confidence between him and the prime minister was broken, and I reported to Chrétien after each of my conversations. The prime minister understood that Martin's resignation would be a political blow, but he saw it as inevitable, and was ready to name John Manley as minister of finance right away. I suggested he wait until Sunday in case Martin changed his mind overnight.

On Sunday morning I reached Martin at his farm in the Eastern Townships. I reminded him that people had been surprised to learn that John Turner's resignation as minister of finance from Trudeau's cabinet in 1976 might have been avoided if Turner and Trudeau had conducted themselves differently at the crucial hour.

"Paul," I asked, "is there anything that can be done to keep you? I don't want to read in the newspapers in the next few days that if only something else had been done, or some call had been made, that you would have stayed."

"No," he replied. "Nothing more can be done. There are a lot of important issues the government has to deal with and they require a prime minister and a minister of finance who have confidence in each other."

I realized that my role for twelve years as the bridge between the two men was over; the chasm had widened so much that it was now unbridgeable. We talked wistfully for a few minutes about what we had been part of together – the Red Book, the turnaround in the finances of the country, the National Child Benefit, the support for learning and higher education. And we talked with some considerable emotion about the friendship in our families that dated back to when our fathers first met in the early 1930s.

Later that morning, Martin called John Manley saying that he expected he would be the next minister of finance and he wanted to wish him well.

That afternoon, I met Chrétien in an office he rarely used in the Langevin Building. Much of the PMO senior staff was present, as was Alex Himelfarb, the new Clerk of the Privy Council. Chrétien told us that he would talk to Martin and, depending on how the conversation went, would appoint Manley to succeed him. He asked Himelfarb to prepare for a swearing-in ceremony at the end of the day, and he asked me to draft a letter for his signature thanking Martin for his services to the government. I prepared the letter, showed it to Chrétien, and then made a few changes at his request. Then he asked me to get Martin on the line. When I couldn't reach him, I finally called his executive assistant, Tim Murphy, who had the nerve to ask me, "What does the prime minister want to talk to him about?"

It took two hours for Martin to return the call from his prime minister.

When he finally called back, Alex Himelfarb picked up the phone and Martin told him, "I have dipped my toes into the Rubicon, but I haven't crossed it yet." (At the same time his staff was shredding their files.) Himelfarb later recalled that Martin had called him late on the fateful Friday to discuss an agricultural issue. They talked for a while and agreed to continue their discussion after the weekend, and then Martin added, "If I am still in the Cabinet on Monday." It was only when Martin went on television later that evening that Himelfarb realized it was more than a bad joke.

Himelfarb passed the phone to Chrétien, who had a brief conversation with his minister, and then said that he had a letter that he wanted me to read to him. I picked up the phone and, in a voice choked with emotion, I began to read a letter praising his contributions to the government and to Canada, and making it clear that he was not leaving the Cabinet because of any policy disagreements. Martin first asked for two minor changes, then said that he didn't want to negotiate a letter, and that Tim Murphy would call me right back to discuss it. Tim never called.

At five o'clock on June 2, 2002, John Manley was sworn in as minister of finance. A few hours later, Paul Martin expressed surprise that he had been "fired."

A Liberated Leader

OVER THE SUMMER of 2002, the Martin forces, through anonymous leaks and organized statements by disgruntled MPs, most of whom had given up hope that Chrétien would ever make them ministers, continued and intensified their pressure on the prime minister to leave office.

Jean Chrétien's schedule for August 20, 2002, was extremely busy – an early-morning flight from Ottawa to Toronto, a speech in mid-morning to a Microsoft Conference on Innovation and Competitiveness, some free time for lunch, a 2:00 p.m. meeting with Bill Gates back at the conference, then a mid-afternoon departure for Chicoutimi where the Liberal caucus was holding its summer retreat, and an evening speech to the caucus.

After his morning speech in the north end of Toronto, Chrétien asked me to join him for lunch. We got into the car and headed downtown to the Four Seasons Hotel in Yorkville. We had only been in the car for a minute when Chrétien turned to me and said, "I have had enough of this nonsense. I don't deserve it and I don't need it any more. Sometimes I think I should just quit now and go home. But I have a mandate and responsibilities as prime minister. I must decide. We can't go on like this. We have to be clear. We'll talk about it over lunch."

For a moment I was speechless. I knew that Jean Chrétien was no quitter. But still, all sorts of thoughts and emotions raced through my head. Mackenzie Bowell in 1896 was the last sitting Canadian prime minister to be forced out of office by his own party, although it had been only a few years since Margaret Thatcher had suffered that fate in Great Britain.

"Jean, don't do it. You should leave on your own terms, not theirs."

Our relationship went back almost thirty years; we had been through a lot together; and this would be a conversation that only old comrades in arms could have. There was a two-room suite waiting for us when we arrived at the hotel. Chrétien ordered a club sandwich and I ordered a hamburger, and then we talked for about ninety minutes.

"Jean, are there any circumstances under which you would like to run again for a fourth mandate?" I asked.

"No. I will be seventy years old in January 2004. The last election was in November 2000. I will be close to seventy-one at the time of the next election, and I don't want to be prime minister at seventy-five."

"So there are no circumstances?" I asked again.

"No, definitely not. I only wanted two terms. Three is more than enough. No one is indispensable."

"Have you done everything you wanted to do, or is there more you want to accomplish in this mandate?"

"Yes, there is more," said Chrétien. "Romanow has his report on health coming and I want to act on it. I want to ratify Kyoto. And we haven't finished our education agenda. Then there is the ethics package I committed to recently in Parliament."

We then came to some conclusions. First, it would take more than a year to complete the agenda for which he had been elected less than two years previously. Second, we talked about the transition of leadership in the Liberal Party. Chrétien wanted his successor to have the best possible chance of winning the next election, and told me that the best time to change leaders would be at the beginning of 2004, which would be the start of the fourth year of the mandate. A new leader would have the flexibility to govern for a while or to call a snap election. We then talked strategy, about how best to deal with the Liberal rebels.

"If you don't take them by surprise, you will die the death of a thousand cuts," I said. "You have a speech to the caucus tonight where you are setting out our agenda for the next session of Parliament. You should make that speech and make it sound like business as usual. Then tomorrow at the opening of caucus at two o'clock, you can drop your bomb, and tell them you will retire, but not before February 2004."

Chrétien was happy. "I like that. It is exactly what we just discussed. Prepare me a statement. But just one more thing," said the old fox. "I want a Throne Speech in the fall. The government will stand or fall on it. If they want to vote against me on it, then it is the one case in which I will run again."

The prime minister went into the other room, called Aline, told her what he wanted to do, and came back to say she was in full agreement. On the flight to Chicoutimi, I was filled with emotion, thinking back on the journey I had accompanied him on ever since my first summer job thirty years earlier. Now I was sitting in the back of the Challenger jet drafting his retirement statement. Meanwhile, the prime minister sat in the front of the plane – as if nothing important was happening – joking and telling stories to PMO staff and to David Collenette and Maurizio Bevilacqua, the two Cabinet ministers who were on board.

In Chicoutimi, Chrétien followed his script to the letter. He made a well-received speech the first evening. The next afternoon, he stunned the caucus and Cabinet – and certainly the Martin forces who wanted him out quickly – with his announcement. Then he met the press and came back upstairs to a small PMO office, where, with a large smile on his face, the prime minister told his assembled staff: "I am not a lame-duck leader. I am a liberated leader."

The next fifteen months bore out that statement – from the ratification of the Kyoto Accord, to a vast expansion of the national parks system, to the creation of thousands of scholarships at the graduate level, to a substantial increase in the National Child Benefit, to the introduction of legislation recognizing same-sex marriage, to a new health accord with the provinces, to a commitment to double aid to Africa, and to the decision to stay out of the war in Iraq.

Political Party Finance Reform

THE MOST IMPORTANT and far-reaching legislative achievement of the last phase of the Chrétien government was a radical reform of political party financing in Canada. In May 2002, the Auditor General issued a scathing report on the sponsorship program of the government. There were allegations of contracts awarded to "Liberal friendly" advertising agencies. Chrétien's reaction was to refer wrongdoing to the RCMP, and to put forward reforms to increase public trust in the institutions of government.

I raised with him the option of banning all corporate and trade union contributions to political parties, and placing limits on the amount individuals could contribute, as had been done in Quebec at the provincial level in 1977 by René Lévesque. Chrétien was receptive to the idea and asked me to explore it. I suggested that corporate funding be replaced by public financing. He listened to me, but said that the Liberal Party was traditionally far more dependent on corporate financing than on individual donations, and he would not proceed unless I could come back with a proposal that did not handcuff the party financially.

In this case, it was difficult for me to turn to the public service for advice – as I would normally have done – because there was no expertise there on the working of political parties or on the conduct of elections. So in the fall of 2002, I looked outside. Gordon Ashworth was a former national director of the Liberal Party, and had managed countless federal and provincial election campaigns, including the three victorious Chrétien elections. Harry Near had long played a similar role in the Progressive Conservative Party, the other party more dependent on corporate than on individual contributions. Despite being on different sides of the political fence, Ashworth and Near were good friends who had a high regard for each other's professional abilities. I asked them if they would meet with me to discuss the feasibility of a ban on corporate contributions. They eagerly agreed.

"Look, guys, you know the costs of election campaigns and the costs of running political parties between elections. You know how both of our parties are financed. Is there a practical way of getting rid of corporate contributions and replacing them with public financing without our parties coming out as net losers?" I asked.

We met a few times and, after examining Elections Canada data on Liberal and Progressive Conservative Party fundraising and spending in every year from 1984 to 2000, they came up with an interesting idea. They determined that a public subsidy of $1.50 per year per vote each party had received in the previous election would fully compensate for the complete removal of corporate funding of parties. Of course, parties such as the Bloc Québécois, the Canadian Alliance, and the NDP would be the overall beneficiaries because they were little dependent on corporate funding, but the Liberal and Progressive Conservative parties would not lose anything.

I reported these findings back to the prime minister. He had confidence that Ashworth and Near would not propose anything impractical, so he asked Don Boudria, the Government House Leader, to test the proposal with Cabinet and caucus. He was met with a storm of protest from ministers and MPs – all comfortable with the existing system, and afraid of a plunge into the unknown. Many MPs actually felt that their own integrity was being unfairly attacked by the very intimation that they were unduly influenced by campaign contributions.

The president of the Liberal Party, who was virulently anti-Chrétien, called the idea "dumb as a bag of hammers." Liberal Party fundraisers were also opposed to the idea of banning corporate contributions. I met with a delegation of fundraisers and explained that public financing would completely compensate for the abolition of corporate contributions. That did not seem to matter to them. I came to the conclusion that their opposition was self-serving. While in my own experience, fundraisers had little or no influence in practice on government policy, the perception that they had influence greatly improved their own status in the business community, which was something they did not want to lose.

It was rare that Chrétien imposed his own authority as prime minister against the wishes of most of the caucus and the Cabinet. He had done so in the case of the Clarity Act, and now he decided that the reform of political party financing was equally important. I kept pressing the prime minister to move quickly. Before Christmas of 2002, he said to me, "I will get this reform done, but I need a little time to deal with caucus." I was impatient and wanted to move immediately, but he had measured the mood of caucus and had determined in his own mind the timing necessary to ensure success.

He asked Don Boudria and me to listen to the complaints of caucus members and to see if any of them could be accommodated without diluting the principles of the reform. We found ways to reduce the resistance in caucus by increasing even more the public financing of election campaigns, and by providing a very limited exemption to the ban on corporate contributions to constituency associations.

In February 2003, Chrétien was ready to introduce a bill in Parliament that would ban all corporate and trade union contributions to national parties (as well as to candidates for party leadership), impose strict limits on individual political contributions, and radically increase public financing of elections. For the first time in almost ten years, he asked me to meet with the caucus to explain the bill, then hold a press conference, and finally to give an interview on national television. Normally, PMO staff should stay in the background, but this time the prime minister put me up front to make clear his absolute commitment to the reform. On February 11, for the first and only time as prime minister, rather than have a minister speak for the government, Chrétien introduced a bill himself in the House of Commons. He called it a bill "that will address the perception that money talks. That big companies and big unions have too much influence on politics. A bill that will reduce cynicism about politics and politicians."

The bill continued to meet with resistance from Liberal members, particularly those supporting Paul Martin, who masked their support for corporate financing with the argument that the public financing in the bill was insufficient for the needs of the Liberal Party. Chrétien warned them that he would call an election and run again if they defeated the bill. That got their attention. Their resistance was totally overcome by a proposal made by Alex Himelfarb and Don Boudria to increase the subsidy to $1.75 per vote. Himelfarb reached me with the proposal in St. Petersburg, where I was accompanying the prime minister at celebrations of the three hundredth anniversary of the founding of the city. I passed it on to Chrétien, who immediately agreed. The final obstacle to the most significant democratic reform of the Chrétien era was overcome in the city that gave birth to a less happy revolution. And the way it works in Canadian politics will never be the same again.

Epilogue

The summer job that I began in May 1972 finally ended on December 12, 2003, when the Chrétien government left office, and I moved into the private sector. I look back with enormous pride at the great privilege I had of working with so many remarkable and dedicated men and women – politicians and public servants – who loved their country and wanted to make it a better place, and I treasure the friendships I made with many of them. Since then, I have enjoyed the opportunity to reflect on my experiences over my thirty years in and around government, as I hope this book reveals.

I have called it *The Way It Works*, and not *The Way It Worked*, for a good reason, because the lessons I learned will continue to apply regardless of which political party is in government or in Opposition and which prime minister is in office.

There are many iron rules of politics and government in Canada. Here are a few:

- Opposition MPs (to the delight of the government in office) will continue to prepare for the next election by refighting the last election campaign as long as they can, until a new party leader drags them kicking and screaming away from their obsession with the past and (to the consternation of the government in office) towards preparing for the future.
- Opposition parties – like lemmings going over the edge of a cliff

– will continue to make popular but irresponsible promises that will get them into trouble if they break them when they eventually reach office; even worse, they will continue, lemminglike, to make other popular but irresponsible promises that will get them into trouble if they keep them.

– Just as Napoleon said that there is a field marshal's baton in every soldier's knapsack, so there will continue to be a ministerial car and driver in the starry-eyed visions of every elected MP. When they don't make Cabinet, they will continue to regard themselves as potentially great ministers, and they will continue to resent those upstarts who do achieve Cabinet status. Eventually their unfulfilled ambitions will create problems for the prime minister who, in their view, and that of their family, friends, and campaign managers, will continue to demonstrate poor judgment in his or her choice of ministers.

– Academics, media pundits, opposition MPs, ministers who like to march to the beat of their own drummers, and certainly government MPs whose Cabinet ambitions have been frustrated, will continue to rant about the dictatorial power of unelected officials in the PMO.

– Political staffers will continue to be criticized for being too political when they focus only on politics, and they will continue to be criticized for being too involved in policy issues when they work closely with public servants on the government's policy agenda.

– Inside Cabinet, ministers – egged on by their public servants – will continue to argue that their department is uniquely deserving of the unlimited generosity of the minister of finance. No matter how often and how rigorously a prime minister tries to enforce his or her own priorities, over time he or she will continue to have to find ways to accommodate the PIMBY (Please In My Backyard) syndrome in the Cabinet, the caucus, and the public service.

– Cabinet ministers will continue to pledge undying fealty to fiscal responsibility at the same time as they unashamedly plot to circumvent the minister of finance; and they will continue to appeal to the prime minister to overrule – "just in this one special case" – the minister of finance "in the greater national interest."

– Prime ministers will continue to be accused of exhibiting dictatorial traits when they set government priorities and make unpopular decisions; and they will continue to be accused of lacking in courage when they don't make such decisions. The buck will continue to stop on the prime minister's desk and nowhere else.

– New prime ministers will continue to denounce the shameful and corrupt patronage appointments of their predecessors, and will continue to pledge to appoint only "highly qualified" Canadians, who, surprise, surprise, will almost invariably happen to belong to their own political party.

– A new government will continue to treat the Auditor General as God until the day arrives when, to its shock and horror, the Auditor General treats the new government as the Devil.

– The Auditor General will continue to claim to be God, or at the very least to be accountable only to God; and the age-old question "who guards the guardians" will continue to remain unanswered.

– Public servants and politicians will continue to proclaim their heartfelt belief in the benefits of consultation and access to information; and they will continue to find reasons to act – "just in this one special case" – without consulting, or without providing the requested information.

– Ministers and MPs will continue to be unable to resist cameras and microphones, and will continue to blame the media for reporting what they wish they hadn't said, and PMO press officers will continue to have to explain the inexplicable.

– Ministers, with the "glint of ambition" in their eyes, will continue to deny with childlike innocence what is obvious to everyone, as they prepare their campaign for the next leadership convention; and prime ministers – who sit in the House of Commons facing the Opposition – will continue to listen ever more intently for footsteps creeping up from behind.

– Quebec's place in Confederation will continue to preoccupy all federal governments; and some new prime ministers will continue to believe that unlike their incompetent and arrogant predecessors, they will solve the problem once and for all by appearing nice and understanding, and by being the new best friend of the Quebec premier.

– Prime ministers will continue to discover to their shock and horror that when push comes to shove, provincial premiers, including the premier of Quebec, will always continue to put their own re-election interests ahead of the re-election interests of the prime minister, no matter how nice and understanding that PM – unlike his or her terrible predecessors – may have tried to be with them.

– Quebeckers will continue to support clarity, to the continued surprise of the separatists, who will continue to want to be called "sovereignists," because it sounds so much less threatening, and makes their objective so much less clear.

– Intergovernmental Affairs officials will continue to see constitutional change as a panacea; Canadians will continue to avoid it like the plague.

– The West will continue to want in, even when it is in.

– The Council of the Federation will continue to sound much like Oliver Mowat and Honoré Mercier in 1886. Unlike Stephen Harper and his five scattered priorities, the provinces meeting under this grand title will continue to have only three focused priorities, namely more federal money, more federal money, and more federal money. They will continue to make the case that a reasonable response from Ottawa is to satisfy at least one of their priorities, and all provincial premiers will naturally continue to want the federal government to levy taxes and send the revenues to the provinces.

– Over and above the three priorities of the Council of the Federation, each individual province will continue to demand more money from the federal government for its own special needs, be it for fish or wheat or industrial subsidies.

– The United States will continue to be, in one wag's famous words, "Canada's best friend whether we like it or not," and governments, unsure if we like it or not, will continue to walk a tightrope in dealing with the Americans.

– The United States will continue to be the whipping boy for the left and a support for the right.

– The Canadian media will continue to attribute all sorts of motives that Washington never thought of to whatever Washington does that affects Canada directly or indirectly; and Canada will continue to have to work hard even to be noticed in Washington.

– The resolution of Canada-U.S. trade disputes will continue to depend far less on relations between prime ministers and presidents and far more on local U.S. politics.

– Government agendas will continue to be torn apart by unanticipated events, such as terrorism, wars, assassinations, natural disasters, and economic spillovers from financial crises around the world.

In dealing with these iron rules of government and politics in Canada, government will continue to work best when issues are put in their proper context, when value is placed on historical perspective and institutional memory, when there is a recognition of the importance of personal relationships and team building to deal with complex issues, when prime ministers focus on what is most important, while delegating the rest, and take time to reflect before deciding on the most important issues.

There will, of course, continue to be a debate about the proper role for the federal government. Neo-conservatives will continue to advocate restricting the role of the federal government, whether through narrow interpretations of its constitutional jurisdictions or through excessive tax cuts or transfers of fiscal resources to the provinces; while others – and I am one – will continue to argue that the federal government has a crucial role to play as a force for good in Canadian society, and will continue to need substantial resources to fulfill its obligations, whether to deal with poverty, or health care or support for learning and higher education, or public infrastructure, and much, much more.

Some will continue to argue that politics doesn't matter and that all politicians are the same. I will continue to hold up the example of Canada's decision not to participate in the war in Iraq as a convincing argument that it matters very much who is in office, and that young people should take an interest in politics and public service because they can make a difference.

Finally, I hope that the rest of the world will continue to look admiringly at Canada as it did at the end of the Chrétien period, when *The Economist* in Great Britain ran a front cover saying, "CANADA IS COOL," and the front cover of *L'Express* in France was entitled "CANADA: LE PAYS QUI FAIT RÊVER LES FRANÇAIS" ("Canada, the country that the French dream about"), and will continue to pass judgment on the Canadian Way as "the way it works."

Acknowledgements

This book is the product of three decades in and around the government of Canada. I am extremely grateful to all those, far too many to name, in government, politics, and public service who taught me so much about the way it works, from my first day in Ottawa as a summer student to my last day as chief of staff to the prime minister of Canada. I am particularly grateful to Jean Chrétien, who gave me an opportunity to participate in government in a way that few others have ever had. I cannot thank him and his wife, Aline, enough for their confidence and friendship over so many years.

When Avie Bennett, chairman of McClelland & Stewart approached me about writing a book, I was both intrigued and intimidated by the prospect. I had written my fair share of memoranda, and once wrote a masters thesis, but a book was in another league. Then he introduced me to Doug Gibson, who convinced me that I should not be intimidated, and who helped make this book possible. Like countless other, far more talented Canadian writers, I am indebted to him for his guidance, patience, friendship, gentle but firm and unmistakable prodding, and for always keeping his iron fist inside his velvet glove. I had long heard of his reputation as Canada's foremost editor and publisher; now that I have benefited from his extraordinary talents, I too can add my name to the long list of those who have expressed their deep appreciation to Doug Gibson. I want also to thank Heather Sangster, the copy editor provided by McClelland & Stewart, Kong Njo, the art director,

Jean Marc Carisse for his cover photograph and for giving permission to reproduce his other photos, and Diana Murphy for giving permission to reproduce her photos in the book.

This book is the product of memory, notes, files, and conversations with many who were, and some who still are, part of the way it works. It reflects my clearest recollection of years of fast-moving events. Many friends and former colleagues encouraged me to write this book and talked to me at length about its contents. They know who they are, and I am grateful to all of them. I particularly want to thank my friends George Anderson, Peter Donolo, John English, Charlotte Gray, Chaviva Hosek, Michael Kergin, Kevin Lynch, Eric Maldoff, and David Zussman for taking time out of their busy schedules to read and comment on my manuscript. They each made many constructive suggestions that I have incorporated, while I remain solely responsible for any errors.

Over ten years in the PMO, I worked with an extraordinary group of men and women. We became more than friends; we became family. The nature of this book is such that some are mentioned more than others, and some will not find their names in the index. But without the contribution of each and every one of them, from the switchboard operators to the prime minister, nothing would have worked. I will always be proud to have been associated with each of them. I would like to particularly thank my three administrative assistants over those years: Claire Read, Adrian Simpson, and Marjo Dutrisac.

This book is dedicated to the memory of my father, Carl Goldenberg, who more than anyone was responsible for my interest in public policy, and who transmitted to me his values of fairness, equity, and small-l liberalism, which I tried to apply as best I could throughout my years in government.

It is also dedicated to my life partner, Caroline Weber, who supported me unfailingly through the countless nights and weekends I devoted to my writing. I will always be grateful to her for her love and encouragement. Her son, Paul Chrusciel, my stepson, was always there to instruct me in what is second nature to him, but for me are the mysteries of the computer. He could find paragraphs and chapters that I feared were lost forever in cyberspace, and I am grateful to him. As an academic and author of scholarly articles and as one who has supervised doctoral theses, Caroline knows far more than me about the way it works for writers. Her criticisms, particularly of early drafts of chapters, were direct, unvarnished, richly deserved, and much appreciated – even when she sent me back to square one – and made this book possible.

Index